the
WEIMAR REPUBLIC

This bibliography was conceived and compiled from the periodicals database of the American Bibliographical Center by editors at ABC-Clio Information Services.

Lance Klass and Susan Kinnell, project coordinators

Roger W. Davis

Pamela R. Byrne
Gail A. Schlachter

the
WEIMAR REPUBLIC
a historical bibliography

ABC-Clio Information Services

Santa Barbara, California
Denver, Colorado
Oxford, England

016.943
W 422

Library of Congress Cataloging in Publication Data
Main entry under title:

The Weimar Republic.

Includes index.
1. Germany—History—1918-1933—Bibliography.
I. ABC-Clio Information Services.
Z2240.W38 1984 [DD237] 016.943085 83-21522
ISBN 0-87436-378-0

ABC-Clio Information Services
2040 Alameda Padre Serra, Box 4397
Santa Barbara, California 93103

Clio Press Ltd.
55 St. Thomas Street
Oxford OX1 1JG, England

Printed and bound in the United States of America

ABC-CLIO RESEARCH GUIDES

The ABC-Clio Research Guides are a new generation of annotated bibliographies that provide comprehensive control of the recent journal literature on high-interest topics in history and related social sciences. These publications are created by editor/historians and other subject specialists who examine every article entry in ABC-Clio Information Services' vast history database and select abstracts of all articles published during the past decade that relate to the particular topic of study.

Each entry selected from this database—the largest history database in the world—has been reedited to ensure consistency in treatment and completeness of coverage. The extensive subject profile index (ABC-SPIndex) accompanying each volume has also been reassessed, specifically in terms of the particular subject presented, to allow precise and rapid access to the entries.

The titles in this series are prepared to save researchers, students, and librarians the considerable time and expense usually associated with accessing materials manually or through online searching. ABC-Clio's Research Guides offer unmatched access to significant scholarly articles on the topics of most current interest to historians and social scientists.

ABC-CLIO RESEARCH GUIDES

Gail Schlachter, **Editor**
Pamela R. Byrne, Executive Editor

1.
World War II from an American Perspective
1982   LC 82-22823   ISBN 0-87436-035-8

6.
Crime and Punishment in America
1983   LC 83-12248   ISBN 0-87436-363-2

2.
The Jewish Experience in America
1982   LC 82-24480   ISBN 0-87436-034-x

7.
The Democratic and Republican Parties
1983   LC 83-12230   ISBN 0-87436-364-0

3.
Nuclear America
1983   LC 83-12227   ISBN 0-87436-360-8

8.
The American Electorate
1983   LC 83-12229   ISBN 0-87436-372-1

4.
The Great Depression
1983   LC 83-12234   ISBN 0-87436-361-6

9.
The Weimar Republic
1984   LC 83-21522   ISBN 0-87436-378-0

5.
Corporate America
1983   LC 83-11232   ISBN 0-87436-362-4

10.
The Third Reich, 1933-1939
1984   LC 83-21527   ISBN 0-87436-379-9

CONTENTS

LIST OF ABBREVIATIONS

A.	Author-prepared Abstract	*Illus.*	Illustrated, Illustration
Acad.	Academy, Academie, Academia	*Inst.*	Institute, Institut-.
Agric.	Agriculture, Agricultural	*Int.*	International, Internacional,
AIA	Abstracts in Anthropology		Internationaal, Internationaux,
Akad.	Akademie		Internazionale
Am.	America, American	*J.*	Journal, Journal-prepared Abstract
Ann.	Annals, Annales, Annual, Annali	*Lib.*	Library, Libraries
Anthrop.	Anthropology, Anthropological	*Mag.*	Magazine
Arch.	Archives	*Mus.*	Museum, Musee, Museo
Archaeol.	Archaeology, Archaeological	*Nac.*	Nacional
Art.	Article	*Natl.*	National, Nationale
Assoc.	Association, Associate	*Naz.*	Nazionale
Biblio.	Bibliography, Bibliographical	*Phil.*	Philosophy, Philosophical
Biog.	Biography, Biographical	*Photo.*	Photograph
Bol.	Boletim, Boletin	*Pol.*	Politics, Political, Politique, Politico
Bull.	Bulletin	*Pr.*	Press
c.	century (in index)	*Pres.*	President
ca.	circa	*Pro.*	Proceedings
Can.	Canada, Canadian, Canadien	*Publ.*	Publishing, Publication
Cent.	Century	*Q.*	Quarterly
Coll.	College	*Rev.*	Review, Revue, Revista, Revised
Com.	Committee	*Riv.*	Rivista
Comm.	Commission	*Res.*	Research
Comp.	Compiler	*RSA*	Romanian Scientific Abstracts
DAI	Dissertation Abstracts	*S.*	Staff-prepared Abstract
	International	*Sci.*	Science, Scientific
Dept.	Department	*Secy.*	Secretary
Dir.	Director, Direktor	*Soc.*	Society, Societe, Sociedad,
Econ.	Economy, Econom-.		Societa
Ed.	Editor, Edition	*Sociol.*	Sociology, Sociological
Educ.	Education, Educational	*Tr.*	Transactions
Geneal.	Genealogy, Genealogical,	*Transl.*	Translator, Translation
	Genealogique	*U.*	University, Universi-.
Grad.	Graduate	*US*	United States
Hist.	History, Hist-.	*Vol.*	Volume
IHE	Indice Historico Espanol	*Y.*	Yearbook

INTRODUCTION

In February, 1919, the National Constituent Assembly met in Weimar, Germany, and created a new constitution which gave Germany her first republican government. For the next 12 years, the bold political experiment known as the Weimar Republic attempted to solve the severe social and political problems of post-war Germany, problems which eventually caused the Weimar government to collapse and allowed Adolf Hitler's National Socialist German Workers' Party (NSDAP) to take control. Among these problems were the difficult terms of the Treaty of Versailles with its war-guilt clause and demand for reparations; the worldwide economic crisis which ended in debilitating international depression; the conflict between the extreme left and the radical right; and the stunned pessimism of a German people still in shock over their humiliating and unexpected loss.

It is in the turmoil of the Weimar years that scholars have looked for the reasons for the growth and victory of the Nazi party, and for the roots of the policies that led a nation, and then a world, into devastating war.

This book, *The Weimar Republic: A Historical Bibliography,* is the ninth volume in the ABC-Clio Research Guide series. It contains 1034 abstracts of journal articles, drawn from ABC-Clio Information Services' vast database—the largest history database in the world. This database includes abstracts of articles from more than 2000 journals in 42 different languages, published in 90 countries.

In order to create this unique bibliographic volume, the editors read the tens of thousands of abstracts of articles written during the decade 1973-1982, and selected every abstract that related to the subject. Thus, this volume offers an in-depth representation of the scholarship published on the topic of the Weimar Republic in the world's journal literature, and far exceeds what one could expect to find through an online search of the database, or even through a manual search of the subject index for the ABC-Clio Information Services' history database as a whole.

The abstracts are divided into nine chapters. The variance in the size of these chapters represents not any predisposition on the part of the editors, but rather the amount of scholarship on each topic that was published in the journal literature during the decade covered by this volume.

The first chapter, *The Weimar Republic in Historical Context,* covers a broad range of topics that is not limited to the specific time periods or subjects covered in the next eight chapters. Chapter two, *The Beginnings of the Republic,* deals specifically with the end of World War I, the Treaty of Versailles, and the events of 1918: the November Revolution, the provisional government set up under Friedrich Ebert, and the insurrections and aspirations of the communist Spartacists.

Chapter three, *Government, Politics and the Economy,* includes abstracts of articles about political party coalitions and factions; foreign policies and relations with other countries; the effects of rampant inflation; biographies of key leaders such as Gustav Stresemann, Chancellor and Foreign Minister; and the economic policies of Walther Rathenau.

Chapter four, *Weimar Culture and Society,* emphasizes the social life and artistic highlights of the era, such as the Bauhaus, the Dada school of art, the role of sports, and the long association of Albert Einstein with the Berlin Academy of Sciences from 1913 to 1933.

In chapter five, *The Jews of Weimar,* the abstracts include not only Jewish life-style and customs, but the beginnings of the antisemite movement. Germany's relationship to the Jews in Palestine, and the work of Martin Buber and other German-Jewish intellectuals, is covered. Chapter six, *Christianity in Transition,* deals with Protestant liberalism, the German Evangelical Church Federation, and the works of such well-known theologians as Reinhold Niebuhr and Karl Barth, as well as the effects of the social and political climate on the various denominations.

Chapter seven, *The Growth of German Communism,* concentrates on the rise of the left as evidenced by the Young Communist League, the workers' council movement, the influence of Lenin on the German Communist Party, and the revolutionary activities of such men as Ernst Thalmann. Chapter eight, *The Road to Nazi Hegemony,* focuses on the roots of the Nazi party and its rise to power, including such topics as the early political career of Adolf Hitler, Nazi party leadership in the 1930's, and the social origins of SA (Sturmabteilung) membership.

Chapter nine, *The End of the Republic,* deals with the last years of the Weimar government, primarily the chancellorship of Heinrich Brüning. Exacerbated by the worldwide economic crisis, challenged by Hitler, the Weimar Republic ceased to function, and an era of democratic government for the German people came to an end.

These chapters are followed by ABC-SPIndex—one of the most advanced and comprehensive indexing systems yet developed. The editors have taken great care to eliminate inconsistencies that might have appeared in the subject index as a result of combining a decade of database material on this special subject. ABC-SPIndex thus allows fast, analytical, and pinpoint access by the user by linking together the key subject terms and historical period of each abstract to form a composite index entry that provides a complete subject profile of the journal article. Each set of index terms is then rotated so that the complete profile appears in the index under each of the subject terms. Thus the number of access points is increased severalfold over conventional hierarchical indexes, and irrelevant material can be eliminated early in the search process, often without recourse to the abstract or article itself. Additional cross-references have been added to ensure fast and accurate searching.

1

THE WEIMAR REPUBLIC IN HISTORICAL CONTEXT

1. Ageron, Charles-Robert. L'IDÉE D'EURAFRIQUE ET LE DÉBAT CO-LONIAL FRANCO-ALLEMAND DE L'ENTRE-DEUX-GUERRES [The concept of Eurafrica and the Franco-German colonial dialogue between the wars]. *Rev. d'Hist. Moderne et Contemporaine [France] 1975 22(3): 446-475.* The concept of a unified international administration of all the African colonies by a Franco-German partnership or by a united Europe originated toward the end of the 19th century, especially among the Socialists, and was later promoted by Count Richard de Coudenhove-Kalergi. After 1920, German colonialists supported Eurafrica as a means of recovering Germany's colonial role, a position taken also by French leftists. After 1930, the need to end the economic depression kept the Eurafrica concept alive. Until the outbreak of World War II, revisionists and appeasers argued for various international solutions of the colonial problem. One of Adolf Hitler's war aims was the establishment of Eurafrica. The decolonization of Africa ended the debate. Primary and secondary sources; 68 notes.

J. S. Gassner

2. Aizin, B. A. and Goroshkova, G. N. EKSPANSIIA GERMANSKOGO IMPERIALIZMA V EVROPE (OBZOR SBORNIKA DOKUMENTOV, OPUBLIKOVANNOGO V FRG) [Expansion of German imperialism in Europe: review of a collection of documents published in West Germany]. *Novaia i Noveishaia Istoriia [USSR] 1978 (3): 159-173.* Review article on Reinhard Opitz, ed., *Europastrategien des deutschen Kapitals: 1900-1945* (Cologne: Pahl-Rugenstein, 1977), a collection of documents with commentaries that reveal the expansionist program of German imperialist capitalism since the turn of the century, change of tactics after the World War I defeat, domestic impact and international spread of German monopolistic capital under the Weimar Republic and Hitler, and West German attempts, 1945-49, to reestablish links with other West European monopolies. 16 notes.

N. Frenkley

3. Albrecht, Willy et al. FRAUENFRAGE UND DEUTSCHE SOZIAL-DEMOKRATIE VOM ENDE DES 19. JAHRHUNDERTS BIS ZUM BE-GINN DER ZWANZIGER JAHRE [The women's question and German Social Democracy from the late 19th century until the 1920's]. *Archiv für Sozialgeschichte [West Germany] 1979 19: 459-510.* At the end of the 19th century the number of women working in agriculture and household diminished and those

working in industry, trade, and transport increased. Their percentage of the total labor force remained stable at about 35%. During World War I women served as an industrial reserve army, but their struggle was not enough to escape the consequences of this role after the war. In 1914, women workers had acquired a definite though moderate role in working class organizations. The November Revolution brought equal rights, but during the next two decades the conditions for working women deteriorated. The conservative image of woman held by the Social Democratic Party and the unions contributed to this development. 22 tables, 174 notes.   H. W. Wurster

4.   Albrecht-Carrié, René.   THE NORTH SEA TRIANGLE.   *Orbis 1974 17(4): 1306-1325.* Discusses foreign relations among Germany, France, and Great Britain since 1914.   S

5.   Baechler, Christian.   LA POLITIQUE EXTÉRIEURE DE L'AL-LEMAGNE 1871-1945 VUE PAR LES HISTORIENS ALLEMANDS [The foreign policy of Germany, 1871-1945, as seen by German historians]. *Rev. d'Allemagne [France] 1978 10(1): 13-23.* Surveys recent works by West German historians on German foreign policy from 1871 to 1945: pre-World War I policy, especially the works of Fritz Fischer and Hans-Ulrich Wehler; Weimar policy centering on the personality of Gustav Stresemann; and Third Reich policy for which there are two dominant schools of historiography: one which sees Adolf Hitler's diplomacy as a continuation of traditional, aggressive German practice, and the other which sees a sharp break in 1933 with traditional German foreign policy. 19 notes.   J. C. Billigmeier

6.   Bald, Detlef.   THE GERMAN OFFICER CORPS: CASTE OR CLASS? *Armed Forces and Soc. 1979 5(4): 642-668.* In view of the traditional caste-like philosophy and behavior, and the policy of exclusive social recruitment of military officers, explores the extent to which the social structure of the officer corps has been able to maintain itself since the end of the Prussian-German army, how professional and vocational mobility has affected the traditional elitist pattern, and how higher education has influenced officer recruitment. Statistical studies reveal a marked decline in the proportion of the nobility or upper middle class previously considered desirable recruitment sources. Since the mid-1960's, education has contributed significantly to the reduction of social inequality. 6 tables, 30 notes.   R. V. Ritter

7.   Beloff, Max.   ARE THE AUTHORITARIANS COMING BACK? *Int. Rev. [Great Britain] 1974 (2): 5-12.* Parallels the political and economic conditions in Europe today with the situation in the 1920's-30's, showing inflation as a danger to the existence of liberal democracy.

8.   Benninghoven, Friedrich et al.   GESCHICHTSQUELLEN ZUR REICHS-UND PREUSSISCHEN POLITIK 1871-1945 IN ARCHIVEN DER BUN-DESREPUBLIK DEUTSCHLAND. ERSATZ UNTERGEGANGENEN ODER UNZUGANGLICHEN ZENTRALEN ARCHIVGUTES DES DEUTSCHEN REICHES UND PREUSSENS AUS SÜD-, WEST-, UND NORDDEUTSCHEN QUELLEN INSBESONDERE DES 20 JAHRHUN-DERTS   [Historical sources for the German Reich and Prussian policy, 1871-1945, from the archives of the German Federal Republic: the restoration of

destroyed or unattainable central archives' documents of the German Reich and Prussia from southwest and north German sources especially from the 20th century]. *Archivar [West Germany] 1978 31(1): 35-46.* Discusses the fate of four large archives and 17 other German records offices housing documents, 1871-1945.

9. Berthold, Rudolf and Hombach, Wilfried. LANDWIRTSCHAFT UND AGRARPOLITIK IM IMPERIALISTISCHEN DEUTSCHLAND WÄH-REND DES ERSTGEN WELTKRIEGES UND DER REVOLUTIONÄREN NACHKRIEGSKRISE [Agriculture and agricultural politics in imperialist Germany during World War I and in the revolutionary crisis after the war]. *Wissenschaftliche Zeitschrift der U. Rostock. Gesellschafts- und Sprachwissen-schaftliche Reihe [East Germany] 1974 23(9): 571-578, (10): 613-631.* Part I. Analyzes the average number of workers and machines and the wheat and meat production of German farms, 1913-23. Part II. The decline of agricultural production during World War I and the lack of foreign currency between 1918 and 1923 caused a series of food supply crises in Germany that could only have been met by massive social changes in German rural society. Neither the bourgeois parties nor the Social Democrats intended to initiate these reforms. Based on secondary literature and printed documents; table, 112 notes.

R. Wagnleitner

10. Berthold, Rudolf. ZUR ENTWICKLUNG DER DEUTSCHEN AGRARPRODUKTION UND DER ERNÄHRUNGSWIRTSCHAFT ZWISCHEN 1907 UND 1925 [The development of German agricultural production and the foodstuffs economy, 1907-25]. *Jahrbuch für Wirtschaftsges-chichte [East Germany] 1974 (4): 83-111.* Analyzes in detail the development of agricultural production and consumption, 1907-25, with special emphasis on the effects of World War I. In 1913 Germany had the highest yield per hectare in Europe, but only the larger landholdings produced efficiently. Because of a lack of human labor, draft animals, and fertilizer, production and therefore consumption declined drastically during the war and even by 1925 had not reached the 1913 level. The author concludes that only through the replacement of capitalist methods in agriculture would it have been possible to more quickly overcome the catastrophe in consumption. Primary and secondary sources; 10 tables, 13 charts, 60 notes.

J. D. Hunley

11. Berthold, Rudolf. ZUR SOZIALÖKONOMISCHEN STRUKTUR DES KAPITALISTISCHEN SYSTEMS DER DEUTSCHEN LANDWIRT-SCHAFT ZWISCHEN 1907 UND 1925 [On the socioeconomic structure of the capitalist system of German agriculture, 1907-25]. *Jahrbuch für Wirtschafts-geschichte [East Germany] 1974 (3): 105-125.* Numerous statistics show the grossly unequal distribution of the soil, farm machinery, and livestock among various categories of agriculturists and the exploitative nature of agriculture on large capitalistic estates, especially east of the Elbe River. These estates formed the economic basis for the political power of the German nobility whose most influential members were the east-Elbian Junkers. World War I brought changes to German agriculture but no fundamental transformation of its socioeconomic structure. Based on official statistics and secondary works; 8 tables, 5 graphs, 41 notes.

J. D. Hunley

12. Bessel, Richard. EASTERN GERMANY AS A STRUCTURAL PROB-LEM IN THE WEIMAR REPUBLIC. *Social Hist. [Great Britain] 1978 3(2): 199-218.* Examines the economic differences which separated eastern Germany from the rest of the German state during the early 20th century, and especially during the 1920's. The backward economic conditions of the eastern regions were closely bound up with social and geographical factors, and these combined to make the eastern question a volatile one in German politics. The development of eastern Germany can indeed be seen as a vital element in the social and political climate of the Weimar Republic. The German leaders' treatment of this problem contributed significantly to the rise of the Nazi regime in the 1930's. Map, 4 tables, 72 notes.   N. Dejevsky

13. Best, Heinrich. RECRUITMENT, CAREERS AND LEGISLATIVE BEHAVIOR OF GERMAN PARLIAMENTARIANS, 1848-1953. *Hist. Social Res. [West Germany] 1982 (23): 20-54.* Based on data collected on the biographies and voting behavior of around 5,250 members of national German parliaments between 1848 and 1953, adds to studies about the social system and power groups in Germany from the mid-19th century to the beginning of the Federal Republic of Germany.

14. Biddiss, Michael D. FROM ILLUSION TO DESTRUCTION: THE GERMANIC BID FOR WORLD POWER, 1897-1945. *British J. of Int. Studies [Great Britain] 1976 2(2): 173-185.* Reviews Fritz Fischer's *Griff nach der Weltmacht: Die Kriegszielpolitik des kaiserlichen Deutschland, 1914-18* (Düsseldorf, 1961), *Weltmacht oder Niedergang: Deutschland in Ersten Weltkrieg* (Hamburg, 1965), and *Krieg der Illusionen: Die deutsche Politik von 1911 bis 1914* (Düsseldorf, 1969), recent works by John Moses on Fischer's revolutionary place in the national historiographical tradition and works by Norman Rich on German aims associated with World War II.

15. Bird, Keith W. THE ORIGINS AND ROLE OF GERMAN NAVAL HISTORY IN THE INTER-WAR PERIOD 1918-1939. *Naval War Coll. Rev. 1979 32(2): 42-58.* To some extent, American perceptions of the German navy were formed or affected by Admiral Erich Raeder's *My Life.* The author analyzes the control of professional perception that was considered vital to the future of the interwar German navy, and Raeder's role in deliberately adopting and encouraging the distortion of history.   J

16. Birk, Gerhard. EIN PROLETARISCHER TURNVEREIN: DER AR-BEITER-TURN-VEREIN BENNECKENBECK 1882-1933 [A proletarian athletic club: the workers' athletic society in Benneckenbeck 1882-1933]. *Jahrbuch für Volkskunde und Kulturgeschichte [East Germany] 1979 22: 149-170.* Proletarian associations, clubs, and societies were an important part of workers' life in pre-1933 Germany. An athletic club near Magdeburg exemplified proletarian physical culture and education. The author examines its structural base, development, and meaning in the daily life of German workers and publishes seven documents. Primary sources; 6 photos, 12 notes.   G. E. Pergl

17. Bloch, Charles. LA CONCEPTION DE L'EUROPE D'APRÈS LES "SOZIALISTISCHE MONATSHEFTE" 1905-1933 [The conception of Europe according to the *Sozialistische Monatshefte,* 1905-33]. *Relations Int.*

[France] 1976 (8): 295-311. In 1905, Joseph Bloch, a young German socialist of Jewish background, founded the *Sozialistische Monatshefte*. Under his editorship, the periodical fought for two principles above all else: European unity and a "revisionist" interpretation of Marxism. Bloch saw unity threatened by Great Britain, which led him to support Germany in World War I as part of a crusade against British and, later, American imperialism. After the war, Bloch was hostile to both the USSR and the Anglo-Saxons, pinning his hopes on France. He saw the fatal weakness of the Weimar Republic, whose collapse before Hitler necessitated his flight from Germany. 32 notes.   J. C. Billigmeier

18. Bloch, Charles. QUELQUES OUVRAGES SUR LA RÉPUBLIQUE DE WEIMAR   [Works on the Weimar Republic]. *Rev. Hist. [France] 1978 260(1): 161-178*. A critique of nine books on Germany during the Weimar and Hitler periods. Includes works on a variety of topics concerning German domestic and foreign relations.   G. H. Davis

19. Böhme, Helmut. NATIONALE EINHEIT ODER SOZIALE GLEICH-HEIT [National unity or social equality]. *Frankfurter Hefte [West Germany] 1973 28(8): 545-554*. Surveys the history of Germany since the Revolution of 1848 in light of the tension between strivings for national unity and social equality, two goals which are unfulfilled today, and one of which never was.

20. Boll, Friedhelm. ZUR SOZIALGESCHICHTE DES WELTKRIEGES UND DER REVOLUTION: NEUERE LOKALSTUDIEN ZUR GE-SCHICHTE DER DEUTSCHEN ARBEITERBEWEGUNG 1914-1920 [The social history of World War I and of the revolution: new local studies into the history of the German working class movement, 1914-20]. *Archiv für Sozialgeschichte [West Germany] 1979 19: 571-578*. Review article of Volker Ullrich's *Die Hamburger Arbeiterbewegung vom Vorabend des Ersten Weltkrieges bis zur Revolution 1918/19* (Hamburg: Hartmut Lüdke, 1976); Klaus-Dieter Schwarz's *Weltkrieg und Revolution in Nürnberg. Ein Beitrag zur Geschichte der deutschen Arbeiterbewegung* (Stuttgart: Ernst Klett, 1971); and Erhard Lucas's *Zwei Formen von Radikalismus in der deutschen Arbeiterbewegung* (Frankfurt: Roter Stern, 1976). 4 notes.   S

21. Borchardt, Knut.   TREND, ZYKLUS, STRUKTURBRÜCHE, ZUFÄLLE: WAS BESTIMMT DIE DEUTSCHE WIRTSCHAFTSGES-CHICHTE DES 20. JAHRHUNDERTS?   [Trend, cycle, structural breaks, chance: What determines German economic history in the 20th century?]. *Vierteljahrschrift für Sozial- und Wirtschaftsgeschichte [West Germany] 1977 64(2): 145-178*. An illustration of the use of trend, cycle, structural break, and chance models in the long-term interpretation of 20th-century German economic history. The choice of long-term models implies different assumptions about the characteristics and causes of short-term developments and vice versa. The economic historian, conscious of the possibilities and limitations of his methods must test models and assumptions carefully. Secondary sources; 11 graphs, 42 notes.
D. Prowe

22.   Borozniak, A. I. and Pavlenko, G. V.   RADIKAL'NO-DEMOKRATI-CHESKAIA ISTORIOGRAFIIA FRG O PROBLEMAKH GERMAN-SKOGO RABOCHEGO DVIZHENIIA   [Radical-democratic historiography

in West Germany on the German working-class movement]. *Voprosy Istorii [USSR] 1981 (6): 64-75.* Radical-democratic historiography emerged in West Germany in the mid-1970's; its representatives (W. Abendroth, among others) opposed the bourgeois, right-socialist interpretation of the history of German working-class movement, Social Democracy, fascism and the antifascist struggle, and the history of the two German states, thus being rather close to Marxist historiography. They participated in the struggle for peace and disarmament and against neo-Nazism and anti-Communism and advocated good-neighborly relations with the socialist community.   J

23. Bosl, Karl. DER BAYRISCHE STAAT VON 1918 BIS 1975 [The Bavarian state 1918-75]. *Archivalische Zeitschrift [West Germany] 1976 72: 177-198.* In the Weimar republic and during the national socialist period Bavaria had lost considerable sovereign rights as compared to the more decentralized structure of administration of the German monarchy. The modern Bavarian state has been met by two basic federal problems since 1945, by the maintenance of the sovereignty over its budget and its cultural autonomy. Based on secondary sources; 21 notes.

24. Breitman, Richard. NEGATIVE INTEGRATION AND PARLIA-MENTARY POLITICS: LITERATURE ON GERMAN SOCIAL DEMOC-RACY, 1890-1933. *Central European Hist. 1980 13(2): 175-197.* Review article on 10 recent books on the Social Democratic Party of Germany (SPD). The party had its roots in the trade unions of the working class and so began as a socialist, revolutionary party. By the 1930's, however, it was a defender of the parliamentary republic. This shift has attracted a range of explanations. Early explanations were basically ahistorical, relying on supposed axioms like "every human organization has oligarchical tendencies," and attributed the transformation of the party to the conservative force of the bureaucratic apparatus of the SPD itelf. A more historical view—and a more modern one—finds the source of the change in the "negative integration" of the SPD. While the SPD tried to avoid alienating either right or left wings of the party, the Reich succeeded in compromising its original principles and goals. 27 notes.   S

25. Campus, Eliza. LA SÉCURITÉ EUROPÉENE PENDANT L'ENTRE-DEUX-GUERRES (1919-1939) [European security between the wars, 1919-39]. *Rev. Roumaine d'Études Int. [Rumania] 1975 9(30): 400-411.* A review of the interwar period in light of several recent studies and with reference to several documents and newspaper articles of the time. In the diplomatic struggle for the defense of peace and security, one sees the simultaneous firmness of the small and middle-sized states and the concessions of the great powers. The power of the threat of force was sufficient to destroy at least temporarily the force of law. But the idea of security was not killed, and after the war it was once again realized that the strength of law in a climate of real democracy can improve the quality of international life. 90 notes.   G. F. Jewsbury

26. Cole, C. Robert. A. J. P. TAYLOR AND THE ORIGINS OF THE SECOND WORLD WAR. Parker, Harold T., ed. *Problems in European History,* (Durham, N.C.: Moore Publ., 1979): 267-282. A. J. P. Taylor's *The Origins of the Second World War* (1961), represented a rejection of the "Nuremberg Thesis," i.e., of the notion that Hitler was personally responsible for the war and

that consequently the governments of Western Europe and the German people were both substantially innocent and could present a morally unassailable front against a Soviet threat much analogous to the former Nazi one. Taylor saw World War II as in the long run inevitable thanks to Versailles and in detail the result of accidents and blunders in which all were more or less equally at fault. F. H. Hinsley accused Taylor of ignoring the role of long-range plans and of conscious choice between available alternatives, and a host of critics found his thesis morally unacceptable. Some of his ideas have been supported by subsequent scholarship. Refs.   L. W. Van Wyk

27. Conze, Werner. ZUR SOZIALGESCHICHTE DES KAISERREICHS UND DER WEIMARER REPUBLIK [On the social history of the German empire and the Weimar Republic]. *Neue Politische Literatur [West Germany] 1976 21(4): 507-515.* Younger German historians of the late 1960's and 1970's working in German history 1870-1933 have concentrated on the organized potential of the state, economy, and society in their growing politicization, polarization, and differentiation instead of describing events and personalities.

28. Craig, Gordon A. THE END OF PRUSSIA. *Pro. of the Am. Phil. Soc. 1980 124(2): 97-99.* Article 1 of the Allied Control Council's 1947 Law No. 46 abolished "the Prussian State with its central government and all its agencies." The author traces Prussia's statehood from Frederick William I to the days of Hitler, concluding that there have been in fact several Prussias that had different ends for different sets of reasons.   H. M. Parker, Jr.

29. Dähn, Horst. NEUERE UNTERSUCHUNGEN ÜBER DIE SPD [Recent studies on the SPD]. *Neue Pol. Literatur [West Germany] 1978 23(3): 313-321.* Reviews new publications on the ideological development of German socialism during the 19th and 20th centuries, the integration of the German social democrats into the systems of the Weimar republic and West Germany, and recent ideological trends in German socialism.

30. Dauphin-Meunier, Achille. WALTHER RATHENAU, VOYANT DES CHOSES À VENIR (1867-1922) [Walther Rathenau, foreseeing things to come, 1867-1922]. *Écrits de Paris [France] 1973 (324): 66-73.* Analyzes the political theory of German statesman Walther Rathenau, who advocated a kind of populism that had nothing in common with either democracy or totalitarianism.

31. Deist, Wilhelm. ARMEE UND ARBEITERSCHAFT 1905-1918 [Army and labor force, 1905-18]. *Francia [France] 1974 2: 458-481.* Before World War I, Germany's army was hostile to the labor movement and socialism. Mass mobilization necessitated by World War I forced on the military heirarchy a policy of cooperation with leaders of the working class. The military actually supported reforms which they hoped would keep the working class loyal to the kaiser and the existing system. The revolution of 1918 saw the working class and the common soldier as inseparable entities acting together. With the military collapse and the loss of the war this solidarity dissolved and was not restored, in the eyes of the military, until the advent of Nazism. 76 notes.
                                                                                            J. C. Billigmeier

32. Dorpalen, Andreas. WEIMAR REPUBLIC AND NAZI ERA IN EAST GERMAN PERSPECTIVE. *Central European Hist. 1978 11(3): 211-230.* Discusses East German Marxist interpretations of the Weimar Republic and the Nazi period. While their doctrinaire approach often distorts the truth, as for example their conclusion that Adolf Hitler was unimportant in the Nazi regime, it also results in new and significant insights which Western historians tend to overlook, especially relating to the activities of the Communist Party. Based on East German secondary literature; 24 notes.   C. R. Lovin

33. Dräger, Werner. BETRIEBLICHE SOZIALPOLITIK ZWISCHEN AUTONOMIE UND REGLEMENTIERUNG (1918 BIS 1977) [Company social policies between autonomy and regimentation, 1918-77]. *Zeitschrift für Unternehmensgeschichte [West Germany] 1978 Beiheft(12): 58-69.* From 1918 to 1932 German firms retained much independence in their social programs in spite of increased state intervention. In contrast, the state dominated employer-employee relations during the Nazi period. The workers made some gains from 1945 to 1948 under the occupying powers and the *Land* governments. From 1949 to 1969 the coalitions dominated by the Christian Democratic Union passed much social legislation but left business with considerable autonomy. Subsequent interference by the Social Democratic Party governments deprived business of flexibility and initiative in their social programs.   J. T. Walker

34. Dreyfus, F. G. MARXISATION, NON-MARXISATION OU DÉMARXISATION DU SOCIALISME ALLEMAND? [Is German socialism Marxist, non-Marxist, or de-Marxed?]. *Rev. d'Allemagne [France] 1977 9(4): 697-713.* There was no element of Marxism in the origin of German socialism, which had its roots in Luther, Kant, Fichte, and Hegel. It owed its subsequent development mainly to Ferdinand Lassalle (1825-64), upon whom the Gotha Program of 1875 was based. Eduard Bernstein (1850-1932) became the father of German revisionism, which was followed by a substantial growth of the German Social Democratic Party (SPD). Under the Weimar Republic, votes cast for the SPD increased while those for the Communist Party decreased. The same trend appeared after 1948. Marxism has always been a secondary element in German socialism while the dominant ideology has been that of Lassalle. Secondary sources; 36 notes.   J. S. Gassner

35. Droz, Jacques. HISTORIOGRAPHIE D'UN SIÈCLE DE SOCIAL-DÉMOCRATIE ALLEMANDE [Historiography covering a century of German Social Democrats]. *Mouvement Social [France] 1976 (95): 3-23.* Although many works exist on the German labor movement, no overall work on the German Social Democrats is available. Ferdinand Lassalle founded an independent workers' party in 1863 as a political weapon to obtain voting rights for the working class. The Party was first tied to the idea of German unity but the Franco-Prussian War, the creation of the German Empire, and the Paris Commune alienated the German Worker Party from the nation. Antisocialist legislation increased Marxist influence on the Social Democrats. By 1905, having grown into a strong political entity, the Social Democratic movement nevertheless showed certain internal weaknesses that led to the schism of 1917. After years of waiting for revolution, the party divided—the minority leading toward the coalition of Weimar, and the revolutionary majority without influence outside the labor movement. Since its reconstruction in 1945, the Social Democratic Party

has been a movement for human emancipation rather than a political force that can solve socioeconomic problems. Secondary sources; 130 notes.

M. de Gialluly

36. Dupeux, Louis. HISTORIOGRAPHIE RÉCENTE DE LA RÉPUBLIQUE DE WEIMAR ET DU "TROISIÈME REICH" [Recent historiography on the Weimar Republic and the Third Reich]. *Rev. d'Allemagne [France] 1981 13(1): 123-136.* Lists recent works on the Weimar Republic and the Third Reich by categories, with brief descriptions and evaluations. 2 notes.

J. S. Gassner

37. Dupeux, Louis. LA RÉPUBLIQUE DE WEIMAR ET LES TROISIÈME REICH. ESSAI DE BIBLIOGRAPHIE ET D'HISTORIOGRAPHIE RÉCENTES (1972-1977) [The Weimar Republic and the Third Reich: essay on recent bibliography and historiography, 1972-77]. *Rev. d'Allemagne [France] 1978 10(1): 24-48.* Part I. The historiography and a bibliography of 1972-77 works on the Weimar Republic, concentrating on politics, especially foreign policy, Communism, and the rise of the Nazi Party, and on the social and economic milieu. Note. Article to be continued.   J. C. Billigmeier

38. Eley, Geoff. RECENT WORK IN MODERN GERMAN HISTORY. *Hist. J. [Great Britain] 1980 23(2): 463-479.* Reviews 14 publications on modern German history by historians of the "new generation."   A. R. Gross

39. Erdmann, Karl Dietrich. "LEBENSUNWERTES LEBEN." TOTALITÄRE LEBENSVERNICHTUNG UND DAS PROBLEM DER EUTHANASIE ["Life not worth living": totalitarian destruction of life and the problem of euthanasia]. *Geschichte in Wissenschaft und Unterricht [West Germany] 1975 26(4): 215-225.* Describes Soviet revolutionary justice after 1917 and the development of euthanasia in Germany from 1920 to the mass extermination during World War II. As totalitarian systems focus on the collective, they dispose of the individual's life according to social criteria. In the USSR the basis for convictions was not guilt but expediency. The phrase "life not worth living" was coined in Germany in 1920. Based on this concept the Nazis finally included everybody who was of no use, needed help, and did not fit their idealized image of Aryan man. They began with sterilization in 1933, followed by the cloaked "children's action" just before the war, in which abnormal infants were killed, and the veiled wartime mass extirpation, the "euthanasia program" aimed at the irremediably ill, which was halted in 1941 after public protest. Primary and secondary sources; 6 notes.   H. W. Wurster

40. Ernst, Volker; Kaun, Anita; and Zeidler, Hans-Jürgen. NEUERSCHLOSSENE BESTÄNDE IM MILITÄRARCHIV DER DDR (ZEITRAUM 1920-1945) [Recently opened holdings in the Military Archives of East Germany for the years 1920-45]. *Militärgeschichte [East Germany] 1981 20(1): 95-97.* Describes the provenance of about 13,000 documents from the years 1920 to 1945 that were opened in 1979.   H. D. Andrews

41. Evans, Richard J. FEMINISM AND FEMALE EMANCIPATION IN GERMANY 1870-1945: SOURCES, METHODS, AND PROBLEMS OF RESEARCH. *Central European Hist. 1976 9(4): 323-351.* Surveys "the sources available to researchers who wish to tackle . . . aspects of German women's

history," discusses problems in evaluating and interpreting these sources, and suggests directions for research. An appendix surveys feminist periodicals in Germany, 1866-1944. 56 notes.   C. R. Lovin

42. Evans, Richard J. GERMAN SOCIAL DEMOCRACY AND WOMEN'S SUFFRAGE 1891-1918. *J. of Contemporary Hist. [Great Britain] 1980 15(3): 533-557.* The most determined suffrage organizations on the Continent were those of working-class women in the socialist movement. The Social Democratic Party had to have its own SD women's group because of the sexist discrimination of the times (1891-1918). The association included Clara Zetkin and Luise Zietz, who kept the issue of woman suffrage in the forefront with the celebration of Women's Days 1911-14, and various demonstrations, 1915-23. Based on archival sources; 39 notes.   M. P. Trauth

43. Evans, Richard J. RETHINKING THE GERMAN PAST. *West European Pol. [Great Britain] 1981 4(2): 134-148.* Presents two contrasting interpretations of recent German history: that of Gerhard Ritter, doyen of German historians in the 1950's and early 1960's, and that of Hans-Ulrich Wehler.

44. Eyll, Klara van. STADTADRESSBÜCHER ALS QUELLE FÜR DIE WIRTSCHAFTS- UND SOZIALHISTORISCHE FORSCHUNG—DAS BEISPIEL KÖLN [City directories as a source for research in economic and social history: the example of Cologne]. *Zeitschrift für Unternehmensgeschichte [West Germany] 1979 24(3): 12-26.* City directories were first published in France at the beginning of the 17th century and subsequently the idea became used throughout Europe. The French occupation of parts of Germany 1794-1814 made a city directory a regular publishing event. There were 124 editions of the directory of Cologne in the Rhineland from 1795 to 1971, and every volume presents an original source of historical facts for economic or social research. 31 notes.   G. E. Pergl

45. Field, Geoffrey G. NORDIC RACISM. *J. of the Hist. of Ideas 1977 38(3): 523-540.* Describes and criticizes Hans-Jurgen Lutzhöft's *Der Nordische Gedanke in Deutschland 1920-1940* (1971). Lutzhöft's work is the first to treat Hans F. K. Gunther and the other Nordic racists who enjoyed "broad popularity in Central Europe after 1918." Based on Lutzhöft, related scholarship, and published primary sources; 41 notes.   D. B. Marti

46. Fischer, Fritz. DER STELLENWERT DES ERSTEN WELTKRIEGS IN DER KONTINUITÄTSPROBLEMATIK DER DEUTSCHEN GESCHICHTE [The place of World War I in the problem of continuity in German history]. *Hist. Zeitschrift [West Germany] 1979 229(1): 25-33.* Whether World War I was a clear break in the historical continuity of structures and tendencies of German history depends on analysis of its relationship to the Prussian-German Empire to 1914, the empire during World War I, and lines connecting the empire to the Third Reich. Lines of continuity are impressive, since the Empire was prepared for World War I and responded to it by developing the Hindenburg-Ludendorff dictatorship. The revolutionary movement and the failed peace were caused more by the weakness of the Weimar Republic than by discontinuities caused by World War I. The principles of the Nazi state show clear connections with the pre-World War I empire.   G. H. Davis

47. Fischer, Fritz. RECENT WORKS ON GERMAN NAVAL POLICY. *European Studies Rev. [Great Britain] 1975 5(4): 443-461.* A review of three recent works by Volker R. Berghahn which stress the role of domestic politics in Admiral Tirpitz's program of naval armament beginning with the years 1898-1900. Tirpitz's Grand Design was predicated on the assumption that the building of a fleet would stabilize the system of Prusso-German constitutionalism. Another study reviewed is by Ekkehard Böhm which analyzes the attitudes of the Hanseatic merchants toward the Kaiser-Tirpitz navy. The fifth study reviewed is a symposium of lectures in response to Berghahn. The last, by Jobst Dülffer, stresses the continuity in naval policy of Imperial Germany, the Weimar Republic, and Hitler and Admiral Raeder. 10 notes.   C. T. Prukop

48. Forster, Gerhard. VOLK UND ARMEE IN DER DEUTSCHEN MILITÄRGESCHICHTE [People and army in German military history]. *Militärgeschichte [East Germany] 1974 13(4): 441-453.* During the Peasants War of 1524-25, the 17th- and 18th-century rebellions, the wars of liberation, the revolution of 1848, the revolution of 1918, and the Weimar Republic, the masses incorporated progressive forces until the National Peoples Army's creation represented the working class in power.   H. D. Andrews

49. Förster, Gerhard and Sperling, Heinz. ZUM PLATZ DER MILITÄRTECHNIK IM KRIEGSBILD IMPERIALISTISCHER DEUTSCHER MILITÄRS IN DEN 20ER UND 30ER JAHREN [The place of military technology in the image of war of imperialist German officers in the 1920's-30's]. *Militärgeschichte [East Germany] 1975 14(3): 323-336.* Publication of speeches by Wilhelm Groener and Gerhard Maltzky and a study by Walter Nehring, Alfred Schemm, and Eugen Müller between 1927 and 1937 in which the German military officers stressed the strategic importance of German industry.

50. Fricke, Dieter. METHODOLOGISCHE PROBLEME DER ERFORSCHUNG DES KAMPFES DER BÜRGERLICHEN PARTEIEN UM EINFLUSS UNTER DEN WERKTÄTIGEN MASSES [Methodological problems in research on the fight of the bourgeois parties for influence among the working masses]. *Jenaer Beiträge zur Parteien Geschichte [East Germany] 1976 39: 1-90.* The history section of the Friedrich Schiller University in Jena is here inaugurating a several-year study of the efforts of the bourgeois parties in Germany to gain influence over the working class, 1840-1945. Many topics must be explored before the purposes and actions of the various political parties and social classes can be accurately understood. There was a capitalist-monopolist nature to middle-class politics, an aspect as well of other social institutions which gave the middle classes their power. Includes a discussion of three chronological periods: 1840-70, 1870-1917, and 1917-45, and a discussion of 20th-century fascism. 120 notes.   M. Faissler

51. Fuchs, Gerald. REALIZACE PRÁVA NA SEBEURČENÍ NÁRODŮ VE VELKÉ ŘÍJNOVÉ SOCIALISTICKÉ REVOLUCI A OTÁZKA "ANŠLUSU" V NĚMECKO-ČESKOSLOVENSKÝCH VTAZÍCH, 1918-1919 [Realization of the right of national self-determination in the Great October Revolution and the *Anschluss* question in German-Czechoslovak relations, 1918-19]. *Slovanský Přehled [Czechoslovakia] 1978 64(4): 257-262.* The idea of self-determination was an intrinsic part of the October Revolution. Immediately after

this revolution, the Ukrainians and Finns among others exercised the right. During the formation of Czechoslovakia the Sudeten Germans demanded union with Germany. Karel Kreibich, leader of the German Communist Party in Liberec, opposed the demands because, unlike the *anschluss* dreams of 1848, unification with post-World War I Germany would have encouraged German imperialist designs. The Czechoslovak republic, despite its bourgeois limitations, did provide opportunity for the growth of a working-class movement and the beginnings of the struggle for socialism. 25 notes. B. Kimmel

52. García de Tudela, Fernando Dodero. EL GRAN LOBO [The grand wolf]. *Rev. General de Marina [Spain] 1978 195(Aug-Sep): 147-160.* Biography of Admiral Karl Doenitz of the German navy. Commissioned in 1912, Doenitz served aboard the cruiser *Breslau* until he joined the submarine service in 1916. He remained on active duty after the war, and eventually led the recreated submarine service. A strong advocate of submarine warfare, he built the German submarine force to formidable proportions, but when war came again he remembered the principles of humanitarianism. Although a man of honor and above the politics of the Third Reich, he was condemned to a ten-year prison sentence at Nuremberg. 3 photos, biblio. W. C. Frank

53. Geary, Dick. THE RUHR: FROM SOCIAL PEACE TO SOCIAL REVOLUTION. *European Studies Rev. [Great Britain] 1980 10(4): 497-511.* Review article on six studies published between 1974 and 1979 on working-class activities in the Ruhr, Germany's industrial heartland, before and immediately after World War I, the radical swing that occurred in 1919, and the failure of the radicals to make a permanent impact on the political developments in Germany in the 1920's. 18 notes. J. G. Smoot

54. Gersdorff, Ursula von. FRAUENARBEIT UND FRAUENEMANZIPATION IM ERSTEN WELTKRIEG [Working women and the emancipation of women in World War I]. *Francia [France] 1974 2: 502-523.* Before World War I, German women rarely worked outside the home. The movement for women's emancipation was in its infancy. The war effort brought women into factories, mines, offices, schools, and public service. After the war, they lost most of the ground gained in these economic sectors to the returning veterans. Only in schools, welfare institutions, and government offices did women continue to occupy the positions they filled during the war. The end of the war also brought the vote for women, and several were elected to the Reichstag. With the coming to power of Hitler, women lost almost all their gains of the preceding 25 years. 69 notes. J. C. Billigmeier

55. Gregor, A. James. FASCISM AND COMPARATIVE POLITICS. *Comparative Pol. Studies 1976 9(2): 207-222.* Discusses recent historical writings on Italian and German fascism.

56. Groehler, Olaf. DIE ENTWICKLUNG DER TECHNISCHEN MITTEL DES CHEMISCHEN KRIEGES IM IMPERIALISTISCHEN DEUTSCHLAND 1915-1945 [The development of the technical means of chemical warfare in imperialist Germany, 1915-45]. *Militärgeschichte [East Germany] 1976 15(6): 718-728.* Describes the first employment of chemical warfare by Germany on the Western front in 1915, and traces the subsequent development

of chemicals, delivery systems, and tactical uses of chemicals in Germany's preparations for further aggressive war. Based on documents in the Federal Archive in Freiburg and in the Military Archive of East Germany and secondary works; 9 photos, 2 tables, 23 notes.   J. B. Street

57. Gruner, Erich. LITERATUR ZUR SOZIALGESCHICHTE UND POLITOLOGIE [Literature on social history and political science]. *Schweizerische Zeitschrift für Geschichte [Switzerland] 1976 26(4): 670-679.* Reviews 12 books, published between 1972 and 1976, dealing with Germany's society and parties in the 20th century. Four of the reviewed works treat similar subjects in Switzerland.   H. K. Meier

58. Haas, Gerhart. MILITÄRISCHE ENTSCHEIDUNGSFINDUNG UND POLITISCHE FÜHRUNG IM FASCHISTISCHEN DEUTSCHLAND [Military decisionmaking and political leadership in fascist Germany]. *Militärgeschichte [East Germany] 1976 15(5): 584-590.* Reprimands bourgeois German historians for their defense of the German military leadership against responsibility for contributing to aggressive imperialist wars in 1914 and 1939. Cites numerous documented examples of German military influence on war policy decisions. Suggests specific areas of research which would further clarify the war responsibility of the military. Based on published documentary collections and secondary works; 22 notes.   J. B. Street

59. Hanrieder, Wolfram F. GERMANY & THE BALANCE OF POWER. *Polity 1981 13(3): 495-504.* According to A. W. DePorte in *Europe Between the Superpowers: The Enduring Balance* (1979) the division of Germany and the Cold War inadvertently solved Europe's problem, since 1871, of having to contain an overly powerful Germany and has resulted in a stable European system. Hans W. Gatzke's *Germany and the United States: A "Special Relationship?"* (1980), a study of German-US relations from the 18th century to the present, suffers from this bilateral treatment. *Nach dreissig Jahren . . . : Geschichte, Gegenwart and Zukunft der Bundesrepublik Deutschland* (1979), edited by Walter Scheel consists of short essays on political matters, whereas *Germany in World Politics* (1979), edited by Viola Herms Drath contains essays on German society and culture as well as politics. *Rückblenden, 1976-1951 Aufzeichnungen eines Augenzeugen deutscher Aussenpolitik von Adenauer bis Schmidt* (1979) contains the memoirs of Wilhelm G. Grewe, who, as counselor to Chancellor Adenauer and German ambassador to the Kennedy administration, helped shape the legal codification of German foreign policy and articulated the orthodox Cold War views that President Kennedy was anxious to dismiss.   E. L. Keyser

60. Hardt, Hanno. THE RISE AND PROBLEMS OF MEDIA RESEARCH IN GERMANY. *J. of Communication 1976 26(3): 90-95.* Discusses research problems in the historiography and sociology of the role of the press in Germany, 1885-1970's.

61. Heideking, Jürgen. OBERSTER RAT—BOTSCHAFTSKONFERENZ —VÖLKERBUND: DREI FORMEN MULTILATERALER DIPLOMATIE NACH DEM ERSTEN WELTKRIEG [Supreme Council, Conference of Ambassadors, League of Nations: three forms of multilateral diplomacy following World War I]. *Hist. Zeitschrift [West Germany] 1980 231(3): 589-630.* Efforts

to establish new types of diplomatic institutions at the end of World War I took the form of multilateral meetings. The Supreme War Council began in November 1917 as an instrument for military coordination and became the Supreme Council of the Paris Peace Conference. At first it functioned as the Council of Ten, then as the Council of Four, and the Foreign Ministers Council of Five. After the Treaty of Versailles the Council of Heads of Delegations functioned until the treaties took effect. In 1919 the United States, Great Britain, France, and Italy established the Conference of Ambassadors to act as a clearing house of opinion about long-term stipulations of the treaties. These two councils were more influential than the League of Nations before 1924. The League had its golden age between 1925 and 1929. The 1930's temporarily checked cooperation among the allies, but it was revived during World War II. Based on the Public Records Office (London) and published documents; 84 notes.   G. H. Davis

62.   Heiland, Helmut.   PROBLEME DER PADAGOGISCHEN LOCK-EFORSCHUNG IN DEUTSCHLAND (1860-1970)   [Problems of educational research on John Locke in Germany, 1860-1970]. *Paedagogica Hist. [Belgium] 1972 12(2): 405-459.* A comprehensive review of research on John Locke's educational theory in Germany during the last century. Topical headings categorize research into such areas as interpretation of Locke to the time of Johann Friedrich Herbart, interpretation by Herbartians, the relation of Locke and Rousseau, and perceptions of Locke by educational reformers. 31 notes, biblio.
                                                                  J. M. McCarthy

63.   Hildebrand, Klaus.   STAATSKUNST ODER SYSTEMZWANG? DIE "DEUTSCHE FRAGE" ALS PROBLEM DER WELTPOLITIK   [Political artistry or pressure of the system? The "German question" as a problem of world politics]. *Hist. Zeitschrift [West Germany] 1979 228(3): 624-644.* Review article on David Calleo's *The German Problem Reconsidered: Germany and the World Order* (Cambridge U., 1978), which raises issues about the German role in international affairs which German scholars cannot do without appearing apologetic. The author asserts that Germany was only a manifestation of the same tragedy that has engulfed all other great powers, stressing similarities with Great Britain and other states through a discussion of the role of idealistic philosophy, the power mentality, and archaic preindustrial leadership. He casts doubt on many historical judgments without completely repudiating them.   Secondary sources; 38 notes.   G. H. Davis

64.   Hildebrand, Klaus.   WELTPOLITIK 1931-1941: INTERNATIONALES SYSTEM UND AUSWÄRTIGE POLITIK DER MÄCHTE   [World politics 1931-41: the international system and Great Power foreign policy]. *Geschichte in Wissenschaft und Unterricht [West Germany] 1977 28(3): 149-156.* The main tasks of the 31st German Historians' Conference committee on foreign policy were to demolish the idea that Europe still decided world policy, to inquire into the internal and external factors of foreign policy, and to examine the state of the international system, 1931-41. Japan, Great Britain, the United States, the USSR, and Germany were considered, as were the economic crisis of 1929, the war coalition problem 1939-41, Great Britain's appeasement policy, the concept of power, and the international system's dissolution into a bipolar world. Secondary works; 9 notes.   H. W. Wurster

65. Holmes, Kim R. WEST GERMANY. *Wilson Q. 1981 5(3): 94-97.* Reviews 18 books published since 1957 covering German literature, history since 1858, politics, and modern painting, with emphasis on Hitler, Nazism, and the history and culture of the Weimar Republic.

66. Hübner, Hans. WESEN UND ERSCHEINUNGSFORMEN DES PREUSSISCH-DEUTSCHEN MILITARISMUS [Essence and forms of Prussian-German militarism]. *Martin-Luther-Universität Halle-Wittenberg. Wissenschaftliche Zeitschrift. Gesellschafts- und Sprachwissenschaftliche Reihe [East Germany] 1975 24(5): 13-21.* The danger of Prussian-German militarism in the 19th and 20th centuries was a result of the combination of reactionary Prussian military traditions with modern forms of imperialist militarism.

R. Wagnleitner

67. Hugonnot, Jean. LES RÉLATIONS FRANCO-ALLEMANDES À LA LUMIÈRE DE L'HISTOIRE [Franco-German relations in the light of history]. *Année Pol. et Écon. [France] 1973 46(232/233): 140-152.* Examines Franco-German relations over the centuries. Despite their historic antagonism, there seems to have been a qualitative change since World War II. Most of the Nazi teachers have been retired, and a completely new set of values has been inculcated into the Germans, a reassertion of a pattern of friendship and revolutionary solidarity between the French and Germans. Alsace was long a source of French Revolutionary sentiment. On the German side, August Bebel's protest in the face of the enraged Junkers at the annexationist peace of 1871 exemplified the negation of Prussian militarism.

G. E. Orchard

68. Hunt, James C. THE BOURGEOIS MIDDLE IN GERMAN POLITICS, 1871-1933: RECENT LITERATURE. *Central European Hist. 1978 11(1): 83-106.* Surveys more than thirty books since 1973 about German middle class politics, 1871-1933, and concludes that they demonstrate that "the middle parties and pressure groups were better organized, more firmly based in social interests, more activist, and more willing to collaborate with Socialists than had long been assumed." 56 notes.

C. R. Lovin

69. Hürten, Heinz. MILITÄRGESCHICHTE IN DEUTSCHLAND: ZUR GESCHICHTE EINER DISZIPLIN IN DER SPANNUNG VON AKADEMISCHER FREIHEIT UND GESELLSCHAFTLICHEM ANSPRUCH [Military history in Germany: the history of an academic subject and the controversy between academic freedom and social demands]. *Hist. Jahrbuch [West Germany] 1975 95(2): 374-392.* Describes the development of military historiography in Germany. Since the 18th century the German general staff supervised official military historiography. Its aim was to provide sources for strategic studies. Universities did not include military history in their curriculum. After World War I the general staff was abolished and state archives took charge of compiling historical documents. Universities also began to treat military history as a branch of general history. During the Nazi regime the subject was again restricted and adjusted. After 1945 military history as an academic subject was enlarged by including political, economic, and social aspects of the history of wars. Research concentrated on the causes of wars and on means of preventing future wars. 30 notes.

R. Vilums

70.   Jaeger, Hans.   BUSINESS HISTORY IN GERMANY: A SURVEY OF RECENT DEVELOPMENTS.   *Business Hist. R. 1974 48(1): 28-48.* This historiograhical essay on German business history, 1918-74, emphasizes the lack of broad views on the subject. Instead there have been company histories and entrepreneurial biographies. The development of the broader view is handicapped by the lack of business schools and chairs of business history in the universities. Company archives, company histories, entrepreneurial biographies, economic history, and social history comprise the available resources. Notes some developments and a developing methodology toward a broader based business history. 90 notes.
R. V. Ritter

71.   Jarausch, Konrad H.   FROM SECOND TO THIRD REICH: THE PROBLEM OF CONTINUITY IN GERMAN FOREIGN POLICY.   *Central European Hist. 1979 12(1): 68-82.* Reviews the issues involved in determining whether or not Hitler's foreign policy represented a continuation of the foreign policy of the German Empire. Citing a number of secondary works which take different points of view, the author concludes that "instead of arguing further whether the Nazi era constitutes 'a revolutionary break' or a part of 'the main course of German history,' it might be more profitable to pursue individual strands of continuity in order to untangle the skein of constancy and change." 45 notes.
C. R. Lovin

72.   Jelowik, Lieselotte.   ZUR GESCHICHTE DES SCHWURGERICHTS IN DEUTSCHLAND UNTER DER SICHT DER JUSTIZREFORMPLÄNE IN DER BRD   [The history of the jury court in Germany in view of the West German plans for the reform of justice]. *Martin-Luther-Universität Halle-Wittenberg. Wissenschaftliche Zeitschrift. Gesellschafts- und Sprachwissenschaftliche Reihe [East Germany] 1975 24(2): 13-22.* Compares the reform of West German jury courts with the judicial practices in the Weimar Republic.
R. Wagnleitner

73.   Joll, James.   THE FOUNDATIONS OF GERMAN FOREIGN POLICY.   *History [Great Britain] 1977 62(205): 253-258.* Reviews six recently published books on Germany's foreign policy and war aims from the 1870's through the Nazi era.
R. P. Sindermann, Jr./S

74.   Kaelble, Hartmut.   LONG-TERM CHANGES IN THE RECRUITMENT OF THE BUSINESS ELITE: GERMANY COMPARED TO THE U.S., GREAT BRITAIN AND FRANCE SINCE THE INDUSTRIAL REVOLUTION.   *J. of Social Hist. 1980 13(3): 404-423.* Examines changes in the recruitment of business leaders as early capitalism matured into managerial-corporate capitalism in four countries. The German experience in the 19th century was distinctive because stronger preindustrial prejudices prevented parents from a broad spectrum of society from sending their sons into business. The maturation of capitalism curtailed but did not eliminate the practice of business leaders of placing their offspring in places of leadership. The differences between nations are disappearing. 4 tables, 24 notes.
M. Hough/S

75.   Kaelble, Hartmut.   SOCIAL MOBILITY IN GERMANY, 1900-1960. *J. of Modern Hist. 1978 50(3): 439-461.* Investigates the long-term trend of social mobility in 20th-century Germany, the relation to economic development, to

social attitudes, and political decisions. The rates of social mobility increased slightly in the long-term perspective. There is no indication that this is mainly due to economic development and occupational change. Cultural and political factors which influenced the recruitment of the middle class and the lower middle class seem to have played a major role. The essay points especially to the reduction of political barriers at the access to the civil service, the expansion of secondary and higher education, and the gradual diminution of the cultural cleavages between blue-collar workers and white-collar employees. In this way social mobility in Germany became more similar to that in other European countries from which it differed because of the social and political structures rather than because of industrialization. Based on large numbers of surveys and statistical accounts from the late Empire and the interwar period.   J

76. Kathe, Heinz.   US-HISTORIKER ÜBER DEN PREUSSISCH-DEUTSCHEN MILITARISMUS [American historians on Prussian-German militarism]. *Martin-Luther-Universität Halle-Wittenberg. Wissenschaftliche Zeitschrift. Gesellschafts- und Sprachwissenschaftliche Reihe [East Germany] 1975 24(5): 29-33.* Recent US historiography on Germany in the 19th and 20th centuries deny the close connection between Prussian-German militarism and imperialism.   R. Wagnleitner

77. Kent, George O.   RESEARCH OPPORTUNITIES IN WEST AND EAST GERMAN ARCHIVES FOR THE WEIMAR PERIOD AND THE THIRD REICH. *Central European Hist. 1979 12(1): 38-67.* Describes archival collections in Germany to suggest a variety of topics on which further research is needed. Lists some major books and articles in the various areas of German history since 1918. 125 notes.   C. R. Lovin

78. Kern, Wolfgang and Sperling, Heinz.   DER DEUTSCHE MILITARISMUS VOM ENDE DES ERSTEN WELTKRIEGES BIS ZUR ZURSCHLAGUNG DER FASCHISTISCHEN DIKTATUR [German militarism from the end of World War I to the smashing of the fascist dictatorship]. *Militärgeschichte [East Germany] 1974 13(4): 562-571.* Describes the role of the armed forces in the November Revolution and their adjustment to the Weimar Republic, role in the establishment of paramilitary formations, ideological influence on the population, drive for rearmament and a war of revenge, relationship to fascism and role in carrying out Nazi foreign policy, and role in the conspiracy of 20 July 1944.   H. D. Andrews

79. Klein, Fritz.   BEMERKUNGEN ZUM RIEZLER TAGEBUCH [Notes on the Riezler diary]. *Zeitschrift für Geschichtswissenschaft [East Germany] 1973 21(6): 671-678.* Review article on the diary of Kurt Riezler, *Tagebücher, Aufsätze, Dokumente* (Göttingen Germany: K. D. Erdmann, Vandenhoeck and Rupprecht, 1972), in the context of the continuity of the German imperialist foreign policy between World War I and World War II. 6 notes.   R. Wagnleitner

80. Klein, Fritz.   STAND UND PROBLEME DER ERFORSCHUNG DER GESCHICHTE DES DEUTSCHEN IMPERIALISMUS BIS 1945 [The position and problems of research into the history of German imperialism until 1945]. *Zeitschrift für Geschichtswissenschaft [East Germany] 1975 23(5): 485-493.* East

German historians have successfully studied aspects of German imperialism, including the role of imperialists in the causes and conduct of the two world wars, the development of German monopoly capital, and the foreign policy of the Weimar Republic. Topics requiring attention are the influence of economic interest groups on government policies, the relationship between various monopoly capitalist groups and fascism, and imperialism after 1945. 13 notes.

J. T. Walker

81. Kocka, Jürgen. WELTKRIEG UND MITTELSTAND. HAND-WERKER UND ANGESTELLTE IN DEUTSCHLAND 1914-1918 [World war and the middle classes: artisans and employees in Germany, 1914-18]. *Francia [France] 1974 2: 431-457.* Traditional Marxist divisions of social groups into working class and petite bourgeoisie, placing employees in the first and artisans and small merchants into the second, are not easy to apply to pre-World War I Germany. But World War I pushed the former into the proletariat and the latter into the bourgeoisie. The inflation after the war ruined both. War and economic dislocation contributed to a dramatic weakening of the middle classes in Germany, a process which fed the rise of Nazism. 73 notes.

J. C. Billigmeier

82. Krasuski, Jerzy. THE GERMAN REICH AND THE BALANCE OF POWER IN EUROPE. *Polish Western Affairs [Poland] 1973 14(1): 33-48.* Chronicles the impact of Germany, in its various empires, unifications, and divisions, 1800-1945, on the balance of power in Europe.

83. Krieger, Leonard. GERMAN HISTORY—IN THE GRAND MAN-NER. *Am. Hist. Rev. 1979 84(4): 1007-1017.* Review essay of four recent books on modern German history: Gordon A. Craig's *Germany, 1806-1945,* James J. Sheehan's *German Liberalism in the Nineteenth Century,* Fritz Stern's *Gold and Iron: Bismarck, Bleichröder, and the Building of the German Empire,* and Hans-Ulrich Wehler's *Das deutsche Kaiserreich, 1871-1918.* These works vary in their commitment to political or social history—Craig is primarily political, Sheehan and Wehler largely social, and Stern an even mix of the two—but all share a unitary point of reference that is ultimately authoritarian and political. This kind of political teleology is characteristic of the contemporary historiography of modern Germany.

A

84. Lehmbruch, Gerhard. PARTY AND FEDERATION IN GERMANY: A DEVELOPMENTAL DILEMMA. *Government and Opposition [Great Britain] 1978 13(2): 151-177.* Examines the course of federalism in Germany from 1916 to the present and concludes that the system has shown a trend from a multiparty system to a two-party system, the latter being somewhat unusual for a federal system, but one which works in Germany because of the minimal regional variations in social and political structures and the strong preference of the elites and the public for national uniformity.

85. Losser, Alphonse. BIBLIOGRAPHIE ÉCONOMIQUE [Economic bibliography]. *Rev. d'Allemagne [France] 1978 10(1): 122-136.* Lists 66 works on the economic and social history of Germany and Austria from the Industrial Revolution to the present, each followed by an abstract in French.

J. C. Billigmeier

86. Loth, Heinrich. ANTIKOMMUNISTISCHE AKTIVITÄTEN DES DEUTSCHEN IMPERIALISMUS IN AFRIKA SÜDLICH DER SAHARA (1919 BIS 1939) [Anticommunist activities of German imperialism in Africa south of the Sahara, 1919-39]. *Zeitschrift für Geschichtswissenschaft [East Germany] 1973 21(9): 1066-1073.* In the years 1919-39 German imperialism, even after the loss of the German colonies, was regarded as an ally against Communism by the Western powers in Africa. The reports of German immigrants and diplomats in Africa to the German foreign ministry were the basis for anticommunist intervention by colonial powers to crush independence movements. Based on documents in the Deutsches Zentralarchiv Potsdam, printed documents, and secondary literature; 35 notes.   R. Wagnleitner

87. Löwenthal, Richard. BONN UND WEIMAR: ZWEI DEUTSCHE DEMOKRATIEN [Bonn and Weimar: two German democracies]. Winkler, Heinrich August, ed. *Politische Weichenstellungen im Nachkriegsdeutschland 1945-1953* (Göttingen: Vandenhoeck & Ruprecht, 1979): 9-25. Outlines common themes in the Weimar Republic and postwar West Germany, describing the problem of the consolidation of a democratic system in an industrial society without a vital democratic-revolutionary tradition. Explores how the cultural peculiarity of Germany influenced the destinies of both these democratic German states. 10 notes.   G. E. Pergl

88. Mahlke, Bernhard. ZUM VERHÄLTNIS VON MILITARISMUS UND HITLERFASCHISMUS [On the relationship between militarism and Hitler-fascism]. *Militärgeschichte [East Germany] 1976 15(2): 206-210.* Summarizes the many similarities and the few differences between modern fascism and militarism using the example of Germany from 1917 to 1945. Modern fascism and militarism are expressions of the internal and external aggressiveness of monopoly capitalism, and both have their roots in imperialism and reactionary class interests. Based on protocols of Communist party conferences, Lenin's writings and secondary works; 25 notes.   J. B. Street

89. Małachowski, Witold. SPD A INTEGRACJA ZACHODNIO-EUROPEJSKA [The German Social Democratic Party and West European integration]. *Przegląd Zachodni [Poland] 1975 31(2): 327-337.* Traces the development of the German Social Democratic Party's attitudes towards Western Europe from the 1925 Heidelberg program to the resignation of Willy Brandt in 1974.

90. McDermott, John. VARIETIES OF INTERNATIONAL HISTORY. *Can. Rev. of Am. Studies [Canada] 1981 12(1): 101-112.* Review article prompted by Hans W. Gatzke's *Germany and the United States: "A Special Relationship?"* (1980); Phyllis Keller's *States of Belonging: German-American Intellectuals and the First World War* (1979); Melvyn P. Leffler's *The Elusive Quest: America's Pursuit of European Stability and French Security, 1919-1933* (1979); and David Strauss's *Menace in the West: Anti-Americanism in Modern Times* (1978). Methodologically different, the books all stress the impact of World War I and how the war inalterably changed American relations with France and Germany. 6 notes.   H. T. Lovin

91. Menger, Manfred; Petrick, Fritz; and Wilhelmus, Wolfgang. GRUND-ZÜGE IMPERIALISTISCHER DEUTSCHER NORDEUROPAPOLITIK BIS 1945 [Basic features of imperialist Germany's Northern Europe policies to 1945]. *Zeitschrift für Geschichtswissenschaft [East Germany] 1973 21(9): 1029-1044.* During the 20th century Northern Europe and Scandinavia became increasingly important to Germany as a market for exports, a source of raw materials, and an area for investment. In World War I and World War II Scandinavia was of great strategic and economic importance, especially after the German invasion of the USSR. Secondary literature; 56 notes.

R. Wagnleitner

92. Mistrorigo, Luigi. LA DEMOCRAZIA IN GERMANIA E LO "SPETTRO" DI WEIMAR [Democracy in Germany and the specter of Weimar]. *Civitas [Italy] 1979 30(1): 33-47.* Many of the attitudes among Germans that doomed the Weimar Republic are still present today in a subtler form in West Germany; only integration into the European community will bury the Nazi past completely.

93. Moisuc, Viorica. PRINCIPIUL NAȚIONALITĂȚILOR ÎN NOUA ORDINE INTERNAȚIONALĂ DE DUPA 1918 ȘI CHESTIUNEA REVIZIONISMULUI [The principle of nationalities in the new international order after 1918 and the question of revisionism]. *Rev. de Istorie [Romania] 1980 33(2): 285-298.* Examines the consequences for Europe of international policies based on the principles of nationalities or the balance of power, rejecting the thesis that various states were merely the creation of the Paris peace treaties of 1919-20. Various revisionist developments after 1921, particularly the Danubian Confederation and the revision of treaties and frontiers, represented attempts to return to the political and territorial order prevailing before 1918. First presented at the international colloquium "L'Europe de Versailles, 1918-1923" in Geneva, September 1979. 42 notes. French summary.

R. O. Khan

94. Morsel, Henri. LA POSITION FINANCIÈRE ET ÉCONOMIQUE DE L'EUROPE, AU LENDEMAIN DE LA PREMIÈRE GUERRE MONDIALE [Europe's financial and economic position immediately after World War I]. *Relations Int. [France] 1976 (8): 313-322.* World War I enormously weakened the financial and economic position of Europe and strengthened that of the United States, already the world's leading industrial power. In the chaos, prices soared, then, in the depression of 1920-21, they plunged, except in Germany, where they rose to fantastic levels. The tendency to return to economic liberalism worsened matters. Eventually economic reconstruction was based on American aid, which enabled the Allies to pay their debts and the Germans to pay the reparations. Table, 3 notes.

J. C. Billigmeier

95. Moses, John. BUREAUCRATS AND PATRIOTS: THE GERMAN SOCIALIST TRADE UNION LEADERSHIP FROM SARAJEVO TO VERSAILLES, 1914-1919. *Labor Hist. [Australia] 1976 (30): 1-21.* Traces the "doggedly loyal policies" of Germany's Social Democratic labor union leadership during World War I, and their reaction to Versailles and the November Revolution.

96. Moses, John A. FROM KAISER TO FÜHRER: NEW WORKS IN MODERN GERMAN HISTORY. *Australian J. of Pol. and Hist. [Australia] 1979 25(1): 112-116.* A review article of seven recent works which illustrate the continuity of German history, the links between the Hitler and the pre-1919 periods. R. J. Evans, *Society and Politics in Wilhelmine Germany* (London, 1978) gathers 11 research essays by British writers. W. Schiefel, *Bernard Dernburg 1865-1937* (Zurich, 1977) is a biography of a liberal Jewish financier who was Colonial Secretary. E. C. Schoek *Arbeitslösigkeit und Rationalisierung* (Frankfurt, 1977) covers the Communist trade union tactics under the Weimar Republic. P. D. Stachura, ed., *The Shaping of the Nazi State* (London, 1978) gathers nine papers from young scholars in Britain and the same author has provided a critical bibliography, *The Weimar Era and Hitler 1918-1933* (Oxford, 1977). J. Thies *Architek der Weltherrschaft* (Dusseldorf, 1976) covers Hitler's expansionist aims, and H. Hanschel, *Ober-Bürgermeister Hermann Luppe* (Nurnberg, 1975) biography of a mayor during the Nazi rise to power.

W. D. McIntyre

97. Nipperdey, Thomas. DER FÖDERALISMUS IN DER DEUTSCHEN GESCHICHTE [Federalism in German history]. *Bijdragen en Mededelingen Betreffende de Geschiedenis der Nederlanden [Netherlands] 1979 94(3): 497-547.* The German Empire of the Middle Ages provided for a federal structure that was considerably weakened in early modern times. The Napoleonic period brought a measure of political unity but the German Bund of 1815 established a confederative system that had no real central organs. More effective was the Zollverein which provided for real cooperation among the German states. The German Empire was not a unitary state but a federation. It was a compromise between unity and diversity. The Weimar Republic retained the federal principle while the National Socialists established a bureaucratic, authoritarian, unitarian state. The West German republic restored federalism although the powers of the federal government have increased in recent years. Biblio.

G. D. Homan

98. Noack, Karl-Heinz. ZUM MILITARISMUSBEGRIFF IN DER GESCHICHTSSCHREIBUNG DER BRD [The concept of militarism in the historiography of West Germany]. *Militärgeschichte [East Germany] 1977 16(6): 725-731.* Examines the views of militarism in Germany of various historians. Friedrich Meinecke, Hans Herzfeld, Hans-Joachim Schoeps and Gerhard Ritter all reject the notion of inherent German militarism; Karl Bucheim saw militarism in Prussia's history, particularly in the use of the army against social democracy; Volker Berghahn, in his historically based 1975 study of militarism adopts a comparative approach. The concept of militarism cannot be determined merely by describing its historical manifestations. Secondary works; 44 notes.

A. Alcock

99. Obermann, Karl. LES MOUVEMENTS PAYSANS ET LES PROBLÈMES AGRAIRES EN ALLEMAGNE, DE LA FIN DU XVIIIe SIÈCLE À NOS JOURS [Peasant movements and agrarian problems in Germany from the end of the 18th century to the present]. *Cahiers Int. d'Hist. Écon. et Sociale [Italy] 1976 6: 253-281.* After 1750 rapid economic growth, especially in Prussia, stimulated the progress and development of agriculture. In 1807 agrarian reform began with the abolition of serfdom. Agrarian reform was second only to national union as an issue. Peasants could buy themselves free from all obligations to the land-

owner, but the process weakened them economically. Increasingly the peasants turned to political activity. Although the peasants reduced their indebtedness during and after World War I, it grew rapidly after 1924 until many peasants became wage laborers; small landholders correspondingly declined. After World War II East Germany restructured agriculture along Marxist lines. Biblio.
F. X. Hartigan

100. Ohno, Eiji. PUROISEN DOITSU NO KINDAIKA TO CHIHŌ JI-CHI: RYŌCHI KUIKI TO SONO KAITAI [Modernization and local self-government in Prussian Germany]. *Keizai Ronsō [Japan] 1979 123(4-5): 1-18, (6): 1-21.* Examines the duality in the local government system of 19th-century East Prussia, that is, the farming districts *(Gutsbezirk)* and the rural communities *(Landgemeinde).* Considers the process in which the *Gutsbezirk* remained independent of the local government structure, the actual state of the *Junker* rule on the local population and relations with nearby *Landgemeinde,* and movements to reform the *Gutsbezirk* system and actions against it. Discusses the decline of the *Gutsbezirk* in the late Weimar era and emphasizes that the *Junker* continued to hold the power base of the district council through the 19th century. Primary sources; 2 tables, 107 notes.
Y. Aoki

101. Overy, R. J. CLASS AND COMMUNITY IN THE THIRD REICH. *Hist. J. [Great Britain] 1979 22(2): 493-504.* A review article on five books published in 1976 and 1977 on the relationship of capitalism and fascism in the Third Reich. They shed light on the question of whether the German capitalist classes needed fascism to sustain growth and contain class conflict and the particular historical reasons why Germany in the 1920's and 1930's failed to take a route that might have functioned in capitalist interests under a more democratic system. 18 notes.
R. V. Ritter

102. Péron, Jean-Paul. LE RÉARMEMENT DE L'ALLEMAGNE ENTRE LES DEUX GUERRES MONDIALES [German rearmament between the two world wars]. *Information Hist. [France] 1974 36(5): 242-249; 1975 37(1): 53-57.* Part I. A succinct chronological review of the disarmament of Germany after 1919, its social problems, anti-Bolshevism, unemployment, military tradition, and pride. The expected and feared result was the development of the Reichswehr as the pivot of rearmament and both camouflaged and open paramilitary groups in secret training. Finally, the failure of the disarmament conference, the unresolved question of equal rights, and proportional arming vis-à-vis France and England led to the ruptures of 1933 and 1934. 7 notes. Part II. Discusses rearmament in 1934, conscription in 1935. Describes the structure of the new Wehrmacht, made economically possible by Hjalmar Schacht (1877-1970), and the integration with Nazism and the purges of 1934 and 1937. Although the German army in 1939 was a formidable force inspired with patriotism and capable of decisive quick blows, it could not, for lack of strategic resources, withstand a world coalition and a prolonged war. Photo, 17 notes, biblio.
R. K. Adams

103. Peterson, Larry. THE ONE BIG UNION IN INTERNATIONAL PERSPECTIVE: REVOLUTIONARY INDUSTRIAL UNIONISM 1900-1925. *Labour [Canada] 1981 7(Spr): 41-66.* Compares and contrasts the attempts by workers in Great Britain, France, Germany, the United States, and Canada to organize industrial unions at the beginning of the 20th century. Revo-

lutionary industrial unionism was an international phenomenon, arising from similar socioeconomic conditions in the advanced capitalist countries, which spawned simultaneous movements to found "one big union" of all industrial workers. Analyzes the different views of industrial unionists on the subjects of dual unionism, organization, and politics. Syndicalism was only one faction active in the movement. Further analyzes the social bases of the movement among unskilled workers and specific groups of skilled workers in the mass production industries. Points out the tactical originality of the movement and why its tactics posed a revolutionary challenge to capitalist control of the economy.   J/S

104. Pohl, Hans.   DIE KONZENTRATION IN DER DEUTSCHEN WIRTSCHAFT VOM AUSGEHENDEN 19. JAHRHUNDERT BIS 1945 [Concentration in the German economy from the late 19th century to 1945]. *Zeitschrift für Unternehmensgeschichte [West Germany] 1978 11: 4-44.* From the 1870's to 1945 the trend in Germany was toward industrial concentration in the form of mergers, cartels, and industrial associations. During World War I government policies furthered this trend and even forced cartelization in some industries. The Nazi government promoted the trend through tax laws, forced cartelization, and centralized control over the economy. 3 tables, 177 notes.
J. T. Walker

105. Pyenson, Lewis.   CULTURAL IMPERIALISM AND EXACT SCIENCES: GERMAN EXPANSION OVERSEAS 1900-1930.   *Hist. of Sci. [Great Britain] 1982 20(1): 1-43.* Technological development enabled the West to exploit other continents, and science supported the process of imperialism. Three principal overseas scientific institutions established by Germany were in Samoa, Argentina, and China. Here German physicists and astronomers carried out research at posts far outside European and North American centers of learning. These efforts were partly fostered by a sense that civilization was being furthered in the colonies while being directed toward legitimizing political power. Studies done by these overseas enterprises were generally variations on a European theme, but discourse in the exact sciences remained largely unaffected by imperialist ideology.   Primary sources; 113 notes.   J. G. Packer

106. Rahne, Hermann.   ZUR TRUPPENGESCHICHTSSCHREIBUNG DES DEUTSCHEN MILITARISMUS IN VERGANGENHEIT UND GEGENWART [On German militarist historiography about troops past and present]. *Militärgeschichte [East Germany] 1980 19(2): 177-189.* Examines the growing flood of military and neofascist literature in West Germany, and investigates the place, role, and significance of German imperialist historiography about troops within the system of political-ideological manipulation of soldiers and civilians. Describes the characteristics and functions of this kind of literature after the First and Second World Wars, and characterizes the authors, initiators, and supporters of reactionary German military historiography from the Weimar Republic through Fascism to West Germany of the seventies. 2 illus., 27 notes.
J/T (H. D. Andrews).

107. Ritter, Gerhard A.   STAAT UND ARBEITERSCHAFT IN DEUTSCHLAND VON DER REVOLUTION 1848/49 BIS ZUR NATIONALSOZIALISTISCHEN MACHTERGREIFUNG   [State and work force in Germany from the revolution of 1848-49 to the National Socialist seizure

of power]. *Hist. Zeitschrift [West Germany] 1980 231(2): 325-368.* Observations of the relationship among German governmental agencies, the working class, and labor organizations provide insights into the entire system. Beginning with an absolutist state that carried out a disciplining process, conscious activity for working-class welfare had to contend with police, army, and school indoctrination. Bismarck's socialist laws failed to restrain the socialist and labor union movements and demonstrated the failure of the German state policy of restraining labor. The social welfare laws of the 1880's were also connected with the idea of the state as a force for labor discipline. The socialist movement began in isolation but came to identify with the empire, demonstrated by their 1914 vote to support war credits. The Majority Socialists who helped establish the Weimar Republic hoped to apply democratic principles to bring about a conversion to a socialist economy, but polarization of parties between 1918 and 1923 destroyed this hope. Based on local German archives and published documents; 134 notes.

G. H. Davis

108.   Rovan, Joseph.   REFLEXIONS SUR LA SOCIAL-DÉMOCRATIE ALLEMANDE   [The German Social Democratic Party]. *Rev. d'Allemagne [France] 1977 9(4): 667-696.* The history of the Social Democratic Party (SPD) can be divided into three main periods. From its 19th-century beginnings to 1918 it was retarded by the aristocratic and bourgeois forces dominant in Germany. During this period the fledgling party grew to early maturity, developing its relationship to other parties, and sought solutions to internal problems, foremost of which was the dilemma of how to be revolutionary without ceasing to be democratic. The October Revolution split the Social Democrats, who were thenceforth opposed by the new Communist Party. During the second period, 1918-45, the SPD at first came to power, then slipped into the opposition, and finally was suppressed by the Nazi regime. From 1945 to the present, the West German SPD, aided by Soviet policies in East Germany, found the key to success in the Godesberg program by opting for reform instead of revolution. The appearance of a new left within the party, however, has prevented the choice between reform and radicalism from becoming a dead issue. Note.   J. S. Gassner

109.   Ruck, Michael.   "AUS DER GESCHICHTE LERNEN—DIE ZUKUNFT GESTALTEN." KONFERENZ ZUR GESCHICHTE DER GEWERKSCHAFTEN AUS ANLASS DES 30. GRÜNDUNGSTAGES DES DGB   ["Learn from history; form the future." Conference on the history of the trade unions on the occasion of the 30th anniversary of the German Federation of Trade Unions (DGB)]. *Geschichte in Wissenschaft und Unterricht [West Germany] 1980 31(6): 378-385.* Since 1974 German trade unions' interest in their own history has been growing and led to a conference of trade unionists, historians, and social scientists at Munich in 1979. The conference covered union policy in 1914, during the 1918-19 revolution, in the final stage of the Weimar Republic, and in the formative years of the Federal Republic. 12 notes.

H. W. Wurster

110.   Rusconi, Gian Enrico.   WEIMAR: UN MODELLO DI CRISI PER L'ITALIA DEGLI ANNI SETTANTA?   [Weimar: a model of crisis for Italy in the 1970's?]. *Quaderni di Sociologia [Italy] 1975 24(1-2): 5-54.* Compares the crisis of the Weimar political and social system with that of Italy in the 1970's, showing the overall diversity in the structure and development of each, while singling out interesting analogies between the two.

111. Salvadori, Massimo L. LA CONCEZIONE DEL PROCESSO RIVOLUZIONARIO IN KAUTSKY (1891-1922) [The conception of the revolutionary process in Kautsky, 1891-1922]. *Ann. dell'Istituto Giangiacomo Feltrinelli [Italy] 1973 15: 26-80.* Traces the evolution of the concept of the revolutionary process in the political theory of Karl Kautsky through examination of his relationship with the Social Democratic Party, his various positions within the party's hierarchy, and political factionalism in which he participated. The theoretical response to Bismarckian reaction was gradually modified to include alliance with the middle class and acceptance of parliamentary democracy. 207 notes.　　　　　　　　　　　　　　　　　　　　　　J. Brown

112. Schmidt-Linsenhoff, Viktoria. FRAUENALLTAG UND FRAUENBEWEGUNG IN FRANKFURT 1890-1980: EINE NEUE AUSSTELLUNG IM HISTORISCHEN MUSEUM FRANKFURT [Women's daily life and the women's movement in Frankfurt, 1890-1980: a new exhibit at the Frankfurt Historical Museum]. *Geschichtsdidaktik [West Germany] 1981 6(3): 291-304.* Describes an exhibit at the Museum of History in Frankfurt and describes the visual presentation of the facts of women's life in Germany.

113. Stegmann, Dirk. HUGENBERG CONTRA STRESEMANN: DIE POLITIK DER INDUSTRIEVERBÄNDE AM ENDE DES KAISERREICHS [Hugenberg versus Stresemann: The politics of industrial associations at the end of the imperial period]. *Vierteljahrshefte für Zeitgeschichte [West Germany] 1976 24(4): 329-378.* The Central Association of German Industrialists (CDI), founded in 1876, represented large industries, but the Chemical Association left in 1890 and in 1895 helped to form the rival League of Industrialists (BdI), representing smaller concerns. Gustav Stresemann, chairman of the BdI, sought to unite the two in 1905 but failed. His policy of free labor unions was repugnant to the CDI. The Hansa League joined Stresemann in 1909, but four years later Alfred Hugenberg, chairman of the CDI, tried to split them. The War Committee formed in 1914 united the rival groups, although the CDI remained politically strongest. Eventually, in 1919, the Imperial Association for German Industry superseded them all. Based on the Historical Archives of the Gutehoffnungshütte, trade newspapers, and secondary works; 253 notes.　　A. Alcock

114. Stegmann, Dirk. QUELLENKUNDEN UND QUELLENSAMMLUNGEN ZUR GESCHICHTE DES KAISERREICHES UND DER WEIMARER REPUBLIK [The study of sources and source collections on the history of Imperial Germany and the Weimar Republic]. *Archiv für Sozialgeschichte [West Germany] 1980 20: 545-551.* Reviews source collections and introductions to the sources published between 1975 and 1977. Note.
　　　　　　　　　　　　　　　　　　　　　　　　H. W. Wurster

115. Stolz, Gerd. DIE GENDARMERIE IN PREUSSEN 1812-1923 [The Prussian constabulary 1812-1923]. *Zeitschrift für Heereskunde [West Germany] 1976 40(266-267): 148-159.* Continued from a previous article. Details the administration, training, and organization of the provincial constabulary, which increased to over 5,000 men by 1902. Regulations changes in 1886 and 1906 did not alter the fundamental organization. With World War I, however, an eighth of the force was sent to the Army field police or occupied territories. After the war Prussia retained an enlarged constabulary in turbulent times; after Versailles,

the Prussian State Ministry converted it to a civilian rural police. Mentions other types of paramilitary security organizations. Secondary sources; 6 illus., biblio., appendix.   K. W. Estes

116.   Szegvári, Katalin N.   A NŐMOZGALMI IRÁNYZATOK HARCA A NŐK EGYENJOGÚSÍTÁSÁÉRT NÉMETORSZÁGBAN A NÁCI HATALOMÁTVÉTELIG   [The struggle of the feminist movement for women's equality in Germany up to the seizure of power by the Nazis]. *Acta Facultatis Politico-Iuridicae U. Scientiarum Budapestinensis de Rolando Eötvös Nominatae [Hungary] 1979 22: 103-145.* Depicts the feminist movement's development in Germany up to the 1930's and its impact on its Hungarian counterpart and compares it with feminist movements internationally.

117.   Thadden, Rudolf von.   L'ALLEMAGNE AU LENDEMAIN DES DEUX GUERRES MONDIALES: UNE COMPARAISON   [Germany after two World Wars: a comparison]. *Int. Jahrbuch für Geschichts- und Geographieunterricht [West Germany] 1977-78 18: 194-200.* Affirms that Bonn is not Weimar and that the political stability of the present Federal Republic is unquestionably greater than its predecessor. Suggests that among the major factors favoring stability are: 1) the immigration of around 10,000,000 Germans into West Germany after World War II as refugees; 2) the lack of influence after 1945 of the *Junkers* who played a major role in governing Germany after World War I; and 3) the exclusion of the Communist Party from any meaningful role in the Federal Republic. Based on a paper presented to the Second German-Tunisian Schoolbook Conference, Tunis, 11-15 April 1977; 5 notes.   J. L. Colwell

118.   Thalmann, Rita.   QUELQUES OUVRAGES SUR LA RÉPUBLIQUE DE WEIMAR (1918-1933)   [Several works on the Weimar Republic, 1918-33]. *Rev. Hist. [France] 1979 262(2): 399-406.* Reviews seven books concerning the *Freikorps* (Free Corps), the *Jungdeutsche Orden* (Young German Order), the pacifist Hellmut von Gerlach, Gustav Noske, Theodor Heuss, Heinrich Brüning, and Alfred Hugenberg. Refers to other recent works concerning the rightist paramilitary movements and the politicians who contributed to the erosion and fall of the Weimar Republic.   G. H. Davis

119.   Tilly, Richard H.   *ANGESTELLTE* AND WHITE COLLAR WORKERS: A REVIEW ARTICLE.   *Comparative Studies in Soc. and Hist. [Great Britain] 1979 21(3): 416-420.* Jürgen Kocka's *Angestellte Zwischen Faschismus und Demokratie: zur Politischen Sozialgeschichte der Angestellten: USA, 1890-1940 im Internationalen Vergleich* (Göttingen: Vandenhoek & Ruprecht, 1977) compares the socioeconomic condition of salaried workers in the United States with that of German white collar workers and determines that the Americans were less susceptible to fascism because their sense of class consciousness was less well developed.

120.   Tipton, Frank B., Jr.   SMALL BUSINESS AND THE RISE OF HITLER: A REVIEW ARTICLE.   *Business Hist. Rev. 1979 53(2): 235-246.* Review article of Shulamit Volkov's *The Rise of Popular Antimodernism in Germany: The Urban Master Artisans, 1873-1896* (Princeton U. Pr., 1978), Robert Gellately's *The Politics of Economic Despair: Shopkeepers and German Politics, 1890-1914* (London: Sage, 1974), and Heinrich A. Winkler's *Mittelstand,*

Demokratie and Nationalsozialismus (Cologne: Kiepenheur & Witsch, 1972). These books all attempt to prove with empirical evidence that German small business formed a key source of support for Nazism. C. J. Pusateri

121. Towle, Philip. REALPOLITIK, DECEIT, AND DISARMAMENT. *Army Q. and Defence J. [Great Britain] 1981 111(1): 62-72.* Discusses the disarmament policies of Germany, Great Britain, France, and the USSR from the 1920's to the present, and compares the nature and results of past efforts with current disarmament negotiations.

122. Turner, H. A. REVIEW. *Central European Hist. 1974 7(1): 84-90.* Reviews Heinrich August Winkler's *Mittelstand, Demokratie und National-sozialismus. Die Politische Entwicklung von Handwerk und Kleinhandel in der Weimarer Republik* (Cologne: Kiepenheuer & Witsch, 1972) and Martin Schumacher's *Mittelstandsfront und Republik. Die Wirtschaftspartei—Reichspartei des deutschen Mittelstandes 1919-1933* (Düsseldorf: Droste Verlag, 1972). The *Mittelstand* (lower middle class), though dissatisfied during the Weimar period, suffered less materially than has been generally thought. Winkler's book is the more ambitious and complete; Schumacher effectively illuminates an anti-republican middle class party. C. R. Lovin

123. Vinogradov, V. N. KRIZIS BURZHUAZNOGO LIBERALIZMA V GODY VEIMARSKOI RESPUBLIKI V OSVESHCHENII ISTORIO-GRAFII FRG [The crisis of bourgeois liberalism in the years of the Weimar Republic as reflected in West German historiography]. *Voprosy Istorii [USSR] 1977 (6): 81-97.* The problem of the crisis of bourgeois liberalism in the years of the Weimar Republic is studied in the Federal Republic of Germany primarily from the viewpoint of class collaboration, which corresponds to the present-day aspirations of the ruling element in that country. The experience of German liberalism in this respect is evaluated as a "great service," a "contribution to the discussion" on enlisting the working class to play a "constructive role" in bourgeois society. The vast majority of West German historians fail to bring out the actual causes responsible for the crisis of the liberal parties, reducing these causes to subjective factors. A number of progressive-minded authors come out against apologetic conceptions and expose the real culprits responsible for the fall of the Weimar Republic. J

124. Voigt, Gerd. OSTFORSCHUNG UND MILITARISMUS [Eastern European research *(Ostforschung)* and militarism]. *Militärgeschichte [East Germany] 1976 15(6): 708-717.* The conjuring of illusory enemies has been an integral part of the ideological manipulation of the masses in Germany and has contributed to a militarist psychology. In pre-World War I imperial Germany, the Weimar Republic, Nazi Germany, and West Germany scholars engaging in Slavic and East European research at institutes and universities have contributed to the imperialist and militarist aggressions of Germany by putting their "science" to work, conjuring a Slavic and Bolshevik danger from the East. Secondary works; 17 notes. J. B. Street

125. Walczak, Antoni Wladyslaw. STOSUNKI NIEMIECKO-CHIŃSKIE, 1897-1939 [Sino-German relations, 1897-1939]. *Przegląd Zachodni [Poland] 1975 31(1): 1-41.* Outlines the history of German involvement in China from the

18th century through the period of colonialism, and examines the period of "colonization without colonies," 1918-39.

126. Waline, Pierre. SYNDICATS, ORGANISATIONS PATRONALES ET RELATIONS SOCIALES EN FRANCE ET EN ALLEMAGNE [Trade unions, employers' associations, and social relations in France and in Germany]. *Rev. d'Allemagne [France] 1980 12(1): 102-116.* By 1914 the German labor unions had made much more progress in organization and collective bargaining than the French. During the interwar period, both the German and French labor movements declined, but for very different reasons. After World War II, the German labor unions achieved a high degree of unity and succeeded in forming a pragmatic partnership with an equally unified set of employers. In contrast, organized labor in France was fragmented, although the French employers were represented by a single agency. Recent developments in Germany augur well for social harmony there, but labor problems in France are troublesome signs.
J. S. Gassner

127. Wasser, Hartmut. ARGUMENTATIVE GRUNDMUSTER LINKER UND RECHTER PARLAMENTARISMUS-KRITIK VOM KAISERREICH ZUR BUNDESREPUBLIK [The basic concepts of left- and right-wing criticism of parliamentarism from the empire to the Federal Republic]. *Geschichte in Wissenschaft und Unterricht [West Germany] 1977 28(9): 513-534.* Analyzes the history of criticism and nonacceptance of parliamentary government in Germany since 1870, where differing concepts of government and the state are basic. Wilhelm Liebknecht initiated left-wing criticism, claiming that parliamentary activity obscures revolutionary objectives, stabilizes the regime, and may lead to neglect of the people's interest. Right-wing criticism, strongest during the Weimar Republic, held that the real representative of the general interest is not party-ridden parliament, but independent government; parliamentary government leads to inefficiency. Right- and left-wing criticism both reject representative systems—the existence of several different and legitimate interests in parliament—and both criticize parliamentary government against an unreal image. Present-day parliamentary self-awareness shows the necessity of reform. 52 notes.
H. W. Wurster

128. Weissbecker, Manfred. DIE "ZEITGESCHICHTLICHEN KONTROVERSEN" KARL DIETRICH BRACHERS: EIN ANTIKOMMUNISTISCHER ZERRSPIEGEL DER GESCHICHTE UND THEORIE DES FASCHISMUS [The "controversies on contemporary history" of Karl Dietrich Bracher: an anticommunist distorting mirror of the history and theory of fascism]. *Wissenschaftliche Zeitschrift der Friedrich-Schiller-Universität Jena. Gesellschafts- und Sprachwissenschaftliche Reihe [East Germany] 1979 29(2): 291-303.* Karl Dietrich Bracher and most other West German historians try to interpret fascism as being contrary to the capitalist system and liberal-democratic society. These authors even attribute to fascism some characteristic revolutionary theories. 75 notes.
R. Wagnleitner

129. Weissbecker, Manfred and Gottwald, Herbert. ZUR ROLLE DER FÜHRER BÜRGERLICHER PARTEIEN: BIOGRAPHISCHE ASPEKTE IN DER GESCHICHTE DER POLITISCHEN PARTEIEN DES DEUTSCHEN IMPERIALISMUS VON DER JAHRHUNDERT-WENDE BIS 1945

[The role of bourgeois party leaders: biographical aspects of the history of German imperialist political parties from the turn of the century until 1945]. *Zeitschrift für Geschichtswissenschaft [East Germany] 1979 27(4): 299-315.* Presents several hypotheses concerning bourgeois party leaders, a topic which has hitherto been neglected in Marxist historiography. These leaders had freedom of action only within their own economic, political, social, and ideological milieu. Successful leaders have had the following characteristics: deep insights into the interests of the ruling class, and a mastery of the tactics needed in the class struggle; ability to exploit the weaknesses of their class opponents; and skill in manipulating the masses. 83 notes. J. T. Walker

130. Wereszycki, Henryk. FROM BISMARCK TO HITLER: THE PROBLEM OF CONTINUITY OF HISTORICAL DEVELOPMENT FROM THE SECOND TO THE THIRD REICH. *Polish Western Affairs [Poland] 1973 14(1): 19-32.* Maintains that there was essentially no break in continuity in German ideological development, 1871-1945, and that careful examination of foreign relations ideology bears out such a hypothesis.

131. Wiener, Johnathan M. WORKING CLASS CONSCIOUSNESS IN GERMANY, 1848-1933. *Marxist Perspectives 1979-80 2(4): 156-169.* Review essay based on Barrington Moore, Jr.,'s *Injustice: The Social Bases of Obedience and Revolt* (White Plains: M. E. Sharpe, 1978).

132. Willey, Thomas E. LIBERAL HISTORIANS AND THE GERMAN PROFESSORIAT: A CONSIDERATION OF SOME RECENT BOOKS ON GERMAN THOUGHT. *Central European Hist. 1976 9(2): 184-197.* Review article on Georg G. Iggers' *The German Conception of History: The National Tradition of Historical Thought from Herder to the Present*, Robert A. Pois's *Friedrich Meinecke and German Politics in the Twentieth Century*, and Fritz K. Ringer's *The Decline of the German Mandarins: The German Academic Community, 1890-1933.* Begins with the 1972 opinion of Geoffrey Barraclough that no new insights could be gained about Germany from "liberal intellectual history" and evaluates the books with this in mind. To the extent that each has modified the intellectual history approach to include more social and economic influences, their works are valuable. 17 notes. C. R. Lovin

133. Willoweit, Dietmar. PREUSSISCHE VERGANGENHEIT UND DEUTSCHE GEGENWART. ÜBERLEGUNGEN ZUM URSPRUNG UND ZUR AKTUALITÄT DER PREUSSISCHEN AUTOKRATIE [Prussian past and German present: reflections on the origin and present relevance of the Prussian autocracy]. *Jahrbuch für die Geschichte Mittel- und Ostdeutschlands [West Germany] 1978 27: 186-205.* It is a commonplace today to blame the worst elements in German history and culture, especially the barbarities of the Nazis, on Prussia and Prussian militarism, but Nazism had other roots, mainly in other parts of Germany. The most that can be said is that the Prussian bureaucracy, dedicated and nonpolitical, having served both the King of Prussia and the Socialist government of Prussia after 1918, served the Nazis equally well after they seized power. The Prussian officer corps did make Hitler's conquests possible, but its members despised the Austrian-born dictator and many lost their lives in the effort to overthrow him. The author calls for a new approach, examining the origins of Prussian autocracy in the Enlightenment, its subsequent develop-

ment along lines of benevolent despotism, and its effects on today's Germany. 75 notes.
                                                                        J. C. Billigmeier

134.   Winkler, Heinrich A.   FROM SOCIAL PROTECTIONISM TO NATIONAL SOCIALISM: THE GERMAN SMALL-BUSINESS MOVEMENT IN COMPARATIVE PERSPECTIVE.   *J. of Modern Hist. 1976 48(1): 1-18.* Argues that the "feudalization of the bourgeoisie," i.e., the social adjustment of the German upper middle classes to the traditional power elites, was not the only aspect of the stability in Imperial Germany and of the structural weakness of Weimar Germany. Discusses the adjustment of another group, the *Mittelstand* (small businessman), which through its stress on social protectionism and antiliberalism reinforced the Empire and supported Nazism. Paper delivered at a conference on 20th century capitalism at Harvard, September, 1974. Secondary sources, especially German; 23 notes.
                                                                        P. J. Beck

135.   Wolf, Armin.   100 JAHRE PUTZGER: 100 JAHRE GESCHICHTS-BILD IN DEUTSCHLAND (1877-1977)   [Putzger's one hundred years: the image of history in Germany, 1877-1977]. *Geschichte in Wissenschaft und Unterricht [West Germany] 1978 29(11): 702-718.* Describes the history of the German *Putzger Historical School Atlas.* Follows the changes of maps, their contents, their interpretations, and their priorities, and relates them to political development in Germany. The editions of 1888, 1901, 1916, 1923, 1931, 1934, 1954, and 1961 underwent important changes. Secondary works; 39 notes.
                                                                        H. W. Wurster

136.   Wozniak, John Stanley.   MODERN GERMAN HISTORY: TWO INTERPRETATIONS.   *Orbis 1973 16(4): 1070-1072.* Reviews Hajo Holborn's *Germany and Europe: Historical Essays* (Doubleday, 1970) and Marshall Dill, Jr.'s *Germany: A Modern History* (U. of Michigan Press, 1970), both dealing with the 19th and 20th centuries.   S

137.   Wróblewski, Mścisław.   SŁUŻBA PRACY W NIEMCZECH HITLEROWSKICH   [Labor service in Hitler's Germany]. *Przegląd Hist. [Poland] 1977 68(2): 313-340.* In the mid-1920's the German Right urged labor service *(arbeitsdienst)* as a substitute for military service, barred under the Treaty of Versailles, but it was the Depression that popularized the idea. Viewed as a means of easing the economic crisis, labor service remained voluntary, much like the American Civilian Conservation Corps, until Hitler came to power. The Nazis methodically subordinated it to the party. Constantine Hierl, a World War I colonel and an early advocate of the idea, oversaw the process. By the time World War II broke out, labor service had become an auxiliary corps whose members graduated to the army. 81 notes.   J. T. Hapak

138.   Zhukov, E. M.   PROISKHOZHDENIE VTOROI MIROVOI VOINY   [The origins of World War II]. *Novaia i Noveishaia Istoriia [USSR] 1980 (1): 3-16.* The author analyzes the causes of the second world war started by international imperialism. The author shows how after the first world war the reactionary ruling circles of Britain, France and the United States embarked on the path of reviving German militarism and conspiring with German fascism. Revealing the reactionary essence of the Munich collusion of the Western powers Zhukov exposes the policy of appeasing the aggressor spearheaded against the Soviet Union. 20 notes.   J

2

THE BEGINNINGS OF THE REPUBLIC

139. Adler, Georg. WISSENSCHAFTLICHE MITTEILUNGEN: NEUES ZUR BIOGRAPHIE ROSA LUXEMBURGS [Scholarly news: new information concerning the biography of Rosa Luxemburg]. *Beiträge zur Gesch. der Arbeiterbewegung [East Germany] 1981 23(1): 79-83.* Contains previously unpublished letters by and about Rosa Luxemburg pertaining to the judicial proceedings against her, Clara Zetkin, Franz Mehring, Peter Berten, and Heinrich Pfeiffer for publication of the periodical, *Die Internationale.* Based on material from Central Party Archives, Institute for Marxism-Leninism; 16 notes.

A. Schuetz

140. Aizin, B. A. OB OSOBENNOSTIAKH NAZREVANIIA REVOLIUTSII V GERMANII V NACHALE XX V (SOOTNOSHENIE OBEKTIVNOGO I SUBEKTIVNOGO FAKTOROV) [Special features of the ripening revolution in Germany at the beginning of the 20th century: the correlation of objective and subjective factors]. *Novaia i Noveishaia Istoriia [USSR] 1981 (2): 55-72.* Discusses the factors that led to the German working class's failure to seize power when the possibility existed in the turbulent years of 1918-19. The Industrial Revolution started later in Germany than elsewhere in Europe but proceeded more rapidly. One result of this recent and rapid growth was that by the beginning of the 20th century the proletariat was plagued by an excess of petit bourgeois ideas and aspirations that gave rise to an "aristocracy" of workers. As a result the working class was split, with a concomitant loss of the unity essential to positive revolutionary action. 69 notes. A. Brown

141. Ambrosius, Lloyd E. WILSON, CLEMENCEAU AND THE GERMAN PROBLEM AT THE PARIS PEACE CONFERENCE OF 1919. *Rocky Mountain Social Science J. 1975 12(2): 69-80.*

142. Arday, Lajos. THE QUESTION OF AN ARMISTICE AND OF THE MILITARY OCCUPATION OF AUSTRIA-HUNGARY IN OCTOBER-NOVEMBER 1918, TRACED IN THE RELEVANT BRITISH DOCUMENTS. *Acta Hist. [Hungary] 1980 26(1-2): 167-178.* On 4 October 1918 Germany and Austria-Hungary asked President Woodrow Wilson for an armistice on the basis of his Fourteen Points. The question was discussed and decided at the highest level of the Allied political and military command. The armistice conditions were laid down at the Interallied Conference at Versailles on 5-9 October. The item of the armistice empowering Allied forces to occupy any strategic zone in the vanquished territories sparked keen debate. The British were

opposed to occupying anything not directly connected with lines of communication and military operations. France would send troops only if the British participated equally in the occupation efforts. The British government declined and thus the Allies missed their opportunity to reorganize East Central Europe in a systematic and reasonable way. Based primarily on the minutes of the War Cabinet, Public Record Office, London; 35 notes.   A. M. Pogany

143. Aretin, Karl Otmar von. VERFASSUNG UND VERFASSUNG-SUNTREUE [Constitution and its betrayers]. *Frankfurter Hefte [West Germany] 1975 30(3): 19-26.* Describes the course of the German revolution of 1918 and the Weimar Republic that followed it.

144. Arndt, Helmut. ZUM 60. JAHRESTAG DER DEUTSCHEN NO-VEMBERREVOLUTION [The 60th anniversary of the German November Revolution]. *Archivmitteilungen [East Germany] 1978 28(5): 161-165.* Despite favorable conditions the November Revolution failed. The author considers its origins, events, and the reasons for its failure indicating the lessons to be learned by the Communist Party and workers' movement.

145. Artaud, Denise. SUR L'ENTRE-DEUX-GUERRES: WILSON À LA CONFÉRENCE DE LA PAIX (1919) [On the interwar period: Wilson at the peace conference]. *Rev. d'Hist. de la Deuxième Guerre Mondiale [France] 1981 31(124): 97-107.* American feelings of rivalry with British financial interests and Woodrow Wilson's lack of realism in dealing with British war debts were the chief causes of the failure of European financial reconstruction at the Paris peace conference in 1919. Based on writings of John Maynard Keynes and other economic history sources; 34 citations.   G. H. Davis

146. Badia, Gilbert. L'ANALISI DELLO SVILUPPO CAPITALISTICO IN ROSA LUXEMBURG [The analysis of capitalist development in Rosa Luxemburg]. *Ann. dell'Istituto Giangiacomo Feltrinelli [Italy] 1973 15: 232-257.* In a review of the central concepts of Rosa Luxemburg's (1870-1919) theory of capitalist development the author stresses Luxemburg's astute capacity of analysis; weaknesses of argumentation included, she is unique, even today, in her ability to identify the principles of the formulation of capital. The review is based on two works: *The Accumulation of Capital* (1913) and the *Anticritique* (1921). Based on the writings of Luxemburg, her contemporaries, the works of Karl Marx, primary documents from the Archiv für die Geschichte des Sozialismus und der Arbeiterbewegung, and secondary sources; 172 notes.   M. T. Wilson

147. Bailey, Stephen. THE BERLIN STRIKE OF JANUARY 1918. *Central European Hist. 1980 13(2): 158-174.* Too little attention has been paid to the Berlin strike of January 1918. The fact that the strike failed allowed the militarist German government to impose an annexationist peace on Russia and launch a new military offensive in the west. The strike also illustrated the divisions within the Left in Germany, which were to reappear in the 1918-19 revolution. Based on secondary works and published documents; 78 notes.
                                    C. R. Lovin

148. Barmeyer, Heide. GESCHICHTE ALS ÜBERLIEFERUNG UND KONSTRUKTION—DAS BEISPIEL DER DOLCHSTOSSLEGENDE [History as tradition and construction: the example of the myth of stabbing the

German army in the back]. *Geschichte in Wissenschaft und Unterricht [West Germany] 1977 28(5): 257-271.* Analyzes the history of the myth of stabbing the German army in the back and its political uses since 1918. Awareness of the home front's importance and old concepts of war combined to explain the unexpected defeat in 1918 to forces other than the army. This explanation played a vital role in the controversies about Germany's sole responsibility for war. After 1945, when historians looked at the stabbing theory from a democratic point of view, it turned into the myth of the stabbing. Secondary works; 31 notes.

H. W. Wurster

149. Bartsch, Günther. DIE AKTUALITÄT ROSA LUXEMBURGS IN OSTEUROPA [The current East European interest in Rosa Luxemburg]. *Osteuropa [West Germany] 1975 25(10): 848-854.* Rosa Luxemburg anticipated the New Left by more than 40 years in criticizing Leninist organizational models. Her emphasis on the self-emancipation and independent mass action of the working class and her advocacy of democratic socialism are being rediscovered by West European Marxists and by Polish, Yugoslav, and Czechoslovak Communist opposition leaders. 30 notes. R. E. Weltsch

150. Bassler, Gerhard P. A RECONSIDERATION OF THE IMPACT OF THE RUSSIAN REVOLUTION ON THE REVOLUTIONARY MOVEMENT IN GERMANY, 1917-1918. *Can. Hist. Assoc. Hist. Papers [Canada] 1976: 67-92.* In 1917-18, there was a genuine revolutionary situation in Germany, and the conservative Weimar Republic was not an inevitable development. Well informed about the Russian Revolution, Germans in early 1917 imitated its forms, symbols, and issues while ignoring the Bolsheviks. By November 1918, Social Democrats and Spartacists along with labor groups were opposed over the question of imitating the Bolshevik example. Based on government archives and secondary sources; 156 notes. G. E. Panting

151. Beier, Gerhard. ROSA LUXEMBURG. ZUR AKTUALITÄT UND HISTORIZITÄT EINER UMSTRITTENEN GRÖSSE [Rosa Luxemburg: on the current relevance and historical reality of a controversial figure]. *Internationale wissenschaftliche Korrespondenz zur Geschichte der deutschen Arbeiterbewegung [West Germany] 1974 10(2): 179-210.* Reflections on the many caricatures of Rosa Luxemburg (1870-1919) and the real Rosa. Dubbed "bloody Rosa" by her detractors, she has, from her first political appearance, been crucified in a "ritualized class struggle" that found its most recent expression in a postage-stamp controversy in West Germany. Deeply humanistic in education and persuasion, she was in reality a radical democrat and socialist whose revisionism was backward-looking and Romanticist and whose greatest personal strength and weakness was overcompensation. Based on speeches, writings, letters of Luxemburg and contemporaries, press and secondary sources; 8 illus., 168 notes.

D. Prowe

152. Bischoff, William L. THE ACTION COMMITTEE OF REVOLUTIONARY ARTISTS IN THE MUNICH REVOLUTION OF 1918-1919. *Studies in Modern European Hist. and Culture 1977 3: 7-35.* The Action Committee of Revolutionary Artists was organized in 1919 by Munich artists who saw themselves as missionaries who could help create a genuine community of individuals. They saw the November Revolution as an opportunity to achieve the

recognition and autonomy which the previous society had denied them. 84 notes, appendix.   S. R. Smith

153. Boll, Friedhelm. SPONTANEITÄT DER BASIS UND POLITISCHE FUNKTION DES STREIKS 1914 BIS 1918. DAS BEISPIEL BRAUNSCH-WEIG [Spontaneity at the grassroots and the political function of the strike, 1914-18: the case of Brunswick]. *Archiv für Sozialgeschichte [West Germany] 1977 17: 337-366*. Analyzes the history of the labor movement in Brunswick during World War I and explains its unique character. Starting with an isolated strike in 1915, the labor movement increased its activity until in 1917 there was a political mass strike. Though Brunswick was not a prewar center of left-wing activity, left Social-Democrats retained dominant influence in the labor movement and were able to rally nearly all the party members. In 1917, the Independent Social Democratic Party assumed dominance. The author explores theoretical considerations on mass activity, and the existence of a "proletarian counter public opinion." Based on unpublished sources from the state archive Wolfenbüttel, contemporary newspapers, other primary, and secondary works; 6 tables, 105 notes.   H. W. Wurster

154. Bostick, Darwin F. DIPLOMACY IN DEFEAT: GERMANY AND THE POLISH BOUNDARY DISPUTE IN 1919. *Hist. Reflections [Canada] 1977 4(2): 171-190.*

155. Bottigelli, Emile. RÉFLEXIONS SUR UN LIVRE: ROSA LUXEM-BURG: MYTHE ET RÉALITÉ [Reflections on a book: Rosa Luxemburg: myth and reality]. *Mouvement Social [France] 1976 (95): 147-152.* Knowledge of the German labor movement has been considerably advanced by the publication of Gilbert Badia's *Rosa Luxemburg, Journaliste, polemiste, revolutionnaire* (Paris: Editions Sociales, 1975). The entire personality and political activity of Rosa Luxemburg is carefully examined, using her published and unpublished documents from her early work in the Polish and German Social Democratic parties to the last days of her life. The volume documents her opposition to party leadership, her divergence from Lenin on the concept of democracy and dictatorship of the proletariat, and her activity as collaborator to *Spartacus* and as the publisher of *Rote Fahn*.   M. de Gialluly

156. Brügel, Johann Wolfgang. ZANKAPFEL DEUTSCHBÖHMEN: EINE ERINNERUNG AN 1918 [German Bohemia, apple of discord: a memento of 1918]. *Bohemia [West Germany] 1980 21(2): 376-382.* From January 1918, when the Czech deputies declared themselves in favor of an independent Czech and Slovak state, until the end of World War I, Sudeten German nationalists debated the question of safeguarding German Bohemia by partition. Their dilemma was that this would have meant abandoning Prague and the outlying German areas to the Czechs. Social Democrats, who rejected partition but wanted democratic local self-determination, remained aloof from this debate. Based on Bohemian and Austrian newspapers; 15 notes.   R. E. Weltsch

157. Buiting, M. H. J. DE DUITSE REVOLUTIE VAN 1918-1919 [The German revolution of 1918-19]. *Spiegel Hist. [Netherlands] 1982 17(6): 322-329.* An analysis of the social forces evolving from the feudal absolutist institutions of 17th-century Brandenburg-Prussia that underlay the German revolution of

1918-19. The 19th-century alliance of industrial middle class and authoritarian military government burst apart in the aftermath of World War I. The rise of the Socialist Party (SPD) and the workers' party (Spartakus-KPD) created the context for the German revolution. Based on primary resources; 15 illus.

C. W. Wood, Jr.

158. Burian, Peter. EIN BAYERISCHER GEHEIMERLASS ZUR SUDE-TENFRAGE AUS DEM OKTOBER 1918 [A Bavarian secret ordinance concerning the Sudeten question, October 1918]. *Bohemia. Jahrbuch des Collegium Carolinum [West Germany] 1974 15: 440-445.* Gives the text of official instructions triggered by the imminent change in Bohemia from Austrian to Czechoslovakian sovereignty. Bavarian local authorities were to keep out of any possible movements among Sudeten Germans and protect public order in border communities. Provincial concerns and correctness in international relations clearly outweighed German national solidarity. Based on documents from the Political Archives of the Foreign Office in Bonn. R. E. Weltsch

159. Castellan, Georges. À PROPOS DE ROSA LUXEMBURG [Apropos of Rosa Luxemburg]. *Rev. d'Hist. Moderne et Contemporaine [France] 1976 23(4): 573-582.* A review article on the monumental work of Gilbert Badia *Rosa Luxemburg, Journaliste, polémiste, révolutionnaire* (Paris: Editions Sociales, 1975). It is an intellectual biography of the German Socialist leader between her arrival in Berlin in 1898 and her assassination there in January 1919. It contains all her writings from those years—840 in all—including telegrams. It is a definitive book on this remarkable figure, who still speaks to the modern world. 14 notes. J. C. Billigmeier

160. Collotti, Enzo. KARL LIEBKNECHT E IL PROBLEMA DELLA RIVOLUZIONE SOCIALISTA IN GERMANIA [Karl Liebknecht and the problem of socialist revolution in Germany]. *Ann. dell'Istituto Giangiacomo Feltrinelli [Italy] 1973 15: 326-343.* Describes the political thought and actions of the German political agitator Karl Liebknecht, 1905-19. Based on primary documents from the Institute of Marxism and Leninism, Berlin, the writings of Liebknecht and his contemporaries and secondary sources; 29 notes.

M. T. Wilson

161. Cronin, James E. LABOR INSURGENCY AND CLASS FORMATION: COMPARATIVE PERSPECTIVES ON THE CRISIS OF 1917-1920 IN EUROPE. *Social Sci. Hist. 1980 4(1): 125-152.* The years 1917-20 witnessed a major labor upheaval throughout Europe. Traditional explanations—war-weariness and economic hardship—fail to account for the magnitude of the crisis. An important factor was the increasingly mechanized nature of industrialism in the early 20th century, deemphasizing the value of skilled artisan workers. Protest against this reshaping and proletarianizing of the working class gave the movement added impetus. 4 tables, 11 notes. L. K. Blaser

162. Crozier, Andrew J. THE ESTABLISHMENT OF THE MANDATES SYSTEM 1919-25: SOME PROBLEMS CREATED BY THE PARIS PEACE CONFERENCE. *J. of Contemporary Hist. [Great Britain] 1979 14(3): 483-513.* Among the compromises of the Paris peace settlements of 1919-20 was the establishment of the mandates system to be applied to Germany's former colonies

and the former Arabian provinces of the Ottoman Empire. The mandatory powers were given only authority, not sovereignty, over the former colonies, even though Britain and France would have preferred outright annexation. Implementation of the system was delayed by the American disapproval of the Versailles Treaty and rejection of League membership. Another complication was the division of mandates into A, B, and C types and allocation of rights and privileges in them. Based on documents in the Public Record Office; 83 notes.

M. P. Trauth

163. Dän, Horst. ZUR KONZEPTION EINES WIRTSCHAFTLICHEN RÄTESYSTEMS IN DER SICHT EINER FÜHRENDEN REPRÄSENTAN-TIN DER DEUTSCHEN LINKEN [The concept of an economic council system by a leading representative of the German Left]. *Zeitschrift für Württembergische Landes-Geschichte [West Germany] 1975-76 34-35: 379-392.* Speech of Clara Zetkin at the second state congress of the workers' and peasants' councils of Württemberg in March 1919. She developed a program for a political and economic system based on council democracy and showed ways to achieve this goal. 41 notes.

M. Geyer

164. Danahar, David C. GERMAN MILITARISM AND EXPANSION-ISM, 1914-1918: GERHARD RITTER AND THE FIRST WORLD WAR. *J. of Baltic Studies 1974 5(3): 237-244.* A review article of Gerhard Ritter's *The Sword and the Scepter: The Problem of Militarism in Germany*, trans. Heinz Norden, Vol. III: *The Tragedy of Statesmanship—Bethmann Hollweg as War Chancellor* (Coral Gables: U. of Miami Press, 1972), Vol. IV: *The Reign of German Militarism and the Disaster of 1918* (1973). Ritter's work details the growth and ultimate predominance of militaristic and expansionist ambitions in German wartime policy, but controverts the thesis of Fritz Fischer, *Germany's Aims in the First World War* (New York: W. W. Norton 1967), that Germany consciously precipitated war to achieve such ambitions. Biblio.

E. W. Jennison, Jr.

165. Danset, Dorthée. L'APPORT DE ROSA LUXEMBURG À LA THÉO-RIE DE SOUS-DÉVELOPPEMENT [The contribution of Rosa Luxemburg to the theory of underdevelopment]. *Pensée [France] 1977 (193): 54-74.* Studies the economic theory of the Socialist leader Rosa Luxemburg, explaining national economic underdevelopment. Based on Luxemburg's *The Accumulation of Capital.*

166. Debo, Richard K., ed. THE 14 NOVEMBER 1918 TELEPRINTER CONVERSATION OF HUGO HAASE WITH GEORGII CHICHERIN AND KARL RADEK: DOCUMENT AND COMMENTARY. *Canadian-American Slavic Studies 1980 14(4): 513-534.* Publishes for the first time in English the full text of the teleprinter conversation about relations between the new German revolutionary government and the Soviet state, with an extensive introduction and commentary. The documents containing the conversation are in the Political Archives of the German Foreign Office in Bonn; 37 notes.

G. E. Munro

167. Decker, Alexander. DIE NOVEMBERREVOLUTION UND DIE GESCHICHTSWISSENSCHAFT IN DER DDR [The November revolution and history in East Germany]. *Int. Wissenschaftliche Korrespondenz zur Geschichte der Deutschen Arbeiterbewegung [West Germany] 1974 10(3): 269-299.* A critical examination of the theory and practice of East German historiography through a case study of its treatment of the German Revolution of 1918, contrasted with West German interpretations. The revolution's importance for a socialist historical consciousness has made its interpretation particularly vulnerable to Party dictates. Thus the stress on the central role of the Communist Party and, like West German anti-Communist histories, the denigration of the workers' and soldiers' councils. Based on East and West German secondary sources; 120 notes. D. Prowe

168. Delany, Sheila. RED ROSA: BREAD AND ROSES. *Massachusetts R. 1975 16(2): 373-386.* Examines the life and philosophy of Rosa Luxemburg, a powerful figure in the early development of communism. She rejected compromise, fought reformist revisionism, and died at the hands of German army officers in 1919, a "revolutionary Communist in theory and practice." Primary and secondary sources. M. J. Barach

169. Diehl, Ernst. DIE GESCHICHTE DES DEUTSCHEN VOLKES IM WELTHISTORISCHEN PROZESS [The history of the German people in the world historic process]. *Zeitschrift für Geschichtswissenschaft [East Germany] 1973 21(3): 272-288.* The revolutionary movements in Germany in 1948-49 and 1918-19 had an important impact on the development of Marxist-Leninist revolutionary principles. A real international classification of the revolutionary history of the German people has to take those processes into account, which, from the perspective of world history, embody the most progressive structures. 10 notes. R. Wagnleitner

170. Dietz, Dieter. VERSUCHE DER DEUTSCHEN MILITÄRISCHEN FÜHRUNG ZUR VERHINDERUNG ODER SOFORTIGEN NIEDERSCHLAGUNG DER NOVEMBERREVOLUTION 1918 [Attempts of the German military leadership to prevent or suppress immediately the November Revolution of 1918]. *Militärgeschichte [East Germany] 1978 17(5): 524-533.* Within the ruling circles of German imperialism, especially in its military leadership, considerable differences arose in the fall of 1918 about how the growing revolutionary crisis could best be prevented. The spectrum of the views then advocated reached from the demand for the ruthless employment of the army to a policy of concessions on subordinate issues. The author sketches the relevant considerations and planning which went on within the German military leadership and demonstrates that they quickly became irrelevant due to the revolutionary upsurge of the masses at the beginning of the November Revolution. 64 notes. J/T (H. D. Andrews)

171. Doerries, Reinhard R. [GERMANY AND THE UNITED STATES AFTER WORLD WAR I]. *Central European Hist. 1975 8(4): 370-374.* Reviews *Deutsche Revolution und Wilson-Frieden: Die Amerikanische und Deutsche Friedensstrategie Zwischen Ideologie und Machtpolitik 1918/19* (Düsseldorf: Droste, 1971) by Klaus Schwabe and *Deutschland und die Reparationen 1918/19: Die Genesis des Reparationsproblems in Deutschland Zwischen*

Waffenstillstand und Versailer Friedensschluss (Stuttgart: Deutsche Verlags-Austalt, 1973) by Peter Krüger. Schwabe's study helps correct a long-distorted image of Woodrow Wilson and sheds new light on many of the negotiations which went on in 1918 between Berlin and Washington. Krüger's work is thorough in looking at reparations from Germany's point of view, but it unfortunately ignores the international forces at work.   C. R. Lovin

172. Drabkin, Ia. S.   NOVYE RABOTY ISTORIKOV GDR O NOIABR'-SKOI REVOLIUTSII V GERMANII   [New works by historians from East Germany on the November Revolution in Germany]. *Novaia i Noveishaia Istoriia [USSR] 1980 (6): 182-188.* Discusses recent East German historiography of the 1918 November Revolution. Though the works are in general given approval, some deficiencies are noted. Some of the books under scrutiny are illustrated histories, others relate developments in Germany to those in Soviet Russia, and others analyze worker-soldier solidarity during the revolution. 15 notes.
D. N. Collins

173. Drabkin, Ia. S.   SORATNITSY V BOR'BE ZA VELIKOE DELO (IZ PEREPISKI KLARY ZETKIN I ROZY LIUKSEMBURG)   [Comrades in the fight for a great cause: from the correspondence between Clara Zetkin and Rosa Luxemburg]. *Novaia i Noveishaia Istoriia [USSR] 1976 (3): 71-90.* Discusses the correspondence between Clara Zetkin and Rosa Luxemburg, November 1918-January 1919. The author provides background material about the two women, who were actively involved in the revolutionary movement during the early part of this century in Germany, as well as information concerning the discovery and first publication of the letters in Bonn in 1969. The letters are particularly illuminating on the relationship of the two women and their views of contemporary events. 99 notes.   R. Permar

174. Dreetz, Dieter.   PROBLEME DER DEUTSCHEN NOVEMBER-REVOLUTION 1918/19 IN NEUEREN MILITÄRHISTORISCHEN PUBLI-KATIONEN IN DER BRD   [Problems of the November Revolution in Germany, 1918-19, in recent military history publications in West Germany]. *Militärgeschichte [East Germany] 1980 19(3): 315-322.* The numerous recent West German works on the November Revolution in growing measure examine questions of military policy, the role of the soldiers' councils, armed forces, and people's defense units, the alliance between the Army High Command and the Council of People's Commissioners, and especially the solution to the military question. The author determines their basic positions and trends as well as their relation to current politics, compares them with Marxist-Leninist historiography, and argues against interpretations that cannot be defended on scholarly grounds. 42 notes.   J/T (H. D. Andrews)

175. Eichenlaub, René.   RÄTE ET RÄTEREPUBLIK EN BAVIÈRE (NOVEMBRE 1918-MAI 1919)   [Soviets and Soviet republic in Bavaria, November 1918 to May 1919]. *Rev. d'Allemagne [France] 1977 9(3): 382-398.* The most serious attempt made in Germany to establish social and economic democracy after the collapse of the old regime in 1918 took place in Munich, where three revolutions, in November 1918, February 1919, and April 1919, attempted to establish a government based upon councils of soldiers, peasants, and workers. The *Räterepublik,* proclaimed in Munich, wavered between Marxism-Leninism

and democratic socialism. Finally settling upon a form of temperate dictatorship, it sought to reorganize society, starting with the economy, education, and the press, but it was forced to give most of its attention to defending itself against opposition both internal and external. Based on primary and secondary sources; 38 notes. J. S. Gassner

176. Feldman, Gerald D. and Steinisch, Irmgard. THE ORIGINS OF THE STINNES-LEGIEN AGREEMENT: A DOCUMENTATION. *Int. Wissenschaftliche Korrespondenz zur Geschichte der Deutschen Arbeiterbewegung [West Germany] 1973 (19/20): 45-103.* Documents the major Berlin and Ruhr negotiations between the German electrical, machine, and coal and steel industry magnates and the trade union leadership on the Stinnes-Legien Agreement (15 November 1918), the creation of a central industry-labor board, (*Zentralausschuss*), and a nearly autonomous Demobilization Office. The 25 letters and minutes chiefly from the Siemens, MAN, Bergbau-Archiv, and Rheinrohr company archives demonstrate the evolution of a new extrademocratic interest group collusion in Germany. This collusion gathered impetus from common wartime fears of revolution, national humiliation, and material need. 96 notes.

D. Prowe

177. Feldman, Gerald D. THE POLITICAL AND SOCIAL FOUNDATIONS OF GERMANY'S ECONOMIC MOBILIZATION, 1914-1916. *Armed Forces and Soc. 1976 3(1): 121-146.* German historian Eckart Kehr postulated that the military and foreign policies of the German Empire before World War I were constrained by domestic special interest groups. Applying the thesis to the years of mobilization, 1914-16, the author found substantial conflict between leadership groups in German society. Based on primary sources, periodicals, and secondary literature; 56 notes. J. P. Harahan

178. Fesser, Gerd; Lüttich, Rosmarie; and Poethe, Lothar. DIE REVOLUTIONEN VON 1848/49 UND 1918 UND DIE ENTWICKLUNG DER NICHTPROLETARISCHEN DEMOKRATISCHEN KRÄFTE IN DEUTSCHLAND [The revolutions of 1848-49 and 1918 and the development of the nonproletarian democratic groups in Germany]. *Zeitschrift für Geschichtswissenschaft [East Germany] 1973 21(1): 71-74.* Reviews the lectures and discussions of the scientific conference on the revolutions of 1848-49 and 1918 and their importance for the development of the nonproletarian democratic, antimilitarist and anti-imperialist groups in Germany at Jena in March and April 1972 which analyzed the dialectic relations between the role of the bourgeoisie and proletariat in the two German revolutions. R. Wagnleitner

179. Foch, Ferdinand. [THE ARMISTICE]. *Magazin Istoric [Rumania] 1975 9(10): 44-49; (11): 23-27, 32.* Part I. OCTOMBRIE-NOIMBRIE 1918 [October-November 1918]. Part II. 11 NOIEMBRIE 1918 [11 November 1918]. Excerpts from the author's *Mémoires pour servir à l'histoiire de la guerre de 1914-1918.*

180. Fricke, Dieter. DIE "SOZIALISTISCHE MONATSHEFTE" UND DIE IMPERIALISTISCHE KONZEPTION EINES KONTINENTALEUROPA (1905-1918) [The *Sozialistische Monatshefte* and the imperialist conception of a continental Europe, 1905-1918]. *Zeitschrift für*

Geschichtswissenschaft [East Germany] 1975 23(5): 528-537. In promoting the economic and political unity of continental Europe, the *Sozialistische Monatshefte* betrayed the working class and proved that opportunism and imperialism were by necessity related. *Monatshefte* writers like Richard Calwer and Ludwig Quessel argued that a "continental imperium" could counter the power of England and Russia and secure additional colonial possessions for Europe, thereby preparing the way for the triumph of socialism. 85 notes. J. T. Walker

181. Fritsch, Werner. DIE BEDEUTUNG DER NOVEMBERREVOLUTION 1918 FÜR DIE ANNÄHERUNG NICHTPROLETARISCHER DEMOKRATISCHER KRÄFTE AN DIE REVOLUTIONÄREN POSITIONEN DER ARBEITERKLASSE (THESEN) [The meaning of the November Revolution of 1918 for the approach of the nonproletarian democratic forces to the revolutionary position of the working classes. (Theses)]. *Jenaer Beiträge zur Parteiengeschichte [East Germany] 1973 (34/35): 1-23.* Only in partnership with the working class could nonproletarian democratic groups attack imperialism and further the 1848-49 goals. But most small bourgeois would not join the radical workers. They supported working class policies in the 1918 revolution, but peasants became disenchanted by the failure of land reform while many small bourgeois believed that the Weimar government met their real demands. Only the Spartacists were politically realistic. In late 1918 the German Communist Party was founded, but it had almost no bourgeois support. The seemingly futile leftist struggle of the Weimar years was simply an important learning experience on which the Communists leaned heavily ever afterwards. M. Faissler

182. Fuchs, Gerhard. DIE POLITISCHEN BEZIEHUNGEN DER WEIMARER REPUBLIK ZUR TSCHECHOSLOWAKEI VOM VERSAILLER FRIEDEN BIS ZUM ENDE DER REVOLUTIONÄREN NACHKRIEGSKRISE [The political connections of the Weimar Republic to Czechoslovakia from the Peace of Versailles to the end of the postwar revolutionary crisis]. *Jahrbuch für Geschichte [East Germany] 1973 9: 281-337.* German imperialism was from its beginnings an implacable foe of the Czech and Slovak peoples and their national aspirations. The military defeat suffered by German imperialism in World War I did not alter its aims. Even during the revolutionary crisis following the war, in the face of efforts by armed workers to seize power and overthrow imperialism, German imperialists continued to propagandize against the newly independent Czechoslovakia and to plan its destruction. Thus the eventual Nazi annexation of Czechoslovakia was the logical culmination not only of Nazi but also of Weimar policy. 122 notes. J. C. Billigmeier

183. Haas, Hanns. TRST IN AVSTRIJA V ČASU PARIŠKE MIROVNE KONFERENCE 1919 [Trieste and Austria at the time of the Paris Peace Conference in 1919]. *Prispevki za Zgodovino Delavskega Gibanja [Yugoslavia] 1981 21(1-2): 49-54.* Discusses the situation in the port of Trieste after the collapse of the Habsburg Empire and the effort of the republic of German Austria to obtain free access to the Adriatic Sea and freedom of transit. Austria achieved this, and following the Renner-Nitti agreement in 1920 the situation of the port of Trieste was of even further benefit for Austrian trade. J

184. Hellige, Hans Dieter. DIE SOZIALISIERUNGSFRAGE IN DER DEUTSCHEN REVOLUTION 1918/19. ZU EINIGEN NEUEREN DARSTELLUNGEN [The socialization question in the German revolution of 1918-19: comments on some recent works]. *Internationale Wissenschaftliche Korrespondenz zur Geschichte der Deutschen Arbeiterbewegung [West Germany] 1975 11(1): 91-100.* Reviews three dissertations (Hans Schieck, Heidelberg, 1958; Kurt Trüschler, Marburg, 1968; Michael William Honhart, Duke, 1972) on the socialization question in Germany, 1918-22. Stresses the need for future analyses which concentrate on the socioeconomic causes for the failure of reformist party and union leaderships. Based on archival research at Bundesarchiv (Koblenz), Zentrales Staatsarchiv (Potsdam), and secondary works; 21 notes.   D. Prowe

185. Himmer, Robert. HARMONICAS FOR LENIN? THE DEVELOPMENT OF GERMAN ECONOMIC POLICY TOWARD SOVIET RUSSIA, DECEMBER 1918 TO JUNE 1919. *J. of Modern Hist. 1977 49(2): iii.* A study of economic factors in early Weimar foreign policy. Germany's policymakers looked to the USSR for the solution to the Reich's economic ills. Foreign Minister Ulrich von Brockdorff-Rantzau tried for the grand prize: dominion over the economy of Russia. Despite criticism he steadily sought success through cooperation with the Entente. Repelled by the Versailles peace terms, Rantzau initiated the movement toward an alignment with Russia by bringing in the Soviet representative, Viktor Kopp, in June 1919. His successors, however, found it difficult to follow Rantzau's path. Abstract only.   R. V. Ritter

186. Hollenberg, Günter. BÜRGERLICHE SAMMLUNG ODER SOZIAL-LIBERALE KOALITION? SOZIALSTRUKTUR, INTERESSENLAGE UND POLITISCHES VERHALTEN DER BÜRGERLICHEN SCHICHTEN 1918/19 AM BEISPIEL DER STADT FRANKFURT AM MAIN [Bourgeois front or social-liberal coalition? Social structure, economic interests, and political behavior of the middle classes in 1918-19, using the example of the city of Frankfurt]. *Vierteljahrshefte für Zeitgeschichte [West Germany] 1979 27(3): 392-430.* A case study of grass roots political activity of the middle classes during the German revolution of 1918-19. Traditionally anti-aristocratic and economically liberal, the Frankfurt bourgeoisie went through a process of cautious reorientation and gradual reassertion in the months after the war without forming a united anti-Socialist front. By 1918-19 the new middle classes moved toward a social-liberal coalition with the Social Democrats, while the old middle classes remained politically conservative. Based on political records of the Frankfurt city archive, government statistics, press, and secondary works; 5 tables, 133 notes.

D. Prowe

187. Hortzschansky, Günter. DIE DEUTSCHE NOVEMBERREVOLUTION 1918-1919: DIE ERSTE GROSSE KLASSENSCHLACHT GEGEN DEN DEUTSCHEN IMPERIALISMUS UND MILITARISMUS [The German November Revolution of 1918-19: the first great class battle against German imperialism and militarism]. *Beiträge zur Geschichte der Arbeiterbewegung [East Germany] 1978 20(6): 819-834.* Considers that the revolution in Germany, 1918-19, was the inevitable result of the influence of the Russian Revolution and the collapse of the old regime of capitalism. Despite the struggles of the revolutionaries to establish a democracy, the capitalist system survived, backed by the

right-wing leaders of the Social Democratic Party (SPD), the Independent Social Democratic Party (USPD), and the labor unions. Although these events suggested that the working class could become the main focus of political progress in society, this could only be realized once divisions within the revolutionary group were overcome, and its aims and ideals more fully defined. 21 notes.

L. H. Schmidt/S

188. Hortzschansky, Günter. VELIKII OKTIABR' I NOIABR'SKAIA REVOLIUTSIIA 1918-19 GG. V GERMANII [The November Revolution of 1918-19 in Germany and its lessons]. *Novaia i Noveishaia Istoriia [USSR] 1978 (6): 3-15.* Describes the close interconnection between the Great October Revolution in Russia and the 1918 revolution in Germany, an important link in the chain of revolutionary events which followed the Great October Revolution, and had undermined the foundations of world imperialism. The author analyzes the development, character, and lessons of the November Revolution and exposes the predatory character of the Right-opportunist leaders. He deals at length with the activities of the German Left and the historic significance of the formation of the Communist Party of Germany.   J

189. Howard, Dick. ROSA LUXEMBURG: THÉORIE ET PRATIQUE [Rosa Luxemburg: theory and practice]. *Esprit [France] 1976 (2): 263-285.* French translation of "Re-reading Luxemburg," *Telos* 1973-74 (18): 89-106, analyzing the German socialist's revolutionary theory and practice (1870-1919).

190. Hürten, Heinz and Schmidt, Ernst Heinrich. DIE ENTSTEHUNG DES KABINETTS DER VOLKSBEAUFTRAGTEN: EINE QUELLENKRITISCHE UNTERSUCHUNG [The origin of the Committee of People's Commissioners: a critical study of sources]. *Hist. Jahrbuch [West Germany] 1979 99: 255-267.* Analyzes the formation of the first revolutionary government in Germany on 10 November 1918. Historians hitherto contended that the new government was formed by both the Majority and the Independent Social Democrats and confirmed at a workers' and soldiers' council meeting on 10 November in the Circus Bush in Berlin. Papers of contemporaries recently discovered, however, reveal that the meeting was utterly disorganized and that only a threat of military intervention saved the government. The government derived its existence not from a democratic process but from military might. Based on the coauthor Schmidt's dissertation and on data in the Central State Archive in Potsdam; 15 notes.   R. Vilums

191. Hürten, Heinz. DIE NOVEMBERREVOLUTION: FRAGEN AN DIE FORSCHUNG [The November Revolution: open questions]. *Geschichte in Wissenschaft und Unterricht [West Germany] 1979 30(3): 158-174.* Proposes a new interpretation of the German revolution of 1918. Present interpretations see 1918 not as mere breakdown, but as a revolution, in which the Social Democratic Party missed its chance and followed the path of a parliamentary instead of a socialist democracy. According to the recognized criteria of revolutions there was no revolutionary situation in 1918, and because of the vulnerability of a developed industrial society, even the revolutionaries hesitated making fundamental changes in politics and society. The workers' and soldiers' councils were no means for a socialist transformation; they lacked the strength and social basis to oust the forces represented in parliament. Thus the Weimar Republic had to

be built on the Social Democratic Party and the parties of the center. 59 notes.

H. W. Wurster

192. Iazhborovskaia, I. S. and Evzerov, R. Ia. ROZA LIUKSEMBURG [Rosa Luxemburg]. *Novaia i Noveishaia Istoriia [USSR] 1974 (5): 98-118, (6): 63-85.* Discredits right-wing social reformist and Trotskyite claims that Luxemburg and V. I. Lenin were antagonists. The author describes Luxemburg's early political activism and ideological work for the Polish and Lithuanian Social Democratic Party. Her attitudes toward party politics were generally not as perceptive as Lenin's, who, nevertheless, held her in very high esteem. Together, they succeeded in defeating the opportunism of the German Social Democrats. During World War I, Luxemburg's *Die Internationale* gave prominence to the ideas of left-wing, antiwar, and procivil war groups. She was expelled from the German Social Democratic Party and imprisoned in 1915 and 1916. She greeted the 1917 Russian Revolution as the beginning of a new era, and participated in the revolutionary movements in Germany and Poland. Luxemburg was assassinated in 1919 because of the political threat she constituted. 223 notes.

D. N. Collins

193. John, Matthias. KARL LIEBKNECHT ÜBER DIE ZENTRALISIERUNG DES POLIZEIWESENS IM SYSTEM DES DEUTSCHEN MILITARISMUS [Karl Liebknecht's views on the centralization of police operations in the system of German militarism]. *Militärgeschichte [East Germany] 1977 16(1): 69-73.* Karl Liebknecht (1871-1919) opposed the centralization of police authority because it was directed against the working class and made the democratization of the police more difficult. This shows that he saw antimilitarism and the struggle for democracy as a unity. H. D. Andrews

194. Katsch, Günter. DIE DEUTSCHE NOVEMBERREVOLUTION IN DER IDEOLOGISCHEN TÄTIGKEIT DER KPD 1919-1933 [The German November Revolution in ideological action of the German Communist Party 1919-33]. *Beiträge zur Geschichte der Arbeiterbewegung [East Germany] 1979 21(6): 841-854.* German working class did not succeed in transforming the 1918 revolution into a social revolution. Consequently a bourgeois republic was born. The article examines how the German Communists coped with the weakness of the proletariat, and other problems, including lack of leadership and what they did to achieve a strong organization. The founding of the Leninist German Communist Party could be viewed as the culmination of the November Revolution. 36 notes.

G. E. Pergl

195. Katsch, Günter. DIE ZEITSCHRIFT *KOMMUNISTISCHE INTERNATIONALE* IN DEN JAHREN 1919-1923 ÜBER DIE NOVEMBERREVOLUTION IN DEUTSCHLAND [The periodical *Kommunistische Internationale,* 1919-23, on the November Revolution in Germany]. *Wissenschaftliche Zeitschrift der Karl-Marx U. Leipzig [East Germany] 1973 22(4): 605-610.* The German Communist journal *Kommunistische Internationale* blamed the Social democrats for the failure of the November Revolution.

196. Kellinger, Cesi. ROSA LUXEMBURG: THE PRISON YEARS. *Res. Studies 1975 43(3): 153-161.* Describes Rosa Luxemburg's life while in a Berlin prison, 1915-18.

S

197. Klein, Fritz. KRIEG—REVOLUTION—FRIEDEN 1914 BIS 1920 [War, revolution, peace: 1914-20]. *Zeitschrift für Geschichtswissenschaft [East Germany] 1980 28(6): 544-554.* World War I could be viewed not only as a phenomenon quite different from previous conflicts because of its total devotion of all forces of the countries involved toward the conduct of war, but for its numerous attempts to restore peace. Reviews the various attempts to terminate the struggle and the actions by quite different political forces to reach the final peace agreements of 1918-20. Secondary sources; 14 notes. G. E. Pergl

198. Klein, Fritz. 1848 UND 1918 [1848 and 1918]. *Jahrbuch für Geschichte [East Germany] 1973 8: 223-250.* In 1918, at the close of World War I, the German monarchy crumbled, and a Republic was proclaimed. The lessons of the Revolution of 1848 in Germany were fresh in the minds of the 1918 revolutionaries, who were determined not to repeat the mistakes of 1848, but to change fundamentally the political and social structure of Germany. In this they were only partly successful, but their struggle was a great inspiration, and their mistakes a great lesson, to the people of the German Democratic Republic in overthrowing capitalism and building a new socialist order. 66 notes.
J. C. Billigmeier

199. Klopčič, France. O ZAPRAVLJENI SOCIALISTIČNI REVOLUCIJI V NEMČIJI LETA 1918-1919 [Germany's wasted socialist revolution, 1918-19]. *Zgodovinski Časopis [Yugoslavia] 1973 21(1/2): 127-131.* Reviews the discussion at the 1971 Linz Conference of the History of the Workers' Movement.
T. Hočevar

200. Kohlhaas, Wilhelm. MACHT UND GRENZEN DER SOLDATEN-RÄTE IN WÜRTTEMBERG 1918/19 [The power and limits of the Soldiers' Councils in Württemberg 1918-19]. *Zeitschrift für Württembergische Landesgeschichte [West Germany] 1973 32(2): 537-543.* The Soldiers' Councils during the years 1918-19 had neither the power, the will, nor the concepts to form a progressive and more democratic alternative to the German army, and in Württemberg never played an important role. They were a diverse lot of soldiers, either subordinate to the democratic government and the officers after the abdication of the monarch, or in Spartacist opposition to republicanism and democracy. Review, 21 notes. M. Geyer

201. Kolejka, Josef. KOMUNISTICKÁ INTERNACIONÁLA O POVÁLEČNÉM USPOŘÁDÁNÍ STŘEDNÍ A JIHOVYCHODNÍ EVROPY. NÁRODNOSTNÍ OTÁZKA V PROGRAMECH KOMUNISTICKÝCH SKUPIN A STRAN Z LET 1918-21-22 [The Comintern's views of the post-World War I organization of Central and Southeast Europe: the nationalities problem in the programs of Communist groups and parties]. *Časopis Matice Moravské [Czechoslovakia] 1976 95(3-4): 209-234.* Analyzes basic Comintern documents, 1918-22, regarding the formulation of its international and nationalities program, and emphasizes the organization's rejection of the Treaty of Versailles. Based on documents; 61 notes. G. E. Pergl

202. Könnemann, Erwin. REAKTIONÄRE STAATSSTREICHPLÄNE UND VERSUCHE ZUR EINRICHTUNG EINER MILITÄRDIKTATUR IN DER NOVEMBERREVOLUTION UND DER REVOLUTIONÄREN

NACHKRIEGSKRISE 1918-23 [Reactionary plans for a coup d'état and attempts to establish a military dictatorship during the November Revolution and the revolutionary postwar crisis, 1918-23]. *Martin-Luther-U. Halle-Wittenberg. Wissenschaftliche Zeitschrift. Gesellschafts- und Sprachwissenschaftliche Reihe [East Germany] 1976 25(1): 29-35.* Examines the two types of counterrevolutionary strategy planned by different sections of the bourgeoisie to prevent the working classes from assuming too much power. Erich Ludendorff and Wolfgang Kapp envisaged a violent military coup, but Paul von Hindenburg took no positive action and Hans von Seeckt preferred the legal parliamentary method. The first putsch attempt by Ludendorff failed because of the workers' resistance in the November Revolution, and it was decided to install Friederich Ebert as a figure-head President of the Reich. Kapp's attempt also failed and by 1923 the workers' resistance had thwarted all bourgeois plans for a coup. Secondary sources; 23 notes. A. Alcock

203. Kováč, Dušan. BOJ O ANŠLUS RAKÚSKA AKO DOSLEDOK NEZDARU NĚMECKEJ "MITTELEUROPY" 1918-1919 [The fight for the Anschluss of Austria caused by the collapse of German "Mitteleuropa" idea 1918-19]. *Slovanské Štúdie [Czechoslovakia] 1978 19: 179-210.* German defeat in 1918 made Berlin's prewar plans for hegemony in Central Europe impossible; the new conception of the old imperial idea was based on annexation of Austria and the Sudeten area of Bohemia. 119 notes. G. E. Pergl

204. Kováč, Dušan. ZÁKULISIE A VÝZNAM SALZBURSKÝCH ROZHOVOROV MEDZI NEMECKOM A RAKÚSKO-UHORSKOM V LÉTE R. 1918. [The background and significance of the Salzburg talks between Germany and Austria-Hungary in the summer of 1918]. *Historický Časopis [Czechoslovakia] 1974 22(1): 25- 48.* The Salzburg talks of 9 July to 10 October 1918 ended without practical results. The problems discussed were the distribution of power in Central Europe, the struggle for decisive influence on Germany's foreign policy, the future development of nationalities in Austria-Hungary, the Polish question, and German-Austro-Hungarian relations. Secondary sources; 94 notes. G. E. Pergl

205. Kurokawa, Kō. DOITSU KAKUMEI TO BAYERN NOMIN [The German revolution and the Bavarian peasantry]. *Seiyo Shigaku [Japan] 1977 (104): 25-42.* Studies three peasants' organizations, the Bauernräte, Bauverein, and Bauernbund, in order to clarify the role of the peasants in Bavaria's revolution of 1918-19. The peasants opposed the Soviet-styled new republic in part because the propaganda efforts of the revolutionary government were inadequate in explaining socialist policy.

206. Kurokawa, Kō. MIYUNHEN-KAKUMEI NI OKERU SHYO-SHAKAISŌ TO RETE-UNDŌ [The social classes and the workers' council movement in the November Revolution]. *Shigaku Zasshi [Japan] 1979 88(12): 1-41.* Studies activities of each social class during the 1918 November Revolution in Germany which proceeded from bourgeois democracy to socialism. At the beginning the bourgeoisie supported parliament and did not act against the revolution. The lower middle classes demanded proletarian democracy, and the working class supported socialism. Combining the demands for democracy and socialism and supported by the Socialists, the Independent Socialists, the

Bavarian Peasant Union, and the anarchists the Soviet Republic declared its independence on 7 April 1919. Suppressing an antirevolutionary riot on 13 April, the German Communist Party took the leadership of the Soviet Republic. Table, 155 notes.   M. Kawaguchi

207.   Laschitza, Annelies.   DOKUMENTE UND MATERIALIEN: BRIEFE ROSA LUXEMBURGS AN KAMPFGEFÄHRTEN   [Documents and materials: Rosa Luxemburg's letters to fellow-fighters]. *Beiträge zur Gesch. der Arbeiterbewegung [East Germany] 1981 23(1): 70-73.* Contains eight previously unpublished letters to Rosi Wolfstein and Friedrich Westmeyer, dated 1913 to 1918. 8 notes.   A. Schuetz

208.   Lwunin, J. A.   ERNST THÄLMANN ÜBER KARL LIEBKNECHT UND ROSA LUXEMBURG   [Ernst Thälmann on Karl Liebknecht and Rosa Luxemburg]. *Beiträge zur Geschichte der Arbeiterbewegung [East Germany] 1977 19(1): 63-66.* Prints and discusses two articles originally published in the Soviet press by Ernst Thälmann. Thälmann notes the martyrs' deaths of Karl Liebknecht and Rosa Luxemburg, stressing the former's firm antimilitarist stance and the profound blow dealt to the cause of world peace by his murder. 4 notes.
                                                                          G. H. Libbey

209.   McCrum, Robert.   FRENCH RHINELAND POLICY AT THE PARIS PEACE CONFERENCE, 1919.   *Hist. J. [Great Britain] 1978 21(3): 623-648.* Disputes interpretations that Georges Clemenceau opposed separating the Rhineland from Germany and that the resulting conflict between Ferdinand Foch (1851-1929) and Clemenceau constituted a breakdown in French civil-military relations. Such interpretations obscure the subtlety of Clemenceau's diplomacy and his willingness to compromise when necessary or advantageous. French military efforts to help the separatists establish an independent Rhineland failed for lack of public support in the affected areas, while Allied opposition led Clemenceau to accept Allied economic and strategic guarantees of French national security. Based on British Cabinet and Foreign Office papers, Clemenceau's secret transcripts in the Peace Commission minutes, the Charles Mangin, André Tardieu, and Ray Stannard Baker papers, Department of State foreign relations papers, published sources, especially Raymond Poincaré's *A la recherche de la paix 1919,* and secondary sources; 134 notes.   L. J. Reith

210.   McIntosh, Douglas C.   MANTOUX VS. KEYNES: A NOTE ON GERMAN INCOME AND THE REPARATIONS CONTROVERSY.   *Economic J. [Great Britain] 1977 87(348): 765-767.* Rebuts E. Mantoux, who accused John Maynard Keynes of conjuring up the image of a desperately low per capita income in Germany to bolster his critique of the Treaty of Versailles, in his *Economic Consequences of the Peace* (1919).

211.   Mičev, Dobrin.   GEORGI DIMITROV UND DIE DEUTSCHE SOZIALDEMOKRATIE (BIS 1919)   [Georgi Dimitrov and German Social Democracy to 1919]. *Bulgarian Hist. Rev. [Bulgaria] 1976 4(1): 3-23.* Dimitrov first met German Social Democrats (SPD) in Geneva in the 1890's. He learned German, translated much German socialist literature into Bulgarian, joined the orthodox Bulgarian Social Democrats in 1902, and became secretary of the General Trade Union League in 1910. During 1910-13 Bulgarian and German

labor unions provided mutual financial support but Dimitrov opposed the amalgamation, suggested by Carl Legien in 1911, of the Free Unions with the General League. Disappointed by SPD support of World War I, Dimitrov abandoned the party after the Russian Revolution. Anti-war activities brought him three years in prison. Based on Central Party Archives, and secondary sources; 107 notes.
A. Alcock

212. Mints, I. I. SOVETSKAIA ROSSIIA I NOIABR'SKAIA REVOLIUT-SIIA V GERMANII [Soviet Russia and the 1918 November Revolution in Germany]. *Voprosy Istorii [USSR] 1974 (11): 3-22*. After the victory of the Great October Socialist Revolution in Russia the gradual strengthening of Soviet power and the growing influence of the ideas of the October Revolution on the working people of the belligerent countries forced the two conflicting imperialist groups, the Entente and the German bloc, to put aside their contradictions and seek to unite their forces for the overthrow of Soviet power. At that critical moment a revolution broke out in Germany, which helped Soviet power to thwart the sinister designs of the interventionists. Notwithstanding the difficulties with regard to food supplies, Soviet power at once came to the assistance of the famished German workers and proposed to the new German authorities to form an alliance for the joint struggle against the internal counterrevolution and the armed intervention launched by the Entente powers. But the right-wing leaders of German Social Democracy turned down the friendly proposals of the young Soviet Republic. The November Revolution, though it did not develop into a socialist revolution, proceeded under the impact of the liberating ideas generated by the October Revolution and, consequently, played an immense role in revolutionizing the working people of Germany. J

213. Muth, Heinrich. DIE ENTSTEHUNG DER BAUERN- UND LAND-ARBEITERRÄTE IM NOVEMBER 1918 UND DIE POLITIK DES BUNDES DER LANDWIRTE [The genesis of the peasants and agricultural workers' councils in November 1918 and the policy of the Farmers' Union]. *Vierteljahrshefte für Zeitgeschichte [West Germany] 1973 21(1): 1-38*. Shows how the Farmers' Union preserved the peasantry as a stronghold of conservatism in the face of the revolutionary events of November 1918. In this the union took advantage of Social Democratic indifference to agricultural policy established since the Breslau convention of 1895. The newly created peasants' councils never achieved the political independence of the workers' councils; they accepted dominance by conservative leaders of traditional organizations. Unlike the Left, the conservatives succeeded in establishing an effective power basis for the coming years. Documentary sources from the Schorlemer-Archiv, Landwirtschaftskammer Rheinland, and regional archives; 108 notes. U. Wengenroth

214. Naumann, Horst. ERNST THÄLMANN IM ERSTEN WELTKRIEG UND IN DER NOVEMBERREVOLUTION. EINE BIOGRAPHISCHE SKIZZE ÜBER SEINE TÄTIGKEIT VOM SOMMER 1914 BIS ZUR WAHL ZUM VORSITZENDEN DER ORTSGRUPPE HAMBURG DER USPD (MAI 1919) [Ernst Thälmann during World War I and the November Revolution: a biographical sketch of his activities from the summer of 1914 to his election as chairman of the Hamburg local organization of the USPD, May 1919]. *Zeitschrift für Geschichtswissenschaft [East Germany] 1976 24(12): 1424-1436*. Ernst Thälmann warned his fellow union and Social Democratic Party (SPD) members

of the impending imperialist war, and after its outbreak he severely criticized the opportunistic party leaders for supporting it. His years on the front confirmed his antiwar and anti-imperialist views. Returning to Hamburg in November 1918 he played a leading role in the Independent Social Democratic Party of Germany (USPD). He strove to preserve and strengthen the Workers' and Soldiers' Councils and censured the right-wing Social Democrats for their support of the counterrevolution. 78 notes.   J. T. Walker

215. Nitzsche, Gerhard. DIE GRÜNDUNG DER KOMMUNISTISCHEN PARTEI DEUTSCHLANDS 1918 [The foundation of the German Communist Party in 1918]. *Archivmitteilungen [East Germany] 1978 28(6): 201-206.* German Spartacists, who opposed the policy of compromise and class cooperation of the German Social Democrats, formed the German Communist Party in 30 December 1918.

216. Opitz, Alfred. BÖHMEN UND DIE DEUTSCHBÖHMISCHE FRAGE IN DER ERSTEN PHASE DER HERAUSBILDUNG DES TSCHECHISCHEN NATIONALSTAATES IM JAHRE 1918; NACH BERICHTEN DER SÄCHSISCHEN GESANDTSCHAFT IN WIEN [Bohemia and the Bohemian-German question during the first phase of the rise of the Czech nation-state in 1918: Saxon embassy dispatches from Vienna]. *Bohemia. Jahrbuch des Collegium Carolinum [West Germany] 1976 17: 193-208.* Between October and December 1918, Saxon diplomatic representatives kept Dresden informed of Austria-Hungary's disintegration and the problems resulting for Austria's German nationals, especially for the north Bohemians adjacent to Saxony. The reports indicate that most Sudeten Germans wished to belong to a German rather than a Czech national community, but lacked the arms and organization necessary to resist Czech encroachments. Defeated Germany maintained an official caution and permitted Czechoslovak control of the German-inhabited border areas. Based on material in Dresden archives.   R. E. Weltsch

217. Orlova, M. I.   MARKSISTSKAIA ISTORIOGRAFIIA NOIABR'-SKOI REVOLUITSII V GERMANII (K VOPROSU O KHARAKTERE REVOLIUTSII) [Marxist historiography of the November Revolution in Germany: the character of the revolution]. *Voprosy Istorii [USSR] 1980 (5): 59-75.* Analyzes the Soviet and German Marxist historiography of the revolution of 1918-19 in Germany. The author focuses attention on the formation of the Marxist-Leninist conception regarding the character of the German revolution and singles out several stages in its development; in the period of the revolution and of the postwar revolutionary crisis a uniform appraisal of the revolution did not yet crystallize in publicistic literature; from the beginning of the temporary, partial stabilization of capitalism to the latter half of the 1930's the viewpoint was fairly widespread that the proletarian revolution in Germany had suffered a defeat; from the second half of the 1930's to the second half of the 1950's the emphasis was laid on the incompleteness of this revolution, on its bourgeois character; from the second half of the 1950's and particularly in the 1970's it became the generally accepted principle to appraise the revolution of 1918-19 in Germany as a bourgeois-democratic revolution which had a tendency to develop into the socialist revolution.   J

218. Orlova, M. I. NOIABR'SKAIA REVOLIUTSIIA V GERMANII V OSVESHCHENII BURZHUAZNOI I SOTSIAL-REFORMISTSKOI ISTORIOGRAFII FRG (ETAPY RAZVITIIA I TENDENTSII) [The November Revolution in Germany as presented by the bourgeois and social-reformist historiography of West Germany: developmental stages and trends]. *Novaia i Noveishaia Istoriia [USSR] 1981 (6): 33-53.* In the 1950's the November Revolution attracted great interest among West German historians. The 1960's saw widespread acceptance in West Germany of the concept of "lost opportunities" and the "third way" of development of the German revolution produced by historians of a Left and moderate social reformist trend. In the late 1970's and early 1980's that concept was opposed by conservatives.   J

219. Ovchinnikova, L. V. NOIABR'SKAIA REVOLIUTSIIA V SOVREMENNOI SOTSIAL-DEMOKRATICHESKOI ISTORIOGRAFII FRG: KONTSEPTSIIA "TRET'EGO PUTI" [The November Revolution in contemporary Social Democratic historiography in the Federal Republic of Germany: the concept of a "third path"]. *Novaia i Noveishaia Istoriia [USSR] 1979 (6): 144-156.* The hypothetical reformist third path which might have emerged from the November Revolution of 1918 in Germany according to recent West German historians of Social Democratic leanings, could not have come about. The workers' soviets could not have entered upon a reformist middle course. However the author welcomes the appearance in studies by E. Matthias, E. Kolb, R. Rürup, and others who support the third path concept of a more critical attitude toward the weaknesses of the anti-Communist Social Democratic Party in 1918-19. 81 notes.   R. J. Ware

220. Pauley, Bruce F. THE PATCHWORK TREATIES: ST. GERMAIN AND TRIANON RECONSIDERED. *Rocky Mountain Social Sci. J. 1972 9(2): 61-70.* Discusses the peace settlements which concluded World War I in Central and Eastern Europe, 1919, the problems they created for ethnic minorities and the cause of nationalism in those politically volatile nations, and the role of the Big Four in formulating the settlement.

221. Petricioli, Marta. L'EUROPA DI VERSAILLES IN DUE CONVEGNI INTERNAZIONALI [Two international conferences on the Europe of Versailles]. *Politico [Italy] 1980 45(1): 151-162.* Reports on conferences held in Geneva, "L'Europe de Versailles 1918-1923: bilan, perspectives et controverse," and in Mainz, "Südosteuropa im Spannungsfeld der Grossmächte 1919-1939." Both focused on the deep forces that influenced international policy in the interwar years.   J/S

222. Poidevin, Raymond. LA MAINMISE SUR LES BIENS ENNEMIS PENDANT LA PREMIÈRE GUERRE MONDIALE [The seizure of enemy property during World War I]. *Francia [France] 1974 2: 566-579.* In World War I, both sides sequestered or seized property belonging to nationals of enemy countries. The German government liquidated many of these, actions which aggravated the situation after the war when the French government was concerned with indemnifying those of its nationals who had lost property in this manner or restoring it to them. Applying Article 297 of the Treaty of Versailles, the French government liquidated German assets in France to pay these indemnifications. 62 notes.   J. C. Billigmeier

223. Poulaine, Marc. QUERELLES D'ALLEMANDS ENTRE LOCAR-
NISTES: LA QUESTION D'EUPEN-ET-MALMÉDY [German quarrels
among Treaty of Locarno supporters: the question of Eupen-et-Malmédy]. *Rev.
Hist. [France] 1977 258(2): 393-439.* The territory of Eupen-et-Malmédy was
ceded to Belgium by Germany as a result of the treaty of Versailles but the
financial and other details were not easy to arrange. Gustav Stresemann responded to pressure from nationalists who insisted that Germany should not
accept the permanent loss of former Prussian territory. After the pact was signed
he brought up new interpretations of the term "status quo" and his efforts to
dilute recognition of Belgian annexation occasioned heated discourse in London
and Paris. 134 notes.   G. H. Davis

224. Pribylov, V. I. LIGA NATSII I GDAN'SKII VOPROS (1919-1926)
[The League of Nations and the Danzig question, 1919-26]. *Sovetskoe Slaviano-
vedenie [USSR] 1980 (4): 27-42.* Historians agree that one of the main reasons
for the establishment of the free city of Danzig by the Versailles Treaty of 1919
was Great Britain's desire to keep Germany from re-emerging as a Great Power.
During the period 1920-26, relations between Danzig and Poland were far from
smooth and the question of the free city and its status were on several occasions
discussed at the League. Secondary sources; 108 notes.   G. Dombrovski

225. Radczun, Evelyn and Radczun, Günter. WIRKLICHKEITSBEWÄL-
TIGUNG IN DEN BRIEFEN ROSA LUXEMBURGS AUS DEM GEFÄNG-
NIS 1915-1918 [Coming to terms with reality in the letters of Rosa Luxemburg
from prison, 1915-18]. *Zeitschrift für Geschichtswissenschaft [East Germany]
1979 27(2): 99-110.* Although censors prevented direct political commentary,
Rosa Luxemburg demonstrated in her prison letters a deep awareness of the
historical importance of World War I and the Russian Revolution. Because of
her understanding of the historical process, she was cheerful and optimistic about
the future of mankind, and understood the interrelationship of man and nature,
both of which she loved passionately, while her hatred of imperialism and militarism led her to her role in the Spartacus League. 49 notes.   J. T. Walker

226. Reisberg, Arnold. LIEBKNECHTS REDE IN DER SOWJETBOT-
SCHAFT 1918 [Liebknecht's speech in the Soviet Embassy in 1918]. *Beiträge
zur Geschichte der Arbeiterbewegung [East Germany] 1973 15(6): 947-949.* Publishes Karl Liebknecht's speech in the Soviet Embassy in Berlin after his release
from prison on 22 October 1918, in which he welcomed the Russian Revolution
which had to be defended against the intervention of world capitalism. Based on
the autobiography of Arthur Holitscher, *Reisen. Ausgewählte Reportagen und
autobiographische Berichte* (Berlin, 1973); note.   R. Wagnleitner

227. Richez, Jean-Claude. LE RÉVOLUTION DE NOVEMBRE 1918 EN
ALSACE DANS LES PETITES VILLES ET LES CAMPAGNES [The No-
vember 1918 revolution in the small towns and the countryside of Alsace]. *Rev.
d'Alsace [France] 1981 (107): 153-168.* In the interval between the signing of the
armistice ending World War I and the arrival of French occupation troops six
to nine days later, Alsace participated in the beginnings of the November Revolution of 1918 in Germany.

228. Ruch, Karl-Heinz. DIE REGENERATIONSBESTREBUNGEN DES REAKTIONÄREN PREUSSENTUMS UND DIE HERAUSBILDUNG DER NEUKONSERVATIVEN "SOZIALISMUS"-AUFFASSUNG [The efforts to regenerate reactionary Prussianism and the development of a new conservative concept of socialism]. *Martin-Luther-Universität Halle-Wittenberg. Wissenschaftliche Zeitschrift. Gesellschafts- und Sprachwissenschaftliche Reihe [East Germany] 1975 24(1): 23-31.* The new conservative conception and interpretation of socialism that became prominent in Germany in 1917-18 replaced proletarian internationalism with a nationalist militarism. R. Wagnleitner

229. Ruge, Wolfgang. FRIEDRICH EBERT AM 10 NOVEMBER 1918 [Friedrich Ebert on 10 November 1918]. *Zeitschrift für Geschichtswissenschaft [East Germany] 1978 26(11): 955-971.* The pact between the Social Democratic leadership and German militarism concluded during the November Revolution is reflected by the agreement between Friedrich Ebert and Wilhelm Groener on 10 November 1918. The Social Democratic leaders still verbally advocated socialism and fought for the revolution but betrayed the German proletariat by allowing the army generals to start a military campaign against the people. S. Boehnke

230. Rüger, Adolf. IMPERIALISMUS, SOZIALREFORMISMUS UND ANTIKOLONIALE DEMOKRATISCHE ALTERNATIVE. ZIELVORSTELLUNGEN VON AFRIKANERN IN DEUTSCHLAND IM JAHRE 1919 [Imperialism, social reformism, and anti-colonial democratic alternatives: goals of Africans in Germany in 1919]. *Zeitschrift für Geschichtswissenschaft [East Germany] 1975 23(11): 1293-1308.* After World War I the German Colonial Ministry attempted to persuade Africans living in the colonies to declare their unconditional loyalty to Germany, but few were willing to do so. Instead, most supported what they mistakenly perceived as the new anti-imperialist Germany, and attempted to persuade the government to grant their colonies national autonomy and civil and social rights, in the event that Germany should regain control of these territories. Pursuing imperialist policies, the Socialist government turned down the Africans' requests. Based on documents in the Central State Archives at Potsdam; 44 notes, appendixes. J. T. Walker

231. Schaper, B. W. REVOLUTIE EN CONTRAREVOLUTIE [Revolution and counterrevolution]. *Spiegel Historiael [Netherlands] 1973 8(1): 9-15.* Surveys the current literature on revolutionary movements in Central Europe, 1917-19, focusing especially on the German Revolution of 1918 and communist uprisings. The Spartacists failed because they were dilettantish, utopian, and uncertain of themselves; they actually strengthened the counterrevolution. The German revolution was a victory of moderate elements supported by the generals. The same development did not occur in Austria where the Socialists did not need the support of the military. Biblio. G. D. Homan

232. Schmidt, Gustav. EFFIZIENZ UND FLEXIBILITÄT POLITISCH-SOZIALER SYSTEME. DIE DEUTSCHE UND DIE ENGLISCHE POLITIK 1918/19 [The efficiency and flexibility of sociopolitical systems: German and English politics, 1918-19]. *Vierteljahrshefte für Zeitgeschichte [West Germany] 1977 25(2): 137-187.* Great Britain's parliamentary system demonstrated no greater flexibility or efficiency in coping with socioeconomic crisis than the

newly improvised democracy in Germany after World War I. Neither system permitted fundamental social change. This was less because of industrial pressure groups than because international political and economic forces severely limited the governments' options and because the primary concern was maintaining productivity, which in turn favored the traditional economic structures. Based on British and German published documents; 211 notes.   D. Prowe

233. Schönhoven, Klaus. DIE WÜRTTEMBERGISCHEN SOLDATEN-RÄTE IN DER REVOLUTION VON 1918/1919 [The Württemberg soldiers' councils in the revolution 1918-19]. *Zeitschrift für Württembergische Landesgeschichte [West Germany] 1974 23: 236-257.* The representatives of the Württemberg Soldiers' Councils were not revolutionaries who pursued class struggle in the barracks. Rather they were cautious administrators and soldiers from a variety of backgrounds who wanted to introduce democratic and trade unionist principles into the Wilhelminian system in Germany. They were stopped both by demobilization and by the policy of the central government in Berlin. 54 notes.
M. Geyer

234. Schramm, Gottfried. MILITARISIERUNG UND DEMOKRATISIERUNG: TYPEN DER MASSENINTEGRATION IM ERSTEN WELTKRIEG [Militarization and democratization: types of mass integration in World War I]. *Francia [France] 1975 3: 476-497.* Germany and Russia in 1914 were both monarchical, predemocratic states, dominated by a coalition of aristocrats and industrialists. The stress of the war effort told heavily on the antiquated social and political structures of both nations, far more so than it did on those of democratic countries. The two responses were militarization and democratization. The masses were militarized, either drafted for the front or organized for war work. Democratization, though feared by the leadership, was unavoidable. The common people had to be propagandized, inspired, given incentives. When first Russia, then Germany lost the war, mass risings led by common soldiers overthrew their social and political systems. Militarization and democratization combined to change the face of Germany and Russia. 27 notes.
J. C. Billigmeier

235. Schütz, Rüdiger. PROLETARISCHER KLASSENKAMPF UND BÜRGERLICHE REVOLUTION: ZUR BEURTEILUNG DER NOVEMBERREVOLUTION IN DER MARXISTISCH-LENINISTISCHEN GESCHICHTSWISSENSCHAFT [Proletarian class struggle and bourgeois revolution: the interpretation of the November Revolution in Marxist-Leninist historiography]. *Saeculum [West Germany] 1979 30(1): 22-44.* Before World War II Marxist-Leninist historians usually interpreted the German November Revolution as a socialist or proletarian revolution. Only later works began to use the term bourgeois revolution, the failure of which resulted in the lack of a revolutionary party of the labor movement and the cooperation of revisionist social democrats with bourgeois and reactionary groups. Secondary literature; 115 notes.
R. Wagnleitner

236. Schwabe, Klaus. WOODROW WILSON AND GERMANY'S MEMBERSHIP IN THE LEAGUE OF NATIONS, 1918-19. *Central European Hist. 1975 8(1): 3-22.* Describes Woodrow Wilson's changes in attitude, and the reasons for the changes, concerning Germany's membership in the League of

Nations, 1918-19. Wilson moved from the position 1) that Germany should be a member, 2) to one that it should not, 3) to a compromise included in the treaty that Germany should only be admitted to the League when it disarmed. Wilson "simply reacted to changing circumstances" in changing his views. Published and unpublished sources; 65 notes.

C. R. Lovin

237. Shinozuka, Toshio. DOITSU SHAKAI MINSHUTŌ TO DOITSU KAKUMEI [The German Social Democratic Party and the German Revolution]. *Shigaku Zasshi [Japan] 1974 83(12): 1-39.* Actions of the German Social Democratic Party (SPD) in the German Revolution are best represented by the alliance (*bündnis*) between Friedrich Ebert and Wilhelm Groener to overcome Bolshevism formed 10 November 1918 and established by the victory in the January 1919 struggle. There is a difference of opinion between West German and East German historians on the character of the alliance. In West Germany, men like W. Sauer and P. C. Witt generally deny that the alliance had an offensive character from the first, while historians in East Germany insist not only on its initial offensive character but also on the early resolution of the individuals on attacks. The author analyzes the formation and development of the alliance. The SPD had resolved to impede the extension of Bolshevism by 10 November but had not come to the decision to suppress Bolsheviks by arms; it was therefore the dawn of 24 December when they finally made a resolution to step into action. 168 notes.

S. Itō

238. Silberner, Edmund. ROSA LUXEMBURG, IHRE PARTEI UND DIE JUDEN FRAGE [Rosa Luxemburg, her party, and the Jewish question]. *Jahrbuch des Inst. für Deutsche Geschichte [Israel] 1978 7: 299-337.* Rosa Luxemburg fled from Poland to Switzerland and then to Germany where she became a foremost radical leader. She had little interest in Jewish problems as such, for she believed that Jewish separateness hindered working-class interests. She saw Zionism as a reactionary utopia. She helped organize the Social Democratic Party of the Kingdom of Poland and Lithuania. Leo Jogiches, Julian Marchlewski, Adolf Warski, Henryk Walecki, and Wera Kostrzewa were among the leaders. Rosa Luxemburg was murdered in 1919 along with Karl Liebknecht as Spartacus party leaders. 131 notes.

M. Faissler

239. Snelling, R. C. PEACEMAKING, 1919: AUSTRALIA, NEW ZEALAND AND THE BRITISH EMPIRE DELEGATION AT VERSAILLES. *J. of Imperial and Commonwealth Hist. [Great Britain] 1975 4(1): 15-28.* Great Britain and the British Empire were represented at the Paris Peace Conference, but Australia and New Zealand also sent representatives who had particular impact on proceedings with the Colonial Office, establishing the basis for future colonial policy which would involve the two member states more extensively.

240. Stoecker, H. ZU DEN POLITISCHEN AUFFASSUNGEN DER ARBEITERKLASSE IN DER NOVEMBER-REVOLUTION [On the political conceptions of the working classes in the November Revolution]. *R. d'Allemagne [France] 1974 6(2): 17-22.* Investigates the character and political objectives of the regional conference of workers' and soldiers' councils in the industrial area of the Rhineland in late 1918. Attempts to establish rule of councils failed due to lack of organization.

R. K. Adams

241. Terraine, John. "AN ACTUAL REVOLUTIONARY SITUATION": GERMANY IN 1917. *Hist. Today [Great Britain] 1978 28(1): 14-22.* Severe shortages of coal, reversals in military policy, and loss after loss on the battlefield brought German home-front morale to its lowest point in 1917 and presented circumstances ripe for domestic revolt.

242. Terraine, John. 'THE WAR MUST BE ENDED.' *Hist. Today [Great Britain] 1978 28(11): 703-711, (12): 783-792.* Part I. Discusses Germany's participation in World War I, 8 August-27 October 1918, assessing the political and military expertise of Germany's leaders. Part II. Focuses on Germany's participation in World War I from 30 October 1918 until 11 November 1918 when the Armistice ending the war was signed.

243. Tokody, Gyula. AUSSENPOLITISCHE BEZIEHUNGEN ZWISCHEN DER UNGARISCHEN RÄTEREPUBLIK UND DEUTSCHLAND [Foreign relations between the Hungarian Soviet Republic and Germany]. *Études Hist. Hongroises [Hungary] 1980 (2): 173-198.* Official relations between the Hungarian Soviet Republic and Germany were assured by the existence and activities of Germany's consulate in Budapest. Consulates of the former Habsburg Empire had been closed and no new Hungarian consulates were established before the first half of 1919. The new situation in southeastern Europe created by the establishment of the Hungarian Soviet Republic at first was conducive to better relations between the two countries, but after the failure of the attempt to establish relations between the Hungarian and Bavarian Soviet Republics, chances for rapprochement became significantly worse. Hungary tried to improve relations after the announcement of the terms of the Treaty of Versailles, but Germany's negative attitude and the imminent collapse of the Hungarian Soviet Republic made any improvement in relations at that time impossible. 58 notes. Russian summary.   S

244. Tokody, Gyula. A POROSZ-NÉMET KONZERVATIVIZMUS POLITIKAI VÁLSÁGA ES UJJÁSZERVEZESINEK KEZDETE 1918 NOVEMBEREBEN [The breakup of Prussian-German conservatism and its rebirth in November 1918]. *Történelmi Szemle [Hungary] 1972 15(1-2): 48-74.* World War I and the revolution of 1918 unsettled the Conservative Party in Germany. Even before 1914 a split had developed between the old Prussian-dominated party core and the newer branches, which were more flexible socially and ideologically. The experience of 1918 convinced the Conservatives of the need to support new democratic ideas while at the same time opposing the Socialists and Communists. A program based on democratic principles was published in November 1918 in the right-wing newspaper *Neue Preussische Zeitung.* 2 tables, 83 notes.   H. Szamuely

245. Tokody, Gyula. A VERSAILLES-I SZERZŐDÉS KÖZZÉTÉTELE ÉS A NÉMET POLITIKAI KÖZVÉLEMÉNY (MAY-JUNE, 1919) [The release of the Versailles treaty and the political atmosphere in Germany, May-June 1919]. *Párttörténeti Közlemények [Hungary] 1976 22(2): 119-143.* The parties of the German parliamentary session of 1919, and the coalition government led by the Social Democrats alike condemned the dictates of the Treaty of Versailles. The Social Democrats and their allies were finally forced to sign the treaty and accept its conditions, and the Right shifted all the blame on them. 39 notes.

CK-AU

246. Trachtenberg, Marc. VERSAILLES AFTER SIXTY YEARS. *J. of Contemporary Hist. [Great Britain] 1982 17(3): 487-506.* All the major works in English on the Paris Peace Conference develop the assumption that an altruistic, moderate Wilson was outfoxed by vindictive, cunning European diplomats who sought to punish Germany. Fresh investigation of the documents of the conference reveals many variations and nuances of opinion. Wilson comes through as a vindicator; the British, for trials of war criminals; the French, as vacillators without plain direction. "This then is the result of the politicization of this field of historiography: historical writing on the peace conference has been used as a vehicle for the projection of political values, and as a result our understanding of the period has been seriously distorted." Based on archival sources; 49 notes.
M. P. Trauth

247. Trotnow, Helmut. THE MISUNDERSTOOD KARL LIEBKNECHT *European Studies R. [Great Britain] 1975 5(2): 171-191.* Studies the life of Karl Liebknecht (1871-1919), famous son of an equally famous father, Wilhelm Liebknecht, and until now largely overshadowed by and usually connected with the political theorist Rosa Luxemburg (1871-1919) as cofounder of the German Communist Party (KPD). Outlines Liebknecht's career as lawyer, elected deputy, and party tactician as well as his ideas on anti-militarism and influence on the rank and file of the KPD. Primary and secondary sources; 81 notes.
C. T. Prukop

248. Tych, Feliks. MASSE, CLASSE E PARTITO IN ROSA LUXEMBURG [Masses, classes, and party in Rosa Luxemburg]. *Ann. dell'Istituto Giangiacomo Feltrinelli [Italy] 1973 15: 258-288.* Analyzes Rosa Luxemburg's (1870-1919) theory of social development, or "the dialectical revolutionary process and the interrelation between social consciousness and the objective flux of history." Despite the fragmentary and often contradictory nature of Luxemburg's writings on social development one idea dominates: "socialism is the first great mass social movement, constructed and reconstructed by the masses themselves." 118 notes.
M. T. Wilson

249. Ullrich, Robert. ZUR FUNCTION DER DEUTSCHEN VATERLANDSPARTEI (DVLP) [About the function of the German Fatherland Party (DVLP)]. *Jenaer Beiträge zur Parteien Geschichte [East Germany] 1974 (36): 56-71.* The Fatherland Party of 1917 was a political party which could place no members in the Reichstag or state legislatures due to the wartime ban on elections. The party stood against parliamentarianism, popular representation, any changes in the Bismarckian constitution, and the Marxist working-class movement. Its efforts to unify pro-imperialist and promilitary annexationist groups created a new political device that became a forerunner of Nazism. A report of the public defense of a dissertation on the German Fatherland Party; 6 notes.
M. Faissler

250. Vadász, Sándor. MEGJEGYZÉSEK AZ ÚJABB ROSA LUXEMBURG-IRODALOMRÓL [Remarks regarding recent literature on Rosa Luxemburg]. *Századok [Hungary] 1980 14(2): 281-290.* Rosa Luxemburg, one of the leaders of the Polish and German labor movement was one of the most influential representatives of the workers' revolutionary movement. She is shown in a somewhat different light by the current contemporary Marxist literature. The beliefs

that she represented traditional democratic attitudes within a Marxist society are gross oversimplifications. Her political opinions and theories, as well as her life, were more complex and deeper than indicated by previous Western literature.

T. Kuner

251. Weissbecker, Manfred. KONSERVATIVE POLITIK UND IDEOLO-GIE IN DER KONTERREVOLUTION 1918-1919 [Conservative politics and ideology in the counterrevolution, 1918-19]. *Zeitschrift für Geschichtswissenschaft [East Germany] 1979 27(8): 707-720.* During the early phase of the German counterrevolution the conservatives pragmatically cooperated with the bourgeois parties and the Social Democrats. However, after the victory of the counterrevolution the Young Conservatives abandoned a defensive position and looked for new ideological models for a long-range restructuring of the state and society, while the old traditional conservatives became increasingly impotent. Various groups, such as the Anti-Bolshevik League, promoted a dictatorship based on a national socialist mass movement, thus preparing the way for the Nazis. 54 notes.

J. T. Walker

252. Wendt, Bernd-Jürgen. DEUTSCHE REVOLUTION—LABOUR UNREST: SYSTEMBEDINGUNGEN DER STREIKBEWEGUNGEN IN DEUTSCHLAND UND ENGLAND 1918-1921 [German revolution—labor unrest: socioeconomic conditions of the strike movements in Germany and England, 1918-21]. *Archiv für Sozialgeschichte [West Germany] 1980 20: 1-55.* Compares the development of the relationship among the working class, unions, and the state in Germany and Great Britain. In both countries war-induced strains exploded because labor considered itself the loser. British labor generally recognized the political system, and unions were able to keep economy and politics apart. The German unions became integrated into an only partially reformed political system without general consensus and lost their freedom to defend the working class. This alienated major segments of German labor and led to radicalization which increased fragmentation and led to aborted attempts at revolution. In Great Britain collective bargaining regained its prewar role as the means of class struggle and kept the working class together. Contemporary journals; 195 notes.

H. W. Wurster

253. Wiederhöft, Harri. DER ARBEITER- UND SOLDATENRAT IN HAMBURG UND DAS SOWJETISCHE KONSULAT IM NOVEMBER 1918 [The workers and soldiers council at Hamburg and the Soviet consulate, November 1918]. *Zeitschrift für Geschichtswissenschaft [East Germany] 1973 21(4): 426-440.* Publication of 16 documents which deal with the relations between the workers and soldiers council at Hamburg and the Soviet consulate during the November Revolution.

254. Wiederhöft, Harri. HERMANN DUNCKER UND DER IDEOLO-GISCHE KLÄRUNGSPROZESS IN DER REVOLUTIONÄREN AR-BEITERJUGENDBEWEGUNG DEUTSCHLANDS 1918 [Hermann Duncker and the ideological process of clarification within the German revolutionary workers' youth movement, 1918]. *Wissenschaftliche Zeitschrift der U. Rostock. Gesellschafts- und Sprachwissenschaftliche Reihe [East Germany] 1974 23(2): 123-127.* In 1918 Hermann Duncker, member of the Spartakus group in Berlin, assisted the functionaries of the workers' youth movement to clarify their

position on the question of the dictatorship of the proletariat. In October 1918, during the founding congress of the Free Socialist Youth, the delegates adopted a revolutionary line and stated that they wanted to follow the revolutionary example of Russia. Based on documents in the Institute for Marxism-Leninism, Berlin, printed documents, and secondary literature; 37 notes.

R. Wagnleitner

255. Witt, Peter Christian. EINE DENKSCHRIFT OTTO HOETZSCHS VOM 5. NOVEMBER 1918 [A memorandum by Otto Hoetzsch of 5 November 1918]. *Vierteljahrshefte für Zeitgeschichte [West Germany] 1973 21(3): 337-353.* Otto Hoetzsch was chief commentator on foreign affairs with the conservative Kreuzzeitung. Later he became foreign affairs spokesman for the German National Peoples Party, in which he belonged to the left wing. His memorandum surveys the previous 20 years of conservative policy and provides the first basic concept for the organization of a conservative mass party. Monarchy as well as ethnic anti-Semitic radicalism is to be abandoned and Tory democracy is held up as a model. 60 notes, and an appendix containing the text of the memorandum.

U. Wengenroth

256. Żarnowski, Janusz. THE EMERGENCE OF THE SYSTEM OF NATIONAL STATES IN CENTRAL EUROPE (1918): THE CHANGE IN THE POLITICAL MAP OF CENTRAL EUROPE. *Acta Poloniae Hist. [Poland] 1972 25: 57-86.* Discusses the factors contributing to the new Versailles order, interpreted to mean "the political situation as a whole in the territories of Central and South Eastern Europe." The emergence of new states was mostly due to the disintegration of the Habsburg Empire. Neither the Central Powers nor the Entente originally wished to create the independent states. The Paris Peace Settlement was the result of a compromise between the principle of self-determination on the one hand, and the tendency to establish frontiers arbitrarily, according to the interests of the victorious powers, on the other. Biblio.

H. Heitzman-Wojcicka

257. Zawadzki, Józef. *DZEŁA ZEBRANE* RÓŻY LUKSEMBURG. UWAGI I REFLEKSJE [Rosa Luxemburg's *Collected Works:* Notes and reflections]. *Ekonomista [Poland] 1977 (5): 1125-1157.* Discusses the merits of the work of the revolutionary Rosa Luxemburg and her influence on Marxist-Leninist thought, particularly in Poland and Germany.

258. —. [ECONOMIC AND SOCIAL PROBLEMS OF THE GERMAN DEMOBILIZATION, 1918-19]. *J. of Modern Hist. 1975 47(1): 1-47.*
Feldman, Gerald D. ECONOMIC AND SOCIAL PROBLEMS OF THE GERMAN DEMOBILIZATION, 1918-19, *pp. 1-23.* Advocates the investigation of German demobilization, 1918-19, as a starting point in explaining the German revolution's failure and the triumph of the conservatives. Although German demobilization must be assessed in the context of the general demobilization of Western industrial society, it had its own peculiar characteristics. The author assesses the role of Joseph Koeth, the "dictator" of German demobilization. Based on German archival material and secondary sources; 61 notes.
Kocka, Jurgen. COMMENT, *pp. 24-27.*
Johnson, Paul B. COMMENT, *pp. 27-29.*

Mommsen, W. J.   COMMENT,   *pp. 29-32.*
Armitage, Susan H.   COMMENT,   *pp. 32-34.*
Hawley, Ellis W.   COMMENT,   *pp. 34-37.*
Winkler, Heinrich August and Homburg, Heidrun.   COMMENT,   *pp. 37-39.*
Aldcroft, Derek H.   COMMENT,   *pp. 39-40.*
Maier, Charles S.   COMMENT,   *pp. 41-44.*
Feldman, Gerald D.   A COMMENT ON THE COMMENTS,   *pp. 44-47.*
P. L. Solodkin

259.   —.   NEUE DOKUMENTE AUS DER GESCHICHTE DER KAMPF-
GEMEINSCHAFT MIT DER PARTEI LENINS   [New documents on the
history of the struggle-alliance with Lenin's party]. *Einheit [East Germany] 1977
32(4): 427-431.* Publication of a letter by Clara Zetkin to Lenin, June 1918, and
an address of Ernst Meyer to the Fifth Congress of Soviets in June 1918, showing
the strong impact of the Russian Revolution on the left wing of the German Social
Democrats.

260.   —.   [POLITICAL ECONOMY VERSUS NATIONAL SOVER-
EIGNTY].   *J. of Modern Hist. 1979 51(1): 4-85.*
McDougall, Walter A.   POLITICAL ECONOMY VERSUS NATIONAL
    SOVEREIGNTY: FRENCH STRUCTURES FOR GERMAN ECO-
    NOMIC INTEGRATION AFTER VERSAILLES,   *pp. 4-23.* Though
    seeking an integrative framework within the Treaty of Versailles, France
    assumed its own course of revisionism, involving permanent restrictions on
    German sovereignty in the Rhineland, a policy more in keeping with the
    balance of power and economic integration Europe required for stability,
    1919-24, than the liberal-internationalist Anglo-American and German for-
    mulations.
Trachtenberg, Marc.   REPARATION AT THE PARIS PEACE CONFER-
    ENCE,   *pp. 24-55.* It was not France but Great Britain alone that prevented
    settlement on a moderate reparations figure at the Paris Peace Conference
    of 1919.
Maier, Charles S.   THE TRUTH ABOUT THE TREATIES?,   *pp. 56-67.*
    Reviews McDougall and Trachtenberg's revision of traditional interpreta-
    tions and suggests other economic methods of evaluating interwar financial
    settlements.
Schwabe, Klaus.   COMMENT ON TRACHTENBERG AND MCDOU-
    GALL,   *pp. 68-73.* Questions the sufficiency of documentary evidence
    offered and asserts that McDougall and Trachtenberg underappraised con-
    temporary diplomatic, psychological, and domestic atmospheres.
Wright, Gordon.   COMMENT,   *pp. 74-77.* The theories offered are not so
    nonsubjective as claimed, yet they possess sufficient credibility to warrant
    further investigation.
McDougall, Walter A.   COMMENT,   *pp 78-81.*
Trachtenberg, Marc.   REPLY,   *pp. 81-85.*

261.   —.   [ROSA LUXEMBURG'S INFLUENCE TODAY].   *Pensée
[France] 1973 (167): 61-79.*
Badia, Gilbert.   ROSA LUXEMBURG AUJOURD'HUI   [Rosa Luxemburg
    today], *pp. 61-71.*

—. LETTRES INEDITÉS DE ROSA LUXEMBURG [Unedited letters of Rosa Luxemburg], *pp. 72-79.* A modern view on the work and influence of Rosa Luxemburg (1870-1919), German socialist leader, journalist, and revolutionary, followed by a selection of her letters written from Breslau Prison during World War I.

3

GOVERNMENT, POLITICS, AND THE ECONOMY

262. Abraham, David. STATE AND CLASSES IN WEIMAR GERMANY. *Pol. and Soc. 1977 7(3): 229-266.* Analyzes actual and possible coalitions of social classes during 1919-32. Mass-based political support for the Weimar state was impossible to achieve. Political instability was the inevitable result as classes ceased to view their political parties as effective representatives of their class interests. In the face of economic crisis and without a mass base, a parliamentary-democratic state could not maintain itself. 8 tables, 85 notes.   D. G. Nielson

263. Ackerl, Isabella. DIE ARBEITSGEMEINSCHAFT DEUTSCHER PARLAMENTARIER: EINIGE ASPEKTE TRANSNATIONALER BEZIE-HUNGEN [The professional association of German parliamentarians: some aspects of transnational relations]. *Rev. d'Allemagne [France] 1981 13(4): 690-701.* Leaders of Pan-German parties in Germany, Austria, and Czechoslovakia met from time to time during the 1920's for an exchange of views and to coordinate their policies on particular political questions, especially on annexation and the promotion of the interests of German minorities in various European states. These meetings, composed almost exclusively of parliamentarians, took place in Germany or Austria and received little publicity. Their main political effect was that the German representatives were informed of the positions of the party leaders in other countries. Based partly on Austrian governmental archives; 20 notes.   J. S. Gassner

264. Adanir, Fikret and Müller, Michael G. SÜDOSTEUROPA IM SPAN-NUNGSFELD DER GROSSMÄCHTE 1919-1939 [Southeast Europe in the spectrum of Great Power tensions 1919-39]. *Südost-Forschungen [West Germany] 1980 39: 242-248.* Report of a December 1979 colloquium at Mainz with participants from the United States and 11 countries in Europe.
       P. J. Adler

265. Akhtamzyan, A. A. PROFILI RAPALL'SKOI DIPLOMATII [Different aspects of Rapallo diplomacy]. *Voprosy Istorii [USSR] 1974 (2): 100-124.* Discusses Soviet-German diplomatic and trade relations in the years 1922-28, while Ulrich von Brockdorff-Rantzau (1869-1928) was German Ambassador to Moscow. Foreign trade development, based on the Rapallo Treaty of 16 June 1922, was of bilateral advantage, and ideological differences and political crises

in 1924-25 did not prevent the signing of new trade agreements in Moscow (1925) and Berlin (1926). However, friction between the pro-Western German Minister of Foreign Affairs, Gustav Stresemann (1878-1929) and Brockdorff-Rantzau, who supported the pro-Soviet Rapallo policy, reached a climax in 1927. Only the untimely death (from throat cancer) of Brockdorff-Rantzau prevented his recall. Based mainly on German primary sources; 96 notes.						N. Frenkley

266.	Albertin, Lothar.	LIBERALISMUS IN DER WEIMARER REPUB-LIK	[Liberalism in the Weimar Republic]. *Neue Politische Literatur [West Germany] 1974 19(2): 220-234.* Review article. In spite of the prominent and successful role of liberal politicians in foreign policy, the liberal parties lost their mass support because they had no answer to the novel economic problems confronting the middle classes. 20 notes.						G. Hollenberg

267.	Alexander, Manfred.	ZUR REISE VON MARSCHALL FOCH NACH WARSCHAU UND PRAG IM FRÜHJAHR 1923	[Marshal Foch's trip to Warsaw and Prague in the spring of 1923]. *Bohemia. Jahrbuch des Collegium Carolinum [West Germany] 1973 14: 289-319.* On his visits to Poland and Czechoslovakia (April-May 1923) Marshal Foch sought active support for the French occupation of the Ruhr. France was also interested in strengthening its East European alliance system and used Foch as an intermediary to encourage a Polish-Czechoslovak agreement and more positive commitments to French international policy. Despite manifestations of enthusiasm, the immediate political success of the trip was minor. Based on the Political Archives of the Foreign Office in Bonn and published sources; 160 notes.						R. E. Weltsch

268.	Alter, Peter.	RAPALLO—GLEICHGEWICHTSPOLITIK UND RE-VISIONISMUS	[Rapallo—balance of power politics and revisionism]. *Neue Politische Literatur [West Germany] 1974 19(4): 509-517.* Reviews several studies on the Rapallo Treaty (1922) and argues that it was not an overture to a revisionist policy towards Poland, but a means for Germany to avoid a decision between West and East. 47 notes.						G. Hollenberg

269.	Altschull, J. Herbert.	CHRONICLE OF A DEMOCRATIC PRESS IN GERMANY BEFORE THE HITLER TAKEOVER. *Journalism Q. 1975 52(2): 229-238.* The German press was as free as any in Europe by the 20th century, although, like earlier German constitutions, the Weimar constitution did not specifically guarantee freedom of the press. During the Weimar Republic political battles were waged in the press, and newspapers on both the right and left were suspended. The Nazis used the press in their attempts to bring down the republic. Secondary sources; 52 notes.						K. J. Puffer

270.	amZehnhoff, H.-W.	DER FALL ERNST VON SALOMON. AK-TIONEN UND STANDORTBESTIMMUNG EINES PREUSSISCHEN AN-ARCHISTEN IN DER WEIMARER REPUBLIK	[The case of Ernst von Salomon: actions and place of a Prussian anarchist in the Weimar Republic]. *Rev. Belge de Philologie et d'Hist. [Belgium] 1977 55(3): 871-896.* Ernst von Salomon was a Prussian anarchist with right-wing leanings. He participated in the conspiracy that led to the assassination of Walther Rathenau in 1922. The author examines von Salomon's "national revolutionary" ideology, a curious mixture of radicalism and reaction. 123 notes.						J. C. Billigmeier

271.   Artaud, Denise.   DIE HINTERGRÜNDE DER RUHRBESETZUNG 1923. DAS PROBLEM DER INTERALLIIERTEN SCHULDEN   [The background of the Ruhr occupation of 1923: the problem of inter-Allied indebtedness]. *Vierteljahrshefte für Zeitgeschichte [West Germany] 1979 27(2): 241-259.* A generally ignored aspect of the French decision to invade the German Ruhr Valley (1923) is the British-French disagreement over inter-Allied indebtedness. In 1922 the British consistently refused to make concessions to the French in the debt question in the hope of strengthening the pound and thus hardened the French determination to extract reparations for the reconstruction of France. Based on the French Finance and Foreign Ministry Archives, the British Cabinet and Foreign Office papers (Public Record Office); 42 notes.   D. Prowe

272.   Artaud, Denise.   LA QUESTION DES DETTES INTERALLIÉES ET LA RECONSTRUCTION DE L'EUROPE   [The question of interallied debts and the reconstruction of Europe]. *Rev. Hist. [France] 1979 261(2): 363-382.* The intentions of US policy relative to the payment of interallied debts during the 1920's may have involved control of Germany and Britain as well as the assumption of German financial interests in Latin America. The results of American insistence on repayment and willingness to lend money to Germany brought a fragile stability to the world balance of payments. But the same policy exacerbated French and British insistence on continued reparations and increased the level of German debts to the point of instability.   43 notes.   G. H. Davis

273.   Ayçoberry, Pierre.   LA GUERRE DE RUES DANS L'ALLEMAGNE DE WEIMAR   [The street war under the Weimar Republic]. *Histoire [France] 1979 (10): 86-88.* Street fighting by political paramilitary forces ranging from the Far Right to the Communists helped bring down the republic in Germany, 1920-32.

274.   Baechler, Christian.   UNE DIFFICILE NEGOCIATION FRANCO-ALLEMANDE AUX CONFÉRENCES DE LA HAYE: LE REGLEMENT DE LA QUESTION DES SANCTIONS (1929-1930)   [The difficult French-German negotiations at The Hague conferences: the settlement of the sanctions question, 1929-30]. *Rev. Allemagne [France] 1980 12(2): 238-260.* The first Versailles Treaty signatories conference met at The Hague in order to discuss problems involved in implementing the Young Plan and the evacuation of the Rhineland. The chief stumbling block was the question of sanctions in the event of German refusal to pay reparations. The inability of the first conference to arrive at a Franco-German agreement led to a second, where the Germans argued against the right of the French to impose sanctions by reoccupation of the Rhineland. Both sides finally agreed that under the Young Plan the creditor states recovered their full freedom of action to collect money owed to them under general international law instead of the Treaty of Versailles by employing economic and not military sanctions, thus bringing to fruition the policy initiated earlier by Gustav Stresemann (1878-1929). Based on French and German Foreign Ministry archives; 75 notes.   J. S. Gassner

275.   Baev, V. G.   VOPROSY REPARATSIONNOI POLITIKI VEIMARSKOI RESPUBLIKI (PO MATERIALAM REIKHSTAGA)   [Problems of the Weimar Republic policy on reparations; based on Reichstag materials]. *Voprosy Istorii [USSR] 1977 (9): 192-199.* Discusses parliamentary debates on

World War I reparations, which reveal divergent political tendencies and philosophies of the German political parties. Contrasts the positive role played by Communist delegates in rejecting demands of the Entente powers and foreign capitalists with inconsistencies within Social Democratic ranks. The Communists opposed both the Dawes Plan of 1924 and the Young Plan of 1929, seeing both as means to exploit and enslave German workers. Bourgeois politicians saw the adoption of the Young Plan mainly as a prelude to the liberation of the Rhineland. Opposition to the Young Plan was also expressed by Social Democrats and National Socialists, but their motives were, respectively, financial and demagogic. Based on published proceedings of Reichstag sessions, 1919-32; 67 notes.

N. Frenkley

276.   Barbati, Vittorio.   DA SCAPA FLOW AL PIANO Z—LA POLITICA NAVALE TEDESCA FRA LE DUE GUERRE MONDIALE   [From Scapa Flow to Plan Z: German naval policy between the two world wars]. *Riv. Marittima [Italy] 1975 108(9): 37-44, (10): 31-38.* Part I. Peace treaty restrictions and Germany's economic problems created difficult conditions for rebuilding the German navy after World War I. Nonetheless the Germans succeeded in laying some very solid technical foundations. On the doctrinal side, this period was characterized by very hard work out of which stemmed the daring theories of Admiral Wolfgang Wegener—the extreme implications of which, however, were never accepted by the German navy, and the building, at the end of the twenties, of the first pocket battleship. Part II. Describes the official rearmament of the German navy from 1935 to 1939.   J/S

277.   Barbati, Vittorio.   IL RIARMO TEDESCO TRA LE DUE GUERRE [German rearmament between the two wars]. *Riv. Militare [Italy] 1977 100(1): 73-84.* Examines German rearmament during the Weimar period under Hans von Seeckt (1866-1936) and during the Nazi regime.

278.   Barclay, C. N.   A TRIP TO EAST PRUSSIA IN 1931.   *Army Q. and Defence J. [Great Britain] 1975 105(4): 472-478.* Describes the author's trip to East Prussia in 1931 as part of a group of army officers from Great Britain's Army Staff College.

279.   Barclay, David E.   A PRUSSIAN SOCIALISM? WICHARD VON MOELLENDORFF AND THE DILEMMAS OF ECONOMIC PLANNING IN GERMANY, 1918-19.   *Central European Hist. 1978 11(1): 50-82.* Discusses the proposal prepared and presented to the German Cabinet by Wichard von Moellendorf, under state secretary and of the Reich Economics Office, in July 1919. The proposal called for economic collectivism in Germany and outlined a system for achieving that state. It was rejected almost unanimously by the Bauer Cabinet, resulting in Moellendorf's resignation and in the loss of any chance Germany might have had in dealing comprehensively with its postwar economic problems. Based on unpublished and published primary sources; 89 notes.

C. R. Lovin

280.   Bariéty, J.   AUX ORIGINES DE LA MANOEUVRE AUTOMOBILE ET DE LA CIRCULATION ROUTIÈRE: LE TRAIN À L'ARMÉE DU RHIN 1919-1929   [On the origins of automobile troop movement and military transportation: Army Service Corps in the Army of the Rhine, 1919-29]. *Rev.*

Hist. des Armées [France] 1978 5(3): 105-134. Recollects the engagement of the French Army Service Corps during the occupation of the Rhineland, 1919-29. Service to the occupation army was provided by a newly created 121st Transportation Squadron. The author presents a detailed history of this unit, its leadership and equipment. Based on official records; 10 illus., map, 46 notes.

G. E. Pergl

281.   Bariéty, J.   LES RÉPARATIONS ALLEMANDES 1919-1924: OBJET OU PRÉTEXTE À UNE POLITIQUE RHÉNANE DE LA FRANCE [German reparations, 1919-24: object or pretext of French Rhine policy]. *Bull. de la Soc. d'Hist. Moderne [France] 1973 72(6): 21-33.* Studies the Rhine as a permanent preoccupation in Franco-German relations between 1919 and 1924 and affecting European international politics, especially in the writing of the armistice agreement of 1918 and the Locarno treaties of 1925. The three centers of concern were the Allied negotiations in Paris for preparation of the peace treaty, events taking place on the Rhine, and administrative problems and economic crisis in the Rhine area. Ferdinand Foch and Georges Clemenceau worked for complete control of the Rhine but their plans were imprecise. Based on German and French documents in German archives; 3 notes.   S. Sevilla

282.   Bariety, Jacques.   INDUSTRIELS ALLEMANDS ET INDUSTRIELS FRANÇAIS À L'ÉPOQUE DE LA RÉPUBLIQUE DE WEIMAR   [German and French industrialists at the time of the Weimar Republic]. *R. d'Allemagne [France] 1974 6(2): 1-16.* It was not the businessmen or metallurgical industrialists who were responsible for Franco-German rapprochement in the 1920's, but the politicians and Westward-looking German economists who achieved a capitalist solidarity, underwritten by English and American banks. Based on documents, primary and secondary sources; 14 notes.   R. K. Adams

283.   Bariety, Jacques.   LA PLACE DE LA FRANCE DANS LA "WESTORIENTIERUNG" DE LA RÉPUBLIQUE DE WEIMAR AU COURS DE SA PHASE DE STABILISATION (1924-1929)   [France's role in the "Westorientierung" of the Weimar Republic during its stabilization phase, 1924-29]. *Rev. d'Allemagne [France] 1976 8(1): 35-50.* Deemphasizes Franco-German relations during the 1924-29 period, and views the dominant strain in Germany's foreign policy as Gustav Stresemann's "Westorientierung"—a dialectical policy of the execution and revision of the Treaty of Versailles—which involved broad negotiation with the West, and pressure on France to accept certain revisions.

284.   Bariéty, Jacques.   LE RÔLE D'ÉMILE MAYRISCH ENTRE LES SIDÉRURGIES ALLEMANDE ET FRANÇAISE APRÈS LA PREMIÈRE GUERRE MONDIALE   [The role of Émile Mayrisch between the German and French steel industries after World War I]. *Relations Int. [France] 1974 (1): 123-134.* Although France received much of Germany's steel industry with the acquisition of Alsace-Lorraine after World War I, Germany still had vast reserves of coal. Émile Mayrisch, a Luxemburger steel producer, played a key role in the 1920's in bringing the French steelmakers and German coal and coke producers together. Mayrisch's contribution came at a time when businessmen played a leading, if not dominant, role in European politics and diplomacy. 12 notes.

J. C. Billigmeier

285. Bariéty, Jacques. STRESEMANN ET LA FRANCE [Stressmann and France]. *Francia [France] 1975 3: 554-583.* Reviews M. O. Maxelon's *Stresemann und Frankreich,* (Düsseldorf: Droste Verlag, 1972). Gustav Stresemann (1878-1929) was always a German nationalist; if his aims in the 1920's were more modest than his hopes during World War I, it was because Germany had lost the war. Always a realist, he based his policy on his current position. His revisionist policies ran counter to his policies of entente with France and peace in Europe, and contributed to maintaining among the German people dangerous hopes and illusions. 60 notes. 						J. C. Billigmeier

286. Beitel, Werner and Nötzold, Jürgen. DEUTSCH-SOWJETISCHE BEZIEHUNGEN IN DER ZEIT VON 1918 BIS 1932 [German-Soviet relations, 1918-32]. *Österreichische Osthefte [Austria] 1975 17(4): 394-397.* The second German-Soviet colloquium of historians in Leningrad in April 1975 discussed the treaties of Rapallo and Berlin, the economic relations between the Soviet Union and Germany, the Soviet policy of peaceful coexistence, 1918-32, and the theory of social fascism. 					R. Wagnleitner

287. Beitel, Werner and Nötzold, Jürgen. DIE DEUTSCH-SOWJETISCHEN BEZIEHUNGEN 1918-1932; ERGEBNISSE EINES HISTORIKER-KOLLOQUIUMS IN LENINGRAD [German-Soviet relations, 1918-32; results of a historians' colloquium in Leningrad, April 1975]. *Osteuropa [West Germany] 1975 25(8-9): 782-785.* The second meeting of West German and Soviet historians dealt with the origins of peaceful coexistence in the 1920's, the Rapallo Treaty (1922) and German-Soviet trade up to the Great Depression. Only on economic topics did the participants reach wide agreement. Further meetings have been planned. 					R. E. Weltsch

288. Beitzel, W. and Nötzold, J. LES RELATIONS ÉCONOMIQUES ENTRE L'ALLEMAGNE ET L'U.R.S.S. AU COURS DE LA PÉRIODE 1918-1932, CONSIDÉRÉES SOUS L'ANGLE DES TRANSFERTS DE TECHNOLOGIE [Economic relations between Germany and the USSR, 1918-32, with respect to the transfer of technology]. *Rev. d'Études Comparatives Est-Ouest [France] 1977 8(2): 97-134.* Studies the USSR's dependence on Germany as the principal supplier of modern technology through the exportation of important equipment goods, before the preference shifted from Germany to the US after 1934, including important commcercial agreements, 1922-25, and credit extended during the first Five-Year Plan.

289. Berg, Volker vom. DIE ARBEITSZEITFRAGE IM RUHRBERGBAU ALS POLITISCHES PROBLEM DER FRÜHEN WEIMARER REPUBLIK [The working-time question in the Ruhr mining industry as a political problem of the early Weimar Republic]. *Geschichte in Wissenschaft und Unterricht [West Germany] 1975 26(6): 360-380.* During the first years of the Weimar Republic the workers in the Ruhr mining industry fought for shorter working hours, whereas industry wanted an increase. The government, pressured by reparations payments and the necessity of economic recovery, supported industry's demand. The May strike of 1924 was the last attempt to build trade union power, and it ended in government-enforced industrial arbitration. Thereafter no industrial agreement was achieved without governmental involvement to the considerable disadvantage of the trade unions. Primary and secondary sources; 103 notes. 					H. W. Wurster

290. Berndt, Roswitha.   RECHTSSOZIALDEMOKRATISCHE KOALI-
TIONSPOLITIK IN DER WEIMARER REPUBLIK   [Right-wing Social
Democratic coalition politics in the Weimar republic].   *Martin-Luther-Universität Halle-Wittenberg. Wissenschaftliche Zeitschrift. Gesellschafts- und Sprachwissenschaftliche Reihe [East Germany] 1977 26(1): 43-52.* Attempts at
cooperation between the German Social Democratic Party and the bourgeois
parties after 1918 were based on the historical compromises of German social
democracy before World War I. These attempts at cooperation by German social
democrat leaders during the era of the Weimar Republic were doomed to fail and
opened the way for national socialism. Based on printed documents and secondary literature; 54 notes.   R. Wagnleitner

291. Bernot, Roswitha.   FÜR UND WIDER PREUSSEN IN DER WEI-
MARER REPUBLIK   [For and against Prussia in the Weimar Republic].
*Martin-Luther-U. Halle-Wittenberg. Wissenschaftlich Zeitschrift. Gesellschafts-
und Sprachwissenschaftliche Reihe [East Germany] 1976 25(1): 13-29.* During
the Revolution of 1918-19 reaction in Germany promoted federalism and particularism in order to isolate working-class dominated Berlin. Subsequently, with the
reinstatement of the prerevolutionary bureaucracy and judiciary and the recovery
of the influence of the ruling class, reactionaries promoted the creation of a
unitary state. By this means it was intended to bring about the dissolution of
Prussia, then under right SPD control, to remove the political gains achieved by
the working class under the Weimar constitution, and to prepare for a war to
reverse the provisions of the Treaty of Versailles. This process helped prepare the
ground for the erection of a fascist dictatorship from 1933. Based on documents
located at the German Central Archives, Merseburg, and secondary sources; 104
notes.   J. A. Perkins

292. Binoux, Paul.   LE MOUVEMENT SÉPARATISTE RHÉNAN (1919-
1923)   [The Rhineland separatist movement, 1919-23]. *Écrits de Paris [France]
1973(327): 2330.* Recounts the struggle of the Rhinelanders to establish an autonomous state within Germany, over US and British objections after World War
I.

293. Birk, Gerhard.   DIE MILITARISTISCHE WEHRORGANISATION
STAHLHELM IN DER MAGDEBURGER BÖRDE   [The militarist defense
organization Stahlhelm in the Magdeburg plain]. *Militärgeschichte [East Ger-
many] 1982 21(4): 443-446.* Traces the origin, function, and activities of the
paramilitary Stahlhelm in the Magdeburg area. This reactionary defense organization was the bearer of the elementary traits of Prussian-German militarism
and a forerunner of fascism.   27 notes.   J/T (H. D. Andrews)

294. Blaich, Fritz.   DIE "FEHLRATIONALISIERUNG" IN DER
DEUTSCHEN AUTOMOBILINDUSTRIE 1924 BIS 1929   ["Misrationaliza-
tion" in the German automobile industry from 1924 to 1929]. *Tradition [West
Germany] 1973 18: 18-33.* German firms manufacturing automobiles in the
1920's produced a large number of work-process models. There was much talk,
and some action in the direction of rationalizing the industry so that it would
produce a greater number of fewer types, thus cutting costs. This was a mistake,
particularly for the luxury car market, where people bought cars as symbols of
social prestige and appreciated fancy, unusual models. The problems of the

industry were due to other factors, such as high costs and lack of highways. 3 tables, 77 notes.   J. C. Billigmeier

295. Blaich, Fritz. "GARANTIERTER KAPITALISMUS": SUBVEN-TIONSPOLITIK UND WIRTSCHAFTSORDNUNG IN DEUTSCHLAND ZWISCHEN 1925 UND 1932 ["Guaranteed capitalism": subvention policy and economic order in Germany, 1925-32]. *Zeitschrift für Unternehmensgeschichte [West Germany] 1977 22(1): 50-70.* During the short period of stability between Germany's financial crisis in the early 1920's and the rise of National Socialism in the 1930's, many medium-sized German firms encouraged state intervention in private industry. A system of guaranteed capitalism emerged in which state financing considerably reduced the risk to private investors. The author discusses particular examples of public subsidies of the shipping, locomotive, trucking, and automotive industries. On balance, unemployment problems were little affected by these efforts. Many businessmen fought against what they saw as socialistic tendencies because they believed they would stifle private initiative. 110 notes.   M. A. Butler

296. Bloch, Charles. DER KAMPF JOSEPH BLOCHS UND DER *SOZIALISTISCHEN MONATSHEFTE* IN DER WEIMARER REPUBLIK [The struggle of Joseph Bloch and the *Sozialistischen Monatshefte* in the Weimar Republic]. *Jahrbuch des Instituts für Deutsche Geschichte [Israel] 1974 (3): 257-287.* Examines the career and political-intellectual development of Joseph Bloch (b. 1871), an assimilated Jew and founder (1897) of the socialist-revisionist journal, the *Sozialistischen Monatshefte*. Bloch was a moderate, an internationalist, and a Francophile, and he tried unsuccessfully to influence Weimar politics in these directions. Based on published primary sources; 56 notes.
                                                                                        J. G. Morrison

297. Boelcke, Willi A. WANDLUNGEN DER DEUTSCHEN AGRARWIRTSCHAFT IN DER FOLGE DES ERSTEN WELTKRIEGS [Changes in the German agricultural economy in the aftermath of World War I]. *Francia [France] 1975 3: 498-532.* World War I was disastrous for German agriculture. Acreage planted dropped by half, the number of cattle by two-thirds. Nearly a million Germans died of starvation. In the brief postwar recovery, the population engaged in agriculture, which had been decreasing since the mid-19th century, actually rose. New technology was introduced. Yet recovery was slow and the increased number of small farms, encouraged by the government for political reasons, hardly made for efficiency. Agricultural prices, high during the war, began to drop, and with the depression, many farmers fell into debt. The cooperative movement grew, but was not strong enough to solve problems such as marketing that it sought to. Price fluctuations caused increased tension between city and country. Despite all crises, however, the family farm remained a model of stability. 99 notes.   J. C. Billigmeier

298. Bonjour, Edgar. NEUTRALE HALTUNG DER SCHWEIZ IN DER DEUTSCHEN REPARATIONSKRISE 1921 [Neutral posture of Switzerland during the German reparations crisis of 1921]. *Schweizerische Zeitschrift für Geschichte [Switzerland] 1976 26(1-2): 184-194.* The Swiss minister in Berlin Alfred von Planta, advocated that Switzerland mediate between the French, with their intransigent demands, and the willing but desperate Germans. Planta in-

formed the Federal Council of his discussions of the German reparations problems with Allied ambassadors in Berlin and members of the German government and parliament. There are no traces of a response by the Swiss Federal Council to this proposal. The author surmises that Federal Councillor Giuseppe Motta gave a negative reply since he wanted to protect Swiss neutrality. Based on diplomatic dispatches; 9 notes.   H. K. Meier

299. Borelli, Giorgio. RATHENAU E LA CRISI DEL PRIMO DOPO-GUERRA [Rathenau and the crisis of the post-World War I period]. *Econ. e Storia [Italy]* 1977 24(2): 213-216. Discusses the life and works of Walther Rathenau, electrotechnician and industrialist, who organized the *Allgemeine Elektrizitäts-Gesellschaft* and the war industries in Germany during World War I. Evaluates his role in the postwar reconstruction. Based mainly on Rathenau's writings.   P. J. Taylorson

300. Brunon, Paul. LE REDRESSEMENT ALLEMAND AU JAPON APRÈS LA GRANDE GUERRE (1919-1922): POINTS DE VUE DIPLO-MATIQUES FRANÇAIS [German renewal of relations with Japan after the Great War (1919-22): viewpoints of French diplomacy]. *Rev. Hist. [France]* 1976 256(520): 419-442. Describes German activities in Japan, 1919-22. Since 1870 a significant element of Japanese public opinion had been pro-German. During World War I, Japanese public opinion was not anti-German, even though Japan was at war with Germany. After the war the Germans were very successful in regaining Japanese goodwill. By asserting that Germany had not really lost the war, the Germans won Japanese respect for their power and acceptance of a critical view of the Versailles Treaty. German Ambassador Wilhelm Solf was successful in a minor propaganda campaign, but secret agent Captain von Knorr took more spectacular actions. German industries benefited, and academic exchange programs proved very effective in gaining Japanese support for Germany's return to the community of nations, including membership in the League of Nations. Based on the French foreign affairs archives; appendix.
                                     G. H. Davis

301. Burens, Peter-Claus. KONTINUITÄT UND WANDEL DER DEUTSCHEN OSTPOLITIK SEIT 1919. EIN UNTERRICHTSENTWURF FÜR DIE SEKUNDARSTUFE II: TEIL I [Continuity and change in German eastern policy since 1919: an educational draft for the "Sekundarstufe" II]. *Zeitgeschichte [Austria]* 1978 6(1): 25-31. Presents a lesson unit for secondary schools. German Eastern Policy during the period of the Weimar Republic is an excellent topic for the study of political movements, group dynamics and the role of leading politicians. Since Eastern Policy is a topic of current interest, students can develop a better understanding of the current debate by studying its historical background. 23 notes. Article to be continued.   G. H. Libbey

302. Burk, Kathleen. ECONOMIC DIPLOMACY BETWEEN THE WARS. *Hist. J. [Great Britain]* 1981 24(4): 1003-1015. A review article of Walter A. McDougall's *France's Rhineland Diplomacy, 1914-1924: the Last Bid for a Balance of Power in Europe* (1978), Marc Trachtenberg's *Reparation in World Politics: France and European Economic Diplomacy, 1916-1923* (1980), Melvyn P. Heffler's *The Elusive Quest: America's Pursuit of European Stability and French Security, 1919-1933* (1979), and David E. Kaiser's *Economic Diplo-*

macy and the Origins of the Second World War: Germany, Britain, France, and Eastern Europe, 1930-1939 (1981), which concentrate on the problem of reparations and economic diplomacy in Europe after World War I. 13 notes.   S

303. Buse, D. K. ECONOMIC INTERESTS AND LOBBYING IN THE EARLY WEIMAR REPUBLIC: HOLTZENDORFF'S POLITICAL SALON. *Social Hist. [Canada] 1981 14(28): 455-484.* During and after World War I, Hapag, one of Germany's largest shipping firms, used the salon or discussion group for lobbying. The elusive Arndt von Holtzendorff (1859-1935) ran the salon. The lobbying was important because German shippers had suffered serious losses in the war and needed government aid to restructure. Holtzendorff was effective because he became a respected social coordinator within the Weimar Republic. His salon, contacts, and advice-giving illustrate the mechanism by which large-scale economic interests can adjust, alter, and subtly affect policy through government officials. Based largely on papers in the Hapag Archiv, Hamburg; 102 notes.   D. F. Chard

304. Caspar, G. A. REICHSWEHR UND WEHRMACHT IN DER DEUTSCHEN GESELLSCHAFT ZWISCHEN DEN BEIDEN WELTKRIE-GEN [The German military establishment in German society between the two world wars]. *Rev. d'Allemagne [France] 1979 11(3): 363-382.* An investigation of the changes in the relationship between the armed services and society during the Weimar Republic and the Nazi regime shows that the army of the Weimar Republic had a self-image of professionalism which greatly resembled that of the pre-1914 army, that in general there was little popular sympathy for the army, and that the social status of the military after 1919 was similar to what it was before 1914. During the Nazi period, however, the armed forces became highly politicized, they were greatly appreciated and esteemed by the public, and the social status of the members of the rapidly expanding armed forces rose considerably.   J. S. Gassner

305. Castellan, Georges. LE RÉARMEMENT CLANDESTIN DE L'AL-LEMAGNE DANS L'ENTRE-DEUX GUERRES [Clandestine rearmament in Germany between the wars]. *Rev. d'Allemagne [France] 1976 8(1): 61-82.* Views the stages of German military rearmament as seen by the Deuxième Bureau during 1930-35, asserting that the French knew of German preparations for World War II and studying France's reaction.

306. Chabert, A. DE LA "GUERRE DE LA RUHR" ET DE SES CONSÉ-QUENCES [On the *War of the Ruhr* and its consequences]. *Rev. d'Allemagne [France] 1975 7(2): 155-166.* Reviews *Guerre de la Ruhr* by Pierre Jolly (Paris, 1974), detailing the occupation of the Ruhr by the French (1923) and the German resistance to the occupation. French politicians did not consider the effects of the humiliation it was imposing on the German people, nor of the power of the United States, which was to force French withdrawal and impose the Dawes Plan. Biblio.
                                                                   J. C. Billigmeier

307. Chamberlin, Brewster S. DER ATTENTATSPLAN GEGEN SEECKT 1924 [The assassination plot against Seeckt, 1924]. *Vierteljahrshefte für Zeitgeschichte [West Germany] 1977 25(4): 425-440.* An analysis of the conception and political exploitation of the January 1924 assassination attempt against Colonel

General Hans von Seeckt (1866-1936), Chief of Army Command, 1920-26, in the post-World War I German Republic. The affair revealed the scheming and bitter conflicts among rightist groups, primarily Heinrich Class's Pan-Germans and Volkish groups close to Hitler, and the disastrous intriguing of the rightist-dominated RKO (Reich Commissioner for Public Order). Based on records in East German (Potsdam) and West German (Bavarian State Archive, Research Center of National Socialism, Hamburg) archives, the contemporary press, and secondary works; 69 notes.   D. Prowe

308. Chappius, Charles William.   GERMANY AND THE ANGLO-FRENCH ACCORD OF CONFIDENCE, JULY 1932.   *German Studies Rev. 1979 2(2): 211-224.* The Anglo-French Accord of Confidence of July 1932 was interpreted as a new entente cordiale directed at Germany. Originally, however, the accord was part of a larger British proposal which included a German suggestion for a consultative pact. Following French rejection of the British proposal, an Anglo-French accord was signed; but the British interpreted the accord in the sense of a consultative pact and invited Germany and Italy to adhere. Based on published and unpublished documents and secondary works; 58 notes.   A

309. Childer, Thomas.   THE SOCIAL BASES OF THE NATIONAL SO-CIALIST VOTE.   *J. of Contemporary Hist. [Great Britain] 1976 11(4): 17-42.* Virtually all analysts have concluded that "German fascism was a middle-class movement supported at the polls primarily by Protestant self-employed proprietors in agriculture, commerce, and handicrafts, as well as by white collar workers in the public and private sectors." A statistical study of the Nazi vote, 1924-33 shows, however, that the National Socialist constituency gradually changed until by 1932 it had become a "catch-all party of protest whose constituents, while concentrated primarily in a socially diverse middle class, were united above all by a vehement rejection of an increasingly threatening present." Primary and secondary sources; 55 notes, appendix with 10 tables of results of Reichstag elections of Weimar Republic, 1920-32.   M. P. Trauth

310. Cienciala, Anna M.   AN ASPECT OF THE GERMAN PROBLEM IN THE INTERWAR PERIOD: THE SECRET ANGLO-FRENCH AGREEMENT ON DANZIG AND THE SAAR, AND ITS CONSEQUENCES, 1919-1926.   *Zeitschrift für Ostforschung [West Germany] 1978 27(3): 434-455.* Discusses secret Franco-English agreements (1919) connected with the Free City of Danzig stating that this area was never really free. The English viewed the idea of a free city as a temporary compromise: Danzig could be used to Great Britain's favor in future British policy toward Germany. Poland never had a chance to establish a genuine influence in Danzig's affairs and Warsaw resented the free city idea from the start as did Berlin. Primary sources; 76 notes.   G. E. Pergl/S

311. Collotti, Enzo.   ITALLIA E WEIMAR: ASPETTI DI UNA POLEMICA E LIMITI DI CERTE ANALOGIE   [Italy and the Weimar Republic: some aspects of a polemical argument and the limitations of certain analogies]. *Italia Contemporanea [Italy] 1978 30(131): 5-18.* Discusses the political and social crisis in Italy during the 1970's in the context of the attitude of the popular press which likened the situation to that of Germany in the 1920's-30's. Both nations faced problems of political and social reform by groups with very

different aims, and the experiences of the Weimar government are instructive for any nation seeking to implement institutional and structural changes in government and the internal balance of power. Based on newspapers, journals, and secondary sources; 16 notes. C. E. King

312. Conte, Francis. LLOYD GEORGE ET LE TRAITÉ DE RAPALLO [Lloyd George and the Treaty of Rapallo]. *Rev. d'Hist. Moderne et Contemporaine [France] 1976 23(1): 44-67.* Describes the inadvertent role played by David Lloyd George in creating the Russo-German Treaty of Rapallo (1922). Lloyd George wanted improved relations with both Germany and the Soviet Union. His object was to open them up as markets for British goods, thus reducing Great Britain's domestic unemployment. His maneuvering with Germany and the USSR for an Anglo-German and/or an Anglo-Russian accord resulted in the Russo-German pact. The signing of the treaty marked the complete failure of Lloyd George's foreign policy, a policy which had aroused Winston Churchill's opposition. Primary sources; 94 notes. K. A. Harvey

313. Cornebise, Alfred E. THE REFINEMENT OF ALLIED PRESS PROPAGANDA: THE CASE OF THE *NACHRICHTENDIENST.* German Studies Rev. 1979 2(1): 30-48. The subject of Allied propaganda during World War I has often been discussed. Less well known is that the French had an opportunity to refine their expertise and to add dimensions to their efforts during the period of the Franco-Belgian Ruhr occupation, 1923-25. In these years, they published and circulated a German-language newspaper, the *Nachrichtendienst.* This was a shrewdly edited paper containing cultural and intellectual articles as well as more flagrant propaganda copy. The publication later influenced Nazi propagandists, as had the earlier Allied successes. Indeed, one Nazi argued that the reason Germany "lost" the *Ruhrkampf* was that the German press, in particular, failed to successfully counter the French propaganda offensive. A

314. Corni, Gustavo. L'AGRICOLTURA NELLA REPUBBLICA DI WEIMAR [Agriculture under the Weimar Republic]. *Studi Storici [Italy] 1979 20(3): 525-545.* Reviews historical work on agriculture in Weimar Germany. The continuing political and ideological influence of the large Junker landowners of the east foiled attempts at fundamental reform. The mass of farmers subscribed to an extreme right, anti-industry ideology and were organized in pressure groups to promote it, while the division into great estates in the east and smallholdings in the west, combined with permanent indebtedness, left no room for a medium-sized capitalist agriculture to develop. The primary sector failed to adapt to an organized capitalist economy and merely defended its own autonomy through ideology and economic protectionism. 45 notes. D. J. Nicholls

315. Corni, Gustavo. LE RELAZIONI INTERNAZIONALI IN EUROPA E LA POLITICA ESTERNA NAZISTA [International relations in Europe and Nazi foreign policy]. *Studi Storici [Italy] 1980 21(1): 211-218.* Examines two study weeks held in West Germany in December 1979, one at Mainz, the other at Cologne. Both were concerned with foreign relations in Europe in the period between the world wars, particularly with the relationship between the Great Powers and the marginal countries. Primary sources. E. E. Ryan

316. Costigliola, Frank. THE UNITED STATES AND THE RECON-
STRUCTION OF GERMANY IN THE 1920'S. *Business Hist. Rev. 1976
50(4): 477-502.* US foreign policy in the 1920's was aimed at reconstructing a
prosperous and stable Europe, and that policy in turn depended upon a German
revival. Especially active in the effort were private American businessmen, semi-
public agencies such as the Federal Reserve Bank of New York, and the first
postwar US ambassador to Germany, Alanson B. Houghton. While American
policy seemed successful at first, Germany's economic health ultimately depended on a continuous flow of capital from the United States, a flow cut off with
the coming of the Depression. Based principally on manuscript materials; 105
notes.   C. J. Pusateri

317. Crozier, Andrew J. THE COLONIAL QUESTION IN STRESE-
MANN'S LOCARNO POLICY. *Int. Hist. Rev. [Canada] 1982 4(1): 37-54.*
Discusses the British reaction to German claims for colonial restitution before,
during, and after the Locarno Conference of 1925. The colonial movement in
Germany was dominated by the conservatives and Prime Minister Gustav Stresemann. British support was not lacking for Germany's colonial aspirations. Some
of the British felt that if the Germans did not have adequate access to colonial
raw materials, they would eventually try to take them by force. The official stance
of the British government was to usurp Germany's desire for colonies. The
colonial question did arise during Locarno, and Stresemann inferred that Germany's right to possess colonies had been recognized. Chamberlain was quick to
counter that the issue had arisen with reference to the League of Nations, under
which Germany, like any other member, would be a *possible* candidate for
mandates. Primary sources; 74 notes.   J. Powell

318. Cziomer, Erhard. DIE POLITISCHEN PARTEIEN DER WEI-
MARER REPUBLIK UND DER KAMPF UM DIE NORMALISIERUNG
DER DEUTSCH-SOWJETISCHEN BEZIEHUNGEN WÄHREND DER
POLNISCH-SOWJETISCHEN KRIEGES 1920 [Political parties of the Weimar Republic and the struggle for a normalization of German-Soviet relations
during the Polish-Soviet war of 1920]. *Jahrbuch für Geschichte der Sozialistischen Länder Europas [East Germany] 1979 23(1): 127-151.* Recollects an important part of Weimar Republic foreign policy, discussing the position of different
German parties on the normalization of relations with the USSR. After the
Reichstag session of January 1921 the government was exposed to constant
political pressure from the parliament. The trade agreement of May 1921 was a
first step toward normalization. Based on records of the Reichstag sessions; 136
notes.   G. E. Pergl

319. Danzl, Erna. DOKUMENTATION: ERINNERUNGEN HANS
SCHÄFFERS AN ERNST TRENDELENBURG [Documentation: Hans
Schäffer's reminiscences of Ernst Trendelenburg]. *Vierteljahrshefte für Zeitgeschichte [West Germany] 1977 25(4): 865-888.* The reminiscences of post-World
War I statesman Hans Schäffer regarding his colleague and friend Ernst Trendelenburg. Trendelenburg remained in key government positions under Hitler
until 1945. The document is significant in relating post-World War I concepts of
a socially planned economy *(Gemeinwirtschaft)* and economic stabilization, and
in relating Schäffer's sensitivity to Trendelenburg's inability to abandon his life-
long vocation as public servant even under Hitler. Based on the Schäffer Papers
at the Institute for Contemporary History (Munich); 78 notes.   D. Prowe

320.   Davidovich, D. S.   ORUDIE GERMANSKOGO IMPERIALIZMA I MILITARIZMA: K ISTORII VOZNIKNOVENIIA GERMANSKOGO FA-SHIZMA (1919-23)   [The tool of German imperialism and militarism: the history of German fascism, 1919-23]. *Novaia i Noveishaia Istoriia [USSR] 1976 (3): 105-124.* Historians have not yet provided sound economic and sociopolitical reasons for the rise of fascism in Germany in 1919. The author attempts to provide these explanations by analyzing aspects of the postwar situation in Germany: the class struggle; the struggle of the political parties during the initial period of the Weimar Republic; and the social structure, politics, and class ideology of the Nazi Party. 68 notes.   R. Permar

321.   Davies, Norman.   AUGUST 1920.   *European Studies Rev. [Great Britain] 1973 3(3): 269-281.* Examines the four-week Soviet invasion of Poland in 1920 and the inaction of Britain, France, and the Eastern European successor states in the face of this attempt to provoke a European revolution. It was the first major challenge to the Versailles peace settlement and paved the way for Russo-German military cooperation and the Rapallo Treaty of 1922. More importantly, it presaged comparable attitudes, arrangements, and inaction when these same states were challenged by Nazi Germany in the late 1930's. 22 notes.
                                                                           C. T. Prukop

322.   Dem'ianenko, A. P.   IZ ISTORII POLITIKI GERMANII NA BLIZH-NEM VOSTOKE NAKANUNE VTOROI MIROVOI VOINY   [German policy in the Middle East on the eve of World War II]. *Narody Azii i Afriki [USSR] 1973 (1): 138-144.* Describes the reemergence of German influence in the Middle East, 1918-39, by economic penetration, and judicious encouragement of opposition movements in Palestine and elsewhere.

323.   Diamond, Sander A.   EIN AMERIKANER IN BERLIN: AUS DEN PAPIEREN DES BOTSCHAFTERS ALANSON B. HOUGHTON 1922-1925 [An American in Berlin: from the papers of Ambassador Alanson B. Houghton, 1922-25]. *Vierteljahrshefte für Zeitgeschichte [West Germany] 1979 27(3): 431-470.* A summary of some of the high points of the detailed diary and correspondence of Corning Glass millionaire Alanson B. Houghton (1863-1941), first post-World War I American ambassador in Germany. The diary's tone is pro-German, anti-Communist, and anti-French. The papers reveal Houghton's impressions of the reparations question, the Ruhr Invasion, the Kapp Putsch, and early Nazi activities, and provide glimpses of German politicians and industrialists. Based on the private Houghton papers (Corning, N.Y.) and secondary works; 111 notes.   D. Prowe

324.   Dichtl, Klaus and Ruge, Wolfgang.   ZU DEN AUSEINANDERSET-ZUNGEN INNERHALB DER REICHSREGIERUNG ÜBER DEN LOCARNOPAKT 1925   [On controversies within the Reich government over the treaty of Locarno of 1925]. *Zeitschrift für Geschichtswissenschaft [East Germany] 1974 22(1): 64-88.* Contains excerpts from German cabinet discussions from 24 June to 23 September 1925, preceded by a short introduction. All the cabinet ministers agreed on strategic matters, e.g., that war was permissible to recover lost German territory and that Germany should have a free hand against Poland and the USSR. However, there were tactical disagreements between the foreign minister Gustav Stresemann and the majority of the cabinet, which did

not share Stresemann's realistic appraisal of German weakness within the imperialist camp. Therefore, they opposed the Locarno treaties. Based on four documents from the Central Archives at Potsdam.   J. T. Walker

325. Diskin, Abraham and Wolffsohn, Michael.   KOALITIONSVERHALTEN IN DER WEIMARER REPUBLIK   [Coalition government in the Weimar Republic]. *Politische Vierteljahresschrift [West Germany] 1980 21(2): 174-185.* A discussion of the parties of the Weimar government, the ideologies that separated them, and their coalitions. Provides a model with rules for survival of the party system which advocates that in times of crisis, moderates should exercise their critical powers outside government, as happened with the Social Democratic Party under Brüning's chancellorship, and not become governing partners with those on the extremes, as occurred under von Papen. The comparatively moderate German National People's Party (DNVP), in throwing in its lot with the Nazis, failed to heed warnings about the Nazi's true nature. Postulates a structural rather than an ideological cause for the failure of the first German democracy.   4 tables, 8 notes, biblio.   S. Bonnycastle

326. Długajczyk, Edward.   UKŁADY O WZAJEMNEJ WYMAINIE AKT MIĘDZY POLSKĄ A NIEMCAMI W ZWIĄZKU Z PODZIAŁEM GÓRNEGO ŚLĄSKA W ROKU 1922   [The Polish-German agreements on exchange of records, 1922]. *Archeion [Poland] 1976 64: 87-103.* Under the Treaty of Versailles, Germany relinquished the eastern part of Upper Silesia to Poland, and should have ceded all records and archives connected with the territory. Germany stalled the negotiations so that it was not until 18 June 1922 that a final agreement was concluded. The author describes the course of the negotiations and quotes the full text of the agreement concluded.   J/S

327. Dow, James Elstone.   THE GERMAN NATIONAL PEOPLE'S PARTY: IN THE CAUSE OF MONARCHY.   *Continuity 1981 (3): 37-50.* The German National People's Party outlined three main goals which it retained throughout its history, 1918-33: 1) raise the integrity of the German state by revising the Versailles Treaty; 2) bring back strong government to Germany by eliminating the parliamentary executive; and 3) restore the monarchy. Strict adherence to the last goal led to the party's ultimate demise. Because party members could not forget the glory of a monarchist past, they were unable to read the German masses accurately during the Weimar years and, as a result, could not forge a viable modern yet constitutionally conservative party.
                                                              W. A. Wiegand

328.   Dreetz, Dieter.   DIE REICHSWEHR UND DIE PROVOKATION IM MITTELDEUTSCHEN INDUSTRIEREVIER IM MÄRZ 1921   [The Reichswehr and the armed provocation in the central industrial district of Germany in March 1921]. *Militärgeschichte [East Germany] 1981 20(2): 169-178.* Assesses documents of the Reichswehr command and some important decisions of the German president and chancellor in the years 1920 and 1921 on the role of the Reichswehr in German domestic affairs. Beginning in May 1920 the Reichswehr command pushed for armed intervention in the central industrial district of Germany and fulfilled more assignments during the March provocation of 1921 than has heretofore been known. On the basis of its assessment of the March events the military command developed the Reichwehr further as the most impor-

tant instrument in upholding imperialist power as well as in achieving the central government interests against the interests of the individual states. Based on documents in the Central State Archives, Potsdam; 52 notes.

J/T (H. D. Andrews)

329. Dreetz, Dieter and Sperling, Heinz. REICHSWEHRFÜHRUNG UND MILITÄRISCHER AUSNAHMEZUSTAND 1923/24 [Reichswehr command and the state of martial law, 1923-24]. *Militärgeschichte [East Germany] 1978 17(6): 711-731.* The memorandum of the defense minister concerning the state of martial law from 26 September 1923 to 29 February 1924 is a fundamental document which characterizes the place and role of the Reichswehr command in the maintenance of conditions of imperialist power. It documents the anti-Communist and antidemocratic thrust in the domestic use of the instrument of military force. The memorandum reflects the views of the Reichswehr command on the state of martial law as well as on the important political questions in the period of transition from the revolutionary postwar crisis to the relative stabilization of capitalism. Illus., 35 notes. H. D. Andrews

330. Dreetz, Dieter and Sperling, Heinz. ZUR MITWIRKUNG DER REICHSWEHR BEI DER ÖKONOMISCHEN FESTIGUNG DER IMPERIALISTISCHEN HERRSCHAFT IN DEUTSCHLAND 1923/24 [On the co-operation of the Reichswehr in the economic stabilization of imperialist rule in Germany, 1923-24]. *Militärgeschichte [East Germany] 1979 18(5): 607-615.* Part II of the *Memorandum* of Reichswehr Minister Otto Gessler of 11 September 1924 concerning martial law in Germany, 26 September 1923 to 29 February 1924. Part II, entitled "Economic Measures of the Holder of Executive Power," shows that the Reichswehr leadership supported the efforts of monopoly capital to maintain political control in the face of protests by the workers led by the Communist Party. H. D. Andrews

331. Droz, Jacques. LES TENDANCES "GROSS-DEUTSCH" EN ALLEMAGNE ET EN AUTRICHE A L'EPOQUE DE LA REPUBLIQUE DE WEIMAR [The "Grossdeutsch" debate in Germany and Austria during the Weimar period]. *Rev. d'Allemagne [France] 1981 13(4): 645-665.* The problem of Austria's relationship to the Germanic community is as old as the effort to unify Germany, but the peace settlement after World War I gave a fresh impetus to the debate over Anschluss. Various versions of it were heatedly endorsed in both Germany and Austria. When the victorious powers vetoed political union, the discussion turned first to a customs union, and when that failed, to other plans, such as cultural cooperation and the formation of a Danubian federation. Eventually certain advocates of union began to support the Nazi movement. Throughout the period, however, some Austrian opinion preferred national independence and opposed annexation. 30 notes. J. S. Gassner

332. Due-Nielsen, Carsten. BROCKDORFF-RANTZAU I TYSK HISTORIOGRAFI [Brockdorff-Rantzau in German historiography]. *Hist. Tidsskrift [Denmark] 1974 74(1): 271-312.* Count Ulrich von Brockdorff-Rantzau (1869-1928) played a significant role in Germany as ambassador to Denmark, foreign minister in 1918-19, and ambassador to the Soviet Union, 1922-28. His role and policies have been continuously debated, receiving more exposure with the availability of the captured German documents. His adherence to principles,

his realpolitik, and his policy of alternating alliances with either the West or the Soviet Union make him subject to controversy. In general his defenders note his adherence to principles and his opponents attack the policy of realism. German historiography about Rantzau is both extensive and diverse, especially on his attempt to control domestic affairs and his relations with the army. Historians after 1945 have fused the traditional and liberal historical schools, but the debate continues over Rantzau's role.   R. E. Lindgren

333. Dülffer, Jost. DETERMINANTEN DER DEUTSCHEN MARINE-ENTWICKLUNG IN DER ZWISCHENKRIEGSZEIT 1920-1939 [Dominant factors of the German Navy's development during the interwar period: 1920-39]. *Marine Rundschau [West Germany] 1975 72(1): 8-19.* Surveys the building of the German Navy, 1920-39, dividing the period into seven phases. Focuses on 1933-39, when naval policy came to be oriented toward future continental expansion. 17 notes.   G. E. Pergl

334. Dupeux, Louis. LA "REVOLUTION CONSERVATRICE" ET LA MONTÉE DE L'ANTICAPITALISME "ALLEMAND" SOUS LA RÉPUBLIQUE DE WEIMAR (1919-1933) [The "conservative revolution" and the rise of German anticapitalism in the Weimar Republic, 1919-33]. *R. d'Allemagne [France] 1974 6(2): 67-86.* Assesses the meaning of Armin Mohler's expression "conservative revolution." Studies how the movement supplanted the traditional Right, and a wave of anticapitalism swept the youth movements and the leftist elements of National Socialism. Primary and secondary sources; 7 notes.
R. K. Adams

335. Ekoko, A. Edho. THE BRITISH ATTITUDE TOWARDS GERMANY'S COLONIAL IRREDENTISM IN AFRICA IN THE INTER-WAR YEARS. *J. of Contemporary Hist. [Great Britain] 1979 14(2): 287-307.* Germany was very dissatisfied with the colonial settlement of the Paris Conference after World War I. Both the Weimar Republic and the early Hitler regime viewed the mandate system as provisional. The colonies could have been used as a sop to Hitler before 1936, but Great Britain always hesitated. After the German occupation of the Rhineland on 7 March 1936, it was too late to give Hitler a colonial pacifier. He then had other ambitions. Based on the Official Journal of the League of Nations and other primary sources; 49 notes.   M. P. Trauth

336. Elliott, Christopher J. THE KRIEGERVEREINE AND THE WEIMAR REPUBLIC. *J. of Contemporary Hist. [Great Britain] 1975 10(1): 109-129.* The Kriegervereine go back to the veterans of Frederick the Great. Their purpose was at once fraternal, social, and benevolent, but their usefulness went beyond welfare services to civil defense and military reserve. After World War I, the veterans' organizations became officially politically neutral; actually, they tended toward a right-wing nationalism and openly opposed all socialist organizations. Their enmity toward the SPD prevented rapprochement with the Weimar government. The 3.5 or more million members gradually moved into rival or splinter groups like officer clubs or *Waffenringe* of old soldiers of particular branches. The 1929-33 period, however, saw a closer connection of Kriegervereine and the Reichswehr in an attempt to keep the veterans out of the Nazi camp. The effort failed. In January 1934, what remained of the Kriegervereine were either dissolved or made to toe the Nazi line. Archival sources; 36 notes.
M. P. Trauth

337.   Enssle, Manfred J.   STRESEMANN'S DIPLOMACY FIFTY YEARS AFTER LOCARNO: SOME RECENT PERSPECTIVES.   *Hist. J. [Great Britain] 1977 20(4): 937-948.* Reexamines the legend of Gustav Stresemann. He contributed both to the international equilibrium of Locarno and to its demise. He was simultaneously cooperative and revisionist on Germany's frontier problem. His foreign policy fluctuated. Based on published primary and secondary sources, and unpublished papers delivered at scholarly meetings; 43 notes.

L. A. McGeoch

338.   Erdmann, Karl Dietrich.   BIOGRAPHISCHES ZU STRESEMANN: VOM NUTZEN UND NACHTEIL DER JUBILÄUMSLITERATUR   [Biographies of Stresemann: virtues and vices of anniversary works]. *Geschichte in Wissenschaft und Unterricht [West Germany] 1979 30(1): 29-32.* Finds fault with Theodor Eschenburg and Ulrich Frank-Planitz's *Gustav Stresemann. Eine Bildbiographie* (1978) and Felix Hirsch's *Stresemann. Ein Lebensbild (1978).* Secondary works; 3 notes.

H. W. Wurster

339.   Erdmann, Karl Dietrich.   DIE DEUTSCH-SOWJETISCHEN BEZIEHUNGEN IN DER ZEIT DER WEIMARER REPUBLIK ALS PROBLEM DER DEUTSCHEN INNENPOLITIK   [Soviet-German relations as a problem of German domestic politics in the Weimar Republic]. *Geschichte in Wissenschaft und Unterricht [West Germany] 1975 26(7): 403-426.* Analyzes the attitudes of German parties and relevant social forces toward the USSR during the Weimar Republic. Treaties with the West were strongly opposed, those with the USSR almost not at all. Except for an uneasy period in the mid-twenties, the Communists were in favor of improved Soviet-German relations. From the SPD to the DNVP, the parties stood for normalization, which represented an intermediate position between East and West. Public opinion was divided and focused around two journals, *Tat* and *Weltbühne.* Though trade unions were critical, they supported normalization while the churches were against the USSR. At the end of Weimar, public opinion was anti-Russian. Primary and secondary works; 57 notes.

H. W. Wurster

340.   Erdmann, Karl Dietrich.   GUSTAV STRESEMANN: SEIN BILD IN DER GESCHICHTE   [Gustav Stresemann: his image in history]. *Hist. Zeitschrift [West Germany] 1978 227(3): 599-616.* Some historical evaluations of Stresemann stress his cooperative "fulfillment" policy while others stress his German nationalism. When seen in the context of his own time of the 1920's, Stresemann emerges as a truly masterful statesman in Germany, but more for his style than for the content of his policies. Under the difficult conditions of his time, the maintenance of stable policy against the influence of rightist extremists and French pressure was a remarkable accomplishment.

G. H. Davis

341.   Erin, M. E.   POLITIKA PARTII TSENTRA V 1928-1933 GG. V OSVESHCHENII ZAPADNOGERMANSKOI ISTORIOGRAFII   [Politics of the Center Party in 1928-33 as presented in West German historiography]. *Voprosy Istorii [USSR] 1979 (11): 155-163.* Reviews over 30 titles published during 1950's-74 on the rise and fall of the Catholic Center Party under Heinrich Brüning (1885-1970), a major topic in West German research on the history of bourgeois parties of the Weimar Republic. Most studies, however, disregard socioeconomic factors and the influence of monopolistic capital. They fail to

consider the class character of the Center Party and its reactionary policy and political tactics which caused its downfall and led to Hitler's seizure of power in 1933. 54 notes.   N. Frenkley

342. Falkus, M. E.   THE GERMAN BUSINESS CYCLE IN THE 1920'S. *Econ. Hist. R. [Great Britain] 1975 28(3): 451-465.* Examines Peter Temin's "The Beginning of the Depression in Germany" and argues that there was a credit shortage in Germany and declines in German capital imports that were exogenously determined. The traditional view of the role of foreign capital in creating these recessions is supported. 5 figs.   B. L. Crapster

343. Fedor, Karol.   DIE DEUTSCHE PAZIFISTISCHE BEWEGUNG UND DAS PROBLEM DER DEUTSCH-POLNISCHEN BEZIEHUNGEN IN DER ZWISCHENKRIEGSZEIT   [The German pacifist movement and the problem of German-Polish relations in the interwar period]. *Jahrbuch für die Geschichte Mittel- und Ostdeutschlands [West Germany] 1975 24: 143-163.* A narrative of the history of German pacifism during the Weimar era with particular emphasis upon the attitudes and actions of the various pacifist organizations in the area of German-Polish relations. Emerging during World War I as expressions of opposition to that conflict, German pacifist organizations in the 1920's devoted considerable attention to combatting the general drift of public opinion toward extreme nationalism. Failure in this respect is ascribed to the multiplicity of competing organizations, which appealed essentially to the intelligentsia and liberal bourgeoisie and lacked influence with the working class and peasantry. Based on Polish archival sources and records of pacifist organizations; 65 notes.
                                                                        J. A. Perkins

344.   Feldenkirchen, Wilfried.   FERNOSTGESCHÄFTE DER FELTEN & GUILLEAUME CARLSWERK AG BIS ZUM BEGINN DES ZWEITEN WELTKRIEGES   [The Far East business of the Felten & Guilleaume Carlswerk AG up to the beginning of World War II]. *Zeitschrift für Unternehmensgeschichte [West Germany] 1977 22(3): 161-182.* Continued from a previous article. Along with other German manufacturers of cable and wire, the firm of Felten and Guilleaume Carlswerk attempted to recapture the Asian markets lost in World War I. Nonetheless, exports of the company to Asia did not exceed 1% of its total exports in the interwar years because of increasing Japanese competition, formidable tariffs and trade restrictions by Asian countries, competition by the larger European companies, and inadequate sales representation in foreign countries. Based on the company's archives; 10 tables, 93 notes.
                                                                        J. T. Walker

345.   Feldman, Gerald D.   ARBEITSKONFLIKTE IM RUHRBERGBAU 1919-1922. ZUR POLITIK VON ZECHENVERBAND UND GEWERKSCHAFTEN IN DER ÜBERSCHICHTENFRAGE   [Labor conflicts in Ruhr Valley mining, 1919-22: the policies of the mine owners' association and the labor unions in the question of overtime shifts]. *Vierteljahrshefte für Zeitgeschichte [West Germany] 1980 28(2): 168-223.* A case study of German labor's gradual loss of power to Ruhr mine owners in a series of tactical encounters from 1919 to 1932. After miners' initial triumphs which brought 7-hour and discussion of 6-hour shifts immediately after World War I, coal shortages and inflation forced the Social Democratic government to join employers in pressuring miners into

accepting three successive overtime arrangements, which eventually led to 8-hour shifts and more at reduced real wages. Based on Bergbau-Archiv (Bochum), Bundesarchiv (Koblenz), GDR Zentralstaatsarchiv (Potsdam), State Archive Münster, and printed sources; 175 notes. D. Prowe

346. Feldman, Gerald D. and Steinisch, Irmgard. DIE WEIMARER REPUBLIK ZWISCHEN SOZIAL- UND WIRTSCHAFTSSTAAT. DIE ENTSCHEIDUNG GEGEN DEN ACHTSTUNDENTAG [The Weimar Republic between social state and economic state: the decision against the eight-hour day]. *Archiv für Sozialgeschichte [West Germany] 1978 18: 353-439.* Analyzes industrial relations, working hours, and salaries in Germany from 1922 to 1924. Led by heavy industry, industry attacked social improvements, mainly the eight-hour working day. Industry increased working hours to prewar levels and reduced salaries massively in three major conflicts: the South German metalworkers' strike in 1922, the heavy industry dictate on working hours in 1923, and the 1924 struggle of the coal miners. Industrial relations suffered badly. Trade unions lost much of their power to protect the workers. At first convinced by industry's "productivity" argument, the government eventually had to intervene to protect the workers. Based on unpublished sources from state archives in East and West Germany, industrial archives, and labor movement archives, other primary and secondary sources; 388 notes. H. W. Wurster

347. Feldman, Gerald D. and Steinisch, Irmgard. NOTWENDIGKEIT UND GRENZEN SOZIALSTAATLICHER INTERVENTION: EINE VER-GLEICHENDE FALLSTUDIE DES RUHREISENSTREITS IN DEUTSCH-LAND UND DES GENERALSTREIKS IN ENGLAND [Necessity and limitations of government intervention in a social state: a comparative case study of the conflict in the Ruhr iron industry in Germany and the general strike in Great Britain]. *Archiv für Sozialgeschichte [West Germany] 1980 20: 57-117.* Compares reasons, course, aims, and results of the conflict in the Ruhr iron industry with the general strike in Great Britain. Whereas the German government eased some of labor's problems during the conflict, the British government used its power against the strike. Both situations required new procedures to solve socioeconomic problems in order to further economic growth and social progress. In their conflict with capital, unions in both countries considered state intervention an effective means of pushing through innovations against outdated capitalist concepts, but their attempts failed. Based on materials in State archives at Koblenz, Merseburg, and business archives at Düsseldorf, Mülheim/Ruhr, and Oberhausen, and contemporary journals; 228 notes. H. W. Wurster

348. Felix, David. WALTER RATHENAU: THE BAD THINKER AND HIS USES. *European Studies R. [Great Britain] 1975 5(1): 69-79.* Examines and contrasts Walther Rathenau (1867-1922), the egregious intellectualizer, with Rathenau, the statesman. Not fully cognizant of his own ideas, Rathenau, nevertheless, did conceive a compromise between free-enterprise capitalism and Marxist socialism as stated in his *Von kommenden Dingen,* ideas refined and brought to fruition by John Maynard Keynes. Primary and secondary sources; 29 notes. C. T. Prukop

349. Felker, Lon S. CONFLICT OF INTEREST THEORY AND SPE-
CIFIC SYSTEMS: POSTWAR ITALY AND WEIMAR GERMANY.
Comparative Pol. Studies 1981 14(3): 357-370. Compares Robert Axlerod's application of conflict of interest theory with other theories, with special reference
to postwar Italian parliamentary coalitions, 1919-31.

350. Fiedor, Karol. CHARAKTER I FUNKCJA OSADNICTWA NA
WSCHODNICH TERENACH NIEMIEC W OKRESIE MIEDZYWOJEN-
NYM [The character and the function of settling Germany's eastern territories
between the wars]. *Przegląd Zachodni [Poland] 1975 31(2): 257-291.* Discusses
the organization and management of the settlement program in the six German
provinces of East Prussia, Brandenburg, Pomerania, Upper and Lower Silesia and
the borderland area (Grenzmark Posen-Westpreussen) during the Weimar era.

351. Fiedor, Karol; Sobczak, Janusz; and Wrzesiński, Wojciech. THE IM-
AGE OF THE POLES IN GERMANY AND OF THE GERMANS IN PO-
LAND IN INTER-WAR YEARS AND ITS ROLE IN SHAPING THE
RELATIONS BETWEEN THE TWO STATES. *Polish Western Affairs [Po-
land] 1978 19(2): 203-228.* The events of World War I, the rebirth of the Polish
state, and the struggle to fix Polish-German boundaries deepened the antagonism
that had already existed between Poland and Germany. Each country intensified
propaganda against its neighbor. The spread of stereotyped ideas based on emotional premises, prejudice, and deliberate distortion exerted an influence on the
public opinion of the two nations. Historical arguments played an important role
in the formulation of ethnic stereotypes in both countries and were practically the
only argument used in contemporary evaluations.   M. Swiecicka-Ziemianek

352. Fiedor, Karol. NIEMIECKI RUCH PACYFISTYCZNY WOBEC
SPRAW POLSKICH W OKRESIE MIEDZYWOJENNYM [German paci-
fism and Poland in the prewar period]. *Przegląd Zachodni [Poland] 1977 33(2):
23-54.* In the 1920's the pacifist movement in Germany had over 100,000 members and was a major political force. Its leaders, like Carl von Ossietzky, H. von
Kessler, and Hellmuth von Gerlach, advocated friendly relations with Poland
and greater understanding of Polish history among German youth. However,
their efforts were boycotted by both right- and left-wing politicians and did not
improve Polish-German relations. 113 notes.   W. Kowalski

353. Fink, Carole. STRESEMANN'S MINORITY POLICIES, 1924-29.
J. of Contemporary Hist. [Great Britain] 1979 14(3): 403-422. As a permanent
member of the League of Nations Council, 1926-29, Gustave Stresemann worked
for improvement in the international system for minority protection. In 1922
Germany and Poland had negotiated the Geneva Convention on Upper Silesia.
It was violations of this Convention and German appeals to the League for redress
that consumed much of Stresemann's time. Actually, Germans in Silesia were
more fortunate than the Poles in East Prussia, Berlin, and the Rhineland, the
Danes in Schleswig, and the Serbs in Saxony who had no protection either in
international law or Reich law. Stresemann's repeated pronouncements in favor
of these national minorities were fruitless. On 2 October 1929, the day before he
died, he proposed a pact with Poland whereby that country would stop liquidat-
ing German properties. Berlin in turn would terminate pending litigation against
the Poles and compensate the claimants. Archival sources; 58 notes.
                                                        M. P. Trauth

354. Finker, Kurt. AUFGABEN UND ROLLE DES ROTEN FRONT-
KÄMPFERBUNDES IN DEN KLASSENSCHLACHTEN DER WEI-
MARER REPUBLIK [The tasks and role of the Red Front Fighters
Federation in the class struggles of the Weimar Republic]. *Militärgeschichte
[East Germany] 1974 13(2): 133-144.* With the founding of the Red Front Fighters Federation (RFB) in July 1924, the Communist Party of Germany (KPD)
created one of its most significant political organizations. As a defense organization against police terror and militarist indoctrination, it was designed to protect
workers and drew its members from those who had experienced trench warfare.
It formed youth and women auxilliaries as well, with Clara Zetkin leading the
latter. A provisional federation leadership was established in August 1924, but
at its first conference, which took place on 1 February 1925, the RFB, finding
the provisional leadership wanting, chose Ernst Thälmann as its new leader.
Although not a military organization, it adopted military rules and forms and
operated according to the tenets of democratic centralism in order better to
propagandize workers and prevent bourgeois units from dominating the scene.
In 1929 the government forbade the RFB which then went underground where
it fought against growing fascism until integrated after 1933 into the KPD's
resistance organization. 4 illus., 17 notes.   H. D. Andrews

355. Fischer, Wolfram. DEZENTRALISATION ODER ZENTRALISA-
TION—KOLLEGIALE ODER AUTORITÄRE FÜHRUNG? DIE AUSEI-
NANDERSETZUNG UM DIE LEITUNGSSTRUKTUR BEI DER
ENTSTEHUNG DES I. G. FARBEN-KONZERNS [Decentralization or centralization: collective or authoritarian leadership? The debates on managerial
structure during the formation of the I. G. Farben concern]. Horn, Norbert and
Kocka, Jürgen, ed. *Recht und Entwicklung der Grossunternehmen im 19. und
frühen 20. Jahrhundert* (Göttingen: Vandenhoeck & Ruprecht, 1979): 476-488.
The debates surrounding the establishment of I. G. Farbenindustrie A. G. show
that centralization and authoritarianism were not necessarily regarded as models
for company organization. Although the fusion of the largest German chemical
firms was intended, among other things, to neutralize the effects of excessive
decentralization, especially in marketing, in the production sector the intention
was to maintain the level of decentralization. Differences of opinion centered
mainly on whether a fixed organizational pattern would diminish flexibility or
increase it, since all management personnel would have their own areas of responsibility. Areas such as marketing, financing, tax considerations, and the political
representation of interests became more centralized, but the member firms which
had previously been independent retained their decisionmaking powers. 24 notes,
16 ref. English summary.   S

356. Flemming, Jens. DIE BEWAFFNUNG DES "LANDVOLKS":
LÄNDLICHE SCHÜTZWEHREN UND AGRARISCHER KONSER-
VATISMUS IN DER ANFANGSPHASE DER WEIMARER REPUBLIK
[The arming of the peasants: rural defense and agrarian conservatism in the
beginning phase of the Weimar Republic]. *Militärgeschichtliche Mitteilungen
[West Germany] 1979 (2): 7-36.* Analyzes the confluence of interests between
conservative political organizations and rural defense movements amid the col-
lapsing fortunes and revolutionary atmosphere of post-1918 Germany. The self-
defense groups assumed an antidemocratic and anti-worker attitude, reflecting

the reinforcing conservative ideals that survived in the countryside. These tendencies proved most vigorous in east Elbian territories, where fear of Bolshevism contributed to the strength of the defense groups. Alarmed by the Kapp Putsch, the government and Allied governments moved to disarm the rural defense bands, leaving the political organs intact as powerful antagonists of the Weimar Republic. Based upon documents in various German archives; 149 notes.

K. W. Estes

357. Fleury, Antoine. LA PÉNÉTRATION ÉCONOMIQUE DE L'ALLEMAGNE EN TURQUIE ET EN IRAN APRÈS LA PREMIÈRE GUERRE MONDIALE: L'IMPACT DE L'ÉVOLUTION DES STRUCTURES ÉCONOMIQUES SUR LES ÉCHANGES COMMERCIAUX [German economic penetration in Turkey and Iran after World War I: the impact of the evolution of economic structures on commercial exchanges]. *Relations Int. [France] 1974 (1): 155-171.* One of the principal aims of the Allies at the close of World War I was to reduce or eliminate German interests and influence in the Balkans and Middle East. The Germans, however, sought to revive their economic interests and influence. During the Nazi period Germany achieved considerable successes in Turkey and Iran due to the similar positions of these countries, the complementarity of their economic structures with respect to Germany, and their desire for greater independence from British and French hegemony. 52 notes.

J. C. Billigmeier

358. Freymond, Jean. GUSTAV STRESEMANN ET L'IDÉE D'UNE "EUROPE ÉCONOMIQUE" (1925-1927) [Gustav Stresemann and the ideal of an "economic Europe," 1925-37]. *Relations Int. [France] 1976 (8): 343-360.* Gustav Stresemann was both a German patriot and a believer in European unity, especially economic unity. In this he saw no contradiction; only international solidarity, dialogue, and economic cooperation could create conditions in which Germany's economic might could find full expression. His vision also extended to the United States. Only on such a stage could Germany's economic and political goals be met. 8 tables, 31 notes.

J. C. Billigmeier

359. Fritzsche, Klaus. KONSERVATISMUS IM GESELLSCHAFT-LICHE-GESCHICHTLICHEN PROZESS [Conservatism in sociohistorical development]. *Neue Politische Literatur [West Germany] 1979 24(1): 1-23, (3): 295-317.* Part I. Conservatism as an ideology in feudal and bourgeois society has been largely a political rather than a theoretical enterprise. Even recent studies on conservatism lack a structural analysis of social conditions in the 19th and 20th centuries. Part II. The philosophical-ideological background of conservatism in the Weimar Republic was based on the universalist theories of Othmar Spann, Edgar Julius Jung, Rudolf Pechel, and Ernst Niekisch. Recent studies prove the structural identity between conservatism and fascism and the gradual transformation of conservative reaction into fascist politics between 1918 and 1933. 76 notes.

R. Wagnleitner

360. Fuchs, Gerhard. IMPERIALISMUS VÝMARSKÉ REPUBLIKY A ŽIVOTNÍ ZÁJMY ČESKÉHO A SLOVENSKÉHO NÁRODA [The Weimar Republic's imperialism and the vital interests of the Czech and Slovak nations]. *Československý Časopis Hist. [Czechoslovakia] 1974 22(3): 361-384.* The "democratic" and "peace-loving" character of the Weimar Republic was a political lie.

Prewar imperialism did not die in the times of the Weimar state. After 1933, Germany continued its policy of imperialism and militarism, which worked against the vital interests of Czechs and Slovaks in their state. Secondary sources; 50 notes. G. E. Pergl

361. Fuchs, Gerhard. VÝZNAM "LOCARNA" V NĚMECKO-ČESKOS-LOVENSKÝCH VZTAZÍCH [The meaning of Locarno in German-Czechoslovak relations]. *Československý Časopis Hist. [Czechoslovakia] 1981 29(6): 847-878.* At the Locarno Conference, October 1925, Gustav Stresemann achieved the readmission of defeated Germany among the great powers, in return for a guarantee of Germany's western border of 1919. The Western Allies insisted on no similar guarantees for the German-Polish and German-Czechoslovak frontiers, though Edvard Beneš, as Czechoslovak foreign minister, had strenously lobbied for them. While trying to avert German revisionism from Czechoslovakia, Beneš even abandoned Poland, though the question vitally concerned both countries. Locarno was not only a stinging defeat for Beneš, but an early phase in the West's anti-Soviet appeasement policy, which was to lead to Munich and to World War II. Based on archives in Prague, Bonn, and Potsdam and on published sources; 113 notes. Russian and German summaries.
R. E. Weltsch

362. Furuuchi, Hiroyuki. WAIMARU-KI DOITSU NŌGYŌ NO KŌZŌ TO KEIEI KIKI [German agricultural structure and the crisis of the farm economy in the Weimar period]. *Tochiseido Shigaku [Japan] 1980 (89): 43-59.* The writer aims to elucidate the background of peasants' support of the Nazis, examining the German agricultural structure in the Weimar period. Agriculture in the Weimar period was biased toward stockraising. The speculative expansion of the breeding of hogs and cattle caused a crisis in that sector, 1927-28, characteristic of Weimar agriculture. Unlike the agricultural crisis in grain in the 1890's, the state took no measures to overcome this crisis, and the peasantry looked in greater numbers to the Nazis. Primary sources; 14 tables, 51 notes.
Y. Imura

363. Furuuchi, Hiroyuki. WAIMARU-KI DOITSU NŌGYŌ NO KIKI TO NŌGYŌ SEISAKU [The crisis of German agriculture and German agricultural policy in the Weimar period]. *Shakaikeizaishigaku (Socio-Economic Hist.) [Japan] 1980 46(2): 19-43.* German agricultural policies, 1924-28, included protective tariffs to prevent foreign competition in grain production and animal husbandry, and resulted in dissatisfaction with the government on the part of the peasants and the Junkers, paving the way for the rise of Nazism.

364. Gessner, Dieter. AGRARIAN PROTECTIONISM IN THE WEIMAR REPUBLIC. *J. of Contemporary Hist. [Great Britain] 1977 12(4): 759-778.* The high imperial tariffs were continued in the early Weimar Republic. The first struggle for the continuation of the tariff came in 1925 with Germany's regaining of international trade rights previously limited by the Versailles Treaty. Both agriculture and heavy industry opposed introduction of free trade. Government after government floundered on the issue and furnished an excellent opportunity to the Nazi leadership to propagate their own ideas. 61 notes. M. P. Trauth

365.   Gintsberg, L. I.   IOSEF VIRT: PUT' K BOR'BE ZA MIR I SOTRUD-NICHESTVO MEZHDU NARODAMI   [Joseph Wirth: the path to the struggle for peace and cooperation between peoples]. *Novaia i Noveishaia Istoriia [USSR] 1981 (1): 105-124, (2): 102-121.* Part I. Biographical sketch of Joseph Wirth (1879-1956), German chancellor, 1921-22, covering the period 1879-1922. Wirth was born and attended university in Freiburg and was elected to the Reichstag as a member of the Catholic Center Party. After two periods as finance minister he became chancellor in 1921. He played a major part in concluding the Treaty of Rapallo in 1922, and throughout his political life he was in favor of friendly relations between Germany and the USSR. Part II. Describes the period from the end of Wirth's chancellorship in 1922 until his death in 1956. Wirth's next important government post was minister of foreign affairs in the Brüning government, 1930, in which he worked to stem the rising tide of Nazism. Eventually removed, he went into exile when Hitler came to power, spending most of his time in Switzerland. Returning to Germany in 1945, he attempted to form a left-wing party but was frustrated by the occupying powers. He spent the last years of his life in campaigning against the reemergence of West Germany as a military power.   223 notes.   A. Brown

366.   Goold, J. Douglas.   LORD HARDINGE AS AMBASSADOR TO FRANCE, AND THE ANGLO-FRENCH DILEMMA OVER GERMANY AND THE NEAR EAST, 1920-1922.   *Hist. J. [Great Britain] 1978 21(4): 913-937.* The two years following the appointment of Charles Hardinge, Baron Hardinge of Penshurst (1858-1944), as ambassador to France in November 1920 were crucial in Anglo-French relations. A breach had developed concerning security against German aggression and the interpretation and enforcement of the peace treaties. Lord Hardinge dealt creatively with the new diplomacy in connection with such problems as reparations, Upper Silesia, the proposed Anglo-French pact, German disarmament, and the dispute in the Near East. His realism, initiative, and sensitivity toward the French leaders had a positive influence on the general course of British policy during this period. Based on the private papers of Lloyd George, Curzon, Hardinge, and Crewe; archival materials from the Public Record Office, the India Office Records, and the Hardinge MSS. in the Kent County Record Office; Hardinge's published reminiscences and published primary sources; contemporary newspaper accounts; and secondary sources; 124 notes.   L. J. Reith

367.   Gotschlich, Helga.   GRÜNDUNG UND ANFÄNGE DES REICHS-BANNERS SCHWARZ-ROT-GOLD   [Founding and beginning of the Reichsbanner Schwarz-Rot-Gold]. *Militärgeschichte [East Germany] 1980 19(1): 33-40.* Presents the history of the Reichsbanner Black-Red-Gold, a paramilitary unit of the Social Democratic Party. The author compares the development of the Reichsbanner with the defense organizations of the Communist Party of Germany and the Alliance of Red Front Fighters. The right-wing leaders of the Social Democratic Party betrayed their class and objectively rendered assistance to reaction. Central State Archives, Merseburg; Central Party Archives, Berlin; 24 notes.   J/T (H. D. Andrews)

368.   Gottschalch, Wilfried.   SVILUPPO E CRISI DEL CAPITALISMO IN RUDOLF HILFERDING   [Development and the crisis of capitalism in Rudolf Hilferding]. *Ann. dell'Istituto Giangiacomo Feltrinelli [Italy] 1973 15: 197-215.*

Rudolf Hilferding (1877-1941) was a militant and theorist within the German Independent Social Democrat Party (USPD) until it split in 1922 at which time he returned to the Social Democrat Party (SPD). The theoretical works of Hilferding can be divided into three phases: in the first he dedicated himself to the analysis of "financial capital" in which he refuted the inevitability of the economic collapse of capitalism; in the second phase, Hilferding realized that he had overestimated the revolutionary will of the working class and subsequently developed his theory of "organized capital" in which he predicted the restructuring of capital instead of its collapse; in his third phase he concerned himself primarily with foreign affairs and the relationship of economics and politics in the national socialist state. 75 notes.

M. T. Wilson

369. Grathwol, Robert. STRESEMANN REVISITED. *European Studies Rev. [Great Britain] 1977 7(3): 341-352.* Reviews three recent books on the policy of German Foreign Minister Gustav Stresemann, 1923-29. Martin Walsdorff, *Westorientierung und Ostpolitik. Stresemanns Russlandpolitik in der Locarno-Ara* (Bremen, 1971), Michael-Olaf Maxelon, *Stresemann und Frankreich. Deutsche Politik der Ost-West-Balance* (Dusseldorf, 1972) and Werner Weidenfeld, *Die Englandpolitik Gustav Stresemanns. Theoretische und praktische Aspekte der Aussenpolitik* (Mainz, 1972). Of the three, Maxelon is the most sympathetic and Walsdorff the most critical of Stresemann. All three authors analyze Stresemann in terms of continuity or change in modern German foreign policy. 4 notes.

J. L. White

370. Grathwol, Robert P. GERMANY AND THE EUPEN-ET-MALMÉDY AFFAIR 1924-26: "HERE LIES THE SPIRIT OF LOCARNO." *Central European Hist. 1975 8(3): 221-250.* The Locarno agreements did not preclude border rectifications. Negotiations between the Germans and the Belgians to effect a return of Eupen-et-Malmédy to Germany in exchange for German financial restitution for the issuance of occupation marks in Belgium continued after the agreements were signed. Great Britain opposed such an agreement and was eventually supported by Poincaré who returned as France's premier in 1926. The failure to work out these problems helped undermine the spirit of Locarno. Based on original sources; 85 notes.

C. R. Lovin

371. Groehler, Olaf. VORBEREITUNGEN FÜR DIE CHEMISCHE KRIEGFÜHRUNG DURCH DIE DEUTSCHE ARMEE ZWISCHEN ERSTEM UND ZWEITEM WELTKRIEG [Preparations for chemical warfare by the German army between the wars]. *Rev. Int. d'Hist. Militaire [France] 1979 (43): 167-180.* After 1918 the German Reichswehr secretly investigated chemical warfare agents, following the other bourgeois armies of the world. The development and mass production of chemical warfare material in Germany's chemical industry was stimulated; militarists in the Weimar Republic planned offensive operations using chemical agents. The Wehrmacht of the Nazi era did not use chemical warfare in World War II due to lack of technical preconditions for its operational use. Based on archival material and published works; 43 notes.

G. E. Pergl

372. Grosfeld, Leon. LA POLOGNE FACE AU PROBLÈME DE L'ÉVACUATION DE LA RHÉNANIE (1926-1929) [Poland faces the problem of the Rhineland evacuation, 1926-29]. *Acta Poloniae Hist. [Poland] 1974 30:*

213-228. Examines Poland's efforts to obtain nonaggression guarantees from Germany, while Germany was demanding Allied evacuation of the Rhineland and the redrawing of its eastern frontier to include Pomerania, Upper Silesia and Danzig. The Hague Conference of 6 August 1929 adopted the Young Plan, which provided for German reparations over 59 years and the withdrawal of Allied troops from the Rhineland in 1930, without any supplementary guarantees for Poland. The diplomatic rebuff suffered by Poland deeply affected its future foreign policy. Based on documents in the Archives des Actes Nouveaux in the Ministry of Foreign Affairs, the archives of the Ministry of Foreign Affairs-European Series 1918-1929 in the Polish Institute of International affairs, and secondary sources; 43 notes.   A. Armstrong

373. Guthke, Karl S. DER "KÖNIG DER WEIMARER REPUBLIK": GERHART HAUPTMANNS ROLLE IN DER ÖFFENTLICHKEIT ZWISCHEN KAISERREICH UND NAZI-REGIME [The "king of the Weimar Republic": Gerhart Hauptmann's public role between the German empire and the Nazi regime]. *Schweizer Monatshefte [Switzerland] 1981 61(10): 787-806.* While Gerhart Hauptmann (1862-1946) had been the enfant terrible and symbol of left-wing opposition in the Wilhelminian period, his confused nationalism and chauvinism made him appear a supporter of Nazism, although many of his public statements and articles show that he favored democratic ideals.

374. Haar, John M., III. JOHANNES HALLER AND THE "RUSSIAN MENACE": BALTIC GERMAN RUSSOPHOBIA DURING WORLD WAR I. *East European Q. 1980 14(1): 75-91.* An analysis of the writings of Johannes Haller, a prominent Baltic German who wrote anti-Russian propaganda during World War I. Haller constructed an elaborate historical structure to demonstrate that Russia was really an Asian state and called for the detachment of all non-Russian territories from Russia, especially the Baltic states. Haller's work helped intensify the anti-Russian attitude of nationalistic Germans. Based on Haller's published works; 72 notes.   C. R. Lovin

375. Hägel, Helmuth. DIE STELLUNG DER SOZIALDEMOKRATISC-HEN JUGENDORGANISATIONEN ZU STAAT UND PARTEI IN DEN ANFANGSJAHREN DER WEIMARER REPUBLIK [The position of the Social Democratic youth organizations toward the state and party in the beginning years of the Weimar Republic]. *Int. Wissenschaftliche Korrespondenz zur Geschichte der Deutschen Arbeiterbewegung [West Germany] 1976 12(2): 166-216.* Strict hierarchies, opposition to democracy, and inflexibility in discussing political questions characterized German Social Democratic youth organizations, 1918-20's. They failed to integrate the left-wing fraction.

376. Hansen, Ernst W. ZUR WAHRNEHMUNG INDUSTRIELLER IN-TERESSEN IN DER WEIMARER REPUBLIK. DIE GESCHÄFTSSTELLE FÜR INDUSTRIELLE ABRÜSTUNG (GEFIA) [Regarding the promotion of industrial interests in the Weimar Republic: the Office for Industrial Disarmament (GEFIA)]. *Vierteljahrshefte für Zeitgeschichte [West Germany] 1980 28(4): 487-501.* In response to the Versailles Treaty's limitations on German armaments production, the German armaments industry set up an extensive organization which in cooperation with the government sought to limit information going to the International Control Commission, prevent unannounced con-

trol visits, and define "armaments" as narrowly as possible. When the government began its policy of reconciliation, this organization allied with the army to resist disarmament and later to promote clandestine rearmament. Based on Bayer, MAN, the German Foreign Ministry, and Federal Archives; 71 notes.
D. Prowe

377. Hårløv, Tyge. DEN DANSK-TYSKE GRAENSEVANDLØBSKOM-MISSION [The Danish-German Border Stream Commission]. *Nordisk Administrativt Tidsskrift [Denmark] 1973 54(2): 82-94.* In 1920, according to the Versailles Treaty and after a plebiscite, a border-line separating Denmark and Germany was laid between Flensborg fjord in the eastern part of Slesvig and the marshland by Siltoft in the west. To a great extent the border followed the central line of small rivers and streams running east and west. In order to have decisions with regard to those common waters binding for all parties concerned on the Danish and the German side of the border, a joint Danish-German commission was established in 1922. Gives the historical background for this commission. Describes the decisions of the commission, especially the successful long-distance straightenings of the streams and decisions regarding exchange of areas between owners on each side of the border and the paying of compensation.   J

378. Heideking, Jürgen. DAS ENDE DER SANKTIONSPOLITIK: DIE ALLIIERTEN MÄCHTE UND DIE RÜCKKEHR DES DEUTSCHEN KRONPRINZEN IM NOVEMBER 1923 [The end of sanctions policy: the allied forces and the return of the German crown prince in November 1923]. *Francia [France] 1979 7: 365-400.* Describes the political and diplomatic background to the November events which changed European politics and ended sanctions against Germany. While French president Poincaré used Crown Prince William's secret return to Germany, 10 November 1923, to press for sanctions to enforce reparations conditions favorable to French interests, the British government was against all sanctions and against independent action by any member of the allied forces' Reparations Commission. Delaying action to win support from France's allies, Italy and Belgium, the British and the Americans isolated the French at the Ambassadors' Conference, 21 November 1923, and forced them to compromise on their reparations demands. Based on the Ambassadors' Conference Acts and other English, French, and German official documents; 125 notes.
G. Herritt

379. Heideking, Jürgen. VOM VERSAILLER VERTRAG ZUR GENFER ABRÜSTUNGSKONFERENZ: DAS SCHEITERN DER ALLIIERTEN MILITÄRKONTROLLPOLITIK GEGENÜBER DEUTSCHLAND NACH DEM ERSTEN WELTKRIEG [From the Versailles Treaty to the Geneva disarmament conference: the failure of allied military control policy toward Germany after World War I]. *Militärgeschichtliche Mitteilungen [West Germany] 1980 (2): 45-68.* The demise of the Allied Military Control Commission occurred not only through the steady opposition of the German government, but through increasing disharmony among the Allies. Such factors as economic policy, the changing character of parliamentary governments, and Anglo-French disagreement over the status of European states all combined to undercut support of the concept and apparatus of controlling and later observing German military power. Based on British foreign policy documents; 96 notes.   K. W. Estes

380.   Helmreich, J. E.   BELGIUM AND THE DECISION TO OCCUPY THE RUHR: DIPLOMACY FROM A MIDDLE POSITION.   *Rev. Belge de Philologie et d'Hist. [Belgium] 1973 51(4): 822-839.* Examines reparations negotiations leading to the Franco-Belgian occupation of the Ruhr basin in 1923 from the Belgian point of view. Between 1920 and 1923, the Belgians often served as mediators between the English and the French. They also had the difficult task of guarding Belgium's own interests and not allowing the powers to ignore their small country. Belgium entered the Ruhr primarily because it was not receiving the required payments from Germany and to protect its Antwerp-Rhine trade from French encirclement. Based on private papers of Paul Hymans, Henri Jaspar, and Georges Theunis; 30 notes.   M. F. Bassman

381.   Hennicke, Otto.   ZUM POLITISCHEN UND MILITÄRISCHEN CHARAKTER DES ROTEN RUHRARMEE   [The political and military character of the Red Ruhr Army]. *Militärgeschichte [East Germany] 1980 19(3): 300-315.* The creation of a working-class army in the Ruhr in response to the Kapp-Lüttwitz Putsch in 1920 was a creative achievement of the German proletariat. Initially supported by a range of center-to-left parties and the unions, it proved impossible to establish a united command because the process of creating the army began at the bottom. Once the putsch was repulsed, the strength of the Red Army declined, in part because only the Communist Party conceived of a role for military action in the class struggle. Documents from the Central State Archives, Potsdam, and secondary sources; 6 photos, 41 notes, list of units.
H. D. Andrews

382.   Hertz-Eichenrode, Dieter.   REICHSKREDITE FÜR DIE OSTSIEDLUNG. EINE INNENPOLITISCHE STREITFRAGE DER JAHRE 1925 BIS 1927   [Reich credits for settlement of the East: domestic political question, 1925-27]. *Jahrbuch für die Geschichte Mittel- und Ostdeutschlands [West Germany] 1978 27: 238-290.* During the late 19th and early 20th centuries, the emigration of German rural populations from the Junker areas east of the Elbe, threatened to weaken Germany's hold on these territories. Societies were formed before World War I to promote the colonization of the East by German farmers from western and southern Germany, an effort that resumed after the war. In 1925-27, eastern colonization was the subject of political rivalry between the central government and the Prussian Socialist government. Eventually, Reich financial credits revived the colonization projects from their stagnation of 1925-27. 160 notes.   J. C. Billigmeier

383.   Herwig, Holger H.   FROM KAISER TO FÜHRER: THE POLITICAL ROAD OF A GERMAN ADMIRAL, 1923-33.   *J. of Contemporary Hist. [Great Britain] 1974 9(2): 107-120.* A study of the efforts of Rear-Admiral Magnus von Levetzow to find a dictator who would be acceptable to the German people and who would open the way to restoration of the Hohenzollern dynasty. Initially Hitler was rejected as a possible candidate. Further contacts allayed earlier fears. Yet the Kaiser was not willing to take the next steps which would have necessitated cooperation with National Socialism and Hitler. Levetzow broke with William II and joined Adolf Hitler. 33 notes.   R. V. Ritter

384. Hess, Jürgen C. EUROPAGEDANKE UND NATIONALER REVI-
SIONISMUS: ÜBERLEGUNGEN ZU IHRER VERKNÜPFUNG IN DER
WEIMARER REPUBLIK AM BEISPIEL WILHELM HEILES [The united
Europe ideal and national revisionism: considerations of connections between
them during the Weimar Republic as exemplified by Wilhelm Heile]. *Hist. Zeits-
chrift [West Germany] 1977 225(3): 572-622.* Wilhelm Heile was extremely
active in the movement for European cooperation, having helped establish the
German Society for European Understanding [Deutscher Verband für europeisc-
hen Verständigung] in 1926. At the same time Heile was very active in the
Austrian-German National League [Österreichisch-Deutsches Volksbund],
which was the leading proponent of Anschluss between Germany and Austria.
Heile's activity and writings from 1919 to about 1930 show the development of
his thought favoring peaceful revision of the Versailles restrictions on a German-
Austrian merger while supporting the international peace movement and remaining within the structure of politics in the Weimar Republic. 210 notes.

G. H. Davis

385. Hiden, John. THE WEIMAR REPUBLIC AND THE PROBLEM OF
THE AUSLANDSDEUTSCHE. *J. of Contemporary Hist. [Great Britain]
1977 12(2): 273-289.* The whole question of Germans living abroad requires far
more study, both as to fact and as to terminology. There were numerous private
organizations, from shooting clubs to the secret, official German Organization
(Deutsche Stiftung). Although the Weimar Republic hoped to use these Germans
abroad to further its foreign policy, it seems that the hope came to naught. There
never existed in Weimar days the professed determination of the Nazis to unite
the Auslandsdeutsche politically. Based on archival sources; 50 notes.

M. P. Trauth

386. Hiden, John W. THE SIGNIFICANCE OF LATVIA: A FORGOT-
TEN ASPECT OF WEIMAR *OSTPOLITIK*. *Slavonic and East European R.
[Great Britain] 1975 53(132): 389-413.* During 1920-22 the German government
negotiated with newly independent Latvia in hopes of gaining a commercial
staging area close to the Russian market, minimizing Polish influence in any
Baltic regional bloc, and promoting German business in Latvia. Even after the
Rapallo Treaty with Soviet Russia, stability and economic recovery were leading
German objectives. Based on material in the German Central Archives (Pots-
dam), British Foreign Office microfilms, and published sources; 91 notes.

R. E. Weltsch

387. Himmer, Robert. RATHENAU, RUSSIA, AND RAPALLO. *Central
European Hist. 1976 9(2): 146-183.* Resolves the historical dilemma which had
the main industrialists of Germany supporting an agreement with Russia in 1922
and the industrialist-foreign minister, Walther Rathenau, opposing it. German
industrialists favored an agreement for the economic exploitation of Russia, but
they realized Germany did not have sufficient capital to pour into Russia, so they
began to develop the idea of a Western consortium. Russia resisted the consortium idea and essentially presented Germany with an ultimatum to make an
agreement or the Soviets would make one with the Entente powers. At the Genoa
Conference, it appeared to Rathenau that the latter was a possibility, so the
Rapallo Treaty was signed. Based on microfilmed German documents and recently published Russian and East German documents; 128 notes.

C. R. Lovin

388.   Hirschfeld, Yair P.   GERMAN POLICY TOWARDS IRAN; CONTI-NUITY AND CHANGE FROM WEIMAR TO HITLER, 1919-1939.   *Jahr-buch des Inst. für Deutsche Geschichte [Israel] 1975 Beiheft 1: 117-141.* Investigation of German-Iranian relations in the Weimar and Nazi periods has disproved two previously accepted theories: 1) that the Weimar government developed a definite policy toward Iran, and 2) that German achievements in Iran were greater under Hitler than under the Weimar government. Evidence has not shown that the Weimar government had any developed strategic or political aims in Iran. Under Hitler increased economic relations with Iran were tied to political considerations but German influences, both economic and political, were greater in Weimar times than under the Nazis. 129 notes.   M. Faissler

389.   Hirszowicz, Lukasz.   THE COURSE OF GERMAN FOREIGN POL-ICY IN THE MIDDLE EAST BETWEEN THE WORLD WARS.   *Jahrbuch des Inst. für Deutsche Geschichte [Israel] 1975 Beiheft 1: 175-190.* Neither the Weimar Republic nor the Nazi regime looked upon the Middle East as of prime importance to Germany. German businessmen sold machinery and technical equipment to Turkey, Iran, and Egypt, but without great encouragement from their government. The government often refrained from pressing some advantage in the Middle East for fear of offending Great Britain. As World War II approached, the Germans abandoned other opportunities in the Middle East for fear of offending the Italians. But when war actually broke out they sought friendship with several Arab states. 20 notes.   M. Faissler

390.   Holder, L. D.   SEECKT AND THE FÜHRERHEER.   *Military Rev. 1976 56(10): 71-79.* Discusses General Hans von Seeckt's supervision, leadership, and military training of the officer corps and armed forces of Germany, 1920-26; considers the impact of his political conflicts with the Weimar Republic on the rise of Nazism.

391.   Holl, Karl.   EUROPAPOLITIK IM VORFELD DER DEUTSCHEN REGIERUNGSPOLITIK: ZUR TÄTIGKEIT PROEUROPÄISCHER OR-GANISATIONEN IN DER WEIMARER REPUBLIK   [European policy on the fringes of German government policy: on the activity of pro-European organizations in the Weimar Republic].   *Hist. Zeitschrift [West Germany] 1974 219(1): 33-94.* Two rival groups promoting European cooperation failed to cooperate with each other or to gain strong influence in German politics. Wilhelm Heile and Alfred Nossig worked together in several organizations, but were never able to cooperate with Count Richard Coudenhove-Kalergi's Pan-European Union or work with the German pacifists. They got no consistent support from the leading German politicians, nor did they achieve any practical results from international conferences. 200 notes.   G. H. Davis

392.   Holtfrerich, Carl-Ludwig.   AMERIKANISCHER KAPITALEXPORT UND WIEDERAUFBAU DER DEUTSCHEN WIRTSCHAFT 1919-23 IM VERGLEICH ZU 1924-29   [American capital export and the economic reconstruction of Germany: 1919-23 compared to 1924-29].   *Vierteljahrschrift für Sozi-al- und Wirtschaftsgeschichte [West Germany] 1977 64(4): 497-529.* Contrary to general belief, German economic development and specifically US investment in Germany was as great in the immediate post-World War I years, 1919-22, as in the years of the Dawes Plan, 1924-29. US investment in 1919-22 in the form of

short-term private export credits and currency speculation actually added more value to the German economy than later aid under the Dawes Plan. Based on documents in the Bundesarchiv Koblenz, the US National Archives, the Federal Reserve Bank of New York, published statistics, and secondary works; 8 tables, 2 graphs, 4 documents, 67 notes.
D. Prowe

393. Holtfrerich, Carl-Ludwig. INTERNATIONALE VERTEILUNGS-FOLGEN DER DEUTSCHEN INFLATION 1918-1923 [International consequences of the German inflation, 1918-23]. *Kyklos [Switzerland] 1977 30(2): 271-292.* The German inflation of 1918-23 was partly a result of foreigners' withdrawing their capital from the German money market; gains by Germany from the depreciation of foreign bank deposits in German banks due to inflation in this period roughly equal German reparations of the same period, including payments in kind, showing that inflation was a rational and effective economic strategy.

394. Hopwood, Robert. PALADINS OF THE BUERGERTUM: CULTURAL CLUBS AND POLITICS IN SMALL GERMAN TOWNS, 1918-1925. *Can. Hist. Assoc. Hist. Papers [Canada] 1974: 213-235.* Discusses the social and political attitudes of middle-class residents of small German towns, 1918-25, and their response to the prospect of social and economic upheaval.

395. Jacobson, Jon and Walker, John T. THE IMPULSE FOR A FRANCO-GERMAN ENTENTE: THE ORIGINS OF THE THOIRY CONFERENCE, 1926. *J. of Contemporary Hist. [Great Britain] 1975 10(1): 157-181.* Aristide Briand and Gustave Stresemann, foreign ministers of France and Germany, met at Thoiry 17 September 1926. They discussed the Saar, German disarmament, Eupen-et-Malmédy, and the termination of Allied military occupation. The Locarno Treaties had been signed only the year before and Germany had entered the League of Nations. The Thoiry Conference might have had comparable historic significance. The meeting was well-prepared and each delegate was at first backed by his government. The heart of the discussions was the Rhineland-reparations deal, a plan to reduce military occupation of the Rhine and ease the French financial difficulties. Neither country followed up the proposals. Thoiry now represents only what might have been. Archival and printed primary sources; 88 notes.
M. P. Trauth

396. James, Harold. STATE, INDUSTRY, AND DEPRESSION IN WEIMAR GERMANY. *Hist. J. [Great Britain] 1981 24(1): 231-241.* A review article on seven books published in Germany in the mid-1970's on problems of 1918-33. Examines the Depression in Germany and what could have been done to lessen its effect. Practical men were on hand, but the problem lay in the ideology and the export-oriented environment, a situation different from today's. 14 notes.
J. P. H. Myers

397. Jones, K. P. STRESEMANN, THE RUHR CRISIS, AND RHENISH SEPARATISM: A CASE STUDY OF WESTPOLITIK. *European Studies Rev. [Great Britain] 1977 7(3): 311-340.* During the Ruhr crisis of 1923-24 German Foreign Minister Gustav Stresemann (1878-1929) was faced with the question of whether or not to approve the creation of an independent government for the Rhineland. France seemed intent on creating an autonomous Rhine

subordinate to it. Separatist uprisings had occurred in the Rhineland. Further, financial payments to the Rhineland threatened to undermine Stresemann's efforts to stabilize the *Rentenmark.* In the course of the crisis Stresemann moved from opposition to acceptance of autonomy. The evolution of German policy represented a retreat for Stresemann, but demonstrated his devotion to a policy of compromise with France. Based on primary sources; 87 notes.

J. L. White

398.   Jones, Kenneth Paul.   ALANSON B. HOUGHTON AND THE RUHR CRISIS: THE DIPLOMACY OF POWER AND MORALITY.   Jones, Kenneth Paul, ed. *U.S. Diplomats in Europe, 1919-1941* (Santa Barbara, Calif.: ABC-Clio, 1981): 25-39. Alanson Bigelow Houghton (1863-1941) was America's ambassador to Germany from February 1922 to February 1925. Describes his role in the Ruhr reparations crisis of 1923-24, an instructive example of what recent scholarship has argued concerning the legend of American isolationism. Republican policymakers were deeply involved in the search for peace in Europe, fearful of Congressional opposition to direct governmental intervention, and confident of the ability of the private sector to provide a businesslike solution to Europe's difficulties.   Based on primary sources; 67 notes.   J. Powell

399.   Jones, Larry Eugene.   ADAM STEGERWALD UND DIE KRISE DES DEUTSCHEN PARTEIENSYSTEMS: EIN BEITRAG ZUR DEUTUNG DES "ESSENER PROGRAMMS" VOM NOVEMBER 1920   [Adam Stegerwald and the crisis of the German party system: an interpretation of the "Essen Program" of November 1920]. *Vierteljahrshefte für Zeitgeschichte [West Germany] 1979 27(1): 1-29.* An analysis of the genesis and ultimate failure of German Christian labor leader Adam Stegerwald's (1874-1945) famous November 1920 Essen Program for the creation of a large centrist Christian People's Party in the Weimar Republic. Motivated by concerns about the Catholic Center Party's internal crisis, poor relations with the German People's Party (DVP), and the Nationalists' (DNVP) shift to the right, the initiative was ultimately frustrated by the established parties and the traditional Catholic labor leadership.   Based on newly discovered Stegerwald papers for 1920-33, papers in the Bundesarchiv (Koblenz), Stadtarchiv Köln, Stegerwald Archive, German Foreign Office, and secondary works; 111 notes.   D. Prowe

400.   Jones, Larry Eugene.   INFLATION, REVALUATION, AND THE CRISIS OF MIDDLE-CLASS POLITICS: A STUDY IN THE DISSOLUTION OF THE GERMAN PARTY SYSTEM, 1923-1928.   *Central European Hist. 1979 12(2): 143-168.* Emphasizes that the German bourgeois parties were in a state of dissolution before the Depression or the Nazi electoral breakthrough. The process was exacerbated by the inflation and the consequent revaluation crises which affected the middle classes in different ways. The inability of these parties "to integrate the diverse and the increasingly antagonistic social and economic interests . . . into a viable and effective social force" led to the dissolution. Special attention is given to new parties formed in 1925 and 1926 to oppose existing bourgeois parties. Based on original sources; 84 notes.   C. R. Lovin

401.   Juhász, Gyula.   AZ 1929-1933-AS GAZDASÁGI VÁLSÁG HATÁSA A NEMZETKÖZI VISZONYOKRA   [The impact of the 1929-33 economic crisis on the international situation]. *Magyar Tudomány [Hungary] 1979 24(10):*

730-734. Many national archives on this period have recently become accessible to historians. This may lead to some revision of the accepted views on how the 1929-33 crisis led to World War II. Around 1930, dictatorial regimes emerged all over Europe. It was not understood that the Nazis sought not only revenge for Germany's losses, but strove for European hegemony.   R. Hetzron

402. Kahl, Monika. ADOLF SCHMALIX UND DIE FASCHISTISCHE "GROSSDEUTSCHE VOLKSPARTEI" [Adolf Schmalix and the fascist Great German People's Party]. *Zeitschrift für Geschichtswissenschaft [East Germany] 1976 24(5): 547-558.* Between 1924 and 1932 the fascist Adolf Schmalix won an influential position in the political life of Erfurt. After 1929 the Great German People's Party stagnated because of the success of the National Socialists. Based on documents in the Stadtarchiv, Erfurt, printed documents, secondary literature and newspapers; 62 notes.   R. Wagnleitner

403. Káňa, Otakar. VĚDA VE SLUŽBÁCH VÝBOJNÉ POLITIKY NĚMECKÉHO IMPERIALISMU V OBDOBÍ VÝMARSKÉ REPUBLIKY [Science in the service of the German policy of aggressive imperialism during the Weimar Republic]. *Slezský Sborník [Czechoslovakia] 1976 74(1): 1-15.* Examines the scientific and historical institutes, already in existence in 1918 or created thereafter, which tended to support German imperialism. They supplied information about all Germans abroad and the various stages of national development and persecution in their countries of residence. The focus is on those institutes that wrote about the Germans in Czechoslovakia. The first of these was the *Deutsches Auslandsinstitut Stuttgart-DAI* in which extensive work was done on the full history of the Germans throughout the world. Second in importance was the *Osteuropa-Institut zu Breslau-OEI* which surveyed Germans in Silesia. It put out a bibliography about Germans in Eastern Europe and provided courses on the history of the area. In 1925 the institute published a polemic against the Poles insisting that they bow down to the Germans and form a united front with them against the Bolsheviks. After Hitler came to power the Institute served the Nazi ideology completely. The *Kulturbodenforschung* in Leipzig was another scientific institute that concentrated on the relationship between Germans living along the borderlands and Germany proper. In the 1920's much work was done here on the prehistoric settlement of the Germans in Slavic areas such as Bohemia. Article to be continued. 53 notes.   B. Kimmel

404. Kanbayashi, Teijiro. ZUR GESCHICHTE DES LEUNA-WERKS DES IG-KONZERNS [The history of the Leuna Works of the I. G. Farben combine]. *Keieishigaku [Japan] 1967 2(2): 1-29.* The history of the Leuna Works in Germany has two parts: the first, 1916-45, is the story of the Leuna Works as a large unit of the I. G. Farben monopoly; the second, 1945 to the present, is the story of a publicly owned operation in East Germany (VEB Leuna Works, Walter Ulbricht). The author describes the earlier period. The establishment of the Farben trust in 1925 was the consequence of a long development process, in which eight great chemical companies coalesced into two groups in 1904 and into one in 1916, to be fused in a single trust in 1925. The Leuna Works was established in 1916 as a plant of the Badische Anilin- und Soda- Fabrik and after 1925 it became the largest unit in the Farben group. The destruction of German imperialism in World War II also marked the destruction of the Leuna Works as a monopoly. Article in Japanese.   J/S

405. Kasper, Martin. BOR'BA LUZHITSKIKH SERBOV ZA NAT-
SIONAL'NOE RAVNOPRAVIE V 1919-1932 GODAKH [The struggle of
the Lusatian Sorbs for their national rights in 1919-32]. *Sovetskoe Slavianovede-
nie [USSR] 1976 (6): 24-31.* In the ideology of German imperialism, anti-Slavism
was particularly strong. With the rebirth of the *Drang nach Osten* policy, anti-
Slavic propaganda increased. Inside the country it was directed against the Polish
and Sorbian national minorities. During the Kaiser's rule, the Sorbs were doomed
as a nationality. Anti-Sorb policies were still in force in 1920, though the means
of their execution had changed. The election of Paul von Hindenburg to the
presidency, which represented the rebirth of German militarism and reaction,
shadowed the Sorb national movement's efforts to preserve Sorb culture and
language. The example of the USSR led to the spread of socialist ideas among
Sorbians and friendly feelings toward Russia and Soviet workers, and in 1929 the
strong anti-Nazi mood among Sorbs led to attacks by the Nazis on their leaders.
Secondary sources; 23 notes.   L. Kalinowski

406. Kater, Michael H. DIE "TECHNISCHE NOTHILFE" IM SPAN-
NUNGSFELD VON ARBEITERUNRUHEN, UNTERNEHMERINTER-
ESSEN UND PARTEIPOLITIK ["Technical Emergency Aid" in the context
of labor unrest, self-interest of employers and party politics]. *Vierteljahrshefte für
Zeitgeschichte [West Germany] 1979 27(1): 30-78.* The *Technische Nothilfe*,
established by the German Social Democratic government in November 1919 to
maintain emergency services in the face of massive labor unrest, evolved into an
organization of strikebreakers of mainly upper middle class and student background closely associated with industry, large landowners, and conservative parties. Ideologically rightist and anti-Communist it was attacked by Social
Democrats and labor after 1920, but survived through the Nazi regime. Based
on records in Bundesarchiv in Koblenz and Bayerisches Hauptstaatsarchiv in
Munich, contemporary press and secondary works; table, 247 notes.
                                                                    D. Prowe

407. Kato, Eiichi. SOTAITEKI ANTEIKI DOITSU NO CHIHOSAI
SHIJO [The local bond market in Weimar Germany]. *Shakaikagaku Kenkyū
[Japan] 1977 28(4-5): 62-110.* Examines German local bonds during the latter
half of the 1920's, on the basis of accounts, lists of creditors, and the proportion
of foreign capital. Due to the worsening issue market, it was difficult for local
governments to secure funds even at high interest, and the autonomy of local
finance diminished after World War I, an expression of the contradiction of
German capitalism. Based on official financial statistics; 21 tables, 48 notes.
                                                                    Y. Aoki

408. Klein, Fritz. ZUR DEUTSCH-FRANZÖSISCHEN AUSEINANDER-
SETZUNG ZWISCHEN 1919 UND 1939 ÜBER DIE URSPRÜNGE DES
ERSTEN WELTKRIEGES [On German-French argumentation between 1919
and 1939 on the origins of the First World War]. *R. d'Allemagne [France] 1974
6(2): 47-57.* Surveys the conflict over the *Kriegschuldfrage* between the wars, the
political intentions involved, the effects, and the claim that Hitler harvested the
fruits of the entire German bourgeois research on the question of war guilt. Based
on documents and primary sources; 15 notes.   R. K. Adams

409. Kohler, Eric D. REVOLUTIONARY POMERANIA, 1919-20: A STUDY IN MAJORITY SOCIALIST AGRICULTURAL POLICY AND CIVIL-MILITARY RELATIONS. *Central European Hist. 1976 9(3): 250-293.* Uses the example of the Pomeranian agricultural situation of 1919 and the response of the Majority Socialist government to it to demonstrate that early leaders of the Weimar Republic had the ability to solve some of its most difficult problems. Prussian Minister of Agriculture Otto Braun was able to develop a viable agricultural policy and to defy the army when it tried to interfere. In time, the policy failed, but it was due to forces beyond Braun's control, rather than the lack of perception or ability. Based on published and unpublished sources; 199 notes.   C. R. Lovin

410. Kollmer, Gert. TENDENZEN DES WIRTSCHAFTLICHEN WACH-STUMS IN SÜDWESTDEUTSCHLAND ZWISCHEN 1918-1945 [Patterns of growth in Southwest Germany, 1918-45]. *Zeitschrift für Württembergische Landesgeschichte [West Germany] 1979 38: 188-216.* The two growth periods of the Southwest-German economy, 1924-30 and 1934-39, had very distinct characters. The first favored a trickle-down effect of wealth, while the second one exclusively favored state sponsored armaments production. In both cases, however, technical efficiency increased. Based on secondary material; 117 notes.
M. Geyer

411. Könnemann, Erwin. ZU NEUEREN EINSCHATZUNGEN DES MILITARISMUS IN DER WEIMARER REPUBLIK DURCH HIS-TORIKER DER BRD [On recent assessments of militarism in the Weimar Republic by historians of the Federal Republic of Germany]. *Militärgeschichte [East Germany] 1980 19(4): 461-466.* Evaluates from a Marxist definition of militarism the papers and commentary of a symposium held in May 1977 by the Hochschule der Bundeswehr in Hamburg as published in K. J. Müller and E. Opitz, ed., *Militär und Militarismus in der Weimarer Republik* (Düsseldorf: Droste Verlag, 1978). 7 notes.   H. D. Andrews

412. Koonz, Claudia. CONFLICTING ALLEGIANCES: POLITICAL IDEOLOGY AND WOMEN LEGISLATORS IN WEIMAR GERMANY. *Signs: J. of Women in Culture and Soc. 1976 1(3 Pt. 1): 663-683.* Women had been legally excluded from politics in Germany before 1919; their prior experience, therefore, differed from that of their male legislative colleagues. While women legislators showed special interest in female-related legislation, they generally left debating to men on key national issues of foreign policy, domestic political crises, and the economy. Women remained outside the ruling cliques and did not represent powerful national interests outside the party organizations during the Weimar period. As the institutional framework of society appeared to disintegrate with the Depression, the need for security overcame any tenuous commitment to women's emancipation, and females were relegated to traditional familial roles. Primary and secondary works; 3 tables, graph; 36 notes.
S. E. Kennedy

413. Koops, Tilman P. HEINRICH BRÜNINGS "POLITISCHE ERFAH-RUNGEN" (ZUM ERSTEN TEIL DER MEMOIREN) [Heinrich Brüning's *Politische Erfahrungen*: the first part of the memoirs]. *Geschichte in Wissenschaft und Unterricht [West Germany] 1973 24(4): 197-221.* Heinrich Brüning's

Memoiren 1918-1934 (Stuttgart 1970) do not prove the thesis that he supported the Müller cabinet until the end by working out a compromise for the coalition parties in March 1930.

414. Korczyk, Henryk. TRAKTAT BERLIŃSKI ZAWARTY POMIĘDZY ZSRR A NIEMCAMI W 1926 R. [Treaty of Berlin contracted between the USSR and Germany in the year 1926]. *Przegląd Zachodni [Poland] 1980 36(5-6): 221-238.* The Treaty of Locarno signed in 1925, among other purposes, aimed to isolate the USSR. Germany considered isolation of the Soviets contrary to its own interests and raised the issue of interpretation of Article 16 of the League of Nations Compact, claiming the freedom to join or not to join any economic or military sanctions against the USSR. In the end, the Western powers offered their own interpretation. Germany, still dissatisfied, entered secret talks with the USSR, leading to a new treaty of friendship and noncooperation in sanctions against either the USSR or Germany. The clear thrust of the treaty was anti-Polish, and questions were raised about the propriety of the treaty clauses. In the end Britain acquiesced, believing the treaty would not violate Locarno or the League Compact. This was a clear defeat for Poland. Based on primary research in Polish, German, British and League of Nations Archives and other primary publications.   M. Krzyzaniak

415. Kotłowski, Tadeusz. THE WEIMAR REPUBLIC IN POLISH HISTORIOGRAPHY. *Polish Western Affairs [Poland] 1979 20(1): 79-101.* Polish research on the history of the Weimar Republic, in spite of the large number of publications, reflects the general lack of work devoted to 20th-century Germany. Much more research still remains to be done to eliminate deficiencies in both fact and interpretation.   M. Swiecicka-Ziemianek

416. Kövics, Emma. COUDENHOVE-KALERGI'S PAN-EUROPE MOVEMENT ON THE QUESTIONS OF INTERNATIONAL POLITICS DURING THE 1920'S. *Acta Hist. [Hungary] 1979 25(3-4): 233-266.* Outlines the history of the Pan-European Union, established in 1924 and led by Count Richard Coudenhove-Kalergi, and European reactions to it. The Pan-European Union wanted an economic and political alliance of European states. Europe's more uniform postwar political systems aided the rise of the movement. However Eastern Europe's and Italy's demands for revision of the peace treaties, particularly in regard to boundaries, France's hatred of Germany, and Germany's discontent and francophobia were insurmountable problems that the economic factors urging integration could not overcome. Based primarily on Coudenhove-Kalergi's writings; 112 notes. Russian summary.   A. M. Pogany

417. Kövics, Emma. A PÁNEURÓPA-MOZGALOM FOGADTATÁSA NÉMETORSZÁGBAN 1924-1932 [The reception of the Pan-European movement in Germany, 1924-32]. *Történelmi Szemle [Hungary] 1981 24(3): 360-384.* In Vienna, 1924, Richard Coudenhove-Kalergi, a Czech citizen, founded the Pan-European Union. Weimar Germany was becoming a great power, hence the importance of its reaction to the idea of European integration. The concept of "little Europe" was rejected. The union wanted to maintain cooperation with Great Britain, the USSR, and the United States. French-German rivalry was also an impeding factor. Each one of these powers believed the other to be striving for hegemony in a Pan-Europe. Opinions were divided over the setting up of a

customs union, which would have favored the modern branches of German industry. Based on contemporary printed documents and newspapers. Russian and German summaries.

R. Hetzron

418. Krohn, Claus-Dieter. HELFFERICH CONTRA HILFERDING. KONSERVATIVE GELDPOLITIK UND DIE SOZIALEN FOLGEN DER DEUTSCHEN INFLATION 1918-1923 [Helfferich vs. Hilferding: Conservative monetary policy and the social consequences of the German inflation, 1918-23]. *Vierteljahrschrift für Sozial- und Wirtschaftsgeschichte [West Germany] 1975 62(1): 62-92.* The German inflation, kindled by the Imperial Government's policy of paying for the war on credit, was used by big industry, banking, and agriculture to regain lost positions of economic power at the expense of wage earners. Under the guise of a monetary theory which identified monetary value with state power and blamed the Allies and German workers for inflation, the same groups were able through the *Rentenmark* scheme to end inflation while assuring the protection of their inflation gains and undermining the parliamentary order. Based on government and private papers in the Bundesarchiv, memoir and secondary literature; 104 notes.

D. Prowe

419. Krüger, Peter. BENEŠ UND DIE EUROPÄISCHE WIRTSCHAFTSKONZEPTION DES DEUTSCHEN STAATSSEKRETÄRS CARL VON SCHUBERT [Beneš and the concept of European economic cooperation as held by Carl von Schubert, German State Secretary]. *Bohemia. Jahrbuch des Collegium Carolinum [West Germany] 1973 14: 320-339.* In May 1928 Foreign Minister Eduard Beneš of Czechoslovakia visited Secretary Schubert at the German Foreign Office. In view of the Franco-German trade agreement of 1927, Schubert and Beneš agreed that Germany, Austria, and Czechoslovakia might cooperative economically within a larger European framework and without any implicit threat of German hegemony. In the charged political atmosphere of the time, Schubert's constructive idea could not bear fruit. Based on the Political Archives of the Foreign Office in Bonn and published sources; 40 notes.

R. E. Weltsch

420. Krüger, Peter. DER DEUTSCH-POLNISCHE SCHIEDSVERTRAG IM RAHMEN DER DEUTSCHEN SICHERHEITSINITIATIVE VON 1925 [The German-Polish arbitration treaty in the context of the German security initiative of 1925]. *Hist. Zeitschrift [West Germany] 1980 230(3): 577-612.* The Locarno Pact is the symbol of Germany's policy of reassurance in 1925, a policy designed to preclude action by France and Great Britain and to build good will for later improvements in Germany's status in Europe. The negotiation of the Polish-German arbitration treaty was also a part of this same initiative. Study of these negotiations reveals motives and techniques in German policy which clarify the overall reassurance program. Based on the Politisches Archiv des Auswärtigen Amtes in Bonn; 76 notes.

G. H. Davis

421. Krüger, Peter. FRIEDENSSICHERUNG UND DEUTSCHE REVISIONSPOLITIK. DIE DEUTSCHE AUSSENPOLITIK UND DIE VERHANDLUNGEN ÜBER DEN KELLOGG-PAKT [The securing of peace and German policy of revision: German foreign policy and the negotiations over the Kellogg Pact]. *Vierteljahrshefte für Zeitgeschichte [West Germany] 1974 22(3): 227-257.* The Kellogg-Briand Pact (1928) was not only a highly significant

concrete step toward the construction of a system of international security in the 1920's because it included for the first time the major Western powers excluded by the Versailles System and the League of Nations; it also represented a high point in German-American relations and a major move by Germany toward a policy of increasing realism. Initiated and chiefly executed during Stresemann's illness in the key years of 1927-28 by State Secretary Carl von Schubert, German foreign policy in its support of the Kellogg Treaty freed itself from a fixation on revision of Versailles and found a basis for an honest security policy without closing off the possibility of revision—a policy which ended with Stresemann's death and the subsequent dismissal of Schubert. Based on records from the Political Archive of the German Foreign Office and other documents and memoirs; 55 notes.   D. Prowe

422.   Kulski, W. W.   THE SOVIET UNION, GERMANY AND POLAND. *Polish Rev. 1978 23(1): 48-57.* Traces the history of German-Soviet maneuvers vis-à-vis Poland in the interwar period. In 1926, the two countries signed a treaty of friendship, but the Nazis were in turn friendly to the USSR and then to Poland. The 1939 Nazi-Soviet Pact included a secret protocol partitioning Poland. In 1941, Germany breached the pact, invading Soviet territory. 48 notes.
                                                                    J. Tull

423.   Kurata, Minoru.   RUDOLF HILFERDING. BIBLIOGRAPHIE SEINER SCHRIFTEN, ARTIKEL UND BRIEFE   [Rudolf Hilferding: a bibliography of his essays, articles, and letters]. *Int. Wissenschaftliche Korrespondenz zur Geschichte der Deutschen Arbeiterbewegung [West Germany] 1974 10(3): 327-346.* A chronological bibliography of 516 writings by Rudolf Hilferding (1877-?1941), Germany's Social Democratic Minister of Finance (1923, 1928-29) and important theorist. The article includes his little-known pamphlets, over 240 articles from *Neuer Vorwärts,* and unpublished letters located mainly at the Socialist Archives in Amsterdam and the Ebert Stiftung Archive in Bonn. Based on library and archival holdings in East and West Germany, Vienna, Amsterdam, London, Paris, Washington; 12 notes, index.   D. Prowe

424.   Kuzko, V. A. and L'vunin, Iu. A.   POMOSHCH TRUDIASH-CHIKHSIA SSSR RABOCHIM GERMANII V 1923-1924 GG   [Aid provided by Soviet workers to German workers, 1923-24]. *Voprosy Istorii [USSR] 1973 (12): 200-204.* The economic difficulties in Germany during 1923-24 caused much suffering among the country's working class, whose predicament aroused wide concern among Soviet workers. Special collections were organized and assistance provided to supply aid to the needy Germans. In 1923 the assistance provided amounted to some 800 wagonloads of grain and 33,000 roubles. In 1924 further aid was given, and a collection among workers in the Urals netted 2,000 gold roubles. Primary sources; 47 notes.   S

425.   Labuda, Gerard.   UMSTRITTENE FRAGEN DER DEUTSCH-POL-NISCHEN BEZIEHUNGEN. ZEHN THESEN ÜBER POLEN UND DEUTSCHLAND BIS 1939   [Controversial questions concerning German-Polish relations: ten theses referring to Poland and Germany up to 1939]. *Internationales Jahrbuch für Geschichts- und Geographie-Unterricht [West Germany] 1972/73 14: 166-177.* Offers a brief sketch of the following ten problems in German-Polish relations: 1) the Germans as heirs of the soil in the east, 2) the

theory of conquest as an explanation of the origins of the Polish state, 3) German colonization in Poland, 4) eminent German personalities in Polish history, 5) the partitions of Poland, 6) Prussia's and Austria's policy of germanization in Poland, 7) the theory of the Polish soil as belonging to and developed by the Germans, 8) the Polish Corridor and Danzig, 9) the German minority in Poland, and 10) the image each has of the other in literature and historiography.

J. B. Street

426. Lakowski, Richard and Wunderlich, Werner. SEEKRIEGSPLANUNG UND FLOTTENRÜSTUNG DES DEUTSCHEN IMPERIALISMUM VOR DEM ZWEITEN WELTKRIEG [Naval war planning and the naval armaments of German imperialism before World War II]. *Militärgeschichte [East Germany] 1974 13(6): 669-678.* The debate among Weimar naval theoreticians about future warfare resulted in the decision to build pocket battleships that could be used in North or Baltic Sea battles or in an Atlantic supply war. In the 1930's the Atlantic naval strategy gained ground but still theoreticians overvalued battleships and undervalued aircraft carriers and submarines. Gradually plans were directed principally against England, leading to the Z-Plan, which called for a navy that could fight both a supply war and against armed ships. At the outbreak of war in 1939 this plan was incomplete so that surface warfare ended in 1941 and submarine warfare in 1943. 37 notes.

H. D. Andrews

427. Laschitza, Annelies. SOZIALDEMOKRATIE UND IMPERIALISTISCHE DEUTSCHE MITTELEUROPA POLITIK. EIN BEITRAG ZUR STELLUNG DER VERSCHIEDENEN STRÖMUNGEN DER DEUTSCHEN SOZIALDEMOKRATIE ZUR IMPERIALISTISCHEN AUSSENPOLITIK [Social democracy and Imperial German Mitteleuropa policy: the positions of the various Social Democratic Party factions on foreign policy]. *Jahrbuch für Geschichte [East Germany] 1977 15: 107-144.* Social Democrats divided into three schools: 1) social imperialists who accepted Germany's status as a colonial and world power, 2) social pacifists who opposed all wars, and 3) left socialists who opposed only imperialist wars. When war came, all of the first group and much of the second voted for, with the others led by Karl Liebknecht voting against, war credits. Some social pacifists supported the idea of a United States of Europe, but Rosa Luxemburg opposed this as un-Marxist. She maintained that a united Europe, like a united Mitteleuropa, would be a front for German hegemony. 140 notes.

J. C. Billigmeier

428. Laubach, Ernst. MALTZANS AUFZEICHNUNGEN ÜBER DIE LETZEN VORGÄNGE VOR DEM ABSCHLUSS DES RAPALLO-VERTRAGES [Maltzan's notes concerning the final proceedings upon the conclusion of the Rapallo Treaty]. *Jahrbücher für Geschichte Osteuropas [West Germany] 1974 22(4): 556-579.* The Rapallo Treaty concluded in Genoa between Germany and the USSR (April 1922) enjoys a unique place in Weimar historiography. New evidence from private notes by Ago von Maltzan, Chief of Eastern Affairs in the Foreign Office, sheds new light on Walther Rathenau's participation in rapprochement with Russia. Heretofore, Rathenau's biographers (Kessler) and students of Rapallo (Linke, D'Abernon, etc.) have argued that Rathenau disagreed with Chancellor Karl J. Wirth's moves toward Russia. Archival and secondary sources; 114 notes.

J. R. Goldman

429.   Lee, Marshall M.   DISARMAMENT AND SECURITY: THE GER-
MAN SECURITY PROPOSALS IN THE LEAGUE OF NATIONS, 1926-
1930. A STUDY IN REVISIONIST AIMS IN AN INTERNATIONAL
ORGANIZATION. *Militärgeschichtliche Mitteilungen [West Germany] 1979
(1): 35-45.* German policy regarding League of Nations deliberations on security
and disarmament aimed at preserving freedom of revision of the Versailles Treaty
and securing parity of European armaments. The ultimate duplicity of German
diplomatic efforts emerged in the expansion of Council membership in an un-
wieldy size, thus assuring its noninterference in German revisionist aims. Based
on archival sources; 30 notes.   K. W. Estes

430.   Lee, Marshall M.   THE GERMAN ATTEMPT TO REFORM THE
LEAGUE: THE FAILURE OF GERMAN LEAGUE OF NATIONS POLICY
1930-1932.   *Francia [France] 1977 5: 473-490.* Germany attempted to reform
the League of Nations by enlarging the contingent of Germans in key positions
of the League's executive structure to gain influence and diminish French and
British domination. After six years of diplomatic activity in Geneva, Berlin
decided to retreat behind a weak and prestigeless "German permanent representative." Germany became further separated from the League. Primary documents; 37 notes.   G. E. Pergl

431.   Lippert, Hans-Joachim.   DOKUMENTE ZUM DEUTSCHEN
BAUERNKRIEG   [Documents on the German Peasants War]. *Archivmitteilungen [East Germany] 1975 25(3): 102-104.* Recalls the 1925 celebration of
the 400th anniversary of the great peasant revolt in Germany led by Thomas
Münzer; this was marked by Communists and Socialists with "proletarian"
dramas, despite police interference, and with other activities.

432.   Lönne, Karl-Egon.   ITALIEN UND DAS DEUTSCHLAND DES
VERSAILLER VERTRAGES   [Italy and Germany of the Versailles Treaty].
*Quellen und Forschungen aus Italienischen Archiven und Bibliotheken [Italy]
1973 53: 318-384.* Analyzes Alfredo Frassati's views of and reports on conditions
and trends in Germany during his service as Italian ambassador in Berlin in
1921-22. Frassati viewed German revival as a natural development after the
defeat of 1918 and argued that Italy and the Allies ought to adapt to this trend
rather than resist it. Postwar French hegemony in Europe narrowed Italian
diplomatic flexibility. Describes Frassati's philosophy of historical development
and how it was reflected in his reports. Based on documents in the historical
archive of the Italian foreign ministry, Frassati's correspondence with Giolitti,
and secondary works; 149 notes, appendix.   J. B. Street

433.   Lucas, Erhard.   DIE WIDERSTANDSBEWEGUNG GEGEN DEN
KAPP PUTSCH IN DER DDR-HISTORIOGRAPHIE   [The resistance
against the Kapp putsch in East German historiography]. *Internationale Wissenschaftliche Korrespondenz zur Geschichte der Deutschen Arbeiterbewegung
[West Germany] 1973 (18): 72-79.* A critical review of the 1972 East German
Kapp putsch study by Erwin Könnemann and Hans-Joachim Krusch, *Aktion-
seinheit contra Kapp-Putsch* (United Front vs. Kapp Putsch). The goal of the
authors is to present historical evidence for the continuing need for unified
progressive, democratic, and proletarian action. This goal has resulted in a distortion of the 1920 events and an account marred by errors, contradictions, and a

general tendency toward glorification and idealization. Based on primary and memoir literature; 17 notes.   D. Prowe

434. Luks, Leonid. DIE WEIMARER REPUBLIK IM SPIEGELBILD DER POLNISCHEN GESCHICHTSSCHREIBUNG NACH 1945 [The Weimar Republic as reflected in Polish historiography since 1945]. *Vierteljahrshefte für Zeitgeschichte [West Germany] 1980 28(4): 410-439.* Polish historians since 1945 have not followed Soviet Marxist interpretations of the Weimar Republic but have strongly criticized not only the Versailles Treaty for its leniency, but also the treaties of Rapallo (1922) and Locarno (1925) for directing Germany's energies toward Poland, and especially Foreign Minister Gustav Stresemann (1923-29) for his anti-Polish revisionism. Interpretations of the Nazi rise to power have, on the other hand, been quite differentiated and influenced by West German scholarship. Based on historical literature published in Poland, 1945-49 and 1956-78; 134 notes.   D. Prowe

435. Mann, Thomas. INFLATION: THE WITCHES' SABBATH: GERMANY 1923. *Encounter [Great Britain] 1975 44(2): 60-63.* Discusses inflation, raw materials shortages, and profiteering in Germany in 1923, emphasizing their relationship to World War I.

436. Marks, Sally and Dulude, Denis. GERMAN-AMERICAN RELATIONS, 1918-1921. *Mid-American 1971 53(4): 211-226.* From the armistice in 1918 until the Treaty of Berlin in 1921, the United States maintained no official diplomatic relations with Germany. It did, however, conduct extensive unofficial relations and maintained several quasi-official agents in Berlin. Ellis Loring Dresel was the central figure representing the United States in Germany but others like Captain W. R. Gherardi and Hague legation senior clerk Charles B. Dyar also served in Berlin. After some concern about rising Bolshevism and internal disorder, the function of Dresel became chiefly that of facilitating the reestablishment of relations, which led to the Treaty of Berlin, securing all the rights of the Versailles Treaty with none of its burdens or costs. Primary sources; 44 notes.
                                                                          T. D. Schoonover

437. Marks, Sally. THE MYTHS OF REPARATIONS. *Central European Hist. 1978 11(3): 231-255.* Argues that the actual amount of reparations required of Germany and its allies after World War I was not the 132 billion marks cited in the London Schedule of 1921 but the 50 million marks stipulated in the A and B Bonds. Germany actually paid very little and most of that was paid for out of loans from Western bankers. The Ruhr occupation was both justified and profitable, but sympathy for Germany and Stresemann's shrewdness led to reductions in the total reparations bill both in the Dawes and the Young Plans. While it may not have been wise to seek reparations from Germany, "it was unwise to inflict the insult without rigorous enforcement." 85 notes.   C. R. Lovin

438. Martin, Bernd. GERMANY BETWEEN CHINA AND JAPAN: GERMAN FAR EASTERN POLICY OF THE INTERWAR PERIOD. *Bull. of the Inst. of Modern Hist. Acad. Sinica [Taiwan] 1978 7: 593-610.* Analyzes the relationships between Germany, Japan, and China between the two World Wars. Argues that historically, German foreign policy was pro-Chinese, and that Germany and Japan were unlikely allies. Hitler's rise to power coincided with the

political ascendancy of the Japanese army, and the two countries embarked on a policy of military expansion which brought them together in the Anti-Comintern Pact of 1936. Secondary sources; 49 notes.   C. C. Brown

439. Mayer, Klaus. WEHRMACHTSGENERÄLE IN DER POLITISCHEN ARENA [German army generals in the political arena]. *Neue Politische Literatur [West Germany] 1979 24(1): 85-93.* During the Weimar Republic, officers of the German army in World War I, including Generals Ludwig Beck, Heinz Guderian, Alfred Jodl, Walter von Seydlitz and Hans Speidel, tried to create a political system that guaranteed a quiet home front in case of war. The opposition of conservative officers to Nazism was not based on democratic political ideas but on the social origins and primitivism of Nazi leaders. 42 notes.   R. Wagnleitner

440. Megerle, Klaus. DANZIG, KORRIDOR UND OBERSCHLESIEN. ZUR DEUTSCHEN REVISIONSPOLITIK GEGENÜBER POLEN IN DER LOCARNODIPLOMATIE [Danzig, the corridor and Upper Silesia: German revisionist policy in relation to Poland in the Locarno negotiations]. *Jahrbuch für die Geschichte Mittel- und Ostdeutschlands [West Germany] 1976 25: 145-178.* From 1925 in the negotiations leading up to the Treaty of Locarno German foreign policy was able to switch from the defensive to the offensive on the question of the eastern frontiers. Here every possible means was exploited to further German objectives, including the exploitation of Poland's economic dependence on Germany and the support of German minorities. However, contrary to the East German view, there is insufficient evidence that the use of force was seriously envisaged in order to achieve a solution. In fact, German policy was based on its own dependence on the Western powers and the creation of a capitalist community of interests to gain support for the enforcement of a solution favoring Germany. Based on German foreign office documents and secondary works; 121 notes.   J. A. Perkins

441. Mendel, Roberta. RAPALLO AND THE SECOND WORLD WAR. *East Europe 1975 24(1): 13-20.* The Treaty of Rapallo (1922) was responsible for Germany's resumed strength by 1939 and the assurgence of Soviet Russia.

442. Merker, Paul. ERINNERUNGEN AN DEN GEWERKSCHAFTLICHEN KAMPF DES BERLINER GASTSTÄTTENPROLETARIATS (1920/1921) [Memoirs of the trade union struggle of the Berlin restaurant workers, 1920-21]. *Beiträge zur Geschichte der Arbeiterbewegung [East Germany] 1973 15(3): 466-471.* The November Revolution mobilized workers in cafés, restaurants, and hotels, and in 1920-21 the class-conscious groups within the trade concentrated on the trade union struggle for the eight-hour day, better working conditions, and better wages. The climax of the strike movement was the strike of 40,000 Berlin restaurant, café, and hotel workers between 30 September and 7 November 1921, in which the author organized the strike in the district Berlin-West. Based on personal recollections.   R. Wagnleitner

443. Meyers, Reinhard. DAS RHEINLAND IN DER POLITIK DER EUROPÄISCHEN MÄCHTE DER ZWISCHENKRIEGSZEIT: ANMERKUNGEN ZUR NEUEREN LITERATUR [The Rhineland in the politics of the European powers of the interwar period: remarks on the recent literature].

Rheinische Vierteljahrsblätter [West Germany] 1979 (43): 303-314. Recent historical studies on the interwar period have increasingly shown the central position of the Rhineland, not only as focus of German domestic policies, but of European strategic and military policies.

444. Michal, Wolfgang. BASISDEMOKRAT DÖBLIN [Alfred Döblin, fundamental democrat]. *Frankfurter Hefte [West Germany] 1982 37(1): 10-12.* In 1919 Alfred Döblin (1878-1957) recognized the coming importance of Africa and China, predicted the convergence of capitalism and communism, interpreted the Weimar Republic as a peaceful form of capitalism, and demanded the democracy of the base in the form of councils and popular initiatives, demands that were strongly opposed by German socialists and communists.

445. Milkowski, Fritz. "DAS FREIE WORT" 1929-1933 [*Das freie Wort* 1929-33]. *Zeitschrift für Geschichtswissenschaft [East Germany] 1976 24(1): 42-48.* The issues of the Social Democratic journal *Das Freie Wort* document the split of the German Social Democratic Party into a social reformist and a revolutionary fraction. Based on the journal *Das Freie Wort,* other primary and secondary sources; 40 notes. R. Wagnleitner

446. Mohler, Armin. DAS BUCH "DIE KONSERVATIVE REVOLUTION IN DEUTSCHLAND" DREI JAHRZEHNTE SPÄTER [*The Conservative Revolution in Germany* 30 years later]. *Rev. d'Allemagne [France] 1982 14(1): 161-164.* Current French research on the conservative revolution prompts Armin Mohler to explain some of the basic assumptions and premises of his *The Conservative Revolution in Germany* (1950), of which a third edition is in preparation. Notes that his identification of National Socialism and the conservative revolution was a naive error, and he now recognizes that there is only a tenuous distinction between conservatism and the conservative revolution. Note. J. S. Gassner

447. Möller, Horst. PREUSSENS DEMOKRATISCHE SENDUNG: ZUR OTTO-BRAUN-BIOGRAPHIE VON HAGEN SCHULZE [Prussia's democratic mission: the Otto Braun biography by Hagen Schulze]. *Jahrbuch für die Geschichte Mittel- und Ostdeutschlands [West Germany] 1980 29: 113-119.* Hagen Schulze's *Otto Braun oder Preussens demokratische Sendung* stands not only as a definitive biography of Otto Braun, Social Democratic Minister-President of Prussia during the Weimar Republic, but as one of the most significant contributions to the history of Prussia as well. Exhausting all possible sources with the exception of unavailable archival materials in the German Democratic Republic, Schulze has dealt with virtually all significant aspects of Prussian politics during the Weimar period. He poignantly depicts the hopelessness of the political situation by the winter of 1931-32 and Braun's increasing inability to influence the course of events. With Franz von Papen's coup of 20 July 1932, the erstwhile capable and determined "red tsar" of Prussia gave up the struggle and went into exile a depressed and broken man. S. A. Welisch

448. Moravocová, Dagmar. POČÁTKY TEORIE "ORGANIZOVANÉHO KAPITALISMU" V NĚMECKU (HOSPODÁŘSKÁ KONCEPCE A POLITIKA WALTHERA RATHENAUA) [Beginnings of the theory of "organized capitalism" in Germany: the economic conception and policy of Walther

Rathenau]. *Československý Časopis Hist. [Czechoslovakia] 1979 27(4): 514-539.* With his rich background in corporate management and his experience as coordinator of supplies during World War I, Walther Rathenau (1867-1922) became Germany's minister of reconstruction in 1921 and foreign minister in 1922. Since 1907 he had elaborated economic reforms which involved greater governmental coordination of business and a stronger partnership between monopoly capital and organized labor. Though in 1918 such policies served to forestall a social revolution, most German monopolists suspected or rejected them. After the Rapallo Treaty with the USSR (1922), the assassination of Rathenau by right-wing nationalists freed German big business from the threat of further government interference. Primary sources; 148 notes.   R. E. Weltsch

449. Morsey, Rudolf. DER STAATSMANN IM KÖLNER OBERBÜR-GERMEISTER KONRAD ADENAUER [The mayor of Cologne, Konrad Adenauer, as statesman]. *Rheinische Vierteljahrsblätter [West Germany] 1976 40(1-4): 199-211.* As mayor of Cologne during the Weimar Republic, Konrad Adenauer's politics were already based on his personal faith in the republican and democratic constitution. For Adenauer, the Rhineland was the center of German culture, politics, and economy. Realizing the danger the great number of parties had for the parliamentary system, Adenauer promoted the establishment of a parliamentary system that was based on a small group of democratic parties. Based on secondary literature; 34 notes.   R. Wagnleitner

450. Moses, John A. THE CONCEPT OF ECONOMIC DEMOCRACY WITHIN THE GERMAN SOCIALIST TRADE UNIONS DURING THE WEIMAR REPUBLIC: THE EMERGENCE OF AN ALTERNATIVE ROUTE TO SOCIALISM. *Labour Hist. [Australia] 1978 (34): 45-57.* The German Free Trade Unions developed a program of economic democracy during the 1920's, a plan which drew strong industrial opposition after 1928. Unions upheld the Weimar Republic, acting as champions and guardians of the national economy, with socialism as the ultimate, not immediate goal. The unions opposed the rightists during the Kapp Putsch of 1924 and rejected the Franco-Belgian occupation of the Ruhr. The 1928 statement by Fritz Naphtali for the democratization of the work force culminated in the conception of economic democracy. From the 1929 economic crash to the Nazi seizure of power, the trade unions clung to the Weimar Republic. Table, 35 notes.   D. F. Schafer

451. Most, Eckhard. PERSPEKTIVEN DER DEUTSCHEN AUSSEN-POLITIK ZWISCHEN LOCARNO UND DEM 2. WELTKRIEG. BEMER-KUNGEN ZU DREI NEUERSCHEININGEN [Perspectives of German foreign policy between Locarno and World War II: remarks on three new works]. *Francia [France] 1975 3: 690-698.* Reviews W. Weidenfeld, *Die Englandpolitik Gustav Stresemanns. Theoretische und praktische Aspekte der Aussenpolitik,* (Mainz: Hase und Koehler, 1972); J. Jacobson, *Locarno Diplomacy: Germany and the West 1925-1929* (Princeton: U. Pr., 1972); and O. Hauser, *England und das Dritte Reich. Eine dokumentierte Geschichte der englisch-deutschen Beziehungen von 1933 bis 1939 auf Grund unveröffentlichter Akten aus dem britischen Staatsarchiv,* Vol. I, 1933-36 (Stuttgart: Seewald, 1972). Comments on these works as they deal with British policy toward Germany, 1920's-30's and its continuing ambiguities. 12 notes.   J. C. Billigmeier

452. Mueller, Gordon H. RAPALLO REEXAMINED: A NEW LOOK AT GERMANY'S SECRET MILITARY COLLABORATION WITH RUSSIA IN 1922. *Military Affairs 1976 40(3): 109-117.* The Rapallo Treaty was closely related to secret military and political objectives that never came to light. Even without conclusive support, records show that Germany's entire military relationship with Russia was far more extensive and important than previously thought. There was some relationship between Rapallo and the subterranean military arrangements, and one agreement may have included either a defensive or offensive military alliance against Poland. The author includes the text of the reported military convention between the USSR and Germany and an analysis of the Joseph Wirth (1879-1956) letters, 1933-45. Primary and secondary sources; 63 notes.
A. M. Osur

453. Müller, Klaus. AGRARISCHE INTERESSENVERBÄNDE IN DER WEIMARER REPUBLIK [Agrarian lobbies in the Weimar Republic]. *Rheinische Vierteljahrsblätter [West Germany] 1974 38(1-4): 386-405.* The breakdown of the German monarchy in 1918 caused deep changes in the attitudes of the German rural population. The different political and economic needs of the peasants of various parts of Germany hindered the establishment of a unified agricultural lobby or party, while the agricultural crises of the 1920's impoverished great parts of the rural population. The Reichslandbund and the Vereinigung der deutschen Bauernvereine opposed the democratic form of government, supported radical right-wing movements, and prepared the victory of the national socialists in the rural areas. Based on secondary literature and newspapers; 90 notes.
R. Wagnleitner

454. Müller, Rolf-Dieter. DIE DEUTSCHEN GASKRIEGVOR-BEREITUNGEN 1919-1945. MIT GIFTGAS ZUR WELTMACHT? [The German chemical warfare preparations 1919-45: toward world power with poison gas?]. *Militärgeschichtliche Mitteilungen [West Germany] 1980 (1): 25-54.* Details German research, stockpiling, and planning for chemical warfare after World War I. The German army planned the use of military gas as the only way to fight a major war under the Versailles limitations. Experimental stations in Russia subverted Versailles prohibitions, and these activities were transferred to Germany in 1933 with the Nazi seizure of power. Major production planned by chemical officers and industrialists did not synchronize with the Blitzkrieg economy and military operations, and proposals for a nerve gas wonder weapon late in the war were thwarted by lack of defensive measures and raw materials and the Allied advance. Based upon documents of the Military Archives, Freiberg; 5 tables, 45 notes.
K. W. Estes

455. Mullin, John Robert. CITY PLANNING IN FRANKFURT, GERMANY, 1925-1932: A STUDY IN PRACTICAL UTOPIANISM. *J. of Urban Hist. 1977 4(1): 3-28.* Weimar Germany is not commonly thought of as a location of governmental innovation, but the city planning programs formulated and carried out in Frankfurt during 1925-32 combined advanced planning and land management concepts, progressive design features, and a socialist political element into an experiment in city planning with lasting impact. Under the tutelage of Ernst May the city formulated a master plan of development and, at least initially, vigorously carried out that plan. Although political changes in Germany ultimately led to the abandonment of the plan, it provided an enduring example of the concept of urban planning on its highest level.
T. W. Smith

456. Muñiz, Jaime Nicolas. NOTAS SOBRE EL SISTEMA ELECTORAL ALEMÁN [Germany's electoral system]. *Rev. Española de la Opinión Pública [Spain] 1976 (45): 111-132.* Examines the electoral system of the Weimar Republic and the background to the creation of West Germany and its subsequent development.

457. Murray, Williamson. BRITISH AND GERMAN AIR DOCTRINE BETWEEN THE WARS. *Air U. Rev. 1980 31(3): 39-58.* Compares the development of German and British air force doctrines during the 1920's and 30's and assesses their effectiveness at the outbreak of World War II.

458. Muth, Heinrich. AKTEN DER REICHSKANZLEI [Documents from the Reichskanzlei]. *Geschichte in Wissenschaft und Unterricht [West Germany] 1976 27(12): 790-792.* Reviews the edition of documents from the Reichskanzlei, 1919-33. They show political development as seen by the cabinet and provide insights into the workings of the cabinet. All volumes have exhaustive commentaries. Based on the cabinet minutes in the federal archive in Koblenz.
H. W. Wurster

459. Nair, M. P. Sreekumar. GERMANY AND INDIA'S STRUGGLE FOR FREEDOM WITH SPECIAL REFERENCE TO THE GERMAN WORKING CLASS MOVEMENT. *J. of Indian Hist. [India] 1978 56(2): 351-363.* Surveys the efforts of Germans and Indians in Germany to gain India's independence. In 1907 Har Dayal, Sadar Singh Rana, and Virenda Chattopadhyaya represented India in the International Socialist Congress held in Stuttgart, Germany. In 1919 M. N. Roy settled in Berlin and associated himself with Socialist, Communist, and other revolutionary groups to struggle for India's independence from the British Empire. During the 1920's Roy worked vigorously with the leaders of the German working class movements including Ernst Meyer, August Thalheimer, and Wilhelm Pieck. Secondary sources; 29 notes.
S. H. Frank

460. Nastovici, Ema. INPLICAȚII ECONOMICE ȘI POLITICE ALE CRIZEI PROBLEMEI REPARAȚIILOR DIN ANUL 1923 [The economic and political implications of the reparations problem crisis, 1923]. *Rev. de Istorie [Rumania] 1977 30(9): 1607-1623.* Examines the worsening social, political, and economic situation in the Weimar Republic immediately before and after the occupation of the Ruhr. Stresses the attitudes of both the defeated working classes, and the lesser allies including Rumania, who were discontented with their inequitable treatment. The remedial measures of the Dawes Plan of 1924 were of a temporary nature, and the problems of the war reparations continued until 1932. 66 notes.
R. O. Khan

461. Naumov, G. V. K ISTORII OTECHESTVENNOI PARTII GERMANII (OBZOR ISTOCHNIKOV) [On the history of the German Fatherland Party: a review of the sources]. *Vestnik Moskovskogo U., Seriia 9: Istoriia [USSR] 1975 30(5): 21-33.* Considers some of the correspondence of Wolfgang Kapp, leader of the Fatherland Party, and examines his personal archive. The latter includes documents emanating from the founding committees of the Party, and provides information on the party's structure, charter, links with the German

government, propaganda machinery, and termination. Though politically adapt-able, the party was guided by the goals of reconciling its members to government policy and gaining peace through victory. Its stake in private industry and the right-wing press helped it to influence the government and prolong the war. 84 notes.

                                                                    M. R. Colenso

462. Niemann, Hans-Werner. DIE ANFÄNGE DER STAATLICHEN ELEKTRIZITÄTSVERSORGUNG IM KÖNIGREICH SACHSEN [The beginnings of state electricity production in the Kingdom of Saxony]. *Zeitschrift für Unternehmensgeschichte [West Germany] 1978 23(2): 98-117.* In 1916 the government of Saxony began to take over the production of electricity in order to promote uniform economic development, to balance the interests of major and minor consumers, and to assure a reliable source of power for the state-owned railroads. The program began gradually, with the purchase of privately-owned companies and the construction of state power lines. By 1936 most electrical production in the state was in public hands, reaping large profits for the govern-ment. Primary and secondary sources; 52 notes.   J. T. Walker

463. Niemann, Heinz. DAS GÖRLITZER PROGRAMM DER SPD VON 1921 [The Görlitz program of the SPD of 1921]. *Zeitschrift für Geschichtswis-senschaft [East Germany] 1975 23(8): 908-919.* The political platform formulated by the German Social Democratic Party (SPD) in Görlitz in July 1921 gave theoretical justification for the opportunist course the SPD has followed since the beginning of the Weimar Republic. Rejecting the Marxist-Leninist concept of the dictatorship of the proletariat, the SPD sought to attract bourgeois voters by proclaiming the reformist thesis of the Third Way between communism and capitalism. The party condemned Bolshevism and promoted the integration of the working class into the capitalist state. 52 notes.   J. T. Walker

464. Niemann, Heinz. DAS HEIDELBERGER PROGRAMM DER SPD VON 1925 [The Heidelberg Program of the German Social Democrats 1925]. *Zeitschrift für Geschichtswissenschaft [East Germany] 1976 24(7): 786-794.* Al-though the Heidelberg program of the German Social Democrats in 1925 was written in Marxist terminology, it was a milestone in the development of demo-cratic socialism. The Heidelberg program supported the tactical position of the opportunists of the right wing of the party. Based on documents in the Interna-tionales Institut für Sozialgeschichte, Amsterdam, printed documents and sec-ondary literature; 29 notes.   R. Wagnleitner

465. Nuss, K. K VOPROSU O REAKTSIONNOI SUSHCHNOSTI VZGLIADOV VOENNYKH DEIATELEI GERMANII (1919-1933 GG.) [The reactionary essence of the views of German militarists, 1919-33]. *Voenno-Istoricheskii Zhurnal [USSR] 1981 23(1): 63-70.* Outlines the main stages in the growth of German militarism and rearmament during the Weimar Republic and analyzes the political and economic factors behind the establishment of the Nazi dictatorship. German militarism was in part an attempt to halt the advance of socialism and conspired with the right wing of the Social Democrats to keep the workers in check. On an international level the strictures of the Treaty of Ver-sailles were instrumental in provoking the crises that in turn led to World War II. Based on material from State Archive Dresden; 8 notes.   A. Brown

466. Orde, Anne. THOIRY REVISITED. *Durham U. J. [Great Britain] 1975 67(2): 205-218.* On 17 September 1926, eleven months after the Locarno conference and a week after Germany's entry into the League of Nations, the foreign ministers of France and Germany held a private meeting at Thoiry near Geneva. For a while Franco-German reconciliation seemed possible, France offered an early evacuation of the Rhineland and the return of the Saar in exchange for a contribution to French finances through the commercialization of part of Germany's reparations. The author reconsiders in detail the Thoiry discussions, utilizing recently released official French archival material together with German and British documentary evidence. She provides fresh insights into the origins of the financial proposal and the aftermath of the meeting, and concludes that the Thoiry proposals rapidly became insignificant because they were far in advance of French public opinion. The article includes a transcript (in French) entitled "Notes On The Thoiry Interview" taken from the archives of the French Ministry of Foreign Affairs. Primary and secondary sources; 48 notes.   R. G. Neville

467. Orlova, M. I. BURZHUAZNAIA ISTORIOGRAFIIA FRG O RA-PALL'SKOI POLITIKE VEIMARSKOI RESPUBLIKI [The Weimar Republic's Rapallo policy as reflected in West German bourgeois historiography]. *Voprosy Istorii [USSR] 1978 (11): 68-84.* Analyzing the principal trends in bourgeois historiography, the author comes to the conclusion that there is no concurrence of opinion among West German historians concerning the Weimar Republic's Rapallo policy. Some of them regard the Rapallo treaty as an instrument for revising the results of the First World War by military means, others as an instrument for maintaining a balance of forces in Europe, which did not preclude the possibility of changing the Versailles system by peaceful means in conjunction with the policy of peaceful coexistence with the Land of Soviets. A number of historians occupy an intermediate position. In defining the driving forces of the Weimar Republic's Rapallo policy, both right-liberal and moderately liberal historians fail to take into account the socioeconomic relations obtaining in Germany during the period under review and ignore the position of the working class—the chief mainstay of the peaceful coexistence policy.   J

468. Orlow, Dietrich. PREUSSEN UND DER KAPP-PUTSCH [Prussia and the Kapp Putsch]. *Viertel Jahrshefte für Zeitgeschichte [West Germany] 1978 26(2): 191-236.* The abortive Kapp Putsch (March 1920) a year and a half after the establishment of the Weimar Republic actually led to the stabilization of parliamentary democracy in the key state of Prussia. By remaining in Berlin, negotiating both with the putschists and with radical leftists and unions, Prussian parliamentary leaders, primarily Social Democrats, gained in stature and were able to strengthen the center parliamentary coalition against both rightist pressures for an antisocialist bloc and leftist and labor union demands for a pure socialist government. Based on Prussian and SPD records, papers in the International Socialist archive (Amsterdam), German federal (Koblenz), state, and other archives, secondary sources; 339 notes.   D. Prowe

469. Orlow, Dietrich. REVIEW ARTICLE. *Central European Hist. 1975 8(2): 188-194.* Lothar Albertin's *Liberalismus und Demokratie am Anfang der Weimarer Republik* (Dusseldorf: Droste Verlag, 1973) is a welcome addition to the growing number of works on the positive effort of "liberals" in the Weimar

Republic. Although the potential of this group was never fully realized, it developed a significant and positive program for the republic which is often overlooked.
                                                                                                                    C. R. Lovin

470. Pachter, Henry. WAS WEIMAR NECESSARY? *Dissent 1977 24(1):* *78-88.* The abortive *Räte* Movement of 1918-21 in Germany might have provided a viable democratic alternative to the Weimar Republic.

471. Petersen, Jens. IL FASCISMO ITALIANO VISTO DALLA REPUBBLICA DI WEIMAR [Italian Fascism as seen by the Weimar Republic]. *Storia Contemporanea [Italy] 1978 9(3): 497-529.* Assesses the reaction of Germans to Italian Fascism, who saw it as a new middle-class attempt to prevent communism from spreading in Europe. The Fascist takeover in Italy was the result of an alliance between the state and the business world. Mussolini was characterized as a man of vigorous opportunism and stubbornness. The power of the party was due to Mussolini and not vice versa. The Germans attributed to the Duce a lack of moral scruples, Latin versatility, tactical flexibility, and a demoniac will power. Fascism brought equilibrium to Europe, and Germans anticipated that Italian common sense would prevent a policy of territorial expansion. Secondary sources; 203 notes.
                                                                                                                    A. Sbacchi

472. Peterson, Brian. THE POLITICS OF WORKING-CLASS WOMEN IN THE WEIMAR REPUBLIC. *Central European Hist. 1977 10(2): 87-111.* A statistical analysis of the role of working women in Germany in the Reichstag elections of 1924. The results are correlated with materials available from the census of 1925. Women workers were important in the labor movement, and tended to support Social Democrats rather than Communists. The home is the key to an understanding of women's politics. Based on published statistics and secondary works; 52 notes, methodological appendix.
                                                                                                                    C. R. Lovin

473. Petta, Paolo. SCHMITT, KELSEN E IL "CUSTODE DELLA COSTITUZIONE" [Schmitt, Kelsen and the "guardian of the constitution"]. *Storia e Politica [Italy] 1977 16(3): 505-551.* According to Carl Schmitt (b. 1888) politics is a struggle between *amicus* (friend) and *hostis* (adversary) and the people may only "acclaim" a leader. According to Hans Kelsen (b. 1881) democracy is necessary and is the only method of guaranteeing the pluralism of positions. Therefore in a discussion in 1931 Schmitt attached importance to the president of the republic in the Weimar constitution whereas Kelsen regarded the Constitutional Court as the guardian of the constitution. 67 notes.
                                                                                                                    A. Canavero

474. Petzina, Dietmar. GEWERKSCHAFTEN UND MONOPOLFRAGE VOR UND WÄHREND DER WEIMARER REPUBLIK [Trade unions and monopolies before and during the Weimar Republic]. *Archiv für Sozialgeschichte [West Germany] 1980 20: 195-217.* Examines how unions reacted to economic concentration and how it determined their policy. Increasing concentration was generally considered an economic necessity, an evolutionary step toward socialism; the unions had only to counteract the negative effects on the working class. World War I increased the concentration process and brought about the unions' participation in economic administration. This cooperation, and concomitant positive judgement of monopolies, continued after the war, but when big business

had regained its economic and political power, the unions had to recognize that their policy was wrong. The *Notverordnung* (emergency decree) against trusts, 1923, was the first step in the new direction. The world economic crisis intensified the problems and led to the *Notverordnung* of 26 July 1930. Contemporary publications; table, 59 notes.   H. W. Wurster

475. Petzold, Joachim.   KONSERVATIVE REVOLUTIONSDEMAGO-GIE. EDGAR JULIUS JUNGS VERHÄLTNIS ZUR WEIMARER REPUB-LIK UND ZUR FASCHISTISCHEN DIKTATUR   [Conservative demagogy on revolution. Edgar Julius Jung's relationship to the Weimar Republic and to fascist dictatorship]. *Zeitschrift für Geschichtswissenschaft [East Germany] 1975 23(3): 284-294.* Examines the "conservative revolution" in post-World War I Germany. Unlike the older conservative element, which sought restoration of the monarchy, the new conservatives wanted a rebuilt Germany to be controlled by middle-class wealth. Edgar Julius Jung was the theoretical founder of this move-ment. In 1923 he tried to ally himself with Adolf Hitler, who, instead turned his energies to the unsuccessful revolt in Munich. Although an important precursor of Hitler's fascist rule, Jung fell in a 1934 purge of potential rivals to the National Socialist leader. Primary and secondary sources; 27 notes.   G. H. Libbey

476. Petzold, Joachim.   MONOPOLKAPITAL UND FASCHISTISCHE IDEOLOGIE. ZUR ROLLE DER JUNGKONSERVATIVEN IN DER WEI-MARER REPUBLIK   [Monopoly capital and fascist ideology. On the role of the young conservatives in the Weimar Republic]. *Zeitschrift für Geschichtswis-senschaft [East Germany] 1977 25(3): 295-304.* During the Weimar Republic conservative capital and fascist ideology came together in political association. Leading this organization was Heinrich Class who, as early as 1912, recognized the value to conservatives of a workers' party such as the Nazi Party later became. Young conservatives funded many antisocialist activities during the 1920's; sup-port for Adolf Hitler was the logical step for wealthy and nationalist young conservatives. 61 notes.   G. H. Libbey

477. Petzold, Joachim.   ZUR KONTINUITÄT DER BALKANPOLITIK DES DEUTSCHEN IMPERIALISMUS IN DER ZEIT DER WEIMARER REPUBLIK   [Continuity of the Balkan policy of German imperialism at the time of the Weimar Republic]. *Jahrbuch für Geschichte der Sozialistischen Länder Europas [East Germany] 1975 19(2): 173-183.* Articles concerning Ger-man policies toward the Balkans published in the political magazine *Die Tat* afford an insight into the discussion and final formulation of imperialist strategies.

478. Pohl, Karl Heinrich.   DIE FINANZKRISE BEI KRUPP UND DIE SICHERHEITSPOLITIK STRESEMANNS. EIN BEITRAG ZUM VER-HÄLTNIS VON WIRTSCHAFT UND AUSSENPOLITIK IN DER WEI-MARER REPUBLIK   [Krupp's financial crisis and the security policy of Stresemann. A contribution to the relationship of economics to foreign policy in the Weimar Republic]. *Vierteljahrschrift für Sozial- und Wirtschaftsgeschichte [West Germany] 1974 61(4): 505-525.* Financially threatened, Gustav Krupp (1870-1950) gained not only a 40 million mark government subsidy and loan package through connections to Chancellor Hans Luther (1879-1962) and the Defense Ministry, but also dodged both a government condition of a simultaneous credit from private sources and bank pressure to join the national steel trust.

Krupp did this by threatening Gustav Stresemann's (1878-1929) goal of economic cooperation with France by proposing the sale of 50% of Krupp's stock to England. Based on archival research (Krupp, Bundesarchiv Koblenz, Auswärtiges Amt, Archives Vienna, Munich, Potsdam) and secondary works; 98 notes.

D. Prowe

479. Pohl, Karl Heinrich. DIE "STRESEMANNSCHE AUSSEN-POLITIK" UND DAS WESTEUROPÄISCHE EISENKARTELL 1926. "EUROPÄISCHE POLITIK" ODER NATIONALES INTERESSE? [Stresemann's foreign policy and the Western European Iron Cartel in 1926: European politics or national interest?]. *Vierteljahrschrift für Sozial- und Wirtschaftsgeschichte [West Germany] 1978 65(4): 511-534.* German heavy industry's promotion of the Western European Iron Cartel of 1926 was a vital part of Germany's drive for recovery of national power under the cloak of Gustav Stresemann's "European policy" in the 1920's. The German Foreign Office saw in the iron industry's efforts, which were actually concerned with profit and expansion, a key tool of its national power politics and paid off industrialists with concessions in economic and social policy at home. Based on Gute Hoffnungshütte, Foreign Office, German Federal, Austrian, and Bavarian state archives and secondary Stresemann literature; 94 notes.

D. Prowe

480. Pohl, Karl Heinrich. RHEINISCHE JAHRTAUSENDFEIER UND DEUTSCHE LOCARNO-POLITIK: ZU EINIGEN VORAUSSETZUNGEN DER AUSSENPOLITIK IN DER WEIMARER REPUBLIK [The millennium celebration in the Rhineland and German Locarno policies: some conditions on foreign policy in the Weimar Republic]. *Rheinische Vierteljahrsblätter [West Germany] 1979 (43): 289-317.* Besides German trading interests, the unsolved problem of disarmament, and the attraction of the League of Nations, German initiatives for an improvement of German-French relations in the early 1920's were hindered by the occupied territories, especially the Cologne Zone. The compromises of the Luther-Stresemann government and the acceptance of the German western border met with rigid opposition not only from the right-wing parties, but also from members of the government. The celebration of the millennium of the Rhineland as part of the German empire in 1924 was planned in order to counteract French plans to annex the Rhineland. Based on documents in the Bundesarchiv Koblenz, secondary literature; 136 notes.

R. Wagnleitner

481. Poniatowska, Anna. ORGANIZACJE POLSKIE W BERLINIE W LATACH REPUBLIKI WEIMARSKIEJ [Polish organizations in Berlin during the Weimar period]. *Przegląd Zachodni [Poland] 1975 31(5-6): 40-66.* Surveys the various Polish social organizations in Berlin in the 1920's. They include the National Committee, educational organizations, choral societies, youth groups, and cultural associations.

482. Poniatowska, Anna. WYBORY I PRACA POLSKICH POSŁÓW W NIEMCZECH W RELACJACH *DZIENNIKA BERLIŃSKIEGO* W LATACH 1923-1933 [Elections and the work of members of parliament in Germany, according to reports by the *Berlin Journal* in the years 1923-1933]. *Przegląd Zachodni [Poland] 1979 35(2): 53-63.* Poles remaining in Germany after World War I organized the Union of Poles in Germany, and its organ the *Berlin*

Journal. A major effort was made to obtain parliamentary representation, thwarted by the too stringent membership requirements for the German parliament. But in the November 1922 elections Poles gained two members in the Prussian parliament. The Polish leader, Jan Baczewski, was a skilled parliamentarian, and after a long fight he obtained financing for Polish schools from the Prussian state. Poles retained their two members only through the 1924 elections. Primary sources.   M. Krzyzaniak

483.   Prehn, Helmut.   DIE ROLLE DER SIEDLUNGSPOLITIK IN DER ZEIT DER WELTWIRTSCHAFTSKRISE 1929 BIS 1932 [The role of settlement policy in the world economic crisis, 1929-32]. *Wissenschaftliche Zeitschrift der U. Rostock. Gesellschafts- und Sprachwissenschaftliche Reihe [East Germany] 1973 22(3): 211-219.* Between 1929 and 1932 the German government continued to subsidize bankrupt landlords. The settlement of unemployed peasants was only carried through on those properties that were impossible to save with public financial support. Based on published documents and secondary literature; 6 tables, 69 notes.   R. Wagnleitner

484.   Pryce, Donald B.   THE REICH GOVERNMENT VERSUS SAXONY, 1923: THE DECISION TO INTERVENE.   *Central European Hist. 1977 10(2): 112-147.* Elaborates on the actions of Saxon and reich leaders in the crisis in Saxony which led to the removal of the Saxon Socialist-Communist coalition government and the appointment of a reich commissioner on 29 October emphasizing the roles of Gustav Stresemann, reich chancellor; Erich Zeigner, Saxon minister-president; and Otto Gessler, Reichswehr minister. Explains the difficulty caused by the independent position of the army in the Weimar Republic for both the national and the Saxon governments. Based on archival research; 87 notes.   C. R. Lovin

485.   Puchert, Berthold.   DIE ENTWICKLUNG DER DEUTSCH-SOWJETISCHEN HANDELSBEZIEHUNGEN VON 1918 BIS 1939 [The development of German-Soviet trade relations from 1918 to 1939]. *Jahrbuch für Wirtschaftsgeschichte [East Germany] 1973 (4): 11-36.* After abandoning the objective of overthrowing the Soviet regime by military force and economic blockade in 1919, Germany emerged in the 1920's as the major trading partner of the USSR. Until the late 1920's this development was both in the political and economic interests of German monopoly capital. Thereafter, although trade continued to expand until 1931 (when German exports to the Soviet Union reached four-fifths of the value of those of 1913), political relations deteriorated. During the prewar years of the Nazi regime declining trade was combined with increasing political antagonism. Based on German archival sources, Russian published documents, and secondary works in German and Russian; 3 tables, 79 notes.
                                                                                                J. A. Perkins

486.   Ránki, György.   THE GREAT POWERS AND THE ECONOMIC REORGANIZATION OF THE DANUBE VALLEY AFTER WORLD WAR I. *Acta Hist. [Hungary] 1981 27(1-2): 63-97.* Before World War I Austria and Germany took the preponderance of Hungary's agricultural exports and provided the bulk of its industrial imports. After the war neither country could maintain that role. Britain attempted to break into southeastern European markets with only partial success. In 1920 the French government began a broad economic

offensive in Hungary, having aleady gained a strong position in Poland and Czechoslovakia, in the hope of gaining hegemony in southeastern Europe. Britain and France could provide credits but not markets to southeastern Europe. The search for markets and credits, both essential to Hungary, pointed clearly to Germany. Primary sources; 92 notes. Russian summary.   A. M. Pogany

487.   Ránki, György.   I PROBLEMI ECONOMICI DELL'EUROPA CEN-TRO-ORIENTALE FRA LE DUE GUERRE   [The economic problems of central and eastern Europe between the two wars]. *Riv. di Studi Pol. Int. [Italy]* *1981 48(2): 225-236.* The economic development of central and eastern Europe following World War I was slowed down by inherited characteristics such as the agro-industrial structure, the state of modernization, the concentration of capital, dependence on foreign resources, the composition of foreign trade, and the level of national income.

488.   Roche, Georges.   NOUVELLES CLASSES MOYENNES ET IDÉOLO-GIE: LES INGÉNIEURS SOUS LA RÉPUBLIQUE DE WEIMAR   [New middle classes and ideology: engineers under the Weimar Republic]. *Rev. d'Al-lemagne [France] 1978 10(1): 49-74.* With the growing role of technology in society, engineers have played an ever-increasing part in modern life. In Weimar Germany they constituted a large (ca. 300,000) group within the new middle classes. They suffered much from both the inflation of the early 1920's and from unemployment during the Great Depression. Ignored politically by the Left, engineers felt they were political and social outcasts (many editorials in their journal, the *Technische Akademiker,* were signed "Philoctetes"). Nazism proved attractive to a great many, and the Hitler regime put engineers to work in areas ranging from war preparations to the Deutsche Arbeitsfront and Kraft durch Freude. 83 notes.   J. C. Billigmeier

489.   Rosenfeld, Günter.   ZUR STELLUNG DES DEUTSCHEN IMPERI-ALISMUS GEGENÜBER DER SOWJETUNION BEI BEGINN DER WELTWIRTSCHAFTSKRISE   [The position of German imperialism toward the USSR at the beginning of the world economic crisis]. *Wissenschaftliche Zeitschrift der Humboldt-U. zu Berlin. Gesellschafts- und Sprachwissenschaft-liche Reihe [East Germany] 1973 22(1-2): 9-18.* Although the depression at the end of the 1920's strengthened the anti-Soviet groups in Germany, the conflict within the capitalist states prevented the German government from developing a totally anti-Soviet policy, as well as the formation of a unified anti-Soviet bloc. Based on documents in the Deutsches Zentralarchiv Potsdam, printed documents and secondary literature; 38 notes.   R. Wagnleitner

490.   Roweyk, Horst.   DIE DEUTSCHE VOLKSPARTEI IN RHEINLAND UND WESTFALEN 1918-1933   [The German People's Party in Rhineland and Westphalia, 1918-33]. *Rheinische Vierteljahrsblätter [West Germany] 1975 39(1-4): 189-236.* In the early 1920's the provincial and local party organizations of the German People's Party of the Rhineland and Westphalia intensified their cooperation within the Rheinisch-Westfälische Arbeitsgemeinschaft. In the late 1920's the party was confronted with an exodus of members and threats from their financial sources to cut off funds because of alleged appeasement of the Social Democrats. With the advance of the National Socialists the party finally broke up in 1933. Based on documents in the Bundesarchiv, Koblenz, HSta, Düsseldorf, StA, Düsseldorf and secondary literature; 248 notes.

R. Wagnleitner

491. Rubanowice, Robert J.   AN INTELLECTUAL IN POLITICS: THE POLITICAL THOUGHT OF ERNST TROELTSCH.   *Montclair J. of Social Sci. and Humanities 1974 3(2): 5-29.* Portrays Ernst Troeltsch's (1865-1923) political writings from World War I through the first third of the Weimar Republic. Presented to the 7th Annual Bloomsburg State College History Conference, Pennsylvania, 1974.   S

492. Ruge, Wolfgang.   DIE AUSSENPOLITIK DER WEIMARER REPUBLIK UND DAS PROBLEM DER EUROPÄISCHEN SICHERHEIT 1925-1932   [The foreign policy of the Weimar Republic and the problem of European security, 1925-32]. *Zeitschrift für Geschichtswissenschaft [East Germany] 1974 22(3): 271-290.* Historians of the Federal Republic of Germany maintain that realization of Gustav Stresemann's (d. 1929) attempts at peaceful revision of the Versailles treaty could have prevented the fascist takeover of Germany and World War II, and hence the revolutionary changes in Eastern Europe. In fact, Stresemann and other Weimar politicians advocated a temporary acceptance of Germany's western borders only in order to pursue aggressive goals in Eastern Europe, which included the revision of the German-Polish borders and the destruction of the USSR. Based on archival materials, published documents, and secondary works;   J. T. Walker

493. Ruge, Wolfgang.   ZUM PLATZ DER REVOLUTIONÄREN NACH-KRIEGSKRISE 1917-1923 IM REVOLUTIONÄREN WELTPROZESS [The place of the revolutionary postwar crisis, 1917-23, in the revolutionary world process]. *Zeitschrift für Geschichtswissenschaft [East Germany] 1978 26(9): 771-784.* Argues that for the first time in southeastern and central Europe during this period were to be found the two principal components of the world revolutionary process. Unlike in the West, the effects of the Russian Revolution on this area were direct and immediate. This, together with emergent national movements which arose as a result of the disintegration of the Habsburg Empire, gradually helped the countries of this area to become popular democracies. In addition the postwar crisis in Western Europe prevented the industrial West from interfering with this development. 16 notes.   A. Alcock

494. Rupieper, Hermann J.   DIE FREIEN GEWERKSCHAFTEN UND DER VERSAILLER VERTRAG 1919-23   [The free trade unions and the Treaty of Versailles, 1919-23]. *Geschichte in Wissenschaft und Unterricht [West Germany] 1978 29(8): 482-499.* Describes the reactions of the German trade unions to the Versailles Treaty's severe conditions and its war guilt clause. The major problems for the unions were treaty revision and fulfilling reparations quotas. The unions combined with industry to fight reparations. International trade unions criticized the German unions for their policies during the war, but were helpful from 1921 onward. Unpublished sources from the A.-Bebel-Institute (Berlin), other primary, and secondary sources; 63 notes.   H. W. Wurster

495. Rusconi, Gian Enrico.   LA PROBLEMATICA DEI CONSIGLI IN KARL KORSCH   [The problem of workers' councils in Karl Korsch]. *Ann. dell'Istituto Giangiacomo Feltrinelli [Italy] 1973 15: 1197-1230.* Analyzes the early theoretical work of Karl Korsch, 1919-22, which was almost exclusively dedicated to the question of workers' councils in Weimar Germany. Korsch visualized a socialization of production that was "a synthesis of vigorous eco-

nomic planning and of political control entrusted simultaneously to the 'top' and to new forms of democracy from the 'bottom' which gave to the workers' council hypothesis that concrete beginning that is absent in many 'pure' council projects, constructed on utopian models." Unfortunately, Korsch overestimated the cooperative will of two antagonistic forces, the forces at the top that would be technically capable of divising an economic plan and the forces at the bottom, participating in the workers' councils, wracked with particularistic and anti-institutional tendencies. This type of gap between movement and leadership characterized the Social Democratic coalition government that followed the November Revolution. 70 notes.   M. T. Wilson

496.   Saage, Richard.   DAS DILEMMA DER SOZIALDEMOKRATIE IN DEUTSCHLAND UND ÖSTERREICH 1918 BIS 1934   [The dilemma of the Social Democrats in Germany and Austria, 1918-34]. *Jahrbuch des Inst. für Deutsche Geschichte [Israel] 1980 9: 429-474.* That the best organized labor movements of the times finally succumbed to the fascists can only be understood after a survey of German and Austrian economic and political history, 1918-34. In those years the new German and Austrian republics seemed at times on the way to economic stability but the failure of the bourgeois industrialists to join forces with the working classes was fateful and the bourgeoisie in the end did not stand firmly against the fascists. 128 notes.   M. Faissler

497.   Saarinen, Hannes.   BETALNINGEN AV FINLANDS "KRIGSSKUL-DER " TILL TYSKLAND EFTER ÅR 1918   [The payment of Finland's war debts to Germany after 1918]. *Hist. Tidskrift för Finland [Finland] 1980 65(4): 305-315.* Describes steps taken by the government of Finland, 1919-22, to transmit funds to the German government in payment for wartime weapons purchases and for costs of the German expeditionary force sent to Finland in 1918. Based on documents in the Finnish State Archives, the Finnish Foreign Ministry archives, and Finnish parliamentary records; 29 notes.   R. G. Selleck

498.   Sakmyster, Thomas L.   THE GREAT POWERS AND THE MAGYAR MINORITIES OF INTERWAR EUROPE.   *Nationalities Papers 1980 8(1): 21-28.* Disregarding David Lloyd George's expressed fears that the carving up of Hungary would create irredentist Magyar minorities in the other states (some of them newly created) of Eastern and Central Europe, the Treaty of Versailles humiliated and shocked Hungarian leaders by reducing Hungary to one third of its pre-World War I territory. Getting little or no sympathy from France, Great Britain, the United States, or the USSR for its cause, Hungary turned increasingly to Germany and Italy for support in the 1920's and 1930's. 17 notes.   S

499.   Salewski, Michael.   REICHSWEHR, STAAT UND REPUBLIK [Army, state, and the Weimar Republic]. *Geschichte in Wissenschaft und Unterricht [West Germany] 1980 31(5): 271-288.* The army did not like the Weimar Republic, but after the defeat of the empire they had to cooperate with the government to save the state. From 1926 army and government joined forces to change the Versailles Treaty, but this involved a growing militarization of civil life and a weakening of the republican spirit under the impact of Reich and Third Reich ideologies. Thus the army had already become prepared for Nazism before Hitler gained power. It was too late when some of the generals recognized that their distinction between the state and the Republic might not only lead to the destruction of the Weimar Republic, but to that of Germany. 40 notes.
                                                              H. W. Wurster

500.   Schieder, Theodor.   DAS DOKUMENTENWERK ZUR DEUTSC-
HEN AUSWÄRTIGEN POLITIK 1918-1945   [Documentary work on German foreign policy 1918-45].   *Hist. Zeitschrift [West Germany] 1974 218(1):
85-95.* The great collection entitled *Akten zur Deutschen Auswärtigen Politik*
[Documents on German foreign policy] grew out of a 1947 agreement between
Britain and France to publish German foreign office documents. Divided into five
series: A:1919-24; B:1925-33; C:1933-37; D:1937-41; E:1941-45. Parts of series C
and D published in English translation. Includes information on personalities and
domestic political issues.   G. H. Davis

501.   Schiffers, Reinhard.   REFERENDUM UND VOLKSINITIATIVE IN
DER WEIMARER REPUBLIK. ZUM PROBLEM DER AUFNAHME UND
UMWANDLUNG VON VERFASSUNGSEINRICHTUNGEN DER WEST-
LICHEN DEMOKRATIEN IN DEUTSCHLAND   [Referendum and initiative in the Weimar Republic: the problem of borrowing and altering the
constitutional arrangements of the Western democracies in Germany]. *Francia
[France] 1973 1: 653-691.* The Weimar constitution of 1919 provided for Western
democratic procedures such as the initiative and the referendum. The parties of
the Right were hostile to these procedures, but were not above using them for
their own ends as did the Nazis, for example, in 1929 in opposing the Young Plan.
Every plebiscite turned into a Left-Right confrontation which weakened Weimar
democracy. For this reason the Basic Law of West Germany has omitted provisions for a national initiative and referendum, an omission for which it has been
often criticized. 190 notes.   J. C. Billigmeier

502.   Schomaekers, G.   GUSTAV STRESEMANN   [Gustav Stresemann].
Spiegel Hist. [Netherlands] 1980 15(3): 165-170. Gustav Stresemann (1878-
1929) became the most important minister for foreign affairs in the German
Weimar Republic. When the National Liberal Party collapsed in 1918 Stresemann founded the German People's Party (DVP). He was Chancellor for one
hundred days in 1923 and then became foreign minister. His death in 1929
marked the end of a foreign policy based on the peaceful revision of the Treaty
of Versailles through improved Franco-German relations. He was an ambitious
politician who became identified with the Treaty of Locarno in 1925, and he
worked for the economic revival of Germany through improved relations with
France.   Based on Stresemann's published writings and secondary sources; 7
photos.   M. K. Hogg

503.   Schreiber, Gerhard.   ZUR KONTINUITÄT DES GROSS- UND
WELTMACHTSTREBENS DER DEUTSCHEN MARINEFÜHRUNG
[On the continuity of great power and imperial aspirations of the German naval
command]. *Militärgeschichtliche Mitteilungen [West Germany] 1979 (2): 101-
171.* Assesses the consistent policy of the German naval leadership to regard
Great Britain as the primary enemy in a struggle at sea for world power, illustrated through documents written during the post-1918 period. From the Versailles Treaty, naval officers planned revision of its provisions and resurrection
of German sea power for renewed struggle with Great Britain and other world
powers. Based upon documents in the Military Archives, Freiburg; 8 documents,
352 notes.   K. W. Estes

504. Schulin, Ernst. L'HISTORIOGRAPHIE ALLEMANDE DE L'É-POQUE DE LA RÉPUBLIQUE DE WEIMAR ET SA POSITION ENVERS LA FRANCE [German historiography from the Weimar Republic era, and its position regarding France]. *Rev. d'Allemagne [France] 1976 8(1): 3-20.* Argues that the origin and growth of difficulties in French-German relations, 1929-30, was based more on psychological factors than on the shock of war, although the political events did complicate Germany's position.

505. Schulze, Hagen. RÜCKBLICK AUF WEIMAR. EIN BRIEFWECH-SEL ZWISCHEN OTTO BRAUN UND JOSEPH WIRTH IM EXIL. DOKU-MENTATION [Looking back to Weimar: an exchange of letters between Otto Braun and Joseph Wirth in exile, a documentation]. *Vierteljahrshefte für Zeitgeschichte [West Germany] 1978 26(1): 144-185.* Reprints with commentary five letters dated July through September 1941 between Social Democrat Otto Braun (1872-1955), former Prussian Prime Minister (1920-33), and Centrist Joseph Wirth (1879-1956), former German Finance Minister (1920-21) and Chancellor (1921-22), during their exile in Switzerland. Prompted by Wirth's reactions to Braun's memoirs, the letters shed light on personal relationships of the Weimar period such as those leading to Wirth's 1922 fall from office, due apparently to a coordinated effort of leading Social Democrats and the pro-industrialist German People's Party (DVP). Based on documents contained in Braun Papers, Geheimes Staatsarchiv, (Berlin-Dahlem), commentary based on personal papers in the SPD Archive (Bonn), the Bundesarchiv (Koblenz), and State Archive Detmold, memoirs, and secondary sources; 196 notes. D. Prowe

506. Schulze, Hagen. STABILITÄT UND INSTABILITÄT IN DER POLI-TISCHEN ORDNUNG VON WEIMAR. DIE SOZIALDEMOKRATISC-HEN PARLAMENTSFRAKTIONEN IM REICH UND IN PREUSSEN [Stability and instability in the political order of the Weimar Republic: the parliamentary groups of the Social Democratic Party in Prussia and the Reich]. *Vierteljahrsh efte für Zeitgeschichte [West Germany] 1978 26(3): 419-432.* A comparative examination of the Prussian and Reichstag Social Democratic parliamentary parties shows that the Weimar Republic was weakened not so much by its constitutional structure, but by the parties. The Reichstag party, composed of individualistic party leaders and ideologues politically shaped by experience in a powerless pre-World War I opposition, found compromise for the sake of political stability difficult, while the Prussian party of younger, disciplined labor functionaries served as the foundation for a stable Prussian government. Based on Social Democratic Archive (Bonn), government publications, secondary works; 25 notes. D. Prowe

507. Schwabe, Klaus. ANTI-AMERICANISM WITHIN THE GERMAN RIGHT 1917-1933. *Amerikastudien/American Studies [West Germany] 1976 21(1): 89-107.* Only with World War I, the Armistice, and the Versailles Treaty did the anti-Americanism of the Right become an issue of potentially larger dimensions in Germany. It became the monopoly of extremist groups to the right of the German nationalists (DNVP). Under the influence of Adolf Halfeld's movement and publications in 1927 and 1928 the term "Americanism" acquired a derogatory connotation in German. Anti-Americanism is examined in terms of its racist, geopolitical, economic, and cultural motivation, and as a function of domestic politics. 108 notes. G. Bassler

508. Shattuck, Petra T.   LAW AS POLITICS.   *Comparative Pol. 1974 7(1):*
127-154. Reviews works by Isaac D. Balbus, Theodore L. Becker, Charles Goo-
dell, and Heinrich Hannover and Elisabeth Hannover dealing with political
prisoners in modern America and in Weimar Germany.   S

509. Sierpowski, Stanisław.   KSZTAŁTOWANIE SIĘ SPOŁECZNEGO
RUCHU POPARCIA DLA LIGI NARODÓW W LATACH 1919-1926
[Formation of the social movement to aid the League of Nations, 1919-26].
Kwartalnik Hist. [Poland] 1981 88(4): 973-991. The pact of the League of Nations had great importance as a new concept in international relations. The mass
media at that time spread the idea of the League. Attitudes toward the League
among the Western European powers, the United States, and Germany (not
admitted to the League) are analyzed and public opinion about the League after
the period of initial enthusiasm are discussed. The League was criticized for not
admitting Germany, the nonparticipation of the USSR, and interference in the
internal affairs of some of the participants such as the problem of national
minorities. Table, 41 notes. Russian summary.   H. Heitzman-Wojcicka

510. Sládek, Zdeněk.   POKUSY O HOSPODÁŘSKOU INTEGRACI
STŘEDNÍ A JIHOVÝCHODNÍ EVROPY V MEZIVÁLEČNÉM OBDOBÍ
[Attempts at the economic integration of Central and Southeast Europe in the
interwar period]. *Časopis Matice Moravské [Czechoslovakia] 1979 98(1-2): 32-*
48. Interwar attempts at economic integration among the successor states to the
Habsburg Empire all eventually foundered on fears of a revival of Austro-Hun-
garian hegemony or on the fears of individual Western powers. Germany eventually succeeded in integrating the economies of the area after appeasement had led
to the withdrawal of other potentially influential Western powers. Based on some
Czech and German archival material, records of proposals and discussions, and
secondary literature; 48 notes.   L. Short

511. Slavenas, Julius P.   STRESEMANN AND LITHUANIA IN THE
NINETEEN TWENTIES.   *Lituanus 1972 18(4): 5-25.* As foreign minister,
1923-29, Gustav Stresemann (1878-1929) capitalized on frictions between Lithuania and Poland and the USSR to improve Germany's position on its eastern flank.

512. Smith, Woodruff D.   THE MIERENDORFF GROUP AND THE
MODERNIZATION OF GERMAN SOCIAL DEMOCRATIC POLITICS,
1928-1933.   *Pol. and Soc. 1975 5(1): 109-129.* Places the Carlo Mierendorff
group of the Social Democratic Party of Germany, which included Julius Leber,
Kurt Schumacher, and Theodore Haubach, in political and biographical perspective. The similarity of their backgrounds helps to explain their significant yet
limited influence on Party ideology and tactics. The author emphasizes the war
experiences of the group, and the 1930-33 Party maneuvers instigated by the
group. Secondary sources; 76 notes.   D. G. Nielson

513. Sobczak, Janusz.   DZIAŁALNOŚĆ NIEMIECKIEGO TOWAR-
ZYSTWA POLITYCZNO-GOSPODARCZEGO W OKRESIE REPUBLIKI
WEIMARSKIEJ   [The activity of the German Wirtschaftspolitische Gesellschaft (WPG) in the Weimar Republic]. *Przegląd Zachodni [Poland] 1973 29(1):*
110-131. Describes the methods of disseminating pro-German propaganda used
by the Wirtschaftspolitische Gesellschaft, founded in January 1922 by the big

industrial firms of Rheinland-Westphalia and the Ruhr region; such propaganda was especially effective in Great Britain and the United States.

514. Southern, David B. THE REVALUATION QUESTION IN THE WEIMAR REPUBLIC. *J. of Modern Hist. 1979 51(1): ii.* Though governments in the Weimar Republic hoped the problem of revaluation would disappear, court attitudes, public opinion, and internal divisions forced the cabinet to pass two laws which provided for the revaluation of debts and obligations from the paper mark to the new Reichsmark, 1922-25. Abstract only.

515. Soutou, Georges. DIE DEUTSCHEN REPARATIONEN UND DAS SEYDOUX-PROJEKT 1920/21 [German reparations and the Seydoux Project, 1920-21]. *Vierteljahrshefte für Zeitgeschichte [West Germany] 1975 23(3): 237-270.* The shift in French reparations policy from the apparent era of good feeling at the Brussels Conference (16-22 December 1920) to the subsequent confrontation at Paris (24-29 January 1921) has been much overestimated. The plan of the French representative at Brussels, Jacques Seydoux, to make reparations both more effective and attractive to German industrialists was never seriously accepted by the Germans, who were rather hoping to come to terms with the British behind the backs of the French. Based on documents in the archives of the French and German foreign ministries, *Bundesarchiv, Archives Nationales,* printed documents and memoirs; 136 notes. D. Prowe

516. Soutou, Georges. LES MINES DE SILÉSIE ET LA RIVALITÉ FRANCO-ALLEMANDE, 1920-1923. ARME ÉCONOMIQUE OU BONNE AFFAIRE? [The mines of Silesia and Franco-German rivalry, 1920-23: economic weapon or good business?]. *Relations Int. [France] 1974 (1): 135-154.* In the dispute between Germany and Poland, 1920-23, the French supported the Poles for political and economic reasons. The steel and coal industry of Upper Silesia without the Germans would require French capital and technical help. The project for French economic penetration in the area was dropped due to lack of support from French industrial circles, who considered the government's approach too ambitious. 78 notes. J. C. Billigmeier

517. Soutou, Georges. PROBLÈMES CONCERNANT LE RÉTABLISSEMENT DES RELATIONS ÉCONOMIQUES FRANCO-ALLEMANDES APRÈS LA PREMIÈRE GUERRE MONDIALE [Problems concerning the reestablishment of economic relations between France and Germany after World War I]. *Francia [France] 1974 2: 580-596.* Much of northern France was in ruins at the end of World War I, and economic relations between the Allies and Germany were totally ruptured. Their restoration was gradual. The blockade was lifted when Germany signed the Treaty of Versailles in 1919. In 1920, the French began to doubt the policy of still treating Germany as an enemy nation in the economic sphere. Problems over coal and steel, however, led to the occupation of the Ruhr in 1923, and what amounted to economic war. The British disassociated themselves from this and were the architects of compromise. With the Dawes Plan of 1924, the formation of the International Steel Cartel in 1926, and the French-German Commercial Treaty of 1927, economic relations were finally normalized. 70 notes. J. C. Billigmeier

518. Soutou, Georges. UNE AUTRE POLITIQUE? LES TENTATIVES FRANÇAIS D'ENTENTE ÉCONOMIQUE AVEC L'ALLEMAGNE (1919-1921) [A new policy? French attempts at an economic understanding with Germany, 1919-21]. *Rev. d'Allemagne [France] 1976 8(1): 21-34.* Reviews the French position toward Germany after World War I which was more friendly and understanding than previously thought. Describes France's endeavors at economic cooperation between the two countries, which ultimately failed.

519. Stambrook, F. "RESOURCEFUL IN EXPEDIENTS"—SOME EX-AMPLES OF AMBASSADORIAL POLICY MAKING IN THE INTER-WAR PERIOD. *Can. Hist. Assoc. Hist. Papers [Canada] 1973: 301-320.* Despite the changing functions of 20th-century ambassadors, they have operated in a 19th-century framework which allows them some initiative. The author examines three instances involving the American and British ambassadors to Germany and the German ambassador to Italy during the 1920's. Each of these men believed that his own judgment of the local situation was better than that of his superiors, and asserted some decisionmaking prerogative. Based on the personal papers of the ambassadors, papers of the British, German, and Italian foreign ministries, periodicals, and secondary works; 99 notes.
G. E. Panting

520. Steiner, Jan. K VYUŽITÍ LITERATURY O HOSPODÁŘSKÉM A SOCIÁLNÍM VÝVOJI V POLSKU, SOVĚTSKÉM SVAZU A NĚMECKU PRO KOMPARATIVNÍ VÝZKUM VÝVOJE PRŮMYSLOVÝCH OBLASTÍ 1918-1945 [Using literature about economic and social development in Poland, the USSR, and Germany for comparing the growth of industrial sectors, 1918-45]. *Slezský Sborník [Czechoslovakia] 1981 79(4): 298-306.* Discusses the available literature on industrial growth in Poland, the USSR, and Germany. Identifies historically reliable sources, materials published by various institutes of the countries, and works that are biased and should be discredited. 90 notes, biblio.
B. Reinfeld

521. Stjerna, Leif. UTVECKLINGEN AV UBÅTSVAPEN OCH UBÅTSK-RIGFÖRING I TYSKLAND 1919-1935 [Development of the U-boat and U-boat war strategy in Germany 1919-35]. *Aktuellt och Historiskt [Sweden] 1976: 123-165.* Captured German documents permit a clearer view of German submarine policy between the wars. Working in secret until 1935, German naval and defense leaders were attentive to submarine strategy and planning, even arranging for a Dutch shipyard to build U-boats for other countries so that this knowledge could be perfected. From 1935 to 1938 the Germans openly built U-boats, and increased their numbers until 1939. Funds were competed for with the surface navy (1939-41), and later this source suffered with the coming of the war with Russia. Building and operations increased again from 1943 to the end of the war. The author briefly discusses World War I strategy and building. After the prohibitions of the Versailles Treaty, the German command hid its submarine operations in TMI (Inspektion des Torpedo- und Minewesens) in Kiel. They cooperated with Russia, Spain, Sweden and other nations in building submarines. This effort was exposed in 1928 but revived with Hitler's coming to power. Summary in German.
R. E. Lindgren

522. Takahashi, Susumu. DOITSU BAISHO MONDAI NO SHITEKI TENKAI (1920 NEN-1924 NEN): KOKUSAI FUNSO OYOBI RENKEI SEIJI NO SHIKAKU KARA [The question of German reparations 1920-24: a historical analysis of the international conflict]. *Kokka Gakkai Zasshi [Japan] 1976 89(9-10): 595-635; 1977 90(1-2): 62-132, (3-4): 155-228, (7-8): 417-497; 1978 91(1-2): 51-115, (3-4): 176-230.* Analyzes German diplomatic policies on reparations for World War I from international and national points of view. The question of reparations on an international level was that of conflicts between the powers, and nationally it was the question of linkage politics between foreign and domestic policies. 1,188 notes.

Y. Aoki

523. Teichova, Alice. VERSAILLES AND THE EXPANSION OF THE BANK OF ENGLAND INTO CENTRAL EUROPE. Horn, Norbert and Kocka, Jürgen, ed. *Recht und Entwicklung der Grossunternehmen im 19. und frühen 20. Jahrhundert* (Göttingen: Vandenhoeck & Ruprecht, 1979): 366-387. As a result of World War I, business interests of France and Great Britain increased their involvement and influence in Central Europe. The Bank of England's expansion into the banking system of the former Habsburg Empire provided the mechanism of organizational changes by which the financial-industrial conglomerates in Central and Southeastern Europe were adapted and integrated into Western business structures and became diversified multinational groups headquartered mainly in Paris and London. Juridical processes played a major role in formalizing the organizational changes taking place in modern businesses. 88 notes, 19 ref. German summary.

S

524. Tilkovszky, Lóránt. DIE WEIMARER REPUBLIK UND DIE DEUTSCHEN MINDERHEITEN IM DONAUBECKEN [The Weimar Republic and the German minorities in the Danube basin]. *Études Hist. Hongroises [Hungary] 1980 (2): 199-231.* After the collapse of the Habsburg Empire in 1918, the German national minority of the Danube basin was divided among Hungary, Czechoslovakia, Romania, Yugoslavia, and Austria. The process of assimilation (Magyarization) which had begun decades earlier continued only in Hungary because of political and educational policies. In Austria the Danube Germans ceased to be a national minority, while in Czechoslovakia, Romania, and Yugoslavia a process of re-Germanization was occurring, aided by the governments in those countries aiming to stifle revanchist movements among their Hungarian minorities. The German minority in Hungary requested similar support from Czechoslovakia, Romania, and Yugoslavia. While István Bethlen was prime minister of Hungary, 1921-31, several attempts were made—against the wishes of chauvinist groups—to regulate the position of the German minority in a mutually satisfactory fashion. Ultimately Germany's influence on this minority became important during the rise of fascism. 104 notes. Russian summary.

S

525. Underdown, Michael. DIE KLEINEN STAATEN AUF DER GENFER ABRÜSTUNGSKONFERENZ [The small states at the Geneva disarmament conference]. *Rev. des Études Sud-Est Européennes [Romania] 1981 19(1): 71-79.* The World Disarmament Conference in Geneva, 1932-33, as recorded by the Germans, reveals the degree to which Germany tried to influence the foreign policy of the European central powers during the period between the two world wars. A brief outline of the discussions of the preparatory commission introduces

this study of the negotiations at the conference. It focuses on the German participation and their efforts to establish a common policy with Austria, Hungary, and Bulgaria, the other members in one of the three power blocs that dominated the conference. Disillusioned at the conference, Germany eventually withdrew from it, as well as from the League of Nations. Based on the documents from the Foreign Office Political Archive, the Federal Archive-Military Archive, and other primary sources; 42 notes.   T. Parker

526.   Vinogradov, V. N.   POLITICHESKAIA "SEREDINA" V VEIMARSKOI RESPUBLIKE I OBRAZOVANIE NEMETSKOI GOSUDARSTVENNOI PARTII   [Political centrism in the Weimar Republic and the formation of the Reichs Partei]. *Voprosy Istorii [USSR] 1981 (12): 81-97.* Anxious to overcome the fragmentary character of the party system in the Weimar Republic and strengthen their positions within the framework of the parliamentary regime, bourgeois forces tried to strengthen the political "center" by establishing a large bourgeois party. The author analyzes the struggle on this issue and the differences between the liberals and moderate conservatives over the key political, social, and ideological questions.   J

527.   Walker, D. P.   THE GERMAN NATIONALIST PEOPLE'S PARTY: THE CONSERVATIVE DILEMMA IN THE WEIMAR REPUBLIC. *J. of Contemporary Hist. [Great Britain] 1979 14(4): 627-647.* The German National People's Party (DNVP) was founded in November 1918 to restore the monarchy. The dilemma was whether or not to cooperate with the Weimar Republic which they regarded as weak and illegitimate. By 1924 the DNVP was the second largest party in the Reichstag. The success of the party engendered divergent views: Walter Lambach, chairman of the DNVP's Employees' Committee, wished to include nonmonarchists in the party and form a new leadership elite of trade unionists; Alfred Hugenberg, the industrialist, still anticipated the disintegration of the republic, and wanted an elite based on the German race and a new government guided by the party and the leadership principle. Recognizing the similarity of principles with those of the Nazis, Hugenberg invited Hitler's group to work with the DNVP in 1929.   Archival sources; 76 notes.
M. P. Trauth

528.   Wallace, John E.   OTTO ABETZ AND THE QUESTION OF A FRANCO-GERMAN RECONCILIATION, 1919-1939.   *Southern Q. 1975 13(3): 189-206.* Examines the life and career of Heinrich Otto Abetz (1903-58) with special reference to activities leading to his war crimes trial of 1949. Primary focus is accorded Abetz's efforts toward Franco-German reconciliation, 1919-40. 75 notes.   R. W. Dubay

529.   Wąsicki,   Jan.   JANUSZ   SOBCZAK: PROPAGANDA   ZAGRANICZNA NIEMIEC WEIMARSKICH WOBEC POLSKI   [Jan Sobczak: Weimar Germany's foreign propaganda against Poland]. *Polish Western Affairs [Poland] 1974 15(1): 140-144.* A valuable contribution to our understanding of Weimer Germany's attitude toward interwar Poland, Sobczak's book reveals the means by which the German foreign ministry influenced the domestic and foreign press and other media toward an anti-Polish view. Despite the extremely wide, diversified, and dangerous range of its propaganda activity, the expected results were not forthcoming. Sobczak unfortunately did not extend his

research beyond 1933, a study which would demonstrate that the Third Reich continued and perfected the Weimer Republic's anti-Polish propaganda campaign. The book is important to all those who take an interest in Polish-German relations during the interwar period.   M. A. J. Swiecicka

530. Weidenfeld, Werner. GUSTAV STRESEMANN: DER MYTHOS VOM ENGAGIERTEN EUROPÄER   [Gustav Stresemann: the myth of the committed European]. *Geschichte in Wissenschaft und Unterricht [West Germany] 1973 24(12): 740-750.* While Gustav Stresemann (1878-1929) was seen as a politician of European conciliation, the National Socialists portrayed him as antinational; in the Allied countries during World War II he was thought of as having been a power hungry opportunist, while after World War II he was mythicized as a fighter for European integration.

531. Weingartner, James J.   MASSACRE AT MECHTERSTÄDT: THE CASE OF THE *MARBURGER STUDENTENCORPS*, 1920.   *Historian 1975 37(4): 598-618.* With governmental encouragement and student enthusiasm the Free Corps, which included university contingents, was created in 1919. Operating in Thuringia, volunteers from Marburg University saw action in March 1920 during the Kapp Putsch. Members of the Marburger Studentencorps shot 15 prisoners, supposedly leftist worker-rebels, on the night of 25 March. The events leading to this "massacre at Mechterstädt," along with the public controversy and the military and civil legal proceedings, are reconstructed. 69 notes.   S

532. Weisbrod, Bernd. ECONOMIC POWER AND POLITICAL STABILITY RECONSIDERED: HEAVY INDUSTRY IN WEIMAR GERMANY. *Social Hist. [Great Britain] 1979 4(2): 241-263.* Questions the view that German heavy industry supported the leaders of the Nazi Party. Although heavy industry was a minority in the Reichsverband der Deutschen Industrie [The Confederation of German Industry], it retained political hegemony by the use of the veto power, which functioned as a lever in central political issues. In the fight against labor unions, the target of heavy industry was the political isolation of social democracy and the basic strategy was to functionalize the pressure of economic collapse to clear the way for the expected boom. This left no alternative but an alignment with the National Socialists after they had attracted a considerable part of the bourgeoisie. Secondary sources; 86 notes.   S. Košak

533. Wessling, Wolfgang. HINDENBURG, NEUDECK UND DIE DEUTSCHE WIRTSCHAFT. TATSACHEN UND ZUSAMMENHÄNGE EINER "AFFÄRE"   [Hindenburg, Neudeck, and the German economy. Facts and circumstances of an "affair"]. *Vierteljahrschrift für Sozial- und Wirtschaftsgeschichte [West Germany] 1977 64(1): 41-73.* An analysis of the political and economic background of the gift of Neudeck estate (East Prussia) to German President Paul von Hindenburg (1847-1934) in 1927. The author argues that the donation did not demonstrably influence Hindenburg's support for East Elbian estate subsidies or his dismissal of Chancellor Heinrich Brüning (1885-1970) over this question, and that Junker lobbyist Elard von Oldenburg-Januschau did not consciously promote the donation to gain influence since the purchase was supported by Chancellor Wilhelm Marx (1863-1946) and financed mainly by industry. Based on documents in the Bundesarchiv (Koblenz) and Bayer Werksarchiv (Leverkusen), memoirs, and secondary sources; 88 notes.   D. Prowe

534. Wette, Wolfram.   NS-PROPAGANDA UND KRIEGSBEREIT-
SCHAFT DER DEUTSCHEN BIS 1936   [German Nazi propaganda and readiness for war to 1936]. *Francia [France] 1977 5: 568-590.* Militarism was not a
Nazi invention in Germany. It existed in the Weimar Republic and grew rapidly
between 1929 and 1933. Militarists were found in all anti-democratic movements
and helped bring about the fall of the republic. A latent readiness for war existed
among a majority of the nation before and needed only to be triggered to action
after the opponents had been silenced by terrorism. 48 notes.   G. E. Pergl

535. Whaley, Barton.   COVERT REARMAMENT IN GERMANY 1919-
1939: DECEPTION AND MISPERCEPTION.   *J. of Strategic Studies [Great
Britain] 1982 5(1): 3-39.* During the period 1919-39, both Weimar leaders and
Adolf Hitler succeeded in rearming Germany using deception and misperception.
The Weimar chancellors, chiefs of the *Reichswehr,* and captains of industry all
shared the slogan *Wehrfreiheit* (military freedom) and saw as its instrument a
strong German army. The 1918-19 period of disarmament was followed by one
of arms evasion, covert because of Allied on-site inspection. The years 1927-35
saw clandestine rearmament, and from 1935 to 1939 Hitler moved toward overt
rearmament and bluff. Also, from 1921 to 1933 there was covert German-Soviet
military collaboration. Based on primary sources; 75 notes.   A. M. Osur

536.   Wheeler, Robert F.   DIE "21 BEDINGUNGEN" UND DIE SPAL-
TUNG DER USPD IM HERBST 1920   [The 21 Conditions and the split of the
USPD in the fall of 1920]. *Vierteljahrshefte für Zeitgeschichte [West Germany]
1975 23(2): 117-154.* An analysis of the split in the German Independent Socialist
Party (USPD) over Lenin's 21 conditions for acceptance into the Comintern. The
party's leadership, the press, and textile workers opposed the 21 conditions; a
larger group of the party's rank and file, especially from the mining and chemical
industries and younger workers, favored them. There was a three-way split in the
USPD in October 1920: a left group ready to join the Communists, a smaller
rump USPD, and lastly about 20% of the membership which left the revolutionary labor movement altogether. Based on private papers in Amsterdam, published
documents, the contemporary press, memoirs, and monographs; 4 tables, 151
notes.   D. Prowe

537.   White, Dan S.   RECONSIDERING EUROPEAN SOCIALISM IN
THE 1920'S.   *J. of Contemporary Hist. [Great Britain] 1981 16(2): 251-272.*
Interwar socialism in France, Germany, and Great Britain has been appraised as
a movement that had lost its pristine fervor and become bourgeois and inactive
as it pushed its ideal to an indeterminate future. The judgment is partly true.
Although membership remained largely working class, the goals became the
advantages of the middle class. Socialism's zeal seemed as faded as antebellum
society, and even the Front Generation of critics of social democracy was unable
to match performance to promise. The most they could do was to try to make
socialism a matter of commitment instead of one of social class.   Based on
published primary sources; 41 notes.   M. P. Trauth

538.   Williamson, D. G.   COLOGNE AND THE BRITISH, 1918-1926.
Hist. Today [Great Britain] 1977 27(11): 695-702. Examines the eight-year military occupation of Cologne, which reflected British restraint and civil rather than
military friction.

539. Witt, Peter-Christian. REICHSFINANZMINISTER UND REICHS-
FINANZVERWALTUNG. ZUM PROBLEM DES VERHÄLTNISSES VON
POLITISCHER FÜHRUNG UND BÜROKRATISCHER HERRSCHAFT
IN DEN ANFANGSJAHREN DER WEIMARER REPUBLIK (1918/19-
1924) [Reich Finance Minister and Reich Fiscal Administration. On the problem of the relationship between political leadership and bureaucratic rule in the
early years of the Weimar Republic, 1918/19-1924]. *Vierteljahrshefte für Zeitgeschichte [West Germany] 1975 23(1): 1-61.* Contrary to the common assumption
that the bureaucracy held the real power and conspired to prop up a conservative
economic system in the early Weimar Republic, evidence suggests that 1) at least
three of the finance ministers were firmly in control of the rapidly rotating fiscal
bureaucracy, 2) the main conflicts were with other ministries and the *Länder* over
budgetary and fiscal powers, and 3) the quality of political leadership, not ideological persuasion of governments, determined the effectiveness of the fiscal
administration. Based on fiscal administration records at Bundesarchiv, Deutsches Zentralarchiv, Länder archives, and printed primary and secondary
sources; 10 tables, 206 notes.   D. Prowe

540. Wittgens, Herman J. WAR GUILT PROPAGANDA CONDUCTED
BY THE GERMAN FOREIGN MINISTRY DURING THE 1920'S. *Hist.
Papers [Canada] 1980: 228-247.* In the 1920's the German Foreign Ministry
coordinated the war guilt propaganda campaign, turning Article 231 from a
simple statement of financial liability into a moral and legal base for the Treaty
of Versailles, and a condemnation of the Germans for having caused the war.
Using apparently nonofficial front organizations, Zentralstelle and Arbeitsausschuss, and exploiting the reactions of foreign scholars who opposed the propaganda of their own governments, the ministry began releasing carefully prepared
German documents for historical scholarship. It also published Russian documents in an effort to shift the guilt. Arbeitsausschuss sought to strengthen both
German public opinion and that of foreign revisionists, like Harry Elmer Barnes.
An assessment of the campaign is difficult. Presented at the Annual Meeting of
the Canadian Historical Association, 1980; 100 notes.   A. Drysdale

541. Wojciechowski, Marian. STANY ZJEDNOCZONE AMERYKI POŁ-
NOCNEJ I EUROPA SRODKOWA MIEDZY DWIEMA WOJNAMI (1918-
1939/41) [The United States and Central Europe in the interwar period,
1918-41]. *Kwartalnik Hist. [Poland] 1976 83(2): 329-337.* Although the United
States was closer to Europe after World War I, it didn't sign the Versailles Treaty
or participate in the League of Nations. The United States in fact felt close ties
with Germany, especially under the Hoover administration, a pro-German parti-
sanship linked with the fear of communism. The Roosevelt administration arrived
as Hitler rose to power. This caused the United States to turn more toward
French and British policy. This period was characterized by a lack of realistic
evaluation of Hitler's aims, due mainly to poor judgment by American diplomats
in Europe. Even the German aggression against Czechoslovakia and Poland
didn't shake that policy—America was ready to approve of German conquests,
and only the collapse of France and war in the Pacific brought the United States
into the world conflict. 33 notes.   H. Heitzman-Wojcicka

542. Wojciechowski, Marian. THE UNITED STATES AND CENTRAL EUROPE BETWEEN THE TWO WORLD WARS (1918-1939/41) *Polish Western Affairs [Poland] 1975 16(1): 65-73.* Robert Gottwald's and Werner Link's works on US isolationism are valuable. The Hoover administration staked its interests on Germany in its Central European interwar foreign policy because Germany was most likely to succumb to a socialist revolution and a communist victory there could mean victory in the whole of Europe. A radical change of sympathies was brought about in 1933 by Franklin D. Roosevelt and Adolf Hitler.   M. A. J. Swiecicka-Ziemianek

543. Wulf, Peter.   DIE AUSEINANDERSETZUNGEN UM DIE SOZIALISIERUNG DER KOHLE IN DEUTSCHLAND 1920/1921 [The conflict over nationalization of the coal industry in Germany, 1920-21]. *Vierteljahrshefte für Zeitgeschichte [West Germany] 1977 25(1): 46-98.* Analyzes the second post-World War I attempt to nationalize the German coal industry. In the often passionate confrontation between industry and labor, Ruhr industrialists not only blocked nationalization, but exploited the movement to promote further industrial concentration. They profited by their influence in government through the German People's Party (DVP); by labor's internal disunity and inability to present a common, concrete program for nationalization; and by the general fear of Allied reparations claims against a nationalized coal industry. Based on government and private records at Bundesarchiv Koblenz, Deutsches Zentralarchiv Potsdam, and the contemporary press; 207 notes.   D. Prowe

544. Ziemke, Earl F.   "HEROIC" NIHILISM IN WEIMAR AND NAZI GERMANY.   *Central European Hist. 1980 13(1): 83-91.* Discusses the major themes of four works: *Paramilitary Politics in Weimar Germany* by James M. Diehl; *Soldiers of Destruction* by Charles W. Sydnor, Jr.; *Hitler's Guard* by James J. Weingartner; and *Hitler's Spanish Legion* by Gerald R. Klinefeld and Lewis A. Tambs. Diehl's work is important because it shows how paramilitary forces "managed only to help open the way for the man who will soon show them what force really is, Adolf Hitler." Although the author finds the other three books well researched, he questions whether any divisional history can be very meaningful. 17 notes.   C. R. Lovin

545. —. [THE CHILD PROTECTION AND SERVICE LAWS IN GERMANY]. *Rev. d'Allemagne [France] 1976 8(3): 476-487.*
Koenig, Pierre. INTRODUCTION: LA LOI ALLEMANDE SUR LE BIEN-ÊTRE DE LA JEUNESSE [Introduction: German law regarding the well-being of youth], *pp. 476-478.*
Olier, Viviane.   LA LOI SUR LE BIEN-ÊTRE DE LA JEUNESSE [The law on the well-being of youth], *pp. 479-487.* Outlines and analyzes the history and function of the *Reichsjugendwohlfahrtgesetz* [Law on the well-being of youth] of 1922 and the *Jugendamt* (Youth Office) from its establishment, viewing legislation concerning juveniles, the formation of voluntary youth groups, protection agencies, and educational activities, 1922-76.

546. —. [CONSTITUTING HEGEMONY: THE BOURGEOIS CRISIS OF WEIMAR GERMANY].   *J. of Modern Hist. 1979 51(3): 417-450.*
Abraham, David.   CONSTITUTING HEGEMONY: THE BOURGEOIS CRISIS OF WEIMAR GERMANY, *pp. 417-433.* Conflicts generated by

the diversity of the various sectors of the dominant class in Weimar Germany made it impossible for a ruling consensus to be formed, and made their attitudes to organized labor diverge widely.

Stegman, Dirk. COMMENT ON ABRAHAM, "CONSTITUTING HEGEMONY," *pp. 434-437.*

Mason, T. W. COMMENT ON ABRAHAM, "CONSTITUTING HEGEMONY," *pp. 438-441.*

Abraham, David. RESPONSE, *pp. 442-450.*

547. —. [THE GERMAN BUSINESS CYCLE IN THE 1920'S]. *Econ. Hist. Rev. [Great Britain] 1977 30(1): 159-165.*

Balderston, T. A COMMENT, *pp. 159-161.* Rejects the hypothesis put forth by Peter Temin and M. E. Falkus that a sharp fall in the real rate of nonagricultural inventory investment, 1927-28, was a contributory factor in causing the Depression in Germany.

Temin, Peter. A COMMENT AND REPLY, *pp. 162-164.* Even if Balderston's new data on inventory turnover is correct, the monetary explanation of the German economic downturn is still faulty.

Falkus, M. E. A REPLY, *pp. 165.* Restates that his basic approach remains intact.   B. L. Crapster

548. —. NAZIS VERSUS NATIONALISTS. *Patterns of Prejudice [Great Britain] 1978 12(2): 5-8.* Although anti-Semitic and nationalistic, Germany's National People's Party supported a return to monarchy and resisted association with the Nazis, 1925-44.

549. —. [NON-TRADED GOODS AND GERMANY'S BALANCE OF PAYMENTS]. *J. of Econ. Lit. 1975 13(2): 475-480.*

Hinshaw, Randall. NON-TRADED GOODS AND THE BALANCE OF PAYMENTS: FURTHER REFLECTIONS, *pp. 475-479.*

Oppenheimer, P. M. NON-TRADED GOODS: A REJOINDER, *pp. 479-480.* Considers whether Frank D. Graham anticipated in 1925 B. Ohlin's 1929 position that transfer of German war reparations would not cause a deterioration of German terms of trade.   S

4

WEIMAR CULTURE AND SOCIETY

550. Anchor, Robert. LUKÁCS AS INTERPRETER OF GERMAN CUL-
TURE. *Hist. and Theory 1980 19(3): 278-293.* Shows that most of Georg
Lukács's works "take Germany, implicitly or explicitly, as their frame of reference" and seeks to explain why he considered German culture so relevant to his
wider critical tasks. In philosophy Lukács has concentrated on retrieving Hegel's
reputation from the idealistic distortions of later neo-Kantians and irrationalists.
His examination of the development of German literature centers on seeing the
continuity between the Enlightenment and the *Sturm und Drang.* Goethe
emerges as Lukács's particular hero. The Goethean corpus is read as an extended
commentary on the alienating, ultimately disastrous, contradictions of the bourgeois world view. By juxtaposing the insights of Hegel, Goethe, and Marx, Lukács
arrived at the cardinal concept of his aesthetic realism—the concept of "concrete
universality." Modern German culture found its greatest creator of concrete
universal literature in Thomas Mann. 68 notes.   W. J. Reedy

551. Ash, Mitchell G. ACADEMIC POLITICS IN THE HISTORY OF
SCIENCE: EXPERIMENTAL PSYCHOLOGY IN GERMANY, 1879-1941.
Central European Hist. 1980 13(3): 255-286. Describes the difficulties of the
experimental psychologists in establishing their scientific legitimacy in the German university system. They were a part of the philosophy faculties, but unless
they had distinguished themselves as "pure" philosophers, they had difficulty
carrying out their experimental work. Outside the notably successful psychological institutes at Leipzig and Berlin under Wilhelm Wundt and Carl Stumpf,
experimental psychologists found themselves without the security in the university system most of their colleagues had. This may have been one reason for the
rapid *Gleichschaltung* in the fall of 1933 of the German Society for Psychology.
Psychology became an independent discipline in Germany in 1941 because the
Wehrmacht required trained psychologists. Based on archival and secondary
sources; 111 notes.   C. R. Lovin

552. Bance, A. F. THE INTELLECTUAL AND THE CRISIS OF WEI-
MAR: HEINRICH MANN'S *KOBES* AND LEONHARD FRANK'S *IM
LETZEN WAGEN.* *J. of European Studies [Great Britain] 1978 8(3): 155-174.*
A comparative study of two texts published in 1925, both of which are allegorical
commentaries on the crisis of the Weimar Republic in 1923. Heinrich Mann
foresaw the rise of fascism from monopoly capitalism, and through the story of
a powerful industrial magnate Mann conveyed his disillusion with the intelligent-

sia's failure to find a role in the new state. Leonhard Frank used the allegory of a runaway railway coach to warn that the last possibility of salvation for Germany might be missed. Both writers espoused a socialism that derived less from Marxist theory than from a personal belief in social justice. The two stories might be seen as an expression of a postrevolutionary depression. 31 notes.

D. J. Nicholls

553. Barkhausen, Hans. VERBLEIB VON DOKUMENTAR UND PROPAGANDAFILMEN DER DEUTSCHEN ARBEITERBEWEGUNG VOR 1933 [The whereabouts of documentary and propaganda movies produced by the German workers' movement before 1933]. *Archivar [West Germany] 1978 31(2): 221-225.* Discusses the whereabouts of those films produced by political parties in Germany up to and beyond 1933 which were confiscated and suppressed by the Nazis.

554. Beilner, Helmut. REICHSIDEE, STÄNDISCHE ERNEUERUNG UND FÜHRERTUM ALS ELEMENTE DES GESCHICHTSBILDES DER WEIMARER ZEIT [The idea of empire, restoration of the social orders, and Führertum: building-stones of the historical concept in the Weimar period]. *Geschichte in Wissenschaft und Unterricht [West Germany] 1977 28(1): 1-16.* Discusses the historical concepts of the state and their political consequences in history teaching in the Weimar era. In various circles, the idea of empire dominated thinking about Germany's place in Europe. Plans for internal reorganization based on the social orders and führer-rule principles were abundant. The führer was thought to bring about the new order through violence. This idea affected even democratic circles. Some of the period's foremost historians did not adhere to these concepts, but in general the teaching of history did not strengthen democratic thinking. 77 notes.

H. W. Wurster

555. Bergius, Hanne. THE AMBIGUOUS AESTHETIC OF DADA: TO-WARDS A DEFINITION OF ITS CATEGORIES. *J. of European Studies [Great Britain] 1979 9(1-2): 26-38.* Examines the presuppositions of Dadaist art, and discusses how the Berlin Dadaists in the 1920's used the press to criticize the medium itself. The Dadaists used chance, the inner logic of the creative process, indifference, and irony to point out the arbitrariness and inadequacy of reality and accepted ideas of art, and criticized the press for creating illusions masquerading as authenticity. In using press material for satirical purposes and creating mechanical works of art, however, they found themselves in the ambiguous situation of experimenters forced to use techniques derived from a familiar context. Based on printed works; 8 illus., 32 notes.

D. J. Nicholls

556. Bernett, Hajo. DAS JAHN-BILD IN DER NATIONALSOZIALIS-TISCHEN WELTANSCHAUUNG [The picture of Jahn in national socialist ideology]. *Stadion [West Germany] 1978 4(1): 225-247.* Friedrich Ludwig Jahn (1778-1852) was incorporated by Adolf Hitler into Nazi ideology as one of the precursors of the movement. Hitler adapted previous moves by the "popular" gymnastics movement in Austria and by the "Jahn Renaissance" of the 1920's. In World War II Jahn was put forward as a heroic example. Several relics of this image of Jahn have survived Germany's defeat in 1945. 71 notes. M. Geyer

557. Bookbinder, Paul. ROOTS OF TOTALITARIAN LAW: THE EARLY WORKS OF CARL SCHMITT. *Social Sci. 1981 56(3): 133-145.* Carl Schmitt provided a significant part of the theoretical legal framework for Germany's transition from a republican to a totalitarian state. Schmitt, whom Herbert Marcuse called the smartest man to support the National Socialists, rejected the liberal and individualist traditions of the 19th century in favor of a state dominated by a new "General Will" reflecting the homogenized uniformity of modern industrial society. In three major early works that explore the nature of guilt, the basis for judicial decisions, and the relationship between the individual and the state, he laid the basis for his later work and for totalitarian law.   J

558. Brady, Martin. WALTER GROPIUS: THE BAUHAUS AND MODERN ARCHITECTURE IN WEIMAR GERMANY. *A.N.U. Hist. J. [Australia] 1972 (9): 32-37.* Describes the Bauhaus architectural school as a whole, rather than centering on individuals. Emphasizes Bauhaus efforts at designing buildings which serve society, rather than following established design traditions or the ideas and conceptions of individual artists. While radical because it rejected 19th-century and earlier building styles, the Bauhaus was also conservative because it sought a return to the creation of honest structures. Also relates Bauhaus to the more progressive intellectual currents in Weimar Germany and their rejection to expressionism. In practice, the Bauhaus was particularly associated with municipal architecture and public housing projects. Since most of its work was commissioned and executed in German cities run by socialist governments, such as Berlin and Frankfurt, the style came to be regarded as leftist by more conservative circles. Concludes with a discussion of how these social and political implications affected the Bauhaus's fortunes under the Nazi government. Based on primary sources; 32 notes.   H. Shields

559. Bridenthal, Renate and Koonz, Claudia. BEYOND *KINDER, KÜCHE, KIRCHE*: WEIMAR WOMEN IN POLITICS AND WORK. Carroll, Berenice A., ed. Liberating Women's Hist. (Chicago: U. of Illinois Pr., 1976): 301-329. The support of women for Hitler's antifeminist ideology was a surprising turnabout after the alleged increase in women's rights during the Weimar period. What had appeared to be improved economic and political conditions, however, were actually tokenism and rhetoric within a patriarchal system. While Germany's political parties appealed to women voters, they did not grant them positions of power nor did they emphasize women's rights. Rather they espoused the primacy of the family and urged that women participate politically to preserve their status within the traditional role. Modernization of techniques and concentration of ownership pressed women into unskilled work with less responsibility. Women were thus not interested in entering male occupations where they were not paid or treated equally. Because no appealing alternative existed, women remained loyal to the values of *Kinder, Küche,* and *Kirche.* secondary sources; 111 notes.   S. Tomlinson-Brown

560. Budd, Michael. CONTRADICTIONS OF EXPRESSIONISM IN *THE CABINET OF DR. CALIGARI. Indiana Social Studies Q. 1981 34(2): 19-25.* Describes the "contradictory, unstable, and transitional phenomenon" of German Expressionism which began in 1910 in painting and poetry and spread to literature and theater, films, opera, and architecture, focusing on the contradictions in the film, *The Cabinet of Dr. Caligari* (1920), adopted by Siegfried Kracauer from a script by Carl Mayer and Hans Janowitz.

561. Carr, G. R. ERNST ROBERT CURTIUS AS AN INTELLECTUAL. *J. of European Studies [Great Britain] 1978 8(4): 231-245.* Rainer Lepsius defined an intellectual as someone who has gained his place in society by competence in a specialized sphere, and who uses that place to criticize the values of that society. The author applies Lepsius's definition to the German cultural critic Ernst Robert Curtius, in particular to Curtius's *Deutscher Geist in Gefahr* (Stuttgart, 1933). Curtius criticized several aspects of 20th-century German society, and in his interpretation of contemporary French writers, attempted to stimulate cultural and political unity in Germany. 51 notes.   D. J. Nicholls

562. Cases, Cesare. L'AUTOCRITICA DEGLI INTELLETTUALI TEDESCHI E IL DIBATTITO SULL'ESPRESSIONISMO [The self-criticism of German intellectuals and the debate on expressionism]. *Quaderni Storici [Italy] 1977 12(1): 12-27.* Discusses the German intellectuals' predicament as revealed by the controversy on expressionism. Since 1933 the German intellectual elite lived in exile. They felt it their task to understand why the culture of the Weimar Republic, in spite of its antibourgeois character, had been incapable of stemming or even of foreseeing the coming of Nazism. The political basis for this exercise in self-criticism was provided by Stalinism and the Popular Front policies; and in the cultural area, by the theories of socialist realism. In the literary periodical *Das Wort* (1937-39) the debate focused on Expressionism, which had been the most important factor in the break between the intelligentsia and bourgeois consciousness. The debate had been launched under Georg Lukàcs's sponsorship, in order to denounce expressionism as containing in its abstract radicalism the seeds of Nazism. In opposition to this, the return and development of the bourgeois inheritance, its humanistic and realistic aspects, was advocated. Many intellectuals, headed by Ernst Bloch, refused to follow this line, but at the same time they were incapable of indicating how expressionist radicalism could now regain its relevance. General political conditions were condemning it to obsolescence.   J

563. Chłosta, Jan. SZKOLNICTWO POLSKIE NA WARMII W LATACH 1919-1920 [Polish education in Warmia, 1919-20]. *Komunikaty Mazursko-Warmińskie [Poland] 1977 (3-4): 377-390.* Before the plebiscite of 1919, local German authorities tried to counteract Polish efforts to promote the Polish language and culture in schools. The School Commission of the Polish People's Council arranged courses for youth and future teachers who were to play a role in later plebiscite activities. A number of kindergartens and schools were opened by 1920, but German measures hindered their operation. Following the plebiscite, Polish schools were closed. Based on archival and secondary material; 3 tables, 60 notes.   R. Seitz

564. Cohen, Arthur A. MANN IN HIS LETTERS. *Commentary 1975 60(5): 62-65.* Discusses the literary letters of German author Thomas Mann, 1901-34, emphasizing his correspondence with Hermann Hesse and Karl Kerenyi.

565. Coupe, W. A. GERMAN CARTOONISTS AND THE PEACE OF VERSAILLES. *Hist. Today [Great Britain] 1982 32(Jan): 46-53.* Describes the German cartoons that were published in German periodicals, *Der wahre Jakob, Kladderadatsch, Ulk, Lustige Blätter,* and *Simplicissimus,* that portrayed the

Germans' bitterness about the terms of the 1919 Treaty of Versailles forced on Germany.

566. Coyner, Sandra J.   CLASS CONSCIOUSNESS AND CONSUMP-
TION: THE NEW MIDDLE CLASS DURING THE WEIMAR REPUBLIC.
J. of Social Hist. 1977 10(3): 310-331. Examines life-style to determine class outlook, noting that previous studies of white-collar union consumption patterns were based on averages and not on good survey methods with the necessary variables held constant. Compares government officials, government white-collar workers, and workers. The four investigated areas are diet, family size and expenses, entertainment and diversion, and savings and security. The author's study indicates the emerging differences between government white-collar workers, and workers as well as government officials. The new middle class, the white-collar worker, had an independent, modern outlook. This study suggests the need to examine the supposed appeal of Nazism to government white-collar labor more critically. 42 notes.   M. Hough

567. DeCosta, Serpil.   FOUNDATION AND DEVELOPMENT OF IFLA,
1926-1939.   *Lib. Q. 1982 52(1): 41-58.* The origins of the International Federation of Library Associations (IFLA) as an international library organization are linked to early internationalist concerns of the American and British library associations. Efforts by the League of Nations in the 1920's, coinciding with those of internationally oriented librarians such as Bishop of the United States, Krüss of Germany, and Collijn of Sweden, were instrumental in the founding of IFLA. The questions of how and why IFLA was founded in 1927 are explored, and the later formalization of the structure of the new federation, as well as its relations with other international organizations is treated in detail.   J

568. Devert, Krystyna.   HERMANN HESSE: APOSTLE OF THE
APOLITICAL "REVOLUTION."   *TriQuarterly 1972 (23/24): 302-317.* Discusses the novels of Hermann Hesse (1877-1962), their current popularity and relevance to popular culture.   S

569. Döring, Herbert.   DEUTSCHE PROFESSOREN ZWISCHEN KAI-
SERREICH UND DRITTEM REICH   [German professors between the Empire and the Third Reich]. *Neue Politische Literatur [West Germany] 1974 19(3): 340-352.* Review article. Demonstrates the unpolitical posture of the German academic "mandarins" and their detachment from the socioeconomic aspects of bourgeois society, and asks whether this was part of a bourgeois ideology or of a professional mentality. 49 notes.   G. Hollenberg

570. Düwell, Kurt.   PROBLEME DES DEUTSCHEN AUSLANDS-
SCHULWESENS IN DER WEIMARER REPUBLIK   [Problems of the German schools in foreign countries during the Weimar Republic]. *Geschichte in Wissenschaft und Unterricht [West Germany] 1975 26(3): 142-154.* The Weimar Republic was a decisive era for the German schools abroad. Their reconstruction was difficult due to the distrust left by the prewar propaganda schools. Everywhere nationalism fostered laws against foreign schools, requiring that they be integrated into the national school system. In Europe these schools perpetuated the cultural autonomy of the German minorities. The reform of teachers' training improved the previously poor quality of teachers abroad. The Nazis returned to

the old propaganda schools. Primary and secondary sources; 2 tables, 23 notes.
H. W. Wurster

571. Eckhardt, Georg. DIE GRÜNDUNG DER PSYCHOLOGISCHEN ANSTALT IN JENA (1923) [The founding of the Psychological Institute at Jena, 1923]. *Wissenschaftliche Zeitschrift der Friedrich-Schiller-Universität Jena. Gesellschafts- und Sprachwissenschaftliche Reihe [East Germany] 1973 22(4): 517-559.* In the late 18th and 19th centuries philosophers and doctors began to study psychology at the University of Jena. Between 1923 and 1933 Wilhelm Peters (1880-1963) established the Psychological Institute as one of the prominent scientific institutions of the university.

572. Eksteins, Modris. WAR, MEMORY, AND POLITICS: THE FATE OF THE FILM *ALL QUIET ON THE WESTERN FRONT.* *Central European Hist. 1980 13(1): 60-82.* Describes the events surrounding the initial approval, subsequent censure, and eventual showing of the edited version of the film, *All Quiet on the Western Front,* in Berlin in 1930-31. Although Remarque's book was a best-seller in Germany and the film maker, Carl Laemmle, was a German American, the edited film provoked an uproar in Germany which led to its subsequent banning. The author argues that those who opposed and those who favored the film did so because of ideology, not because it represented the truth about war. When the film was resubmitted to the censors in 1931 with minor cuts, it was approved with little commotion. Based largely on contemporary accounts and archival material; 55 notes.
C. R. Lovin

573. Eliaeson, Sven. MAX WEBER—EN SELEKTIV, KOMMENTERAD BIBLIOGRAFI [Max Weber—a selective, annotated bibliography]. *Statsvetenskaplig Tidskrift [Sweden] 1976 79(3): 268-288.* A bibliographical essay focusing on items relevant to issues in the contemporary debate on the German sociologist, Max Weber (1864-1920), with particular attention to Weber's political participation and methodological contribution. Works both by and about Weber are included.
R. G. Selleck

574. Epstein, Fritz T. OTTO HOETZSCH UND SEIN "OSTEUROPA" 1925-1930 [Otto Hoetzsch and his *Osteuropa,* 1925-30]. *Osteuropa [West Germany] 1975 25(8-9): 541-554.* Appraises Otto Hoetzsch's (1876-1946) leading role in the German Society for East European Studies and his founding and editorship of the new journal, *Osteuropa.* The journal quickly commanded respect, even among Soviet readers, because of its objectivity and the expertise of its contributors. The early volumes of *Osteuropa* remain an impressive source for German-Russian cultural rapprochement under the Weimar Republic. 85 notes with additional documentation on pp. A433-A440.
R. E. Weltsch

575. Fé, Franco. LA DIFFICILE COERENZA DEL "RINNEGATO" KAUTSKY [The difficult coherence of the renegade Kautsky]. *Ponte [Italy] 1977 33(6): 679-685.* Reviews Massimo L. Salvadori's *Kautsky e La Rivoluzione Socialista 1880-1938* (Milan: Feltrinelli, 1976) with a specific discussion of one of Kautsky's central themes, the transition from capitalism to socialism.

576. Field, Geoffrey G. RELIGION IN THE GERMAN VOLKSSCHULE: 1890-1928. *Leo Baeck Inst. Year Book [Great Britain] 1980 25: 41-72.* Since religious and moral training was the cornerstone of German elementary educa-

tion, confessional control was part of the system as it developed in the 19th century. Liberal Germans and advocates of a unified national system placed their hopes for improvement on the growth of *Simultanschulen* (nondenominational schools). By 1900 demands of teacher organizations for reforms and elimination of clerical control became widespread. Between 1918 and 1933 some minor improvements were accomplished, always enmeshed with the party politics of the republican governments. Jewish pupils and teachers played a minor part in the system apart from the few confessional Jewish schools. Commentary by Fritz Stern, pp. 73-77. 96 notes.   F. Rosenthal

577.   Frye, Northrop.   THE DECLINE OF THE WEST BY OSWALD SPENGLER.   *Daedalus 1974 103(1): 1-13.* In his classic work *The Decline of the West* (1918-22) Oswald Spengler opined that Western culture had moved into its winter, "with the world-states of the future fighting it out for supremacy. Of these world-states, only the Prussian tradition that runs through Bismarck seems really to have grasped the facts of the contemporary world, and to have embarked on the 'self-determination' which Spengler sees as essential to a state in the winter phase of its culture." He hoped that Germany might emerge as the Rome of the future.   E. McCarthy

578.   Gajek, Bernhard.   DER POET ALS POLITIKER   [The poet as politician].   *Schweizer Monatshefte [Switzerland] 1974 54(5): 343-354.* The letters of Herman Hesse (1877-1962), today a literary hero of the counterculture, show his struggle against war, ultranationalism, and totalitarianism, and for individual liberty before and after World War I.

579.   Gandouly, Jacques.   HANS GRIMM ET LA MODERNITE: POUR UNE LITTERATURE NATIONALE AU SERVICE DES MASSES   [Hans Grimm and modernity: toward a popular literature for the masses]. *Rev. d'Allemagne [France] 1982 14(1): 165-174.* The experience of living in southern Africa from 1898 to 1908 and the shock of the Treaty of Versailles led Hans Grimm (1875-1955) to develop the concept of literature as a means of propaganda directed at the masses and intended to bring about a national awakening which would enable Germany to recover its place in the sun. His successful novel, *Volke ohne Raum,* reflects his cultural pessimism and his idealization of the first German colonists in Africa. 24 notes.   J. S. Gassner

580.   Gilbert, Felix.   EINSTEIN UND DAS EUROPA SEINER ZEIT [Einstein and the Europe of his time]. *Hist. Zeits. [West Germany] 1981 233(1): 1-33.* Albert Einstein's career was exceptional in many ways. Aside from his scientific accomplishments, he also seemed to rise above forces of nationalism. Born in Ulm in 1879, he moved to Switzerland at age 15 and became a Swiss citizen. He refused to sign a prowar manifesto in 1914, although he permitted Germany to claim him as a citizen when he received the Nobel Prize in 1922. Einstein encouraged scientists and intellectuals to speak out against the forces that disrupted the international scientific community. After World War I, Einstein was the only German scientist with close ties to scientists in formerly enemy countries. He participated in an international commission of scientists for international cooperation. He became associated with Zionism and was deeply affected by the intensification of anti-Semitism in Germany. Based on Einstein's correspondence; 62 notes.   G. H. Davis

581. Gladen, Albin. BERUFLICHE BILDUNG IN DER DEUTSCHEN WIRTSCHAFT 1918-1945 [Vocational training in the German economy, 1918-45]. *Zeitschrift für Unternehmensgeschichte [West Germany] 1979 (Beiheft 15): 53-73.* Analyzes the development and structures of vocational education under the Weimar Republic and Nazism. Continued through World War I, the dual system of separating practical training at the workplace from school education, failing the demands of postwar youth for vocational training and employment, began to be eliminated (1931) with the founding of the German Institute for Technical Training. Nazi vocational training was directed by regional state employment offices, but the highly organized training program of private industry was left intact. Based on state and regional labor department reports and other primary sources; 5 tables, 74 notes.   G. Herritt

582. Glass, Bentley. A HIDDEN CHAPTER OF GERMAN EUGENICS BETWEEN THE TWO WORLD WARS. *Pro. of the Am. Phil. Soc. 1981 125(5): 357-367.* In 1923 the esteemed German plant geneticist Erwin Baur collaborated with Eugen Fischer and Fritz Lenz to write the influential book, *Menschliche Erblichkeitslehre und Rassenhygiene,* which later became the cornerstone of Nazi eugenics. Implicit in it was the assumption that certain characteristics of mental capacity, energy, or leadership are inherited to some extent, and that the absence of these qualities in the proletariat is likewise genetic. Two years earlier Baur had written a brief article in which he viewed Germany as on the brink of eugenic disaster, due to the depredations of colored French troops that had occupied portions of Germany. However, its bitterness toward the Allies was so strong that it was never published. US geneticist Albert F. Blakeslee offered to publish a less extreme version of the article, but Baur rejected his offer, and the book appeared two years later. Contains both Baur's and Blakeslee's versions of the disputed article. Based on the writings of Baur and the Albert Blakeslee Papers in the genetics archives of the American Philosophical Society; 38 notes.   H. M. Parker, Jr.

583. Graham, Loren R. SCIENCE AND VALUES: THE EUGENICS MOVEMENT IN GERMANY AND RUSSIA IN THE 1920'S. *Am. Hist. Rev. 1977 82(5): 1133-1164.* During the 1920's, in both Germany and the USSR, debates on genetics often portrayed Mendelian and Lamarckian theories of heredity as diametrically opposed. A German Mendelian advocate of eugenics, Alfred Ploetz, called for selective abortion to improve the species, an anticipation of current practice using amniocentesis. A Soviet scholar, Iu. Filipchenko, showed that the inheritance of acquired characteristics would harm the lower classes. These debates took place long before the advent of Lysenkoism or of National Socialism; at this time eugenics, based on Mendelian genetics, was as popular with Marxists as with the Right.   S

584. Guenther, Peter W. THE AESTHETICS OF THE BAUHAUS. *Texas Q. 1973 16(1): 162-173.* Walter Gropius founded the Bauhaus to allow artists to use new ideas, new materials, learn to live together, and improve man and environment. Additionally, the school strove to combine innovation and craftsmanship. Freedom at school led to social responsibility, not atomization. The school succeeded in the Weimar period, but Hitler closed it in 1933.   R. H. Tomlinson

585.   Hayman, Ronald.   IN SEARCH OF KAFKA: BERLIN, PRAGUE, VIENNA, LONDON, TEL AVIV.   *Encounter [Great Britain] 1981 56(5): 52-59.* Relates the author's visits with Vera Saudková (Kafka's niece) and Esther Hoffe, a friend of Max Brod, Kafka's main biographer, and discusses the relation of Kafka's writing to his personal life and indications that Kafka's rapprochement with Judaism had progressed much further than was previously thought.

586.   Hegbom, Anna.   OM OG AV KURT TUCHOLSKY   [Of and by Kurt Tucholsky].   *Samtiden [Norway] 1974 83(2): 98-120.* Biography of the German Jewish radical writer, Kurt Tucholsky (1890-1935), with translations of selections of his prose and poetry into Norwegian.   R. G. Selleck

587.   Held, Joseph.   DIE VOLKSGEMEINSCHAFTSIDEE IN DER DEUTSCHEN JUGENDBEWEGUNG: TÄTIGKEIT UND WELTANSCHAUUNG EINIGER JUGENDVEREINE ZUR ZEIT DER WEIMARER REPUBLIK   [The idea of national unity in the youth movement: activity and philosophy of some youth organizations at the time of the Weimar Republic]. *Jahrbuch des Inst. für Deutsche Geschichte [Israel] 1977 6: 458-476.* The German youth movement of the Weimar period had more in common with the utopian communities of 19th-century America than with the ubiquitous youth culture of the 1960's. A variety of youth organizations, loosely connected or not connected at all, sprang up in Germany in the 1920's. Some were long-lived; others frequently reorganized or soon died. Most were critical of Weimar society and most sought to develop "New Men" able to regenerate Germany. Individual youth organizations varied from the summer's-long singing, dancing, and sermonizing group led by Friedrich Lamberty (the Kronacher band), to the Habertshof colony with its sober community living, orphanage, and educational institutions. 52 notes.   M. Faissler

588.   Hendry, John.   WEIMAR CULTURE AND QUANTUM CAUSALITY.   *Hist. of Sci. [Great Britain] 1980 18(3): 155-180.* Examines the conclusions of Paul Forman "Weimar Culture, Causality, and Quantum Theory, 1918-1927: Adaptation by German Physicists and Mathematicians to a Hostile Intellectual Environment" *[Historical Studies in the Physical Sciences* 3 (1971): 1-116] that following World War I and before the development of an acausal quantum mechanics, many German physicists either avoided or repudiated causality in physics as a result of the "currents of thought" then present rather than because of developments in physics. Based on scientific publications and correspondence of the period; 115 notes.   L. R. Maxted

589.   Hinrichs, Ernst.   DIE LEGENDE ALS GLEICHNIS   [Legend as allegory].   *Geschichte in Wissenschaft und Unterricht [West Germany] 1974 25(7): 395-410.* Discusses the message of Heinrich Mann's novels about the French king Henry IV and its relationship with the political reality of the Weimar Republic and the French Third Republic. These novels are fairly popular, mainly because of their subject, though these are no proper historical novels. The obvious parallels between France before Henry IV and the Nazis in Germany have aroused criticism. But Mann was not interested in historical truthfulness; he made a political statement couched in a historical situation. Gives an account of varying interpretations of Henry IV. 39 notes.   H. W. Wurster

590. Horn, Daniel. REFORM AND REVOLUTION IN GERMAN EDU-CATION, 1890-1935. *Hist. of Educ. Q. 1979 19(4): 485-490.* Reviews two books on unsuccessful reforms and destructive revolutions that marked turning points in the history of German education in the late Wilhelmine and Weimar periods. Sterling Fishman's *Struggle for German Youth: The Search for Educational Reform in Imperial Germany* examines the educational ideas of Alfred Lichtwark, a reformer of art education, Herman Lietz, the founder of the German country boarding school movement, and Ludwig Gurlitt, the proponent of the Wandervogel youth movement. Michael S. Steinberg's *Sabers and Brown Shirts: The German Students' Path to National Socialism* traces the rise in university enrollments during the economic depressions of 1922-23 and 1929-31, the role of dueling fraternities such as the Burschenschaften, and the revival of racist ideas which lead to the burning of books and the end of academic freedom.

S. H. Frank

591. Hsu Nan-hu. TÊ-KUO HSIEN TAI CHIAO YÜ SSÜ HSIANG CHIH PIEN CH'IEN [Changes in modern educational thought in Germany]. *Shih-ta Hsüeh-pao (Bull., Natl. Taiwan Normal U.) [Taiwan] 1974 19: 121-133.* The history of modern German educational theories can be divided into three phases: 1) 1870-1918, when German education was reformed and expanded to raise the literacy standard of the population and to implement the nationalist policies of the Bismarckian era, 2) 1918-45, when free and personalized education of the Weimar years gave way to the political-racial programs of the Nazi regime, and 3) 1945 to the present, when educational ideologies reflect the politics of a divided nation. The child-centered Montessori system, the youth culture, and vocational schools were all products of the first phase of educational reforms. During the Weimar Republic, a variety of educational theories flourished but they all shared a basic scientific spirit. However, education became monolithic under the Nazis. During the third phase, educational theory in East Germany evolved from universally Communist to nationalist and socialist. In West Germany, educational ideas have been highly influenced by political and economic democratic theories as well as by the philosophy of existentialism. Based on published German works; 11 notes.

R. C. Houston

592. Jaegerschmid, Adelgundis. GESPRÄCHE MIT EDMUND HUSSERL 1931-1936 [Conversations with Edmund Husserl 1931-36]. *Stimmen der Zeit [West Germany] 1981 199(1): 48-58.* Personal recollection of conversations with the German philosopher Edmund Husserl (1859-1938), who revealed his increasing anxiety with Nazism and sought the working out of a system of universal science.

593. Jay, Martin. KURT MANDELBAUM: HIS DECADE AT THE IN-STITUTE OF SOCIAL RESEARCH. *Development and Change [Netherlands] 1979 10(4): 545-552.* Examines Kurt Mandelbaum's tenure at the German Institute of Social Research from the mid-1920's and his contributions to the *Zeitschrift für Sozialforschung,* the earliest being a review of a Festschrift dedicated to Carl Grünberg, the first director of the institute.

594. Kahlenberg, Friedrich. ERKENNTNISINTERESSEN UND WEGE DER RUNDFUNKFORSCHUNG IN DER BUNDESREPUBLIK DEUTSCHLAND [Fields of activity and progress of broadcasting research in

the Federal Republic of Germany]. *Hist. J. of Film, Radio and Television [Great Britain] 1982 2(1): 65-89.* An account of the development of research in West Germany on broadcasting from the first transmission by Deutsche FunkStunde-AG from Berlin (1923), with comment on the past and future value of the study of broadcasting research history. 92 notes.   A. E. Standley

595. Káňa, Otakar.   VĚDA VE SLUŽBÁCH VÝBOJNÉ POLITIKY NĚMECKÉHO IMPERIALISMU V OBDOBÍ VÝMARSKÉ REPUBLIKY [Science in the service of Germany's aggressive imperialism, 1918-33]. *Slezský Sborník [Czechoslovakia] 1976 74(2): 98-109.* Describes the cultivation of German irredentism during the Weimar Republic. German bourgeois politicians could not openly advocate annexation, yet they labored through the scientific and academic community preparing German support for revision of the Treaty of Versailles. Old institutions of German imperialism such as the Verein für das Deutschtum im Ausland and the Deutsches Auslandinstitut received private funds to encourage German studies. This heightened national consciousness among Germans living abroad and at home. Emphasis on German language alienated Germans living abroad from citizens of the country of their residence. 66 notes.   B. Kimmel

596. Kane, Martin.   THE ART AND COMMITMENT OF GEORGE GROSZ.   *Twentieth Cent. Studies [Great Britain] 1975 (13/14): 110-128.* Discusses political and social satire in the cartoons and caricatures of George Grosz (1893-1959) in Germany, 1917-32, emphasizing socialist ideology in his depictions of social classes and poverty.

597. Kantzenbach, Friedrich Wilhelm.   DAS WISSENSCHAFTLICHE WERDEN VON HANS-JOACHIM SCHOEPS UND SEINE VERTREIBUNG AUS DEUTSCHLAND 1938   [The scholarly development of Hans-Joachim Schoeps and his expulsion from Germany in 1938]. *Zeitschrift für Religions- und Geistesgeschichte [West Germany] 1980 32(4): 319-352.* These 37 letters and one card that Schoeps wrote to Professor Martin Rade between January 1928 and June 1939 deal in the early years with Schoeps' course of studies towards his doctorate of philosophy, awarded in 1932. Also discussed are Schoeps, early scholarly writings. After 1933 the main themes are Schoeps' experiences with discrimination against him as a Jew and his plans to leave Germany. Also contains a letter by Schoeps' mother, his *curriculum vitae,* and an introduction by Professor Kantzenbach.   J. D. Hunley

598. Kater, Michael H.   JUGEND, ERZIEHUNG, WISSENSCHAFT: STUDIEN ZUR IDEOLOGIE UND PÄDAGOGIK IN DEUTSCHLAND ZWISCHEN 1918 UND 1945   [Youth, education, science: studies on ideology and teaching in Germany, 1918-45]. *Archiv für Sozialgeschichte [West Germany] 1979 19: 660-671.* Review article of Ulrich Linse's *Die anarchistische und anarcho-syndikalistische Jugendbewegung 1919-1933. Zur Geschichte und Ideologie der anarchistischen, syndikalistischen und unionistischen Kinder- und Jugendorganisationen von 1919-1933* (Frankfurt, 1976), Kurt-Ingo Flessau's *Schule der Diktatur. Lehrpläne und Schulbucher des Nationalsozialismus* (Munich, 1977), and Uwe Dietrich Adam's *Hochschule und Nationalsozialismus. Die Universität Tübingen im Dritten Reich* (Tübingen, 1977). 69 notes.   S

599. Kater, Michael H. KRISIS DES FRAUENSTUDIUMS IN DER WEI-
MARER REPUBLIK [The crisis of women's university attendance in the
Weimar Republic]. *Vierteljahrschrift für Sozial- und Wirtschaftsgeschichte [West
Germany] 1972 59(2): 207-255.* Although the outbreak of World War I and the
"enlightened" atmosphere of the Weimar Republic resulted in an increase in the
number of female students in the German universities, an exact analysis of the
position of female students during the years 1918-33 shows that female academi-
cians remained underprivileged. The main arguments against female students
were that women would take away men's jobs, especially in times of recession,
and that academic study would hinder women's fulfillment of their real profession, namely, the bearing and care of as many children as possible—a sociobiolog-
ical theory which culminated in the antifemale ideology of the German Nazis.
Based on documents in the Bundesarchiv Koblenz and the US National Archives,
published sources, and secondary material; 7 tables, 224 notes.

R. Wagnleitner

600. Kater, Michael H. THE WORK STUDENT: A SOCIO-ECONOMIC
PHENOMENON OF EARLY WEIMAR GERMANY. *J. of Contemporary
Hist. [Great Britain] 1975 10(1): 71-94.* Among the groups most seriously affected by World War I and its aftermath were the students of Germany. Once
privileged, they now frequently had to work their way through the university.
Difficulties abounded. Unaccustomed to heavy manual labor, they experienced
the disdain of the old hands. Should the students' efforts result in out-producing
the ordinary laborers, there was open hostility engendered by fear of displace-
ment. The *werkstudenten* were appreciated most often only by the managers; to
their fellow-workers, they were just potential or sub-managers. Large numbers of
students came to the United States for experience and greater earning power.
They returned to a Germany depressed and hopeless. The inflation of the 1920's
further eroded morale. No wonder that the National Socialist German Student
League seemed initially attractive. Archival and printed primary sources; 59
notes.

M. P. Trauth

601. Ketels, Violet B. THE DISILLUSIONED AS PREY OF POWER:
ÖDÖN VON HORVÁTH'S DRAMA AND THE RISE OF NAZISM.
Soundings 1979 59(4): 480-499. A study of the drama of German playwright
Ödön von Horváth, 1926-36, and the rise of Nazism as displayed in his characters,
who suffered from the postwar German anomie that was the result of economic
pressure and which erupted into the fascist mentality.

602. Knaack, Rudolf. QUELLEN IM STAATSARCHIV POTSDAM ZUR
BERLINER THEATERGESCHICHTE [Sources in the State Archives of
Potsdam on the history of the Berlin theater]. *Archivmitteilungen [East Ger-
many] 1976 26(6): 223-226.* A survey of the sources in the State Archives of
Potsdam concerning the history of the theater in Berlin during the 19th and 20th
centuries.

603. Küppers, Heinrich. WEIMARER SCHULPOLITIK IN DER WIRT-
SCHAFTS- UND STAATSKRISE DER REPUBLIK [Weimar educational
policy during the economic and political crisis of the republic]. *Vierteljahrshefte
für Zeitgeschichte [West Germany] 1980 28(1): 20-46.* An analysis of the
dilemma of educational reformers struggling against strong authoritarian forces

in the Weimar Republic, describing the 1928-31 efforts for the introduction of the *Mittlere Reife* (a higher education 10th grade diploma) as a way of breaking the vicious circle of increasing educational job requirements and ever larger numbers rushing to college preparatory schools and universities owing to measures to equalize educational opportunities and the dramatic reduction of state and other jobs. Based on minutes of the Committee for Education (State Archive Hamburg), state educational records, and secondary sources; 108 notes.   D. Prowe

604. Kurzweil, Zwi Erich. DIE ODENWALDSCHULE (1910-1934) [The Odenwald School (1910-34)]. *Paedogogica Historica [Belgium] 1973 13(1): 23-56*. In 1910 Paul Geheeb founded the Oldenwaldschule in Oberhambach near Darmstadt. Its career was notable for progressive experiments in education until its closing in 1934. 23 notes.   J. M. McCarthy.

605. Labisch, Alfons. THE WORKINGMEN'S SAMARITAN FEDERATION (ARBEITER-SAMARITER-BUND) 1888-1933. *J. of Contemporary Hist. [Great Britain] 1978 13(2): 297-322*. The Workingmen's Samaritan Federation (ASB) developed out of a Berlin first aid course given in 1888. The organization functioned as ambulance service and general emergency unit, much like a peacetime Red Cross. The ASB had its own ensign of a white, later a gold, cross on a red background together with the letters ASB. It had an enormously rapid, widespread growth until 1933 when the Nazis annexed it to the Red Cross. Based on archival sources; 11 notes.   M. P. Trauth

606. Laqueur, Walter. AMERICA AND THE WEIMAR ANALOGY: LETTER FROM NEW YORK. *Encounter [Great Britain] 1972 38(5): 19-25*. Discusses the role of intellectuals and liberals in the Weimar Republic of Germany, 1918-33, and the possible relevance of historical analogies to elements of fascism in the United States in the 1970's.

607. Läuter, Peter. "BARRIKADEN AN DER RUHR." ÜBER EINE BISHER UNGEDRUCKTE SCHRIFT DES VERLAGES DER JUGENDINTERNATIONALE [*"Barrikaden an der Ruhr"*: an unpublished book of the publishing company of the Communist Youth International]. *Beiträge zur Geschichte der Arbeiterbewegung [East Germany] 1976 18(1): 78-86*. Publication of comments by the German authors Johannes R. Becher, Gerhart Hauptmann, Hermann Hesse, Alfred Kerr, Käthe Kollwitz, Thomas Mann, Heinrich Mann, and Erich Mühsam in July and August 1925. They protested the prohibition by German authorities of Kurt Kläber's *Barrikaden an der Ruhr* (Berlin, 1925).   R. Wagnleitner

608. Luhr, William. *NOSFERATU* AND POSTWAR GERMAN FILM. *Michigan Acad. 1982 14(4): 453-458*. A comparison of Werner Herzog's *Nosferatu* of 1977 and F. W. Murnau's *Nosferatu* of 1922 show epidemic vampirism as a metaphor for postwar cultural decay, the draining of vitality from a society, a society emasculated even before the vampire arrives and which proves incapable of resisting him.

609. Lurz, Meinhold. DER BAU DER NEUEN UNIVERSITÄT IM BRENNPUNKT GEGENSÄTZLICHER INTERESSEN [The building of the new university as the focal point of contrary interests]. *Ruperto Carola [West Germany] 1975 27(55/56): 39-45*. Plans for the construction of new buildings for

Heidelberg University appeared to be stymied in 1927 by financial difficulties. The then American ambassador to Germany, Jacob Gould Schurman, collected $500,000 from American donors. On 17 December 1928, this gift was transferred at a ceremony which hailed international cooperation. The state of Baden sponsored a prize competition for architectural plans which Carl Gruber won. His plan was criticized by Schurman for emphasizing the old buildings with which the new were to be integrated and by the mayor of Heidelberg for being too massive. Gruber revised the plans, and the cornerstone was laid. The new building was dedicated with speeches emphasizing more national than international goals. In November 1933 a memorial to students killed in the war was erected in part of the new building and dedicated with a speech by the chancellor of the university that demonstrated how the ideas of national socialism had overcome those of nationalism. H. D. Andrews

610. Matamoro, Blas. THOMAS MANN, EN SUS DIARIOS [Thomas Mann in his diaries]. *Cuadernos Hispanoamericanos [Spain] 1981 124(371): 227-265.* The novelist Thomas Mann (1875-1955) kept a diary from early adolescence onwards. After he left Germany in 1933 some of his journals were passed to the Nazi authorities, but subsequently he regained them. Mann destroyed much of this material in 1945. The author quotes extracts from some of the surviving diaries, for the years 1918 to 1921 and 1933 to 1936. The diaries kept in the Thomas Mann archive in Zürich were opened in 1975. They add insight into Mann's ideological development, lifestyle, attitude toward Germany, views on society, World War I, Spengler, Nazism and Hitler, his relationship with his brother Heinrich, comments on his own writings, and his homosexual leanings. Based on Thomas Mann's diaries and correspondence. P. J. Durell

611. Mazza, Mario. CRISI TEDESCA E CULTURA CLASSICA: INTEL-LETTUALI TRA REAZIONE E RIVOLUZIONE [The German crisis and classical culture: intellectuals between reaction and revolution]. *Studi Storici [Italy] 1980 21(2): 255-272.* Many of the outstanding scholars of ancient Greek culture in Germany during the Weimar era opposed both parliamentary power and a democratic constitution. One of the leaders of this antidemocratic group was Ulrich von Wilamowitz-Moellendorff (1848-1931). Wilamowitz was active in the Deutsche Vaterlandspartei and later in the Nationale Vereinigung. He based his opposition to a democratic, liberal, or constitutional state on his interpretation of Plato's ideal state. Primary sources; 78 notes. E. E. Ryan

612. Meier-Cronemeyer, Hermann. GEMEINSCHAFT UND GLAUBE: REFLEXIONEN ÜBER DIE DEUTSCHE JUGENDBEWEGUNG [Community and belief: reflections on the German youth movement]. *Jahrbuch des Inst. für Deutsche Geschichte [Israel] 1977 6: 422-455.* This survey of German youth groups of the 1920's analyzes youth organizations ranging from far Left to far Right, including anarchists, socialists, Marxists, various Jewish groups, Nazis, conservatives, imperialists, and others. Discusses each with enough ideological-philosophical depth to provide a broad spectrum of changing and often contradictory German thought. Also mentions individual leaders and thinkers, most notably Martin Buber and Gustav Landauer. 111 notes. M. Faissler

613. Messner, Johannes. FIFTY YEARS AFTER THE DEATH OF HEIN-RICH PESCH. *Rev. of Social Econ. 1976 34(2): 117-124.* The validity of the political economic theory of Heinrich Pesch remains solid 50 years after his death, 1926-76.

614. Moles, Abraham A. DESSIN EXPRESSIONISTE ET CARICATURE POLITIQUE EN ALLEMAGNE (1920-1970) [Graphic expressionism and political caricature in Germany, 1920-70]. *Rev. Allemagne [France] 1980 12(2): 178-199.* Graphic expressionism is best defined as a method which expresses reality better than reality itself and which strengthens form by using the Gestalt properties of the black line upon a white surface. Because the movement was engendered by opposition to social conditions in the German Empire, its themes were often slaughter houses, jails, and streets and its formats political caricatures and posters. It exploited the creative value of *Schadenfreude.* These characteristics are exemplified in the works of Käthe Kollwitz (1867-1945), Alfred Kubin (1877-1959), and especially Paul Weber (b. 1893). 14 illus., biblio.

J. S. Gassner

615. Moses, Stephane. FRANZ ROSENZWEIG HEUTE: ANLÄSSLICH SEINES 50 JÄHRIGEN TODESTAGES [Franz Rosenzweig today: on the anniversary of his death]. *Bull. des Leo Baeck Inst. [Israel] 1981 (58): 11-16.* Franz Rosenzweig's principal work was *Der Stern der Erlösung* (1921). As a student he was influenced by Hegel and by his teacher Friedrich Meinicke. After World War I he rejected the philosophical and political model of the great western countries in favor of the mythical traditions of ancient Greece, Judaism, and Christianity. 15 notes.

M. Faissler

616. Müller, Hans-Harald. PARTEILITERATUR ODER LINK-SRADIKALISMUS? UNTERSUCHUNGEN ZU QUELLEN UND REZEP-TION VON THEODOR PLIEVIERS "DES KAISERS KULIS" [Party literature or left radicalism? Investigations into the sources and reception of Theodor Plievier's *The Emperor's Coolies*]. *Rev. d'Allemagne [France] 1975 7(3): 351-378.* Theodor Plievier's 1929 novel *Des Kaisers Kulis* [The emperor's coolies] describes the rebellion of German sailors in 1917 and again, successfully, in 1918. The book was popular in left-wing circles, including those dominated by Communists, but Plievier was an individual anarchist and avoided having his work published by a Party publishing house. *Des Kaisers Kulis* is not party literature. 92 notes.

J. C. Billigmeier

617. Münz, Rudolf. ZWEI DOKUMENTE ZUR GESCHICHTE DER THEATERWISSENSCHAFT AN DER BERLINER UNIVERSITÄT [Two documents concerning the history of theater science in the University of Berlin]. *Wissenschaftliche Zeitschrift der Humboldt U. zu Berlin [East Germany] 1974 23(3/4): 349-356.* Summarizes the steps initially taken to establish the Institute for Theater Science in Berlin in introduction to two documents. The first, a lecture given by Max Herrmann on 27 June 1920 and again approved by him just before he was carried off by the Nazis, argued for an institute of theater science in a university, since related departments required courses useless to theater science and failed to provide what was uniquely essential to students in that field. The second is a statement from the university (1921) making clear the purpose of the proposed institute and describing its expected relations with the rest of the university. 4 notes.

M. Faissler

618. Nelson, Benjamin. MAX WEBER'S "AUTHOR'S INTRODUCTION" (1920): A MASTER CLUE TO HIS MAIN AIMS. *Sociol. Inquiry 1974 44(4): 269-277.* To understand Max Weber's (1864-1920) research goals requires careful analysis of his major works, especially *The Protestant Ethic and The Spirit of Capitalism* (New York, 1930); *Economy and Society* (Totowa, New Jersey: Bedminster Press, 1968), and *Gesammelte Aufsätze zur Religionssoziologie* (1920).
S

619. Nemitz, Kurt. JULIUS MOSES: NACHLASS UND BIBLIOGRA-PHIE [Julius Moses: papers and bibliography]. *Int. Wissenschaftliche Korrespondenz zur Geschichte der Deutschen Arbeiterbewegung [West Germany] 1974 10(2): 219-247.* A summary listing of the papers of Dr. Julius Moses (1868-1942), physician, *Reichstag* deputy (1920-1932), executive committee member and health policy expert first for the Independent Socialists and later for the Social Democrats. The collection, located at the apartment of Dr. Kurt Nemitz (Bremen), contains books and articles by Moses, a volume of reminiscences, and 69 folders of collected materials and commentaries. Biblio.
D. Prowe

620. Niebuhr, Reinhold. GERMANY. *Worldview 1973 16(6): 13-18.* An overview of Germany's cultural milieu, 1921-31, which touches on political figures and religion, and characterizes politics as inept and spiritualism as heroic, yet ineffectual.

621. Pachter, Henry. THE AMBIGUOUS LEGACY OF EDUARD BERN-STEIN. *Dissent 1981 28(2): 203-216.* Discusses the life and political career of Eduard Bernstein (1850-1932) and his independent interpretation of socialist theory and contribution to the development of socialism in Western Europe, particularly West Germany.

622. Pachter, Henry. NOSTALGIA AND REVISION: THE VOGUE OF WEIMAR CULTURE. *Dissent 1976 23(3): 279-283.* Seeks to establish a link between the two extremes of Weimar culture in Germany during the 1920's, showing that both the vulgarity and the more noble aspects of the culture stem from the same background in society and politics.

623. Perrotti, Gabriele. DEMOCRAZIA, LIBERTÀ E POTERE IN MANNHEIM [Democracy, liberty, and power in Mannheim]. *Studi Storici [Italy] 1981 22(1): 151-178.* Studies the concepts of democracy, liberty, and power in some of the writings of the German sociologist, Karl Mannheim (1893-1947). Mannheim did not aim to supply a foundation for political decisions that remained irrational choices. He attempted, rather, to isolate in a theoretical way the institutional conditions necessary for the autonomous forms of the rationalization of society to find a limit in a superior political instance. 82 notes.
E. E. Ryan

624. Poor, Harold Lloyd. CITY VERSUS COUNTRY: ANTI-URBANISM IN THE WEIMAR REPUBLIC. *Societas 1976 6 (3): 177-192.* A comparative analysis of German history textbooks before and after 1918 reveals a growth of "anti-urban, anti-modern, anti-technological" feeling between the two periods. This helps to explain the rise to power of the Nazis, whose ideology glorified the countryside over the city. Based on sources in the Internationales Schulbuchinstitut in Braunschweig; 51 notes.
J. D. Hunley

625. Raddatz, Fritz J. PROLETARISCHE LYRIK IN DER WEIMARER REPUBLIK [Proletarian lyricism in the Weimar Republic]. *Frankfurter Hefte [West Germany] 1973 28(12): 897-906.* Weimar proletarian poetry 1918-33 was mainly rhymed propaganda of the crudest sort.

626. Raff, Dieter. EIN HALBES JAHRHUNDERT INTERNATION-ALER FERIENKURSE [Half a century of international vacation courses]. *Ruperto Carola [West Germany] 1978 30(61): 32-46.* Foreign students, especially from the United States, studied in Germany in the 1920's and 1930's but the international vacation courses at the University of Heidelberg became problematic during and after World War II.

627. Reishaus-Etzold, Heike. DIE EINFLUSSNAHME DER CHEMIEMONOPOLE AUF DIE "KAISER-WILHELM-GESELLSCHAFT ZUR FÖRDERUNG DER WISSENSCHAFTEN E.V." WÄHREND DER WEIMARER REPUBLIK [The influence of the chemical monopolies on the Emperor Wilhelm Society for the Advancement of Science during the Weimar Republic]. *Jahrbuch für Wirtschaftsgeschichte [East Germany] 1973 (1): 37-61.* The development of scientific research during the Weimar Republic, as exemplified by the history of the Kaiser-Wilhelm-Gesellschaft—Germany's largest research organization and predecessor of the Max-Planck-Gesellschaft of 1948—was characterized by a combination of increased reliance on public funds and the extension of control by private industry. In particular, with the formation of the monopolistic I. G. Farben in 1925, the chemical industry came to assume a dominant role in scientific research. Based on documents in the Deutsches Zentralarchiv Potsdam, archives of firms in the GDR, publications of the society, and secondary sources; 4 tables, 133 notes. J. A. Perkins

628. Rich, B. Ruby. *MAEDCHEN IN UNIFORM:* FROM REPRESSIVE TOLERANCE TO EROTIC LIBERATION. *Radical Am. 1981 15(6): 17-36.* Socially tolerant Weimar Germany, seen through a careful study of Leotine Sagan's fine film *Mädchen In Uniform* (1931), had a wider lesbian culture than is often remembered. The film itself, despite its prominence at the time, has been largely forgotten or misunderstood. The first truly radical lesbian film, *Mädchen's* message is that the momentary victories for tolerance are likely to be attacked. Traces the lives of those involved in the filming through the Nazi period. 26 notes, 8 illus. C. M. Hough

629. Rippley, La Vern. AMERICAN MILK COWS FOR GERMANY: A SEQUEL. *North Dakota Hist. 1977 44(3): 15-23.* Following World War I German-American farmers contributed milk cows to Germany to help counter a serious shortage of milk. Local organizations sprang up to receive dairy cattle donations and facilitate the shipment of the animals to Germany. In April 1921, the Lebanon-Ixonia, Wisconsin, *Committee zur Hilfeleistung der Notleidenden in Deutschland und Österreich* sent a shipment of cattle to German orphanages and hospitals accompanied by a large contingent of German-American farmers from South Dakota and Wisconsin. The venture was successfully undertaken, but no further shipments of cattle to Germany took place. The events of the trip are based on a diary kept by Vilas Behl, a participant, as well as on interviews with surviving members of the delegation. N. Lederer

630. Ritzer, George. PROFESSIONALIZATION, BUREAUCRATIZA-
TION AND RATIONALIZATION: THE VIEWS OF MAX WEBER.
Social Forces 1975 53(4): 627-634. Max Weber (1864-1920) said much about the
professions and the relationship between professionalization, bureaucratization
and rationalization. He recognized that professionalization, like bureaucratization, is an aspect of the rationalization of society. Unlike some contemporary
sociologists, Weber saw that professionalization and bureaucratization are not
antithetical. He understood that a profession must be viewed from the structural,
processual, and power perspectives. Weber's rich understanding of the professions is attributed to two factors. First, he saw them as part of the rationalization
process. Second, his thinking was not distorted, as was the case with American
sociologists, by the aberrant case of the physician in private practice as the
prototype of the professions.   J

631. Roche, Georges. INGENIEURS ET MODERNITE SOUS LA
REPUBLIQUE DE WEIMAR [Engineers and modernity during the Weimar
Republic]. *Rev. d'Allemagne [France] 1982 14(1): 113-126.* Modernity as understood by the engineers was the growth of productivity and the advent of industrial
rationality in a harmonious society guided by technocrats. The world economic
crisis which challenged these assumptions was followed by the victory of National
Socialism, which some engineers vainly hoped to synthesize with technocracy.
This study raises the questions of how these concepts of modernity were transmit-
ted and of what relation there may have been between the actual experiences of
the engineers and the fantasies of the conservative revolution. 51 notes.
                                                                        J. S. Gassner

632. Roper, Katherine Larson. IMAGES OF GERMAN YOUTH IN WEI-
MAR NOVELS. *J. of Contemporary Hist. [Great Britain] 1978 13(3): 499-516.*
The German novels of the Weimar period mirror the crises of the youth at the
time. The hero is usually an adolescent or young adult experiencing personal
difficulty with an authority figure of the home or the school. In the early 1920's,
the problem was generally resolved passively by a return to the precrisis ideal.
In the later 1920's, the solution was activity, revolt, and commitment to a new
order. 39 notes.   M. P. Trauth

633. Rühl, Joachim K. DAS JAHNBILD DES "ZENTRALAUS-
SCHUSSES ZUR FÖRDERUNG DER VOLKS- UND JUGENDSPIELE IN
DEUTSCHLAND" (1892-1921) [The image of Jahn in the Central Committee
for the Promotion of Popular and Youth Games in Germany, 1892-1921]. *Stadion [West Germany] 1978 4(1): 202-224.* Friedrich Ludwig Jahn (1778-1852)
and his writings formed the basis of the arguments brought forward by the
Central Committee for the Promotion of Popular and Youth Games in Germany.
Jahn's writings were used to sanction existing structures, but also made innovation possible. 172 notes.   M. Geyer

634. Schiller, Dieter. OKTOBER—ERFAHRUNGEN [October: experi-
ences]. *Einheit [East Germany] 1977 32(5): 583-589.* Analyzes the impact of the
Russian Revolution on German bourgeois and left-wing authors, scientists, and
intellectuals in the 1920's and 1930's.

635.   Schlichting, Uta von.   DIE WEIMARER SCHULARTIKEL. IHRE
ENTSTEHUNG UND BEDEUTUNG   [Legislation concerning schools in the
Weimar constitution: genesis and importance]. *Internationales Jahrbuch für Ges-
chichts- und Geographie-Unterricht [West Germany] 1972/73 14: 27-94.* Analyzes the origins and content of the legislation concerning the organization and
ideological principles of the educational system in Weimar Germany. Reviews the
debates of the committee to draft a constitution and of the plenary sessions of the
National Assembly, and describes the compromises reached on educational issues, particularly federal versus central jurisdiction, denominational versus nondenominational and private versus public schools. Based on German published
documents, the German constitution, and on secondary works; 338 notes, biblio.,
2 appendixes.   J. B. Street

636.   Schlicker, Wolfgang.   KONZEPTIONEN UND AKTIONEN BÜR-
GERLICHER DEUTSCHER WISSENSCHAFTSPOLITIK. ZUM GESELL-
SCHAFTLICHEN STELLENWERT DER FORSCHUNG NACH 1918 UND
ZUR GRÜNDUNG DER NOTGEMEINSCHAFT DER DEUTSCHEN WIS-
SENSCHAFT   [Conceptions and actions of bourgeois German economic policy:
on the social position of scientific research after 1918 and the founding of the
Notgemeinschaft der Deutschen Wissenschaft]. *Zeitschrift für Geschichtswissenschaft [East Germany] 1979 27(5): 423-438.* Because World War I had had
adverse effects on German science, the chemist Fritz Haber took the lead in
establishing an organization to promote and coordinate scientific research. In
1920 the universities and various scientific organizations formed the Notgemeinschaft der deutschen Wissenschaft [Emergency Union of German Science], which
was supported by the government and private capital. Through this allegedly
independent organization monopoly capital decisively influenced the direction of
scientific research.   74 notes.   J. T. Walker

637.   Schlicker, Wolfgang.   ZU MAX PLANCKS BEDEUTUNG FÜR DIE
LEITUNG DER WISSENSCHAFT UND ORGANIZATION DER FOR-
SCHUNG   [The significance of Max Planck for the leadership of science and
the organization of research]. *Jahrbuch für Wirtschaftsgeschichte [East Ger-
many] 1975 (2): 161-185.* Assesses the scientific career of Max Planck (1858-
1947) during the Weimar period, when he taught at the University of Berlin and
belonged to the Kaiser-Wilhelm-Gesellschaft. Although Planck was personally
committed to preserving the bourgeois social order, he nevertheless often found
himself opposed to its antihumanist and unprogressive attitudes. These conflicts
were reflected in his leadership of the scientific community, distinguished by his
efforts to maintain international scientific collaboration during World War I and
by his defense of Albert Einstein against Nazi persecution. Primary and secondary sources; 70 notes.   R. J. Bazillion

638.   Schödl, Günter.   PAUL SAMASSA: EIN BIOGRAPHISCHER BEI-
TRAG ZUR VORGESCHICHTE DES "EXTREMEN NATIONALISMUS"
IN DEUTSCHLAND UND ÖSTERREICH   [Paul Samassa: a biographical
contribution to the early history of "extreme nationalism" in Germany and
Austria]. *Südostdeutsches Archiv [West Germany] 1978 21: 75-104.* Provides a
biographical sketch of Paul Samassa (1868-1941), a representative of the "intellectual bourgeoisie" and harbinger of extreme German nationalism. The son of
a patrician family in Ljubljana, Yugoslavia, he became associate professor of

Zoology at Heidelberg University. Examines his political and propagandist activity as one of the most important members of the All-German Union. Based on the unpublished papers of Samassa and other primary sources in the Österreichisches Staatsarchiv in Vienna; 149 notes.   A. A. Strnad

639. Schroeter, Gerd. MAX WEBER AS OUTSIDER: HIS NOMINAL INFLUENCE ON GERMAN SOCIOLOGY IN THE TWENTIES. *J. of the Hist. of the Behavioral Sci. 1980 16(4): 317-332.* An assessment of the influence that Max Weber's writings had on the growth of German sociology after World War I. The author isolates those themes which were of major importance during the Weimar Republic: the concern with social integration; the shattered faith in reason; and the attempt to create a uniquely "German" sociology. It becomes clear that neither Weber's conception of sociology nor his methodological formulations had much impact on the next generation. These findings can be accounted for in three different ways: 1) that he died too early; 2) that German sociology lacked the necessary institutionalization; or 3) that there was a reorientation in scholarship following World War I, which Weber's opus could not bridge.   J

640. Schulze, Franz. COLD FACTS. *Art in Am. 1981 69(7): 142-147.* Explores the themes and major artists of the German Realist movement of the 1920's, known as *Neue Sachlichkeit,* discussing the work of Max Beckmann, George Grosz, Otto Dix, Christian Schad, Rudolph Schlichter, and others, and their role as social critics.

641. Schumacher, Martin. QUELLEN ZUR GESCHICHTE DER LANDWIRTSCHAFTKAMMERN UND LANDWIRTSHAFTLICHEN GENOSSENSCHAFTEN IN DER WEIMARER REPUBLIK [Sources for the history of agricultural chambers of commerce and agricultural cooperative associations in the Weimar Republic]. *Archivar [West Germany] 1977 30(3): 273-280.* Considers the loss of documents from West German archives since 1933, in particular those sources dealing with agricultural cooperatives, 1918-33.

642. Schumann, Rosemarie. KURT HILLER ZWISCHEN PAZIFISMUS UND REAKTION. WELTANSCHAULICHE POSITION UND POLITISCHE ROLLE EINES BÜRGERLICHEN INTELLEKTUELLEN [Kurt Hiller between pacifism and reaction: philosophical position and political role of a bourgeois intellectual]. *Zeitschrift für Geschichtswissenschaft [East Germany] 1980 28(10) 957-969.* In 1926 Kurt Hiller founded the Group of Revolutionary Pacifists, a splinter organization from the German Peace Society (Deutsche Friedensgesellschaft), the chief German pacifist organization. Although Hiller opposed the capitalist system, he also rejected Marxism-Leninism and was latently anti-Soviet. The so-called revolution he advocated was to result in an elitist intellectual utopia. While in exile during the Nazi period, Hiller continued to be a divisive influence among those who promoted peace and opposed fascism. 48 notes.   J. T. Walker

643. Schuppan, Peter. HAUPTENTWICKLUNGSLINIEN DER KULTUR IN DER WEIMARER REPUBLIK [Chief lines of cultural development in the Weimar Republic]. *Jahrbuch für Volkskunde und Kulturgeschichte [East Germany] 1973 16: 92-141.* The 1920's were not years of artistic and cultural freedom. For the working class it was a period of financial and even physical

hardship. The proletariat was excluded from much of bourgeois intellectual and cultural life. Under the flowers of the intellect, there was much that was diseased. Only the working class, led by the Communist Party of Germany, was fighting for true cultural freedom. 74 notes.   J. C. Billigmeier

644. Seeligmann, Chaim. DER DEUTSCHE REPUBLIKANISCHE LEHRER BUND IN DER WEIMARER REPUBLIK [The German Republican Teachers' Organization]. *Jahrbuch des Inst. für Deutsche Geschichte [Israel] 1979 8: 365-387.* After the assassination of Walther Rathenau in 1922 an educational group, the German Republican Teachers' Organization, came into being with the purpose of encouraging acceptance of the new German republic. Persons in any way connected with education could become members, but membership was small and the greater number were interested in the education of younger children. The first open congress of the organization took place in 1928. The task of changing the whole way of thought of the German people from imperial to republican was overwhelming. Efforts were made to encourage local groups and to get new textbooks written and to substitute new symbols for old, but time was too short. 33 notes.   M. Faissler

645. Shils, Edward. *IDEOLOGY AND UTOPIA* BY KARL MANNHEIM. *Daedalus 1974 103(1): 83-89.* Karl Mannheim, author of *Ideologie und Utopie* (Bonn, 1929), hoped to escape Hegelian idealism by opting for Marxist determinism, but failed. In his new discipline, the sociology of knowledge, he insisted that objective knowledge was impossible and thought was a "creature of social circumstance." He never satisfactorily developed his theory. Primary and secondary sources; 7 notes.   E. McCarthy

646. Spender, Stephen. HERBERT LIST. *Horizon 1981 24(4): 54-63.* Memoirs of the anti-intellectual German photographer Herbert List and his circle of friends in Weimar Germany, 1929-33, called by Spender "the Children of the Sun."

647. Stackelberg, Roderick. VÖLKISCH IDEALISM AND NATIONAL SOCIALISM: THE CASE OF FRIEDRICH LIENHARD. *Wiener Lib. Bull. [Great Britain] 1976 29(39-40): 34-41.* A biographical sketch of Friedrich Lienhard (1865-1929), dramatist, novelist, and journalist, and a founder of the antiurban, nativist movement in Germany in the 1900's, which was conservative and authoritarian in nature.

648. Stark, Gary D. PUBLISHERS AND CULTURAL PATRONAGE IN GERMANY, 1890-1933. *German Studies Rev. 1978 1(1): 56-71.* Patronage of writers, a role once filled by princely patrons, fell increasingly to publishers in the late 19th and early 20th centuries. The nobility had supported artists and authors regardless of popularity, and, though most publishers might pander to the people's whims and prejudices, some, like Eugen Diederichs and Julius F. Lehmann, took their role as patrons seriously and sought to encourage artistic and intellectual creativity. Others, such as Samuel Fischer, Kurt Wolff, and Ernst Rowohlt, promoted and protected particular groups of writers and painters. Ultimately, the successful writer became independent of his publisher. 45 notes.   J. C. Billigmeier

649. Stenzel, R. BEGRÜNDUNG FÜR DIE VERSCHMELZUNG DER *REICHSANSTALT FÜR MASS UND GEWICHT* MIT DER *PHYSIKA-LISCH-TECHNISCHEN REICHSANSTALT* IN BERLIN IM JAHRE 1923 [Origins of the fusion of the National Laboratory for Weights and Measures with the Physical-Technical Imperial Laboratories in Berlin in 1923]. *Ann. of Sci. [Great Britain] 1976 33(3): 289-306.* Examines the genesis and development of both *Reichsanstalten* [imperial laboratories] up to 1922. The Reichsanstalt für Mass und Gewicht [National Laboratory for Weights and Measures] is treated at some length, because its development is not well-known. Arguments for and against the fusion of the *Reichsanstalten* are reviewed from the points of view not only of these laboratories but also of the gauger's office, industry, various parliamentary committees of the *Deutscher Reichstag* and the appropriate authorities of the *Reichsregierung.* Looks briefly at the problems in Germany during the inflation of 1923, assessing the union of 53 years ago in terms of subsequent developments.   J/S

650. Stern, Guy. TOWARDS FASCISM: A STUDY OF UNPUBLISHED LETTERS OF FRIEDRICH LIENHARD. *Studies in Modern European Hist. and Culture 1976 2: 193-210.* Analysis of and excerpts from 48 unpublished letters and postcards written by Friedrich Lienhard, 1910-19. Lienhard was an Alsatian German, the author of novels popular with the middle class. The letters reveal the writer's bitterness about the loss of Alsace, his inability to accept defeat in World War I, and his willingness to use the Jews as scapegoats. Primary sources; 46 notes.   S. R. Smith

651. Tessitore, Fulvio. LA SVOLTA DELLO STORICISMO NEGLI ANNI DI WEIMAR   [The development of historicism during the Weimar Period]. *Riv. Storica Italiana [Italy] 1979 91(4): 591-616.* Analyzes historicism in the context of German culture during the 1920's. 98 notes.   J. J. Renaldo

652. Tobler, Douglas F. SCHOLAR BETWEEN WORLDS: ADOLF VON HARNACK AND THE WEIMAR REPUBLIC. *Zeitschrift für Religions- und Geistesgeschichte [West Germany] 1976 28(3): 193-222.* For Adolf von Harnack (1851-1930), who was firmly rooted in the bourgeois-nationalist culture by his family background and his immensely successful career as a church historian, the German defeat and revolution of 1918 was a traumatic experience. Yet he interpreted it as an irreversible transition from a monarchical, capitalist, and imperialist age to a democratic and socialist one. Germany's rebirth in his view required 1) a national spirit free from chauvinist narrowness, 2) leadership and authority, combined with democracy, 3) individualism, 4) conciliation between the classes, 5) private wealth as a precondition for the advancement of letters, arts, and learning, 6) a state above society and economy, and 7) Christian fear of God. His views alienated him from the more conservative academic community without winning him friends among the democratic intelligentsia. Thus his influence, which had been paramount in the academic world of pre-1914 Germany, waned in the Weimar Republic. Based on published sources; 131 notes.

G. Hollenberg

653. Treder, Hans-Jürgen and Kirsten, Christa. ALBERT EINSTEIN AN DER BERLINER AKADEMIE DER WISSENSCHAFTEN. 1913-1933 [Albert Einstein at the Berlin Academy of Sciences, 1913-33]. *Archivmitteilungen*

[East Germany] 1978 28(4): 141-144. Considers the archive material relating to Albert Einstein's work for, and involvement with, the Berlin Academy of Sciences, 1913-33.

654. Unser, Jutta.   "OSTEUROPA." BIOGRAPHIE EINER ZEITS-CHRIFT   [*Osteuropa*: biography of a periodical]. *Osteuropa [West Germany] 1975 25(8-9): 555-602.* A survey of the first 14 years of *Osteuropa*, 1925-39, emphasizing the members of its editorial boards and its policies under Otto Hoetzsch, Klaus Mehnert, and their successors under the Nazi régime. Beginning with a staff of outstanding collaborators such as Otto Auhagen and Arthur Luther, the journal supplied to the German public a comprehensive insight into Soviet political, economic, and cultural developments. In the mid-1930's Eastern and Central European topics tended to displace the Soviet focus. Publication of *Osteuropa* ceased at the outbreak of World War II, but in 1951 was revived under Mehnert's leadership. Table, 157 notes.   R. E. Weltsch

655. Verseput, J.   LUDWIG QUIDDE ALS CRITICUS VAN ZIJN TIJD [Ludwig Quidde as critic of his time]. *Spiegel Hist. [Netherlands] 1975 10(9): 458-463.* One of the most important critics of his age was the German historian Ludwig Quidde (1858-1941). He decried anti-Semitism, militarism, and the excessive influence of the emperor. He went into exile in 1933 and died in Geneva. Illus, biblio.   G. D. Homan

656. Villari, Lucio.   CRISI DEL CAPITALISMO E AUTOCRITICA BORGHESE: WALTHER RATHENAU   [Capitalist crisis and bourgeois self-criticism: Walther Rathenau]. *Studi Storici [Italy] 1976 17(1): 41-57.* Discusses the managerial capitalism of Walther Rathenau and his proposals for its application to the German economy during World War I and after. Distinguishes Rathenau's conception of socialism from other capitalist and Marxist-Leninist views. Based mostly on secondary sources; 39 notes.   E. J. Craver

657. Voeltz, Richard A.   SPORT, CULTURE, AND SOCIETY IN LATE IMPERIAL AND WEIMAR GERMANY: SOME SUGGESTIONS FOR FUTURE RESEARCH.   *J. of Sport Hist. 1977 4(3): 295-316.* Describes several areas and approaches for further research into sport, culture, and society in late Imperial and Weimar Germany, including analysis of the rise of sports, sporting clubs in the late 19th century, the relation between sport and the new hedonism, and sports in the military. German sports owed a debt to the American experience, with Carl Diem visiting America with a commission and recommending ways to advance German sport. Sports became more popular, and sporting motifs in advertising increased. The beginning of World War I had a profound impact on the growth of sports in Germany. 68 notes.   M. Kaufman

658. Volkov, Shulamit.   CULTURAL ELITISM AND DEMOCRACY: NOTES ON FRIEDRICH MEINECKE'S POLITICAL THOUGHT.   *Jahrbuch des Inst. für Deutsche Geschichte [Israel] 1976 5: 383-418.* Friedrich Meinecke (1862-1954) belonged to the cultural elite of Wilhelmine Germany. The author seeks to show "the effects of Meinecke's social standing and his environment upon his opinions." Meinecke was deeply interested in the concept of German culture, which he defended in World War I. The central concept for him was individuality, and in time he developed the concept of national individuality

and its culture, which it was, he said, "the highest moral obligation" of the educated citizenry to protect. In the Weimar period he declared himself to be a *Vernünftrepublican,* one who dislikes republicanism but for common sense accepts it. He believed in the political emancipation of the masses only after they had absorbed more of German ideals. 113 notes.   M. Faissler

659. Weisstein, Ulrich. LE TERME ET LE CONCEPT D'AVANT-GARDE EN ALLEMAGNE [The term and concept of avant-garde in Germany]. *Rev. de l'U. de Bruxelles [Belgium] 1975 (1): 10-37.* Although the term "avant-garde" was used for literary and artistic descriptions in France, Italy, and England early in the 20th century, in Germany the term did not become common until the 1930's. This is because the Germanic movement of Expressionism was not conceived as a unified movement at first, nor did it see itself making a distinct break with the past. The Expressionists felt themselves part of an international movement rather than isolated, and in Germany the avant-garde in art and politics were distinct. After 1940, when the term was used in Germany, it has become a term of derision and criticism associated with bourgeois decadence and materialism. 77 notes.   J. Buschen

660. Welch, David. THE PROLETARIAN CINEMA AND THE WEIMAR REPUBLIC. *Hist. J. of Film, Radio and Television [Great Britain] 1981 1(1): 3-18.* Discusses the development of left-wing films in Germany, 1920-30, emphasizing the role of the Social Democratic Party and Communist Party, and pointing to the difficulties caused by censorship.

661. Williamson, David Graham. WALTER RATHENAU: REALIST, PEDAGOGUE AND PROPHET, NOVEMBER 1918-MAY 1921. *European Studies Rev. [Great Britain] 1976 6(1): 99-121.* Examines the ideas and endeavors of Walther Rathenau (1867-1922) as industrialist, reformer, and advocate of a new socioeconomic order in Weimar Germany. Primary and secondary sources; 133 notes.   C. T. Prukop

662. Williamson, David Graham. WALTHER RATHENAU: PATRON SAINT OF THE GERMAN LIBERAL ESTABLISHMENT (1922-1972). *Leo Baeck Inst. Year Book, [Great Britain] 1975 20: 207-222.* Analyzes the major biographies of Walther Rathenau (1867-1922) that appeared before 1933 and since 1945. What emerges is a Wilhelmian who understood the industrial world of the 20th century. 89 notes.   F. Rosenthal

663. Wolf, Günther. VERTEIDIGUNGSVORTRAG ZUR DISSERTATIONSSCHRIFT: "DIE ENTSTEHUNG DER WARTBURGSTIFTUNG. DIE POLITISCHE ROLLE DER WARTBURGSTIFTUNG IN DER WEIMARER REPUBLIK (1922-1933)", GEHALTEN AM 17. MAI 1973 [Lecture in defense of a dissertation on "The origin of the Wartburg Foundation. The political role of the Wartburg Foundation in the Weimar Republic, 1922-33," delivered 17 May, 1973]. *Janaer Beiträge zur Parteiengeschichte [East Germany] 1974 (36): 28-55.* Studies the role of the Wartburg Foundation in German political life, 1922-33. After 1918 the old ruling classes, with Lutheranism as an ever-important influence, attempted to preserve their former position in German society. In the late 19th century the Wartburg had functioned as a symbol of German national greatness and conservatism. Now its influence was enhanced by

the establishment of the Wartburg Foundation. The board of directors was not accountable to outside control, although the former grand ducal house managed at times to veto its decisions. The Foundation became the center of the myth of German greatness based on monarchy, conservatism, and imperialism. 20 notes.

M. Faissler

664. Wolff-Powęska, Anna. POLITYCZNE ASPEKTY BADAŃ GEO-GRAFICZNYCH W NIEMCZECH (1919-1939) [The political aspect of geographical research in Germany, 1919-39]. *Przegląd Zachodni [Poland] 1973 29(3): 17-40.* Examines the political pressures which distorted geography teaching in schools, and the effect of geopolitical theories and the Darwinian theory of natural selection on geographical research.

665. Zerges, Kristina. LITERATURVERMITTLUNG IN DER SOZIAL-DEMOKRATISCHEN PRESSE: 1876-1933 [Literature mediation in the Social Democratic press, 1876-1933]. *Hist. Social Res. [West Germany] 1980 (16): 39-56.* Examines the theoretical concepts of the Social Democratic Party in respect to the communication and reception of literature in the worker's press, using three types of publications dating from 1884 to 1933 as a sample.

666. Zunkel, Friedrich. KÖLN WÄHREND DER WELTWIRT-SCHAFTSKRISE 1929-1933 [Cologne in the world depression, 1929-33]. *Zeitschrift für Unternehmensgeschichte [West Germany] 1981 26(2): 104-128.* Traces the effects of the world depression on the economic and social situation of the people in Cologne as well as on the social and financial policy of the city's administration. Cologne's relatively balanced industrial and social structure meant that the city could do better in the Depression than other big cities. Describes the effects of the crisis on industry by firm size and sector, unemployment, banking, housing, and social conditions and analyzes the response of the city government and its financial situation.   J/S

667. —. [OTTO HOETZSCH, 1876-1946]. *Osteuropa [West Germany] 1975 25(8-9): 603-635.*
Kuebart, Friedrich. OTTO HOETZSCH—HISTORIKER, PUBLIZIST, POLITIKER. EINE KRITISCHE BIOGRAPHISCHE STUDIE [Otto Hoetzsch, historian, journalist, politician: a critical biographical essay], *pp. 603-621.* Saxon by birth, Otto Hoetzsch (1876-1946) early identified himself with a Prussian, Bismarckian, pro-Russian outlook, which motivated his life-long interest in Russian studies and his editorship from 1925 to 1930 of *Osteuropa,* the journal founded by him. After World War I Hoetzsch was active in the German National People's Party, which he hoped in vain to shape into a force for Tory democracy in Germany. His positive though conservative approach to the USSR alienated him from the Nazi regime, which retired him from his university chair in 1935. His vast study of Alexander II remains unpublished. 82 notes with additional documentation on pp. A442-A462.
Heppe, Hans von. ERINNERUNGEN AN OTTO HOETZSCH [Memories of Otto Hoetzsch], *pp. 622-630.* Reminiscences by Hoetzsch's nephew, emphasizing Hoetzsch's political attitudes and differences with the Nazis, whose domestic impact he tended to underestimate. The need for good Russo-German relations, the continuity of Russian history, and Russia's

predominantly European character were three of his basic convictions. Illus., 11 notes.

Pochhammer, Wilhelm. MEIN NACHBAR HOETZSCH [My neighbor Hoetzsch], *pp. 631-632.* Reminiscences of a former German diplomatic representative to the USSR, who knew Hoetzsch socially.

Stupperich, Robert. OTTO HOETZSCH IN MEMORIAM, *pp. 633-635.* Personal reminiscences by a former contributor to *Osteuropa,* and two letters written by Hoetzsch shortly before his death (1946).

668. —. [WEBER'S INFLUENCE IN WEIMAR GERMANY]. *J. of the Hist. of the Behavioral Sci. 1982 18(2): 147-162.*

Factor, Regis A. and Turner, Stephen P. WEBER'S INFLUENCE IN WEIMAR GERMANY, *pp. 147-156.* Response to G. Schroeter, whose thesis that Weber was without influence in Weimar Germany is examined. It is shown that in contemporary published assessments and in private statements in interviews contemporary sociologists regarded him as important. The many dissertations on Weber and the enormous secondary literature are noted. This literature, which was contributed by some of the best minds of the day, included both the philosophical and sociological aspects of Weber's work. It is concluded that the thesis that Weber was without influence is false.

Schroeter, Gerd. WEBER AND WEIMAR: A RESPONSE TO FACTOR AND TURNER, *pp. 157-162.* In their critique, Factor and Turner attempt to substitute one commonplace for another by merely supplying long lists of publications that mention Max Weber. While accepting their reproof that I applied the concept of "influence" too narrowly, my response endeavors to map out the directions that further research in this area will need to follow if the controversy is ever to move beyond jejune polemics.   J

5

THE JEWS OF WEIMAR

669. Altmann, Alexander. THE GERMAN RABBI: 1910-1939. *Leo Baeck Inst. Year Book [Great Britain] 1974 19: 31-49.* A historic and sociologically descriptive image of the German rabbi, 1910-39. Overriding similarities were common to the three religious trends in Judaism, and with few exceptions the modern rabbi became a supporter of the establishment. The German rabbi, as late as 1936, was expected to remain apolitical. F. Rosenthal

670. Aronsfeld, C. C. EXTERMINATION, NOT EMIGRATION. *Patterns of Prejudice [Great Britain] 1975 9(3): 20-24.* Adolf Hitler decided in the twenties and not in 1940 that all Jews in Germany were to be exterminated.

671. Aronsfeld, C. C. "PERISH JUDAH": NAZI EXTERMINATION PROPAGANDA 1920-1945. *Patterns of Prejudice [Great Britain] 1978 12(5): 17-26.* Illustrates the tactics of the Nazi genocide of the Jews as a carefully organized propaganda campaign via the mass media.

672. Bacharach, Walter Zwi. JEWS IN CONFRONTATION WITH RACIST ANTISEMITISM, 1879-1933. *Leo Baeck Inst. Year Book [Great Britain] 1980 25: 197-219.* Existing research on Jewish reaction to German anti-Semitism deals with the cultural, religious, social, organizational, and political aspects without concentrating on the Jewish position on the theory of racism. The theoretical basis of anti-Semitism was already recognized by Wilhelm Marr, who coined the term, when he emphasized the power of race and the primary factor of blood. Jewish writers disputed racist premises with rational argument and by unmasking the contradictions inherent in racist thought, realizing too little and too late that racism was nurtured by a theory that from the outset declined to be rational, scientific, and consistent. 127 notes. F. Rosenthal

673. Baron, Lawrence. ERICH MÜHSAM'S JEWISH IDENTITY. *Leo Baeck Inst. Year Book [Great Britain] 1980 25: 269-284.* The German anarchist and author Erich Mühsam (1878-1934), a prominent participant in the Bavarian Revolution of 1918, grew up in a prosperous middle-class family, committed to assimilation, even as anti-Semitism spread in Germany. Mühsam often sensed that he was ostracized because of his Jewish descent; after 1918 he expressed his views on anti-Semitism in his many writings and in his admiration for certain aspects of Jewish ethics and history. Mühsam was murdered by the Nazis in Oranienburg concentration camp. Photo, 105 notes. F. Rosenthal

674. Bloch, Charles. JOSEPH BLOCH—DER JÜDISCHE VOR-KÄMPFER FÜR KONTINENTAL-EUROPA [Joseph Bloch, the Jewish pioneer of Continental Europe]. *Jahrbuch des Inst. für Deutsche Geschichte [Israel] 1977 (Beiheft 2): 147-164.* Born in Königsberg, Prussia in an orthodox Jewish family, Joseph Bloch became one of the original thinkers of the German Social Democratic Party and from 1895 to 1933 functioned as the publisher of its leading magazine *Sozialistische Monatshefte.* Researches Bloch's work in pioneering European unity and his role in the Zionist movement. G. E. Pergl

675. Bytwerk, Randall L. JULIUS STREICHER AND THE EARLY HISTORY OF *DER STÜRMER,* 1923-1933. *Journalism Hist. 1978 5(3): 74-79.* Early history of the anti-Semitic newspaper published in Nuremberg by Julius Streicher includes samples of writing and cartoons, and chronicles the paper's legal entanglements, 1923-33.

676. Cecil, Lamar. WILHELM II UND DIE JUDEN [William II and the Jews]. Mosse, Werner E. and Paucker, Arnold, eds. *Juden im Wilhelminischen Deutschland 1890-1914* (Tübingen: Mohr, 1976): 313-347. The identification of William II with the Prussian army, a center of German anti-Semitism, promoted the growth of his anti-Semitic opinions. Wilhelm II's closest friends and advisors, Herbert von Bismarck, Alfred von Waldsee, and Philipp von Eulenburg, were extremely anti-Jewish. William's anti-Semitism was an integral part of his animosity toward everything non-German and the essence of his dislike of the opposition to his autocratic regime, which he primarily blamed on the German Jews. Based on documents in the Royal Archives, Windsor; Bundesarchiv Koblenz; National Archives, Washington, D.C.; Geheimes Staatsarchiv Preussischer Kulturbesitz, Berlin-Dahlem, printed documents, and secondary literature; 130 notes. R. Wagnleitner

677. Earley, George and Earley, Roberta. BAVARIAN PRELUDE 1923: A MODEL FOR NAZISM? *Wiener Lib. Bull. [Great Britain] 1977 30(43-44): 53-60.* Traces the contours of the demographic situation of the Jews in Bavaria. Many East European Jews had immigrated, and there was much friction with German Jews. Many Bavarians believed that revolution and Judaism were synonymous; others complained of having to compete with Jews for jobs, and inflation exacerbated the situation. In the crisis, Gustav von Kahr became temporary dictator. An important part of his program was expulsion of "Jews and troublesome foreigners." Von Kahr also put many Jews into special concentration camps. The Nazis attacked von Kahr on the ground that his measures were inadequate. This attack reflected a different kind of anti-Semitism. The Nazi anti-Semitism drew no distinction between German and foreign Jews and also claimed to be rational, in that it was based on biological knowledge about the racial characteristics of Jews. The authors hold that the Nazi anti-Semitic model derives from having to formulate a position different from that of von Kahr. 57 notes. R. V. Layton

678. Eckstein, George Gunther. THE FREIE DEUTSCH-JÜDISCHE JUGEND (FDJJ) 1932-1933. *Leo Baeck Inst. Year Book [Great Britain] 1981 26: 231-239.* The breakup of the Kameraden, the most assimilationist of the German-Jewish *bündisch* youth movements, in 1932 led to the formation of three successor groups: the Kreis, with its identification of the Jewish element and learning,

became part of the Zionist movement and of the new Palestine. The Rote Fähnlein, with its Marxist ideology, came more and more under the control of the Communist Party and suffered further splintering. The FDJJ, trying to adapt the ethical socialism of a Buber and Tillich to an affirmation of its German roots, was suppressed in 1933. A good number of its college-age leadership suffered persecution and death by the hands of the new government or the Nazi Party. Based on personal reminiscenses and organizational publications of the period; 11 notes.

F. Rosenthal

679.   Eloni, Jehuda.   DIE ZIONISTISCHE BEWEGUNG IN DEUTSCH-LAND UND DIE SPD 1897-1918   [The Zionist movement in Germany and the German Social Democratic Party 1897-1918]. *Jahrbuch des Inst. für Deutsche Geschichte [Israel] 1977 (Beiheft 2): 85-112.* Depicts the development of the Zionist movement, 1900-20, and its relationship to the German Social Democrats. Karl Kautsky, among others, viewed Zionism as an ideology without any possibility of realization. There was a sharp discussion about Kautsky's book *Race and Jewry* when Socialists refused to support the national liberation of the Jewish nation. 85 notes.   G. E. Pergl

680.   Foster, Claude R., Jr.   HISTORICAL ANTECEDENTS: WHY THE HOLOCAUST?   *Ann. of the Am. Acad. of Pol. and Social Sci. 1980 (450): 1-19.* The antecedents to the Holocaust lie in anti-Semitism's long history, the 19th-century Jewish struggle to identify with the European Christian community, the latter 19th-century appearance of violent racial anti-Semitism that rejected assimilation, tensions among the Jews themselves, economic crises, the need to find a scapegoat for national humiliation, the identification of Jews with Marxists, and the swing to the political right. With Hitler, ideological anti-Semitism captured a state. Hitler's monopoly of political power, the endemic anti-Semitism in every European state, and the world's indifference to the increasing persecution in Germany were the immediate antecedents of genocide.   J/S

681.   Friesel, Evyatar.   CRITERIA AND CONCEPTION IN THE HISTORIOGRAPHY OF GERMAN AND AMERICAN ZIONISM.   *Zionism [Israel] 1980 1(2): 285-302.* Discusses the history of Zionism as the movement developed in both Germany and the United States. American Zionist historians claim that Zionism in America fulfilled many important functions in American Jewish life. German Zionists perceived their work toward a Zionist entity as a rationalization to continue their lives in Germany without consideration of Aliya themselves. Statistics of Aliya are not germane to the success or failure of the Zionist movement. Historical and philosophical questions face the historiographer examining Zionism because of the ambiguous nature of the Zionist movement. Based partially on Central Zionist Archives materials; 43 notes.

T. Koppel

682.   Frye, Bruce B.   THE GERMAN DEMOCRATIC PARTY AND THE "JEWISH PROBLEM" IN THE WEIMAR REPUBLIC.   *Leo Baeck Inst. Year Book [Great Britain] 1976 21: 143-172.* The German Democratic Party (DDP), the political party favored by most German Jews, 1918-30, was the most philo-Semitic of the middle-class parties; nevertheless the Jewish problem became a major source of division and contributed to the party's decline. Almost from its earliest days in 1919 its competitors fixed its image as a party of Jews tied to

Marxism, the Revolution, and Versailles. Its close connection to the three Jewish-owned newspapers of Berlin and Frankfurt and its association with urban rather than rural pressure groups alientated the party's leadership and left wing from the more conservative and slightly anti-Semitic right wing. 132 notes.

F. Rosenthal

683. Glatzer, Nahum N. REFLECTIONS ON BUBER'S IMPACT ON GERMAN JEWRY. *Leo Baeck Inst. Year Book [Great Britain] 1980 25: 301-311.* Martin Buber saw himself as an atypical man, a dissenter, nonconformist, heterodox, and independent. Only thus could he teach the reality of a personal god in the 20th century, in contrast to Hermann Cohen's rationalism. Buber rediscovered East European Hasidism with its personal god, its attitude of faith, and its dialog between man and the divine, and considered it a new religious possibility. 42 notes.

F. Rosenthal

684. Grunfeld, Frederic V. THE JEWS IN THE WEIMAR REPUBLIC. *Midstream 1979 25(8): 29-31.* The flowering of culture in which the Jews participated in Germany was destroyed by Nazism, 1920's-30's.

685. Grunfeld, Frederic V. PROPHETS WITHOUT HONOR: THE LOST WORLD OF GERMAN-JEWISH INTELLECTUALS. *Present Tense 1979 6(4): 27-35.* Sketches the lives and works of three German-Jewish writers—Else Lasker-Schüler (1869-1945), Erich Mühsam (1878-1934), and Ernst Toller (1893-1939)—whose works were suppressed and largely forgotten and who died in exile or in prison (at least one—Toller—by his own hand) because they were Jews during the Nazi period in Germany.

686. Hamburger, Ernest. HUGO PREUSS: SCHOLAR AND STATES-MAN. *Leo Baeck Inst. Year Book [Great Britain] 1975 20: 179-206.* Hugo Preuss (1860-1925) was one of the seven Jewish ministers in Germany, 1919-32. He drafted the Weimar Republic constitution, introduced the draft into the National Assembly, and guided its deliberations. Men of Jewish descent played a prominent part in the constitutional labors of these years, because of legal excellence as well as disqualification of many non-Jewish scholars due to monarchic, annexationist, and extreme radical right positions. Preuss also became the target of exceedingly vicious anti-Semitic attacks. He was convinced that he had derived the concept of the state and nation from the fountainhead of German constitutional and legal development; it was the tragedy of his life, which he shared with other German Jews, to witness the swelling of the tide that would not admit that a Jew could have German national sentiments. F. Rosenthal

687. Hildesheimer, Esriel. DIE VERSUCHE ZUR SCHAFFUNG EINER JÜDISCHEN GESAMTORGANISATION WÄHREND DER WEIMARER REPUBLIK 1919-1933 [Attempts to establish a general Jewish organization during the Weimar Republic, 1919-33]. *Jahrbuch des Inst. für Deutsche Geschichte [Israel] 1979 8: 335-364.* With provision for religious freedom written into the Weimar constitution, German Jews looked forward to guarantees similar to those enjoyed by the churches and hoped also to create a comprehensive Jewish religious organization that could encompass all Jews and all synagogues. In 1920 Ismar Freund drafted a sketch for such a structure. Until 1933 there was some hope of its being realized but the obstacles were too many, including arguments

with government officials, conflicting views among already existing Jewish organizations, differences between orthodox and more liberal Jews or between Jews
of different regions of Germany, to mention a few. 26 notes.   M. Faissler

688. Hoffmann, Banesh. ALBERT EINSTEIN. *Leo Baeck Inst. Year Book
[Great Britain] 1976 20: 279-288.* Reinterprets Albert Einstein's (1879-1955) life
with emphasis on his religious and artistic sides. His writings and his major
scientific achievements show the lucidity of his mind and his genius to see even
the most complicated matters simply and artistically. The last 30 years of his life
were devoted to futhering peace and strengthening human freedom. Einstein, the
nonreligious Jew, shared the full burden of his Jewishness since he felt responsible
for his people and their fate. 22 notes.   F. Rosenthal

689. Horkheimer, Max. ESPRIT JUIF ET ESPRIT ALLEMAND [Jewish
spirit and German spirit]. *Esprit [France] 1979 (5): 19-27.* Extracts from Horkheimer's discussion relative to Thilo Koch, ed., *Portraits zur deutsch-jüdischen
Geistesgeschichte* (Cologne: Dumont Schanberg, 1961), in a special issue of
Esprit on Jews and modernity.

690. Horwitz, Rivka. ADELE ROSENZWEIGS JUGENDERINNERUN-
GEN [Youthful reminiscences of Adele Rosenzweig]. *Bull. des Leo Baeck Inst.
[Israel] 1977-78 16-17(53-54): 133-146.* The memoirs of A. Rosenzweig should
be viewed as a history of assimilation, of the abandonment of the Jewish life style
and of a strong desire to rise socially. She also discusses her son, Franz Rosenzweig, a well-known Jewish author. The article reproduces part of Adele's diary
starting 2 August 1922. 146 notes.   G. E. Pergl

691. Jay, Martin. ANTI-SEMITISM AND THE WEIMAR LEFT. *Midstream 1974 20(1): 42-50.* Explores the response of German Marxists to Judeo-
phobia in the Weimar Republic.   S

692. Jay, Martin. POLITICS OF TRANSLATION—SIEGFRIED
KRACAUER AND WALTER BENJAMIN ON THE BUBER-ROSENZ-
WEIG BIBLE. *Leo Baeck Inst. Year Book [Great Britain] 1976 21: 3-24.* The
Buber-Rosenzweig Bible, produced in the waning years of German Jewry, provoked considerable controversy when it appeared. This controversy expressed
many of the dilemmas faced by intellectuals after 1918. For Siegfried Kracauer
of the *Frankfurter Zeitung* the new translation was an escape into fundamentalist
religion without roots in social, economic, or political reality. The refutation of
his charges and the ensuing discussions projected a fundamental antipathy to the
antihistorical Jewish existentialism these critics saw at the root of the translation.
99 notes.   F. Rosenthal

693. Jochmann, Werner. DIE DEUTSCHE ARBEITERBEWEGUNG
UND DER ZIONISMUS 1897-1918 [The German workers' movement and
Zionism, 1897-1918]. *Jahrbuch des Inst. für Deutsche Geschichte [Israel] 1977
(Beiheft 2): 113-130.* Explains the basic positions influencing the relationship of
the German Social Democrats toward the Zionist movement. Zionism was con-
sidered by socialist leadership as an unimportant theory and the creation of a
Jewish national statehood was viewed as a "petit-bourgeois utopia." 27 notes,
appendix.   G. E. Pergl

694. Jospe, Alfred. A PROFESSION IN TRANSITION—THE GERMAN RABBINATE 1910-1939. *Leo Baeck Inst. Year Book [Great Britain] 1974 19: 51-61.* The changing nature of the rabbinate raised the problems of role definition and self-image. Tensions arose between traditionalists and innovators, between the rabbinical functions as preserver and initiator of new modes of service. The creation of the direct rabbinate in Prussia in the 1920's was designed to provide the smaller communities with vocational, health, and emigration services, usually not thought of as pastoral functions. The members of the rabbinate found their time was frequently absorbed by immediate concerns and less with academic work. F. Rosenthal

695. Kaplan, Marion A. GERMAN-JEWISH FEMINISM IN THE TWENTIETH CENTURY. *Jewish Social Studies 1976 38(1): 39-53.* The Judischer Frauenbund (JFB), or League of Jewish Women, came to include in its membership 20% of Germany's Jewish women and played a vital role in German-Jewish affairs, 1904-38. Predominantly middle-class and housewife oriented, the JFB was founded and led for 20 years by Bertha Pappenheim. Pappenheim and her associates directed the activities of the JFB into educational enterprises. Their object was to inform Jews of their culture and heritage and thus slow down assimilation, provide career training for Jewish women, wage warfare against Jewish involvement in prostitution, and obtain suffrage for Jewish women in Jewish communal affairs. Based on manuscript and other primary sources. N. Lederer

696. Katz, Jacob. "ENTSCHEIDUNGSJAHR 1932" [Year of decision]. *Bull. des Leo Baeck Inst. [Israel] 1979 18(55): 1-10.* A festschrift in honor of the 60th birthday of Leo Baeck, 23 May 1933, was planned as an outline of the sociology of the German Jews and was to be edited by Max Kreutzberger. Under the circumstances of the times the festschrift was not published. In 1979 Jacob Katz revived four of the intended articles and updated them for the present-day reader who would need help to understand that the year 1932 was indeed a year of decision for all German Jews. 13 notes. M. Faissler

697. Kaufmann, Walter. MARTIN BUBER: OF HIS FAILURES AND TRIUMPH. *Encounter [Great Britain] 1979 52(5): 31-38.* Discusses the broad range of the work of Martin Buber, Jewish religious writer born in Germany in 1878 whose subjects include Judaism, Zionism, the Bible, teaching, philosophy, Hasidism, and a German translation of the Hebrew Bible.

698. Lamberti, Marjorie. [GERMAN JEWRY]. *Central European Hist. 1974 7(4): 365-371.* Reviews two books edited by Werner E. Mosse: *Deutsches Judentum in Krieg und Revolution 1916-1923. Ein Sammelband* and *Entscheidungsjahr 1932. Zur Judenfrage in der Endphase der Weimarer Republik. Ein Sammelband* (Tübingen: J. C. B. Mohr (Paul Siebeck), 1971 and 1966). The first work "achieves distinction in its multifaceted account of the rise of the Jewish problem in the Republic," while the second "makes its mark by providing an astute and approximate assessment of the proportions in which this problem loomed during the Weimar era." C. R. Lovin

699. Loewenberg, Peter. DISTORTED IMAGE. *Hist. and Theory 1977 16(3): 361-367.* Reviews Sidney M. Bolkosky's *The Distorted Image: German Jewish Perceptions of Germans and Germany, 1918-1935* (New York: Elsevier, 1975). Denies the validity of Bolkosky's thesis that the German-Jewish community accepted as myth their assimilation. 21 notes.   D. A. Yanchisin.

700. Löwy, Michael. MESSIANISME JUIF ET UTOPIES LIBERTAIRES EN EUROPE CENTRALE (1905-1923) [Jewish messianism and libertarian utopias in central Europe, 1905-23]. *Arch. de Sci. Sociales des Religions [France] 1981 51(1): 5-47.* There is a deep elective affinity between Jewish messianism and the anarchist utopias, resulting mainly from three common aspects: a) the restorative utopian dimension; b) the catastrophic character of redemption, and c) the utopia of a world emancipated from the bondage of law. This structural homology between both cultural universes grows on the same historical ground: the neoromantic trends in Central Europe at the dawn of the 20th century, to which many Jewish intellectuals were attracted. One can distinguish three groups of Central European Jewish intelligentsia where this elective affinity can be found: 1) semilibertarian religious Jews: Franz Rosenzweig, Martin Buber, Gerschom Scholem; 2) semi-Jewish religious anarchists: Gustav Landauer, Franz Kafka, Walter Benjamin; 3) religious atheist and anarcho-Bolshevik assimilated Jews: Georg Lukacs, Ernst Toller, Ernst Bloch. To understand this phenomenon, one has to examine the contradictory social and cultural conditions of the Jewish intellectuals in Central Europe; assimilated and marginalized at one and the same time, deeply linked to German culture, and truly cosmopolitan. Influenced by Romanticism and its nostalgia for the past, a whole generation of Jewish writers was also attracted by the great revolutionary wave of the years 1917-23.   J

701. Margalith, Elkana. THE DILEMMAS OF GUSTAV LANDAUER. *Jahrbuch des Inst. für Deutsche Geschichte [Israel] 1977 (Beiheft 2): 131-146.* Deals with three aspects of the multifaceted profile of Jewish publicist Gustav Landauer: the revolutionary, the Jew, and the mystic. Born in the western part of Germany, Landauer (1870-1919) viewed himself as a "Weltbürger" and—at the same time—as a Jew bound by tradition. Basically a revolutionary and social thinker, he got involved in post-World War I disturbances in Bavaria which would not have been risked by a skilled politician. Rejecting assimilation, Landauer asserted his Jewishness to his last days. 51 notes, appendix.
G. E. Pergl

702. Mayer, Paul Yogi. EQUALITY—EGALITY: JEWS AND SPORT IN GERMANY. *Leo Baeck Inst. Year Book [Great Britain] 1980 25: 221-242.* The desire of German Jewish youth to prove their equality as individuals and as a group may explain Jewish achievements in sports and their full participation in various German clubs and associations until 1933. Then Jews were expelled and existing Jewish clubs (Der Schild and Makkabi) became the organizational structure for intensive physical training until 1938-39. Examines the hypocrisy surrounding Jewish participation in the 1936 Olympics, in which only two "half-Aryans," Helene Mayer and Rudi Ball, actually competed and reviews the achievements of Kurt Hahn and Sir Ludwig Guttman, both German Jews. 46 notes.
F. Rosenthal

703. Merchav, Peretz. JÜDISCHE ASPEKTE IN DER EINSCHÄTZUNG VON ROSA LUXEMBURG [The Jewish aspect in the evaluation of Rosa Luxemburg]. *Jahrbuch des Inst. für Deutsche Geschichte [Israel] 1977 (Beiheft 2): 185-202.* No interest in the Jewish problem is to be found in the whole career of Rosa Luxemburg, nor were there any contacts with Jewish nationalism. Luxemburg totally ignored her own Jewish background, and she declared the creation of the Jewish Bund a clear case of separatism. Her antinationalism can be explained by her association to two oppressed nations—the Polish and Jewish. 30 notes, appendix.   G. E. Pergl

704. Miller, Susanne. ZUR HALTUNG JÜDISCHER SOZIALDEMOKRATEN IM ERSTEN WELTKRIEG [On the attitude of Jewish Social Democrats in World War I]. *Jahrbuch des Inst. für Deutsche Geschichte [Israel] 1977 (Beiheft 2): 229-246.* A critical review of the attitude of leading Jewish members of the German Social Democratic Party during the critical weeks before the outbreak of World War I and afterwards. There were strong opponents of the war in the party who at the same time declared the defense of the homeland a duty. The ideological conflicts that erupted after 3 August 1914 clearly signaled the later division within the party.   G. E. Pergl

705. Mosse, George L. and Lampert, Steven George. WEIMAR INTELLECTUALS AND THE RISE OF NATIONAL SOCIALISM. Dimsdale, Joel E., ed. *Survivors, Victims, and Perpetrators: Essays on the Nazi Holocaust* (Washington: Hemisphere Publ., 1980): 79-105. Discusses the appeal of fascism to nonacademic intellectuals in Weimar Germany and examines leftist intellectuals' positions on the Jewish question, which "became a test of their firmness in fighting the Nazi menace."

706. Nicosia, Francis R. J. WEIMAR GERMANY AND THE PALESTINE QUESTION. *Lao Baeck Inst. Y. [Great Britain] 1979 24: 321-345.* In the quest for markets for German goods, the Jewish segment of Palestine under the British mandate seemed to be increasingly significant. Thus, sympathy for Zionist efforts remained a constant of Weimar German diplomacy which in turn strengthened Zionism in the German-Jewish community. Based on formerly unavailable archival and diplomatic sources; photo, 89 notes.   F. Rosenthal

707. Niewyk, Donald L. JEWS AND THE COURTS IN WEIMAR GERMANY. *Jewish Social Studies 1975 37(2): 99-113.* An analysis of Weimar court cases involving the prosecution of persons for a variety of crimes against Jews and public order reveals that in the overwhelming number of instances judges acted in a fair and impartial manner in rendering decisions based on the evidence at hand. The allegation that Weimar justice was anti-Jewish is unsubstantiated. A few indications of anti-Jewish judicial prejudice were found in Bavaria and East Prussia but they were exceptions to the rule. Larger obstacles to the legal removal of anti-Semitism included the failure of Jews to organize effectively to present class action suits against anti-Semites, judicial immunity to members of legislatures, and general amnesties for defendants. Based primarily on the published records of the *Central Verein deutscher Staatsbürger jüdischen Glaubens* and the *Verein zur Abwehr des Antisemitismus.*   N. Lederer

708. Paucker, Arnold. DOCUMENTS ON THE FIGHT OF JEWISH OR-
GANIZATIONS AGAINST RIGHT-WING EXTREMISM. *Michael: On the
Hist. of Jews in the Diaspora [Israel] 1973 2: 216-246.* The most representative
organization of German Jews was the *Centralverein deutscher Staatsbürger jü-
dischen Glaubens* (CV). The documents on the CV from its inception in 1932
until its dissolution in November 1938 are very scanty but several German
documents from files on the activities of the CV regional organizations in Bremen
and Nuremberg, and a document from the German Foreign Office relating to the
violent outbreaks in Berlin in 1931 survive and are reproduced here. 24 notes, 6
appendixes.   Y. Sassoon

709. Paucker, Arnold. JEWISH DEFENCE AGAINST NAZISM IN THE
WEIMAR REPUBLIC. *Wiener Lib. Bull. [Great Britain] 1972 26(26-27):
21-31.* Argues that in the 1920's and 1930's politically alert Jews attempted to
oppose the development of the anti-Semitic movement in Weimar Germany, in
organizations and as individuals.

710. Pierson, Ruth. EMBATTLED VETERANS—THE REICHSBUND
JUDISCHER FRONTSOLDATEN. *Leo Baeck Inst. Year Book [Great Brit-
ain] 1974 19: 139-154.* The founding and history of the Jewish Veterans' Association (RJF) from 1919 until its dissolution by the Nazis reflects both the
resurgence of anti-Semitism in Germany during World War I and the will of
German Jewry to defend its good name and its claim to a place in German affairs.
The organization was both a defense organization and a veteran's group. As such
it collected the names of Jewish dead of World War I, emphasized the long history
of Jews in Germany, and called attention to their common fate.

F. Rosenthal

711. Reinharz, Jehuda. IDEOLOGY AND STRUCTURE IN GERMAN
ZIONISM, 1882-1933. *Jewish Social Studies 1980 4(2): 119-146.* Examines the
origins, history, ideology, activities, and structure of the German branch (Zionistische Vereinigung für Deutschland) of the World Zionist Organization, 1882-
1933. After 1933, Zionists were deprived of their freedom of action, and forced
to adapt to changing external conditions. Five years later, the Germans forced
the Zionistische Vereinigung für Deutschland to close down. Based on materials
in Jerusalem's Central Zionist Archives, newspaper articles, and other primary
and secondary sources; 82 notes.   J. D. Sarna

712. Reinharz, Jehuda. THREE GENERATIONS OF GERMAN ZION-
ISM. *Jerusalem Q. [Israel] 1978 (9): 95-110.* Divides German Zionism into
three different generations: 1897-1910, 1910-18, 1918-33.

713. Rheins, Carl J. DEUTSCHER VORTRUPP, GEFOLGSCHAFT
DEUTSCHER JUDEN 1933-1935 [Deutscher Vortrupp, League of German
Jews 1933-35]. *Leo Baeck Inst Year Book [Great Britain] 1981 26: 207-229.* Hans
Joachim Schoeps (1909-80), founder and intellectual driving force of the
Deutscher Vortrupp (1933-35), arrived at his extreme pro-German position as the
result of family background, university education, and the influence of Eberhard
Beyer. Beyer directed his attention to the writings of the early 19th-century
Jewish theologian Salomon Ludwig Steinheim, who established a distinction
between revelation and later Biblical-rabbinic interpretation. By individualizing

the Jewish experience Schoeps provided a system of religious belief based on inward experience that allowed anti-Zionists to remain loyal to their Jewish heritage and to their German fatherland. The Vortrupp's attempts to influence either the attitude of the Nazi government or to reshape the Jewish community were unsuccessful. By 1935 it had dwindled to less than 20 members and was dissolved. Based in part on Schoep's memoirs and secondary sources; 126 notes.

F. Rosenthal

714. Rheins, Carl J. THE SCHWARZES FÄHNLEIN, JUNGENSCHAFT, 1932-1934. *Leo Baeck Inst. Year Book [Great Britain] 1978 23: 173-197.* During the last years of the Weimar Republic a small group of non-Zionist German Jewish youth under the leadership of Günther Ballin and Paul "Yogi" Mayer reaffirmed its German identity and its place within a German Volksgemeinschaft. Totally oblivious to the reality of the Nazi menace, the group engaged in various political activities with the Jewish community and made repeated efforts to impress the government with its German spirit. Actually this ultra-German emphasis ran counter to basic Nazi doctrine and the group was dissolved in 1934. 6 photos, 133 notes.

F. Rosenthal

715. Rheins, Carl J. THE VERBAND NATIONALDEUTSCHER JUDEN, 1921-1933. *Leo Baeck Inst. Year Book [Great Britain] 1980 25: 243-268.* Dr. Max Naumann, lawyer and World War I captain, founded the League of National-German Jews in 1921 as a vehicle for Jews who regarded themselves as totally German and therefore acceptable to the nationalists. Some 89 Jewish professionals and businessmen joined him as founding members of this group which numbered about 3,500 during the days of the Weimar Republic. Convinced that anti-Semitism could only be diminished by total assimilation, the league's relationship to Judaism remained vague and ill-defined. The aim of the group's campaign against East European Jews, Zionism, and Jewish leftists was to convince the German Right that nationalist German Jews, despite their origin, were trustworthy and acceptable. These hopes remained unfulfilled, the Nazi government dissolved the organization in 1935 and arrested its founder. Photo, 148 notes.

F. Rosenthal

716. Rosenthal, Bernard M. CARTEL, CLAN, OR DYNASTY? THE OLSCHKIS AND THE ROSENTHALS, 1859-1976. *Harvard Lib. Bull. 1977 25(4): 381-398.* An historical account of two prominent families in the rare and antiquarian book trade by a leading member of the current generation. Discusses the economic situation of post-World War I Germany and the effects of the rise of Nazism on Jewish businessmen. Illus.

W. H. Mulligan, Jr.

717. Schallenberger, E. Horst and Stein, Gerd. JEWISH HISTORY IN GERMAN TEXTBOOKS. *Patterns of Prejudice [Great Britain] 1976 10(5): 15-17.* Examines the role of textbooks in the formation of public opinion on Jews, 1920's-72.

718. Schatzker, Chaim. THE HISTORY OF THE "BLAU-WEISS": THE PATH TO ZIONISM OF THE FIRST GERMAN JEWISH YOUTH MOVEMENT. *Zion [Israel] 1973 38(1-4): 137-168.* Joseph Marcus organized the first group of Blau-Weiss in 1907. In 1912 it merged with a similar group founded in Berlin by Drs. A. Sachs and L. Weissenberg. In 1914 five such groups proclaimed

a united Jewish German youth movement. The anti-Semitic stance taken by the Wandervogel and other German youth movements aided the growth of the Jewish movement. The principles of the Blau-Weiss were: 1) Nature, natural behavior, true humanity, and nationalism are connected; 2) The Jewish people by going away from nature had turned into a people lacking in inner truth. It was a people that refused to admit the truth about itself and its Jewishness; and 3) A return to nature by means of hiking would bring about a changed attitude and a reordering of emotional life. This change would come about through immanent laws. Hiking was therefore seen as an end in itself. From the beginning some of its members saw it as a Zionist movement. There were others who conceived of it mainly as a youth movement whose purpose was to shape attitudes which would influence Jewish youth towards Zionism. After World War I, the Blau-Weiss underwent great change under the leadership of Walter Moses. The new outlook brought about a new attitude towards Judaism, Eastern European Jews, and Zionism.   J/S

719.   Schatzker, Chaim.   MARTIN BUBER'S INFLUENCE ON THE JEW-ISH YOUTH MOVEMENT IN GERMANY.   *Leo Baeck Inst. Year Book [Great Britain] 1978 23: 151-171.* Examines the influence of Martin Buber (1878-1965) on the Jewish youth movement in Germany from World War I to the mid-1930's. Jewish youth ultimately rejected Buber's mystic and antinomian interpretation of Judaism. Based on youth movement sources; 76 notes.
                                                                F. Rosenthal

720.   Schieffer, Theodor.   WILHELM LEVISON   [Wilhelm Levison]. *Rheinische Vierteljahrsblätter [West Germany] 1976 40(1-4): 225-242.* The German historian Wilhelm Levison, who specialized in medieval history and worked on the publication of the Monumenta Germaniae Historica, was forced after 1933 to emigrate to Great Britain because of his Jewish origin and died in 1947 before he was able to return to the University of Bonn.   R. Wagnleitner

721.   Schulin, Ernst.   DIE RATHENAUS. ZWEI GENERATIONEN JÜ-DISCHEN ANTEILS AN DER INDUSTRIELLEN ENTWICKLUNG DEUTSCHLANDS   [The Rathenaus: two Jewish generations' role in the industrial development of Germany]. Mosse, Werner E. and Paucker, Arnold, eds. *Juden im Wilhelminischen Deutschland 1890-1914* (Tübingen: Mohr, 1976): 115-142. Emil Rathenau established the Allgemeine Elektrizitätsgesellschaft (AEG) as one of the dominating German electrical concerns in the late 19th century. By 1913 the German electrical industry produced 46.6 percent of world exports. Walther Rathenau, his son, was a prominent author before he organized the German war economy in World War I. As foreign secretary and secretary for reconstruction in the Weimar Republic, Walther Rathenau developed a scheme for European economic association. Secondary literature; 81 notes.
                                                                R. Wagnleitner

722.   Schumacher, Martin.   JÜDISCHE PRESSESTIMMEN ZUM TODE VON FRIEDRICH EBERT UND ZUR NEUWAHL DES REICHSPRÄSI-DENTEN 1925   [Jewish press opinion on the death of Friedrich Ebert and the new presidential elections of 1925]. *Jahrbuch des Instituts für Deutsche Geschichte [Israel] 1975 4: 339-367.* Discusses Jewish press coverage of the events of 1925. The German Social Democratic Party and its first president, Friedrich

Ebert, were opposed to open or hidden anti-Semitism. Therefore, it came as no surprise that the death of Ebert caused many genuine statements of sympathy and sorrow in the Jewish press regardless of its political affiliations. The Jewish press greatly feared that anti-Semitic groups would have a deciding influence in the selection and election of candidates for the presidency. The main function of the press during the elections was to combat anti-Semitism. The largest percentage of the Jewish vote probably supported Wilhelm Marx, a Catholic, who was the Center candidate. Many Jews worried about the possible connections between the conservative Paul von Hindenburg and the anti-Semitic groups. Based on Jewish newspapers, and published primary and secondary sources; 72 notes.

E. F. Stocker

723. Sichel, Frieda H. THE RISE AND FALL OF THE KASSELER TAGEBLATT. *Leo Baeck Inst. Y. [Great Britain] 1974 19: 237-243.* The record of the *Kasseler Tageblatt* also tells the story of a German-Jewish family over three generations and across a span of some 80 years. Herz Gotthelft initiated the family's long involvement with the printing trade and newspaper publication when he purchased a small printing press for his son Carl in 1841. Succeeding members of the Gotthelft family published the newspaper until 1932, when it was taken over by the Nazis.

F. Rosenthal

724. Sonn, Moses. SCHULGESCHICHTLICHE AUFZEICHNUNGEN ÜBER DIE ISRAELITISCHE VOLKSSCHULE BUTTENWIESEN [Historical records of the Jewish school in Buttenwiesen]. *Bull. des Leo Baecks Inst. [Israel] 1969 12(48): 221-252.* A documentary history of the Jewish school in Buttenwiesen from its foundation in 1842 to its dissolution in 1932. The documents illustrate the role of the school in Jewish community life, the status of Jewish teachers, the nature of instruction used in Jewish schools, and the Jewish legends and stories prevalant during the period. The material was collected by Moses Sonn (1881-1969), who taught at the school, 1917-32. 30 notes.

R. L. Bytwerk

725. Stern, Eliahu. THE AFFAIR OF RABBI SAGALOVICH (RELATIONS BETWEEN GERMAN JEWS AND "OSTJUDEN" IN THE INTERWAR PERIOD). *Gal-Ed: On the Hist. of the Jews in Poland [Israel] 1978 4-5: 345-363.* An influx of Russian and Polish Jewish refugees in Danzig led to the appointment of Rabbi Jaakov Meir Sagalovich which caused hostility from the native Jewish community. This was due to his Zionist activities, the imposition of Yiddish-language services, permission to campaign for church funds, and various smaller misunderstandings which arose, 1923-33.

726. Tal, Uriel. NAZISM AS A "POLITICAL FAITH." *Jerusalem Q. [Israel] 1980 (15): 70-90.* Discusses Nazism as a messianic belief system and world view which depended upon the elimination of the Jews for its culmination.

727. Walk, Joseph. DAS "DEUTSCHE KOMITEE PRO PALÄSTINA" 1926-1933 [The German Committee for Palestine, 1926-33]. *Bull. des Leo Baeck Inst. [Israel] 1976 15(52): 162-193.* The German Committee for Palestine included Jews and gentiles, Zionists and non-Zionists. Working with the Keren Hayessod, an organization that raised money to support Jewish work in Palestine, the committee attempted to build support in Germany for Jewish efforts in Palestine. 102 notes.

R. L. Bytwerk

728.   Winkler, Enno A.   ERNST UNGER: A PIONEER IN MODERN SUR-
GERY.   *J. of the Hist. of Medicine and Allied Sci. 1982 37(3): 269-286.* Ernst
Unger (1875-1938) was a pioneering surgeon, who is recalled for his contributions
to vascular catheterization, thoracic surgery, organ transplantation, neurosurg-
ery, and organization of blood donor pools. Unger was born to Jewish parents
in Berlin, Germany, became a physician, trained in surgery, and opened up a
private surgical clinic in Berlin. The Unger Clinic became a center of modern
German surgery. He married a Catholic nurse, and had four children, who were
brought up in the Protestant faith. In 1919 Unger was awarded a professorship,
and in 1920 he became director of a surgical clinic in the Rudolf Virchow
Hospital (Berlin). When Hitler came to power, Unger's suffering began. In 1933
he was dismissed from his hospital post, and the anti-Semitic propaganda made
it hard to keep his clinic going. He died in 1938, after Jewish doctors lost the right
to practice medicine. Based on Unger's correspondence and on published medical
journals in German; 79 notes, 3 fig.   M. Kaufman

729.   Yisraeli, David.   GERMANY AND ZIONISM.   *Jahrbuch des Inst. für
Deutsche Geschichte [Israel] 1975 Beiheft 1: 142-166.* Germany never gave
official support to Zionism. Until 1918 the German government feared that the
Zionists might endanger the German-Turkish alliance. Weimar officials were
somewhat more interested in the Zionist cause but primarily as a means of
cementing good relations with Great Britain. Under Hitler hatred of Jews added
a new element to the Zionist problem. At times the government encouraged
Jewish settlement in Palestine in spite of opposition from the Germans resident
there. Later the Nazis feared that Jewish immigration would lead to a Jewish state
that would strengthen Judaism the world over. Differences of opinion within the
government prevented any consistent policy.   M. Faissler

730.   —.   [THE JEWISH TEACHER IN GERMANY].   *Leo Baeck Inst. Y.
[Great Britain] 1974 19: 63-76.*
Gruenewald, Max.   THE JEWISH TEACHER,   *pp. 63-69.*
Ginat, Jochanan.   THE JEWISH TEACHER IN GERMANY,   *pp. 71-75.*
    Solid diversified training in Judaica and the general pedagogic field made the
    Jewish teacher a dependable force in the network of Jewish education. Yet
    in terms of professional status and remuneration the teacher occupied an
    inferior position compared with the rabbi. Only in the waning days of
    German Jewry when the Jewish community was forced to provide general
    schooling for all its children, did the teacher's influence and status rise.
    Presented at the Arden House Conference on "Exploring a Typology of
    German Jewry," New York, 1973.   F. Rosenthal

731.   —.   [JEWISH YOUTH MOVEMENTS IN GERMANY].   *Leo Baeck
Inst. Y. [Great Britain] 1974 19: 77-105.*
Rinott, Chanoch.   MAJOR TRENDS IN JEWISH YOUTH MOVEMENTS
    IN GERMANY,   *pp. 77-95.* 7 photos, 48 notes.
Rosenstock, Werner.   THE JEWISH YOUTH MOVEMENT,   *pp. 97-102.*
    Photo.
DISCUSSION,   *pp. 102-105.*
The phenomenon of the Jewish youth movement first appeared in Germany with
the organization of the Blau-Weiss Wanderbund in 1912. The original member-
ship was mostly middle class, but later included the socialist chalutzic (Palestine-

oriented) children of Eastern Jewish immigrants. All Jewish youth movements, whether Zionist or not, searched for a reinterpretation of their Jewish identity, attempted to create a living Jewish experience, and served as a channel of provocative criticism of society and of the Jewish establishment in particular.

F. Rosenthal

6

CHRISTIANITY IN TRANSITION

732. Bagge, Sverre. DEN KATOLSKE KIRKE OG HITLERS MAK-TOVERTAGELSE [The Catholic Church and Hitler's seizure of power]. *Norsk Teologisk Tidsskrift [Norway] 1972 73(3-4): 137-174.* Analyzes the attitudes of the Catholic clergy in Germany, the Vatican, and the Catholic party *Zentrum* toward the Nazi Party, from the 1930 election to Hitler's concordat with the papacy in September 1933. Before Hitler's seizure of power, the Catholic Church had condemned the Party, particularly for its racial policy, but regarded the Communists as the real threat. Catholic attitudes changed in 1933 because of pressure put on *Zentrum* members, because of the need to preserve the freedom of the Church and its ideology, and because the clergy believed that they shared the Party's belief in authority, national self-pride, and Germany's right to become a major world power. 130 notes.   U. G. Jeyes/S

733. Besier, Gerhard. THE ATTITUDE OF THE CONTINUATION COM-MITTEE ON LIFE AND WORK IN BERNE IN 1926 CONCERNING THE QUESTION OF GERMAN WAR GUILT. *Kyrkohistorisk Årsskrift [Sweden] 1981: 120-152.* Comments on the historical background of the Continuation Committee on Life and Work, which took up the issue of German war guilt in Bern in 1926 at the instigation of the German delegation to the Universal Christian Conference on Life and Work at Stockholm in 1925, and cites material, principally letters sent by the committee's members to one another, in which the nationalistic prejudices of the authors are clearly evident.

734. Besier, Gerhard. DEUTSCHER EVANGELISCHER KIRCHENAUS-SCHUSS (DEKA) UND KRIEGSSCHULDFRAGE 1922-1933 [The German Evangelical Church Federation (GECF) and the war guilt question, 1922-33]. *Kyrkohistorisk Årsskrift [Sweden] 1977 77: 262-269.* After the Versailles Treaty, German nationalist movements exerted strong pressure on the German Evangelical Church Federation, the highest church administration, to protest against Germany alone being found guilty of starting World War I. After some hesitation the Church Federation again assumed its traditional role of supporting the state, sharing the nationalists' resentment against the treaty and disregarding the protests of pacifist groups. The federation avoided ecumenical efforts, and contact with such movements abroad, until international investigations had relieved Germany of bearing the war guilt alone. Primary sources.   G. Herritt

735. Bettis, Joseph. THEOLOGY AND POLITICS: KARL BARTH AND REINHOLD NIEBUHR ON SOCIAL ETHICS AFTER LIBERALISM. *Religion in Life 1979 48(1): 53-62.* Discusses the fundamental differences in the viewpoints of Karl Barth and Reinhold Niebuhr, politically influential theologians of the 1920's-30's concerned with social ethics and alternatives to Protestant liberalism, Barth in Europe, and Niebuhr in America.

736. Bois, Jean Pierre. L'OPINION CATHOLIQUE RHÉNANE DEVANT LE SÉPARATISME EN 1923 [Rhenish Catholic opinion faced with separatism in 1923]. *Rev. d'Hist. Moderne et Contemporaine [France] 1974 21(2): 221-251.* Studies Catholic reaction to the separatist movement in south and western Germany during the German crisis of 1923. Distinguishes various levels of thought and political division in France, where opposition to Prussia and the obvious strategic benefits to France of a separate Rhine State gave rise to pressure tactics to encourage and support the movement. Outlines the formation of two opposing camps: under Adenauer, with a policy of action in accordance with Berlin, and under Dorton, with militant action to force decision. French support was vital in the renewal of the movement after an earlier unsuccessful attempt at separatism (1919). Based on regional German newspapers and secondary sources; 2 maps, 55 notes.   S. Sevilla

737. Brecht, Alfred. ERINNERUNGEN AUS 60 JAHREN URACHER SEMINARGESCHICHTE [Memoirs of 60 years of the Urach Seminary's history]. *Blätter für Württembergische Kirchengeschichte [West Germany] 1977 77: 149-160.* Personal recollections of the development of this Protestant theological seminary, which reflect Brecht's view of German Protestantism during World War I, the Weimar Republic, World War II, and the postwar period.

738. Bussmann, Walter. KIRCHE UND THEOLOGIE ZWISCHEN WEIMAR UND DRITTEN REICH [Church and theology between Weimar and the Third Reich]. *Hist. Zeitschrift [West Germany] 1978 227(3): 617-630.* Review article of Klaus Scholder's *Die Kirchen und das Dritte Reich,* vol. 1, which deals with the background of the Third Reich and the "era of illusions," 1918-34, in German theological circles. Protestant theologians were divided over questions involving anti-Semitism, the relationship between God and the people, and the völkisch movement in general. The Nazis developed a greater appeal to Protestants than to Catholics, yet Protestants refused to accept the German Christian movement, primarily because it was poorly conceived. Scholder is weakest in dealing with the Catholics. Note.   G. H. Davis

739. Campenhausen, Axel. ENTSTEHUNG UND FUNKTION DES BISCHÖFLICHEN AMTES IN DEN EVANGELISCHEN KIRCHEN DEUTSCHLANDS [Origin and function of the office of bishop in the Evangelical Churches in Germany]. *Österreichisches Archiv für Kirchenrecht [Austria] 1975 26(1): 3-24.* Analyzes the development of the independent Evangelical (protestant) office of bishop in Germany between the 16th century and the 20th. 49 notes.   R. Wagnleitner

740. Davies, Alan. RACISM AND GERMAN PROTESTANT THEOLOGY: A PRELUDE TO THE HOLOCAUST. *Ann. of the Am. Acad. of Pol. and Social Sci. 1980 (450): 20-34.* The success of racism in modern Europe

had a great deal to do with the experience of military defeat and political collapse as in France after 1870 and Germany after 1918. As a modern ideology, racism begins in the 19th century, but older modes of race thinking are rooted in European ethnocentrism. When the old Christian universe was replaced by modern secular ideas, racism emerged as a secular myth, the Aryan myth, in which the alienated European found reassurance during a decadent age. German Protestant theology during the 19th century was slowly colored by romantic nationalistic ideas that eventually would open the door to racism. The nation, rather than the state, became an "order of creation," and in this way racist doctrines swept into Protestant theology.   J/S

741. Dülmen, Richard van.   DIE DEUTSCHE KATHOLIZISMUS UND DER ERSTE WELTKRIEG   [German Catholicism and World War I]. *Francia [France] 1974 2: 347-376.* German Catholics rallied to the national banners in 1914 with boundless enthusiasm. The kaiser, though a Protestant, was practically deified. The doctrine of the "just war" was used to justify Germany's entrance into and participation in World War I. The collapse in 1918, followed by Revolution and the fall of the dynasty, left German Catholicism shocked and divided. They rejected both socialism and, for the most part, a restoration of the monarchy. After 1920, most Catholics tended toward the Right, which caused much difficulty for the Center Party, which strove to uphold Weimar democracy. 109 notes.   J. C. Billigmeier

742. Gordon, Frank J.   THE GERMAN EVANGELICAL CHURCHES AND THE STRUGGLE FOR THE SCHOOLS IN THE WEIMAR REPUBLIC.   *Church Hist. 1980 49(1): 47-61.* The German Evangelical Church did not hold the Weimar Republic in the highest esteem. The republic's treatment of issues of vital concern to the churches played a crucial role in shaping church political opinion. An important issue was the question of religious education in the schools. Since the republican regime gave the church no satisfaction, churchmen saw little reason to help the faltering republic. Based on Evangelical newspapers, and official church proceedings and proclamations.   M. D. Dibert

743. Gordon, Frank J.   LIBERAL GERMAN CHURCHMEN AND THE FIRST WORLD WAR.   *German Studies Rev. 1981 4(1): 39-62.* Liberal Protestant churchmen, such as Martin Rade (1857-1940), the editor of *Die Christliche Welt,* and Otto Baumgarten (1858-1934), the editor of *Evangelische Freiheit,* supported Germany's war efforts in World War I, though they insisted that the war be fought without hate and extreme nationalism. They opposed the annexationist schemes of the Pan-Germans and argued that the war should bring about international understanding. Although they initially opposed political democracy, they eventually supported the Weimar Republic.   94 notes.
                                                               J. T. Walker

744. Hafstad, Kjetil.   TEOLOGISK EKSISTENS I DAG. FRAGMENTER AV EN DEBATT MELLOM KARL BARTH OG RUDOLF BULTMANN OM TEOLOGI OG SAMFUNN   [Theological existence today: fragments of a debate between Karl Barth and Rudolf Bultmann about theology and society]. *Norsk Teologisk Tidsskrift [Norway] 1975 76(3): 129-168.* Summarizes the debate between Karl Barth and Rudolf Bultmann, ca. 1920-40, centered around the Günther Dehn case, 1929-32, and the oath of loyalty to Hitler 1934, and investi-

gates the assumption that the former was influenced by socialism, while the latter was idealistic and apolitical. The letters between them indicate that Barth misunderstood Bultmann to a large extent, that Bultmann did engage himself in the political conflict, and that Barth's membership in the Social Democratic Party was of a more formal nature. 167 notes. U. G. Jeyes

745. Hammer, Karl. DER DEUTSCHE PROTESTANTISMUS UND DER ERSTE WELTKRIEG [German Protestantism and World War I]. *Francia [France] 1974 2: 398-414.* German Protestantism, with its historic links to the state and tradition of subservience to it, stood enthusiastically behind the war effort when World War I broke out. The eventual collapse of imperial Germany caught most Protestants unprepared and deeply traumatized them. After the war, organized Protestantism came to be largely identified with the political and cultural Right, a position from which it only began to escape during the Nazi years. 80 notes. J. C. Billigmeier

746. Hollerbach, Alexander. STREIFLICHTER ZUR ENTSTEHUNGS-GESCHICHTE DER BADISCHEN STAATSKIRCHENVERTRÄGE VON 1932 [Sidelights on the origins of the Baden church-state treaties of 1932]. *Zeitschrift der Savigny-Stiftung für Rechtsgeschichte: Kanonistische Abteilung [Germany] 1975 92: 324-347.* Analyzes the origins and the significance of the treaties which the Baden government signed with the Vatican and the United Evangelical Protestant Church in 1932. The correspondence between Ulrich Stutz, a Prussian privy councillor, and Eugen Baumgartner, Baden minister of culture, reveals the importance of these agreements. The treaties mark the emergence of a new understanding of church-state relations; the Catholic and Protestant churches were no longer treated as established state churches, but as autonomous corporate religious bodies whose rights and privileges were guaranteed by the state. Based on documents in the Freiburger Erzbischöfliche Ordinariat, and other primary and secondary sources; 79 notes. B. Nischan

747. Jacke, Jochen. KIRCHE, STAAT, PARTEIEN IN DER WEIMARER REPUBLIK. ZUR INSTITUTIONELLEN PROBLEMATIK DES DEUTSC-HEN PROTESTANTISMUS NACH DEM ENDE DES STAATSKIRCHEN-TUMS 1918 [Church, state, and political parties during the Weimar era: the institutional problem of German Protestantism after the demise of the established church, 1918]. *Zeitgeschichte [Austria] 1976 3(11-12): 346-363.* Research on the German Evangelical Church of the 20th century has concentrated on the *Kirchenkampf* during the Third Reich. The immediate background to the political and religious struggles under Adolf Hitler began with the Weimar Republic, which ended the state-church in Germany. This brought the churches more deeply into active politics than ever before. Various combinations of religion and nationalism emerged, serving in general to cloud the political arena. Primary sources; 39 notes. G. H. Libbey

748. Junker, Théo. LE SYMBOLE DE ROYAUME DE DIEU ET LES CONVICTIONS SOCIALISTES DE TILLICH: L'ESPÉRANCE CONTRE L'UTOPIE [The symbol of the Kingdom of God and the socialist beliefs of Tillich: hope versus utopia]. *Rev. d'Hist. et de Philosophie Religieuses [France] 1978 58(1): 90-102.* Discusses Paul Tillich's involvement in German socialist politics in the 1920's and his view that socialism most closely approximated the religious and political symbol of the Kingdom of God.

749. Knapp, Thomas A. THE RED AND THE BLACK: CATHOLIC SO-
CIALISTS IN THE WEIMAR REPUBLIC. *Catholic Hist. Rev. 1975 61(3):*
386-408. In post-1918 Germany various attempts were made by young Catholics
to overcome the historic opposition between Catholicism and the socialist movement. The difficulties inherent in these attempts, as well as the problem of
growing class conflict in German Catholicism, are well illustrated in the fate of
the *Bund katholischer Sozialisten* of Heinrich Mertens and the Christian-Social
Party of Vitus Heller. Mertens tried to establish a Catholic position within the
Social Democratic Party, whereas Heller concentrated on founding a separate
political alternative. Neither effort succeeded, but they were nevertheless important symptoms of the crisis in German Catholicism.   A

750. Kosian, Jozef. POSTAWA D. BONHOEFFERA WOBEC ROD-
ZAĘGO SIĘ W NIEMCZECH FASZYZMU [Dietrich Bonhoeffer's attitude
to the rise of Nazism in Germany]. *Przegląd Zachodni [Poland] 1975 31(2):*
313-326. Examines the moral attitudes of the German theologian as expressed
in his *Letters and Notes from Prison* (1951).

751. Lorenz, Eckehart. PROTESTANTISCHE REAKTIONEN AUF DIE
ENTWICKLUNG DER SOZIALISTISCHEN ARBEITERBEWEGUNG.
MANNHEIM 1890-1933 [Protestant reactions to the development of the Socialist labor movement: Mannheim, 1890-1933]. *Archiv für Sozialgeschichte*
[West Germany] 1976 16: 371-416. Describes the Protestant Church's reaction
to the Socialist labor movement in Mannheim, the industrial center of Baden-
Württemberg. Several organizations were founded, all in times of crisis. Between
1890 and 1918 a class compromise was first envisaged through religious integration, and later through a union of moderate forces against extremes. After the
revolution of 1918 several streams came into existence: religious socialists, democrats, and a fascist group. The author gives political biographies of four prominent priests, Th. Steltz, Erwin Eckert, Ernst Lehmann, and Hermann Teutsch.
After 1933 all organizations except the fascist Evangelischer Volksbund ceased
to exist. Based on unpublished sources and secondary works; 347 notes.
                                                            H. W. Wurster

752. Lynch, James. POLITICAL AND RELIGIOUS CONSTRAINTS ON
EDUCATIONAL POLICY IN THE WEIMAR REPUBLIC. *Hist. of Educ.*
[Great Britain] 1975 4(2): 49-65. In the political flux of the Weimar Republic
there were initially three major political parties, each of which allocated a high
priority to educational policy, although they were deeply divided on the issue.
Two of the parties held irreconcilable views on education: the Socialist Party
advocated a nondenominational community school, which was anathema to the
Center Party, which was attached to the Catholic Church. An analysis of the
political controversy surrounding the drafting of the Weimar constitution illustrates the polarization of Socialist and Catholic opinion. This polarization contributed to the political uncertainty characteristic of the Weimar Republic and
resulted in a situation in which the central government was in no position to
control the educational policies of the German provinces. These conditions frustrated all attempts at nationwide educational reforms during the Weimar period,
although successful individual initiatives were made in some provinces. Secondary sources; 55 notes.   K. Dobson

753. Norden, Günther van. POLITISCHER PROTESTANTISMUS IN DEUTSCHLAND [Political protestantism in Germany]. *Neue Pol. Literatur [West Germany] 1978 23(1): 34-45.* In contrast to German Catholicism, the German Lutheran Church did not achieve the formation of a typical political party representing protestant interests in the 19th and 20th centuries.

754. Pierard, Richard V. WHY DID GERMAN PROTESTANTS WELCOME HITLER? *Fides et Hist. 1978 10(2): 8-29.* All elements of German Protestantism embraced Hitler, Nazism, and anti-Semitism. The author traces their abrogation of Christian testimony to facets of Germany's theology that fused conservative nationalism, monarchy, the state, and Christian belief. Prominent theologians spelled out clearly the terms of the theology in the 1920's and 1930's. Explores briefly the contradictions between Nazism and Christianity. 52 notes.
R. E. Butchart

755. Thevs, Hildegard. EDUARD CAMPARTERS BEITRAG ZUR ABWEHR DES ANTISEMITISMUS [Eduard Camparter's contribution to the fight against anti-semitism]. *Blätter für Württembergische Kirchengeschichte [West Germany] 1978 78: 146-186.* Describes the work of the German protestant priest and liberal member of parliament, Eduard Camparter (1860-1945), who, particularly since the 1920's, published philosemitic studies on the history of the Jews, supported the League Against Anti-Semitism and tried to win German public support for antiracist policies.

756. Tillich, Paul. THE RELIGIOUS SITUATION IN GERMANY TODAY. *Religion in Life 1978 47(3): 361-370.* Written in 1934. Examines the juxtaposition of increased secularism and decreased humanism in Germany in the 1930's, placing it in a context of political upheaval and social conflict.

757. Tommissen, Piet. CARL SCHMITT E IL *RENOUVEAU* CATTOLICO NELLA GERMANIA DEGLI ANNI VENTI [Carl Schmitt and the Catholic *Renouveau* in Germany during the 1920's]. *Storia e Politica [Italy] 1975 14(4): 481-500.* The 1920's were a period of rebirth for German Catholics, coming forth into the world after their dormancy under the Second Reich (1871-1918). For his role as an apologist for the Roman Church, and as an acute writer on political theology, Carl Schmitt deserves an important place in the history of the German Catholic revival. 74 notes.
J. C. Billigmeier

758. Waldman, Loren K. MASS-SOCIETY THEORY AND RELIGION: THE CASE OF THE NAZIS. *Am. J. of Pol. Sci. 1976 20(2): 319-326.* Contra mass-society theory, whether integration is a buffer to social-movement support depends partially on the content of integration. Those integrated into groups that failed to communicate their position to their members (e.g., church-integrated Protestants), or opposed the Nazi movement (e.g., church-integrated Catholics before November, 1933), voted against the movement; those integrated into groups that favored the movement (e.g., church-integrated Catholics in November, 1933) voted for the movement. Conditions under which integration and support may not be the same as predicted here and found for the Nazi case are discussed.
J

759. —.   CONFESSION ET COMPORTEMENT DANS LES CAM-
PAGNES D'ALSACE ET DE BADE (1871-1939): CATHOLIQUES, PROT-
ESTANTS ET JUIFS: DÉMOGRAPHIE, DYNAMISME ÉCONOMIQUE ET
SOCIAL, VIE DE RELATIONS ET ATTITUDE POLITIQUE   [Religion and
behavior in rural Alsace and Baden, 1871-1939: Catholics, Protestants, and Jews:
demography, economic and social dynamism, interreligious relationships, and
political attitude]. *Rev. d'Alsace [France] 1981 (107): 245-252.* Attempts to
measure the significance of religious affiliation in Alsace and Baden, concluding
that Catholics, Jews, and Protestants confronted each other in order to preserve
their identity and to impose or reject domination, using religion as a kind of
second nationality.

THE GROWTH OF GERMAN
COMMUNISM

760. Abusch, Alexander. CLARA ZETKIN AN DER WENDE DER
WELTGESCHICHTE [Clara Zetkin at the turning point of world history].
Einheit [East Germany] 1977 32(6): 693-701. Clara Zetkin (1857-1933) promoted
solidarity with the USSR in the Weimar parliament, strengthened by her personal
friendship with Lenin and Nadezhda Krupskaya.

761. Arendt, Hans-Jürgen. WEIBLICHE MITGLIEDER DER KPD IN
DER WEIMARER REPUBLIK—ZAHLENMÄSSIGE STÄRKE UND SO-
ZIALE STELLUNG [Female members of the Communist Party of Germany
in the Weimar Republic: numerical strength and social position]. *Beiträge zur
Geschichte der Arbeiterbewegung [East Germany] 1977 19(4): 652-660.* Women
made up 7-17% of the membership of the Communist Party of Germany from
1919 to 1933. The figures must often be deduced from indirect source material.
The social composition can also only be deduced from a small sample. The Party
had difficulty recruiting working-class women. A high percentage of women in
the Party were housewives, unemployed, or from the intelligentsia. Based on
Party conference reports, other Party publications, documents in the archives of
the Institute for Marxism-Leninism, Berlin, and secondary works; 3 tables, 55
notes.   J. B. Street

762. Arns, Günter. DIE LINKE IN DER SPD-REICHSTAGSFRAKTION
IM HERBST 1923 [The left in the SPD-Reichstag delegation in the fall of
1923]. *Vierteljahrshefte für Zeitgeschichte [West Germany] 1974 22(2): 191-203.*
A quantitative analysis of the Social Democratic Party's left wing in the German
parliament according to USPD (Independent Socialist Party) membership and
key 1923 votes and petitions. Over 30% of the parliamentary group, mostly
former independents, were consistently in opposition to the Social Democratic
leadership. And two-thirds of all former Independents were in the opposition
group, suggesting that the SPD-USPD fusion was the key factor in the parliamentary SPD's instability. Based on Reichstag records, press, and secondary sources;
46 notes.   D. Prowe

763. Aue, Dorit and Nitzsche, Gerhard. BRIEFE DER BRÜDERLICHEN
VERBUNDENHEIT UND SOLIDARITÄT ZWISCHEN DEUTSCHEN
UND SOWJETISCHEN WERKTÄTIGEN 1925-1931 [Letters of brotherly

ties and solidarity between German and Soviet workers, 1925-31]. *Beiträge zur Geschichte der Arbeiterbewegung [East Germany] 1977 19(6): 995-1002.* Introduces and publishes for the first time seven letters between German and Soviet labor organizations. The letters express the principles of proletarian internationalism and solidarity between the working class and Communist parties of both countries. The documents are from the archives of the Institute for Marxism-Leninism in Berlin; 5 notes.   J. B. Street

764. Awrus, A. and Babitschenko, L. WILHELM PIECK UND DIE ROTE HILFE (1922 BIS 1941) [Wilhelm Pieck and the Red Aid, 1922-41]. *Beiträge zur Geschichte der Arbeiterbewegung [East Germany] 1975 17(6): 1022-1033.* The International Red Aid benefited from Wilhelm Pieck's participation from its initiation by the Comintern in 1922. His participation began in coordinating the work of the German Red Aid with that of the International. Later he headed the entire organization, the major efforts of which were directed against German fascist oppression throughout Europe. His long conviction that German-Russian friendship was of utmost importance to the socialist revolution found a fruitful means of expression in this vital activity. Based on Pieck's writings; 59 notes.
                                                                G. H. Libbey

765. Babitschenko, L. G. CLARA ZETKIN UND DIE INTERNATIONALE ROTE HILFE [Clara Zetkin and the International Red Aid]. *Beiträge zur Geschichte der Arbeiterbewegung [East Germany] 1977 19(3): 371-382.* Describes Clara Zetkin's leading role in the development of the International Red Aid (IRH) as a mass organization for helping political prisoners and persecuted revolutionaries and her contributions to the strengthening of proletarian solidarity against imperialist reaction. As chairman of the executive committee from 1925 Zetkin was the leading spirit of the organization. Based on Zetkin's published writings and stenographic reports of IRH meetings; 79 notes.
                                                                J. B. Street

766. Bartel, V. VIL'GELM PIK: OT PODMASTER'IA DO PREZIDENTA [Wilhelm Pieck: from apprentice to president]. *Novaia i Noveishaia Istoriia [USSR] 1973 (6): 57-67; 1974 (1): 73-84.* Part I. Describes the career of Wilhelm Pieck (1876-1960), President of East Germany. A member of the Social Democratic Party, he settled in Bremen in 1896, beginning his political career with Karl Liebknecht (1871-1919) and Rosa Luxemburg (1870-1919). In 1906 he became Party secretary in Bremen and was transferred to Berlin in 1910. After the revolution of November 1918, he was elected to the central committee of the German Communist Party and in 1921 he made the first of many visits to Moscow, and met V. I. Lenin. 8 notes. Part II. Continues the career of Pieck, from his denunciation of the Nazis in February 1922 to his death in 1960. With the German Communist Party, he led the resistance to Adolf Hitler, replacing Ernst Thälmann as Party chairman when Thälmann was arrested. He left Germany in May 1933, working underground for the Party, returning to Germany in 1939 on the conclusion of the Soviet-German pact, and continued antifascist work during World War II. He joined Otto Grotewohl to form the Socialist Unity Party of Germany and in 1949 became President of East Germany. 2 illus., 17 notes.
                                                                L. Smith/C. R. Pike

767. Bartel, Walter. UNSER ERNST THÄLMANN [Our Ernst Thälmann]. *Einheit [East Germany] 1974 29(8): 942-950.* After 1925 Ernst Thälmann (1886-1944) worked out the Leninist strategies for the German Communist Party, and after his imprisonment he became a worldwide symbol of resistance to Nazism. After 11 years in prisons and concentration camps he was shot.

768. Bartel, Walter. WILHELM PIECK—EIN KAMPFERFÜLLTES LEBEN FÜR DIE INTERESSEN DER ARBEITERKLASSE UND ALLER WERKTÄTIGEN [Wilhelm Pieck: a life of struggle for the interests of the working class and all working people]. *Einheit [East Germany] 1975 30(12): 1361-1368.* Reviews Wilhelm Pieck's (1876-1960) activities as Communist politician and trade unionist in the Weimar Republic, in the Comintern, in Soviet exile, and his role in the unification of East German Communists and Socialists after World War II.

769. Bartolini, Stefano. LA SINISTRA NEI SISTEMI PARTITICI EUROPEI (1917-1978): UNA ANALISI COMPARATA DELLA SUA DIMENSIONE E COMPOSIZIONE E DEI PROBLEMI DI SVILUPPO ELETTORALE [The Left in the European party systems, 1917-78: a comparative analysis of size, composition, and electoral development]. *Riv. Italiana di Sci. Pol. [Italy] 1979 9(1): 137-169.* Systematically presents the composition and the electoral size of the Left in all European countries. Through the use of simple statistical analysis the article clarifies the differences in national patterns of electoral development of the Left and the extent of the Communist Socialist monopoly of class representation in the various countries as well as the impact of other Left forces.   J

770. Baumann, Helga and Lautenschlag, Kurt. DOKUMENTE DER BRÜDERLICHEN VERBUNDENHEIT DES DEUTSCHEN PROLETARIATS MIT DEN KÄMPFERN DER ROTEN ARMEE [Documents of brotherly ties of the German proletariat with the fighters of the Red Army]. *Beiträge zur Geschichte der Arbeiterbewegung [East Germany] 1977 19(5): 827-836.* Publishes for the first time eight letters, greetings, and telegrams between representatives of the Communist Party of Germany and units of the Red Army of the Soviet Union. The documents, dated 1923-32, express the strong bonds of international proletarianism uniting the workers and peasants of Germany and the USSR. The documents are from the archives of the Institute for Marxism-Leninism, Berlin.   J. B. Street

771. Becker, Rolf. DIE IAH AN DER SEITE DER KPD BEI DER SCHAFFUNG DER EINHEITSFRONT DER ARBEITERKLASSE UND ALLER WERKTÄTIGEN (1929 BIS 1932) [The Workers' International Relief side by side with the Communist Party of Germany in the effort to organize the united front of the working class and all the working people, 1929-32]. *Beiträge zur Geschichte der Arbeiterbewegung [East Germany] 1977 19(2): 279-289.* During 1929-32 the Workers' International Relief and the Communist Party of Germany worked together to organize workers and the labor movement. Facing strong opposition from German fascists and capitalists, the combined efforts required organization to survive in the struggle against the Hitler movement, which was dominated by racist and bourgeois interests. 28 notes.
                                                                                         G. H. Libbey

772.   Blanke, Detlev.   ÜBER DIE ARBEITER-ESPERANTISTEN—BEWE-
GUNG IN DER WEIMARER REPUBLIK UND IHREN BEITRAG ZUR
ENTWICKLUNG DER DEUTSCH-SOWJETISCHEN FREUNDSCHAFT
[On the workers Esperanto movement in the Weimar Republic and its contribution to German-Soviet friendship]. *Beiträge zur Geschichte der Arbeiterbewegung [East Germany] 1976 18(4): 683-691.* Until World War I Esperanto
was primarily used by bourgeois-pacifist groups. After 1930 the workers' Esperanto clubs became influenced by the German Communist Party. The contacts
of the German workers with foreign comrades, especially with Russians, via
Esperanto influenced the development of the ideology of the German workers and
strengthened the ties of friendship. Based on printed documents, secondary literature, and newspapers; 66 notes.   R. Wagnleitner

773.   Bramke, Werner.   ANTIMILITARISMUS UND TRADITIONSP-
FLEGE IN DER IDEOLOGISCHEN ARBEIT DER KPD (1920-1932)
[Antimilitarism and cultivation of tradition within the Communist Party of Germany's ideological activity, 1920-32]. *Militärgeschichte [East Germany] 1978
17(1): 32-42.* In the years of the Weimar Republic, the struggle against militarism
and the danger of imperialist war, which especially threatened the Soviet Union,
belonged to the fundamental components of the ideological activity of the Communist Party of Germany. It therefore took up a broad area in the revolutionary
nurturing of tradition in the Party. The author points out the intimate reciprocal
relationship of the nurturing of tradition and the antimilitary struggle of the
Party, in the process of which he especially deals with the antimilitarist campaign.
Explains at the same time how the resulting antimilitarist struggle contributed
in essential ways to the fact that under the leadership of Ernst Thälmann the
Leninist interpretation finally prevailed. 50 notes.   J/T (H. D. Andrews)

774.   Bramke, Werner.   KOLLOQUIUM ÜBER ERNST THÄLMANNS
KAMPF GEGEN DEN FASCHISMUS   [Colloquium on Ernst Thälmann's
struggle against fascism]. *Beiträge zur Geschichte der Arbeiterbewegung [East
Germany] 1976 18(4): 713-715.* Reviews the lectures and discussions of the
colloquium on Ernst Thälmann's struggle against fascism, Berlin, April 1976,
which analyzed Thälmann's theoretical and practical efforts for the unification
of the German working class in the 1920's and 1930's.   R. Wagnleitner

775.   Broué, Pierre.   SPARTAKISME, BOLCHEVISME, GAUCHISME
FACE AU PROBLÈMES DE LA RÉVOLUTION PROLÉTARIENNE EN
ALLEMAGNE (1918-1923)   [Spartacism, Bolshevism, leftism and the problems of the proletarian revolution in Germany]. *Mouvement Social [France] 1973
(84): 87-96.* Describes the formation of the Communist Party in Germany after
World War I, the diverse currents it united, and its similarities to and differences
from its Russian counterpart. Perceived by its founders as part of an international
Bolshevik revolution, it consisted of three elements: Spartacism, or the pure
product of social democracy in its earliest stages; Bolshevism, or the Russian
influence on the formation of the party; and Leftism, originating in the violent
strikes of the times and in attitudes toward World War I. The first major problem
of the new party was to synthesize these elements. Demonstrates how the militant
Communists played a greater role in organizing the party than official philosophical spokesmen. Based on sources from the Institute of Marxism-Leninism and
the Paul Levi archives in the Buttinger Library.   J. Terhune

776. Büchner, Robert. ERINNERUNGEN AN EIN KAMPFBANNER DES PROLETARISCHEN INTERNATIONALISMUS [Memories of a fighting banner of proletarian internationalism]. *Beiträge zur Geschichte der Arbeiterbewegung [East Germany] 1978 20(6): 876-880.* Describes the fate of a banner presented by the Young Communist League area committee in Kazan in 1923 to the Communist Youth Organization of Germany in Neuss for its help in the international hunger aid program for the Volga district, 1921-23. The banner accompanied the youth group throughout its antimilitary activities and was ultimately burnt in an Anglo-American air raid which destroyed the house where it had been hidden. 2 notes. L. H. Schmidt/S

777. Carsten, Francis L. ARTHUR ROSENBERG ALS POLITIKER [Arthur Rosenberg as politician]. Botz, Gerhard; Hautmann, Hans; and Konrad, Helmut, eds. *Geschichte und Gesellschaft. Festschrift für Karl R. Stadler zum 60. Geburtstag* (Linz-Wien: Europa Verlag, 1974): 267-280. Arthur Rosenberg (1889-1943) played an important role in the German left wing during the Weimar Republic both as a historian and as a Communist politician. Rosenberg, who had been a member of the ultraleft opposition within the German Communist Party until 1926, became a member of the party leadership under Ernst Thälmann (1866-1944). Rosenberg left the party in 1927 because he thought that the romantic philosophy, phraseology, and unrealistic position of the German Communists diverted the workers from their real goals. After 1928 Rosenberg worked as a historian in Berlin and, after 1933, in Liverpool and New York. Based on interviews, published documents, and secondary literature; 29 notes.

R. Wagnleitner

778. Carsten, Francis L. ARTHUR ROSENBERG: ANCIENT HISTORIAN INTO LEADING COMMUNIST. *J. of Contemporary Hist. [Great Britain] 1973 8(1): 63-75.* After beginning a career as a somewhat conservative ancient historian, Arthur Rosenberg (1889-1943) became after World War I an enthusiastic communist, an ultra-left wing functionary of the KPD and the Comintern, and a deputy in the Reichstag. Discouraged by political in-fighting, he left the KPD in 1927. His subsequent books on the history of Bolshevism and of the Weimar Republic displayed sound historical judgement and have influenced the younger generation of German historians. Primary and secondary sources; 27 notes. B. A. Block

779. Charius, Albrecht; Forster, Gerhard; Otto, Helmut; and Schmiedel, Karl. ZUR GENESIS UND ENTWICKLUNG DES DEUTSCHEN MILITARISMUS. PROBLEME SEINER ERFORSCHUNG UND DARSTELLUNG [On the genesis and development of German militarism: problems of investigation and presentation]. *Militärgeschichte [East Germany] 1974 13(3): 306-313.* It is the task of Marxist social scientists to investigate the class nature and forms of militarism on the basis of already established Marxist theoretical foundations. Karl Liebknecht was one of the first to deal extensively with militarism, and his basic explanation, together with Lenin's formulation, is the place to begin. Eight topics deserve attention as do two complex questions: the international effect of German militarism and the dialectic of militarism whereby it creates its own destruction. H. D. Andrews

780. Czubiński, Antoni. TRADITIONEN DER POLNISCH-DEUTSC-HEN REVOLUTIONÄREN ZUSAMMENARBEIT IN DEN JAHREN 1918-1945 [Traditions of Polish-German revolutionary cooperation during the years 1918-45]. *Beiträge zur Geschichte der Arbeiterbewegung [East Germany] 1974 16(1): 31-45.* Cooperation among Polish and German Communists can be traced to the mid-19th century. Rosa Luxemburg, Karl Liebknecht, and Karl Radek, among others, were their mutual intellectual leaders. Territorial changes placed many Poles under German administration and many Germans under Polish administration, increasing the opportunity and need for cooperation. The Polish and German Communist parties supported each other as their legal positions fluctuated, and together opposed the Hitler regime. Based on the papers of the Polish and German Communist parties and on their leaders' correspondence; 71 notes.   G. H. Libbey

781. Czubiński, Antoni. TRADYCJE POLSKO-NIEMIECKIEJ WSPÓŁ-PRACY REWOLUCYJNEJ Z LAT 1918-1945 [Traditions of Polish-German revolutionary collaboration, 1918-45]. *Z Pola Walki [Poland] 1974 17(65): 35-51.* Polish-German revolutionary cooperation was formed under the influence of the founders of scientific socialism as long ago as the mid-19th century. The collaboration was continued by revolutionary Social Democratic activists of both nations; after 1918 the collaboration was consolidated and developed by Communists. The revolutionary Polish-German collaboration was aimed against the propertied classes and their nationalistic ideology. Sometimes the cooperation was direct and intensive; in others, restrained and retarded. Poles took part in the November Revolution of 1918 in Germany. The Communist Party of Poland (KPP) and Communist Party of Germany (KPD) were connected with homogeneous ideological and organizational principles. Both parties went through a difficult evolution of their views on the national question, especially in relation to Upper Silesia. In the 1920's, the KPP availed itself of organizational assistance from the KPD on German territory, mainly in border towns. The political and economic struggle of Poles residing in Germany was carried on with the cooperation of the KPD. After Hitler's seizure of power, the KPP came to the KPD's help in shifting to illegal activities. Both parties were struggling against fascist dictatorship. German Communists declared themselves against Hitler's aggression in Poland and the USSR. The wartime resistance movement organized by German communists on German territory led to contacts between Poles and Germans. Complete elaboration of Polish-German cooperation in the resistance movement requires further research and closer collaboration between historians from Poland and East Germany.   J/S

782. David, Fritz. ZUR GESCHICHTE DER ZEITSCHRIFT "DIE INTERNATIONALE" (1919-1933) [The history of the journal *Die Internationale*, 1919-33]. *Beiträge zur Geschichte der Arbeiterbewegung [East Germany] 1973 15(6): 967-986.* The main topics of the theoretical journal of the German Communist Party *Die Internationale* were the history of the Party and the workers' movement, trade union problems, economic and financial problems, the struggle against the war policies of German imperialism, the work of the Comintern and the struggle of Communist parties in various countries. German and foreign authors, including Ernst Thälmann, Walter Ulbricht, Clara Zetkin, G. I. Zinoviev, K. Radek, and Georg Lukács contributed articles. Based on documents

in the Institute for Marxism-Leninism, newspapers, and secondary sources; 7 tables, 70 notes.

R. Wagnleitner

783. Dillwitz, Sigrid. EDWIN HOERNLE—AGRARPOLITIKER DER REVOLUTIONÄREN DEUTSCHEN ARBEITERBEWEGUNG [Edwin Hoernle: agrarian politician of the revolutionary German workers' movement]. *Wissenschaftliche Zeitschrift der U. Rostock. Gesellschafts- und Sprachwissenschaftliche Reihe [East Germany] 1974 23(9): 547-550.* In the 1920's and 1930's the German Communist expert on agriculture, Edwin Hoernle, analyzed the connection between capital and production and the impact of the world economic crisis on German agriculture. After 1956 Hoernle became an important proponent of unity between workers and peasants.

R. Wagnleitner

784. Dingel, Frank. RÄTEKOMMUNISMUS UND ANARCHISMUS. ZU EINIGEN NEUEREN ARBEITEN UND NACHDRUCKEN [Council communism and anarchism: recent works and reprints]. *Int. Wissenschaftliche Korrespondenz zur Geschichte der Deutschen Arbeiterbewegung [West Germany] 1976 12(1): 71-84.* The pauperized lower working class was the common social strata for left-wing radicalism, immanent in anarchist syndicalism and left-wing communism in Germany between 1918 and 1923.

785. Dobek, Reiner and Kolmsee, Peter. MAXIM ZETKIN—ARTZ, KRIEGSCHIRURG UND KOMMUNIST [Maxim Zetkin: physician, military surgeon, and Communist]. *Militärgeschichte [East Germany] 1978 17(5): 595-603.* Maxim Zetkin (1883-1965) was the son of Clara Zetkin. Following his medical training, he served in the German army in World War I. Politically he moved from the Social Democrats to the Independent Socialists to the Communists. In 1920 he went to the Soviet Union where he worked as a military surgeon during the Civil War and thereafter as clinician, professor, and researcher. During the Spanish Civil War he spent six months organizing medical services in Spain before returning to the Soviet Union as a chief of surgery. During World War II he worked in various Soviet hospitals, and after 1945 he was a medical adviser and policy maker in the Soviet occupation zone and in the German Democratic Republic. 7 illus., 23 notes.

H. D. Andrews

786. Doehler, Edgar. DIE MILITÄFRAGE AUF DEM 12. PARTEITAG DER KPD [The military question at the 12th party congress of the Communist Party of Germany (KPD)]. *Militärgeschichte [East Germany] 1976 15(2): 190-198.* Outlines the decisions on military policy taken by the Communist Party congress at Berlin in June, 1929. The Party criticized past antimilitarist propaganda efforts and called for renewed resistance to fascist trends in Germany, defense of the Soviet Union, and opposition to German militarism and imperialism. Based on Party publications and documents in the Institute for Marxism-Leninism in Berlin; 37 notes.

J. B. Street

787. Doehler, Edgar. DIE MILITÄRPOLITISCHEN RICHTLINIEN VON KPD UND SPD 1929 [The military policy guidelines of the Communist Party and of the Social Democratic Party in Germany, 1929]. *Militärgeschichte [East Germany] 1977 16(3): 306-314.* In the face of the growth of reaction, working class parties were forced to reassess their military policy goals. These goals show the principal differences between the Communists and Social Demo-

crats. The Social Democrats attempted to integrate the military forces and armaments into the parliamentary system on the assumption of a class-neutral state.
The Communist Party oriented itself clearly in the interest of the working masses
and thus served the goal of defending democratic and social rights and achievements of workers against the attack of imperialist, militarist, and fascist forces.
26 notes.   H. D. Andrews

788. Doehler, Edgar and Fischer, Egbert. ERNST THÄLMANNS BEI-
TRAG ZUR ENTWICKLUNG DES WEHRHAFTEN KAMPFES DER
DEUTSCHEN ARBEITERBEWEGUNG GEGEN DIE WACHSENDE FAS-
CHISTISCHE GEFAHR (1929-1933) [Ernst Thälmann's contribution to the
development of the defensive struggle of the German workers' movement against
the growing fascist danger, 1929-33]. *Militärgeschichte [East Germany] 1976
15(3): 274-285.* Reviews the role of Ernst Thälmann, chairman of the Communist
Party of Germany (KPD), in the struggle against German fascism, militarism,
and imperialism during the economic crisis of 1929-33. Thälmann and KPD
devised the united front strategy of mass resistance to fascism, organized self-
defense organizations, and developed ideological arguments to combat the fascist
trend. Lack of support from right-wing socialists and trade unionists hindered the
united front strategy. Based on Thälmann's writings, documents in the Institute
for Marxism-Leninism in Berlin, and secondary works; 33 notes.
                                                                       J. B. Street

789. Doehler, Edgar. ZUR ROLLE DES WEHRHAFTEN ANTIFAS-
CHISTISCHEN KAMPFES IN DER POLITIK DER KPD (1929-1933)
[The role of the armed antifascist struggle in the policy of the Communist Party
of Germany, 1929-33]. *Militärgeschichte [East Germany] 1978 17(5): 534-541.*
With the rise of the fascist danger arose the necessity for the working class to
defend itself against armed acts of terror by fascist forces. On the basis of extensive resource materials the author shows how the Communist Party of Germany
organized the antifascist self defense. At the same time he shows that the defense
against fascist terror was an inseparable part of the antifascist mass struggle and
could achieve full effect only within this greater framework. 27 notes.
                                                                J/T (H. D. Andrews)

790. Döke, Wolfgang. ZUR GESCHICHTE DER BRÜDERLICHEN
ZUSAMMENARBEIT ZWISCHEN DEM LENINSCHEN KOMSOMOL
UND DER REVOLUTIONÄREN DEUTSCHEN ARBEITERJUGEND-
BEWEGUNG IN DEN JAHREN DER WEIMARER REPUBLIK [Frater-
nal cooperation between the Leninist Komsomol and the revolutionary German
workers youth movement during the years of the Weimar Republic]. *Wissenschaftliche Zeitschrift der U. Rostock. Gesellschafts- und Sprachwissenschaftliche Reihe [East Germany] 1973 22(6): 545-549.* Between 1929 and 1933 the
USSR's Young Communist League (Komsomol) and the Communist Youth
League of Germany carried through a revolutionary competition that strengthened proletarian internationalism.

791. Eley, Geoff. THE LEGACY OF ROSA LUXEMBURG. *Critique
[Great Britain] 1979-80 (12): 139-149.* Reviews Norman Gera's *The Legacy of
Rosa Luxemburg* (London: New Left Books, 1976) on the development of Lux-
emburg's political theory in response to events in Germany.

792. Elsen, Heinz. DIE DEUTSCHE KOMMUNISTISCHE KINDEROR-GANISATION—UNTRENNBARER BESTANDTEIL DER REVOLU-TIONÄREN PROLETARISCHEN JUGENDBEWEGUNG [The German Communist children's organization—inseparable part of the revolutionary prole-tarian youth movement]. *Wissenschaftliche Zeitschrift der U. Rostock. Gesell-schafts- und Sprachwissenschaftliche Reihe [East Germany] 1974 23(2): 137-142.* The German Communist children's organization was founded in 1920. It was supervised by the Communist youth organization and was intended to appeal to children with cultural and social programs. Based on printed documents and secondary literature; 19 notes. R. Wagnleitner

793. Ernst, J. and Gassner, K., comps. AUSWAHLBIBLIOGRAPHIE ZUR REVOLUTIONÄREN DEUTSCHEN MATROSENBEWEGUNG (1917-1919) [Select bibliography on the revolutionary German sailors' movement, 1917-19]. *Militärgeschichte [East Germany] 1978 17(6): 747-749.* The bibliogra-phy lists 131 publications that appeared in East Germany under the following headings: works of V. I. Lenin; writings of other leading personalities of the revolutionary workers movement; general accounts and document publications; special topics; first-hand accounts; and fiction. H. D. Andrews

794. Finker, Kurt. ZUM 50. JAHRESTAG DER GRÜNDUNG DES ROTEN FRONTKÄMPFERBUNDES [50th anniversary of the foundation of *Roter Frontkämpferbund*]. *Archivmitteilungen [East Germany] 1974 24(2): 43-46.* Surveys the history of the Antimilitaristic Defense and Protective Organiza-tion of the German Working Class, an association of war veterans, founded and inspired by the German Communist Party in 1924. The organization grew steadily (51,000 members in June 1925); by 1928, 60% of its members did not belong to the Party. Following bloodshed in May 1929, the organization was abolished by official pressure and gradually merged into Party itself. 2 illus., 5 notes. G. E. Pergl

795. Finker, Kurt. ZUR ERFORSCHUNG DER KAMPFES DER KPD GEGEN MILITARISMUS, FASCHISMUS UND IMPERIALISTISCHE KRIEGSVORBEREITUNG (1919 BIS 1933) [Research on the struggle of the Communist Party of Germany against militarism, fascism, and imperialist prepa-ration for war, 1919-33]. *Beiträge zur Geschichte der Arbeiterbewegung [East Germany] 1977 19(6): 947-965.* Reviews the contribution of numerous historical studies, primarily in East Germany in the 1970's, to an understanding of the leading role of the Communist Party of Germany in the struggle against milita-rism and fascism under the Weimar Republic. The many general and specialized studies reviewed show that only the working class under the leadership of its Marxist-Leninist party provided a real alternative to fascism and imperialism. Based on doctoral dissertations, published documentary collections, and second-ary works; 62 notes. J. B. Street

796. Finker, Kurt and Mahlke, Bernhard. ZUR WEHRDEBATTE IN DER DEUTSCHEN ARBEITERBEWEGUNG AM ENDE DER ZWANZIGER JAHRE [On the debate on defense in the German workers' movement at the end of the twenties]. *Militärgeschichte [East Germany] 1979 18(1): 41-49.* The authors show that the defense policy guidelines of the Communist Party of Germany (KPD) of 1929 were the result of ten years' experience of the KPD in

the military policy struggle. Using the example of the development and effect of the Social Democratic Party's "Guidelines for Defense Policy," also worked out in 1929, the authors also clarify the opposing position of the SPD.   35 notes.

J/T (H. D. Andrews)

797. Fölster, Elfriede.   DIE ARBEITSGEMEINSCHAFT SOZIAL-POLITISCHER ORGANISATIONEN (ARSO) VON 1927-1929: ZUR GE-SCHICHTE DER SOZIALPOLITIK DER KPD   [The Work Group of Sociopolitical Organizations (ARSO), 1927-29: the social policy of the Communist Party of Germany]. *Beiträge zur Geschichte der Arbeiterbewegung [East Germany] 1978 20(2): 222-236.* In the face of attacks by monopoly capital on the living conditions and well-being of the working classes, the Communist Party of Germany and other organizations united to form the Work Group of Sociopolitical Organizations (ARSO) in 1927. ARSO organized units on the national, regional, and local levels to educate, publish, and demonstrate. They supported the unemployed and politically persecuted, health and housing programs, and mother and child care for the working classes. Based on documents in the archives of the Institute for Marxism-Leninism, Berlin, published documents, and journals; 49 notes.   J. B. Street

798. Fölster, Elfriede.   SOZIALPOLITIK DER KPD IN DEN JAHREN 1927 UND 1928   [The social policy of the Communist Party of Germany during the years 1927-28]. *Beiträge zur Geschichte der Arbeiterbewegung [East Germany] 1974 16(6): 1015-1032.* Analyzes and prints five documents which present part of the social policy of the Communist Party of Germany during 1927-28. They reveal the nature of Communist efforts to improve social conditions, one of the major goals of the international workers' movement. The documents propose legislation which would provide child support and medical and educational assistance to families. Western historians rarely acknowledge these parliamentary efforts of the Communist Party of Germany. Primary sources; table, 36 notes.   G. H. Libbey

799. Fölster, Elfriede.   VORKÄMPFERIN UND MITGESTALTERIN EINES LEBENS IN FRIEDEN UND SOZIALER SICHERHEIT FÜR ALLE WERKTÄTIGEN   [Fighter for and cocreator of a life in peace and social security for all workers: Martha Arendsee]. *Beiträge zur Geschichte der Arbeiterbewegung [East Germany] 1976 18(4): 701-709.* Beginning her political career in the first decade of the 20th century, Martha Arendsee (1885-1953) joined the left wing of the German Social Democrats. She organized socialist propaganda in World War I, became a Communist parliamentarian in 1924, and between 1934 and 1945 organized antifascist resistance in the Soviet Union. After the liberation of Germany she assisted in the construction of the social system of East Germany. Based on documents in the archive of the Institute of Marxism-Leninism, Berlin, published documents, and secondary literature; 26 notes.   R. Wagnleitner

800. Fosske, Geints.   VIL'GEL'M PIK: ZHIZN', OTDANNAIA BOR'BE ZA SOTSIALIZM (K 100-LETIIU SO DNIA ROZHDENIIA)   [Wilhelm Pieck: a life devoted to the struggle for socialism]. *Novaia i Noveishaia Istoriia [USSR] 1975 (6): 69-84.* On the 100th anniversary of the birthday of the outstanding figure of the German and international Communist movement, the author shows the basic stages of his life and his tireless struggle against fascism and war

for the triumph of peace, democracy and socialism and also his historical role in the formation and development of the German Democratic Republic. J

801. Fritsch, Werner. DER KAMPF DER KPD UM DIE MASSEN UND FÜR DEN SCHUTZ DER SOWJETUNION 1926/1927 IN THÜRINGEN [The struggle of the German Communist Party (KPD) for the protection of the USSR in Thuringia, 1926-27]. *Wissenschaftliche Zeitschrift der Friedrich-Schiller-U. Jena. Gesellschafts- und Sprachwissenschaftliche Reihe [East Germany] 1974 23(6): 811-826.* In 1926 the Thuringian Communists were able to strengthen their support by an uncompromising antifascist strategy in the trade treunions. In addition to the struggle for the satisfaction of the needs of the unemployed the central political issue was the prevention of an anti-Soviet German foreign policy. Based on documents in the Institute for Marxism-Leninism, Central Party Archives, Berlin, printed documents and secondary literature; 62 notes.

R. Wagnleitner

802. Gemkow, Heinrich. WSPÓLNE TRADYCJE NIEMIECKIEGO I POLSKIEGO RUCHU REWOLUCYJNEGO 1917/1918-1945 [Common traditions of Polish and German revolutionary movements 1917-1918-45]. *Z Pola Walki [Poland] 1974 17(65): 3-33.* International working class solidarity found an expression in the collaboration between the German and Polish social democratic Left. Influenced by the October Revolution, the newly created Communist Party of Germany (KPD) and the Communist Party of Poland (KPP) mobilized the working class for the revolutionary struggle and defense of Soviet Russia. Both parties were among the cofounders of the Third International and participated in its activities. After Hitler's seizure of power the KPD was forced to shift into underground activity. With Polish Communist help, the KPD struggled against Hitler's dictatorship in the name of proletarian internationalism. German and Polish Communists fought for republican Spain. During World War II, especially after Hitler's aggression against the USSR, the struggle of German Communists and antifascists intensified, and they collaborated with the Polish Workers' Party (PPR) and other Polish patriots in various forms of resistance. Collaboration took place in the partisan movement, among prisoners in concentration camps, and in joint sabotage and intelligence actions aimed against the Nazi regime.

J/S

803. Gibas, Monika. DIE BEWAFFENETEN KÄMPFE DER REVOLU-TIONÄREN NACHKRIEGSKRISE IM GESCHICHTSBILD DER KPD IN DEN JAHREN DER WEIMARER REPUBLIK [The armed struggles of the revolutionary postwar crisis in the historical view of the Communist Party of Germany in the years of the Weimar Republic]. *Militärgeschichte [East Germany] 1980 19(5): 554-563.* Right opportunist and left sectarian groups in the Communist Party of Germany hindered the Leninist analysis of the major events of German working-class history in the post-World War I period. Based on contemporary books, brochures, and newspapers; 38 notes. H. D. Andrews

804. Gombin, Richard. COMMUNISME DE PARTI ET COMMUNISME DE CONSEILS: L'EXEMPLE DE LA REPUBLIQUE DE WEIMAR [Party and council communism in the Weimar Republic]. *Rev. d'Hist. Moderne et Contemporaine [France] 1976 23(1): 32-43.* Council communism, as distinct from party communism which it opposed on ideological and theoretical grounds,

was extra-institutional, and its proponents were ideological rather than practical. Council communism was born in World War I Germany in opposition to socialism, but its confederation of unions was not popular until the general strikes of 1917-18, which witnessed the establishment of workers' councils. Revolutionary exuberance led the extreme left to unite under the banner of the German Communist Party (KPD). Before its constitutional congress scheduled for December 1918 the KPD fractured into the Bolshevik Party and the council communists, some of whom founded the Communist Worker Party of Germany (KAPD), or merged with other organizations. The author outlines both the opposition to the Third International and the KPD and the rejection of the Fourth International. After 1922, the number of council communists declined precipitously, although it was a period of considerable ideological fertility. Secondary sources; 37 notes.

K. A. Harvey

805. Götze, Dieter. DIE ORGANISATORISCHE VORBEREITUNG FÜR DIE SCHAFFUNG DER KOMMUNISTISCHEN FRAUENBEWEGUNG 1919-1921 [Organizational arrangements to create a Communist women's movement in 1919-21]. *Zeitschrift für Geschichtswissenschaft [East Germany] 1975 23(10): 1165-1176.* Little was done to formulate the ideological and historical basis of the role of women in the international class struggle until Clara Zetkin (d. 1933) wrote the *Guidelines for the Communist Women's Movement* in the fall of 1920. Inspired by Lenin, Zetkin stated that the emancipation of women would take place only after the victory of the working class. At the Second International Women's Congress, held in Moscow in June 1921, Zetkin continued to offer ideological guidance to the international women's movement. 35 notes.

J. T. Walker

806. Griepentrog, Gisela. POLITISCHE ERINNERUNGEN ALS BESTANDTEIL DES ERZÄHLGUTS [Political memoirs as a component of literary narrative]. *Jahrbuch für Volkskunde und Kulturgeschichte [East Germany] 1980 23: 80-83.* Considers reports about Communist and Social Democratic Party activists during their political struggle in prewar Germany against the reactionary forces of the ultra-rightists. Even during times of despair there were moments of real humor; comic anecdotes of political clashes and street fights are typical of this folklore prose, still alive after decades. 15 notes.

G. E. Pergl

807. Grinshtein, B. I. V GERMANSKOM PLENU (1914-1920 GG) [In German captivity, 1914-20]. *Voprosy Istorii [USSR] 1975 (9): 115-126.* The author describes his experiences as a German prisoner of war, 1914, the unsanitary conditions in the camps, and the fierce camp discipline. After the Kaiser's removal, the prisoners created their own executive committee and were attracted by Communist propaganda. The German Communist Party assisted them with materials and worked for their release. The author returned from the camp at Krosno in September 1920.

R. J. Service

808. Grunwald, Manfred. DIE BEDEUTUNG DER MARXISTISCH-LENINISTISCHEN FORDERUNG NACH ENGER VERBINDUNG DER NAH- UND FERNZIELE DER KÄMPFENDEN ARBEITERKLASSE FÜR DIE AUSEINANDERSETZUNG MIT DEM RECHTEN REVISIONISMUS [The importance of the Marxist-Leninist demand for the close connection of

immediate- and long-range objectives of the fighting working class in the confrontation with right-wing revisionism]. *Wissenschaftliche Zeitschrift der Friedrich-Schiller-Universität Jena. Gesellschafts- und Sprachwissenschaftliche Reihe [East Germany] 1976 25(4-5): 549-554.* Eduard Bernstein's (1850-1932) criticism of Marx and Engels's long-range socialist objectives as utopian and his concentration on the immediate political day-by-day problems introduced a conformist general liberal trend within German social democracy. Based on Marx, Engels, and Bernstein's works and secondary sources; 22 notes.   R. Wagnleitner

809.   Gutsche, Willibald and Seeber, Gustav.   BOURGEOISIE, ARBEITERKLASSE, VOLKSMASSEN VON DER PARISER KOMMUNE BIS ZUR GROSSEN SOZIALISTISCHEN OKTOBERREVOLUTION   [Bourgeoisie, working class, and popular masses from the Paris Commune to the October Revolution]. *Zeitschrift für Geschichtswissenschaft [East Germany] 1977 25(10): 1194-1211.* With the Paris Commune the proletariat became the main agent of progress. At the same time the suppression of the Commune resulted in German preeminence in the workers' movement. The rise of imperialism led to even greater polarization between the middle classes and the proletariat. Inspired by V. I. Lenin's call for a new type of revolutionary party, the German Left, led by the Spartacus League, opposed World War I and led the struggle for socialism. Based on 31 theses presented to the Sixth Historical Congress of the German Democratic Republic in 1977. 10 notes.

J. T. Walker

810.   Haferkorn, Katja.   BIOGRAPHISCHE SKIZZEN. "WIR HABEN DAS RECHT, STOLZ ZU SEIN AUF EINEN SOLCHEN KÄMPFER . . .": HANS BEIMLER   [Biographical sketches. "We have the right to be proud of such a fighter . . .": Hans Beimler]. *Beiträge zur Gesch. der Arbeiterbewegung [East Germany] 1981 23(1): 84-93.* Hans Beimler (1895-1936), a Bavarian mechanic, joined the Spartacists in 1918, participated in the navy uprising, became a member of the Bavarian Soviet Republic, a union activist, city councilman at Augsburg, and representative in the Bavarian state parliament. In April 1933, he was arrested and held at Dachau. He escaped to the Soviet Union and from there went to Prague, Zurich, and Paris to support German exiles and strengthen the anti-fascist forces. He was killed during the Spanish Civil War. Based on party archives and published sources; 43 notes.   A. Schuetz

811.   Haferkorn, Katja and Leidigkeit, Karl-Heinz.   DIE KPD IM REICHSTAG DER WEIMARER REPUBLIK   [German Communist Party in the Weimar Republic parliament]. *Beiträge zur Geschichte der Arbeiterbewegung [East Germany] 1979 21(3): 372-388.* Reflects on participation of German Communist representatives in the parliament and explains the potential and the limits of Communist activities. The Communist minority developed a good working system for its parliamentary work against the hostile majority. Based on documents; 50 notes.

G. E. Pergl

812.   Haferkorn, Katja.   EIN DOKUMENT DER DEUTSCHEN SEKTION DER "INTERNATIONALEN ARBEITERHILFE" AUS DEM JAHRE 1925 [A document of the German section of the Workers' International Relief, 1925]. *Beiträge zur Geschichte der Arbeiterbewegung [East Germany] 1973 15(6): 963-966.* Publishes a letter of the League of the Friends of the Workers' International

Relief, March 1925, which seeks assistance in defeating hunger in Germany and other capitalist countries and in establishing practical solidarity with the workers and peasants of the Soviet Union. Publication of a document in the Institute for Marxism-Leninism, Berlin; 6 notes.   R. Wagnleitner

813. Heider, Paul. DER INTERNATIONALISMUS IN DER MILITÄR-POLITIK DER KPD IM KAMPF GEGEN FASCHISMUS UND KRIEGS-GEFAHR [Internationalism of the military policy of the Communist Party of Germany in the struggle against fascism and danger of war]. *Zeitschrift für Geschichtswissenschaft [East Germany] 1973 21(11): 1342-1351.* In the 1920's the German Communists stressed the importance of the defense of the USSR by all Communists in the case of an anti-Soviet imperialist war. Therefore the education of the German workers in the spirit of proletarian internationalism and the development of an alliance between the revolutionary German workers and the Red Army became one of the most important problems of the German Communist Party. Secondary literature; 30 notes.   R. Wagnleitner

814. Heider, Paul. PROBLEME DER MILITÄRPOLITIK DER KOM-MUNISTISCHEN PARTEI DEUTSCHLANDS (1919-1945) [Problems of the military policy of the Communist Party of Germany (KPD), 1919-45]. *Militärgeschichte [East Germany] 1982 21(1): 5-28.* Summarizes the extensive source material and literature and sketches the basic outlines of the development and execution of the military policy of the KPD. Describes the changing relations between the concrete situation in the Weimar Republic and under the fascist dictatorship and the policy responses of the KPD and traces the continuity in the struggle of the KPD against imperialism, militarism, armaments, and war and for peace, democracy, and socialism. 86 notes.   J/T (H. D. Andrews)

815. Hess, U. and Kinner, K. DIE PARISER KOMMUNE IM GES-CHICHTSBILD UND GESCHICHTSDENKEN DER KPD IN DEN JAHREN DER WEIMARER REPUBLIK [The image of the Paris Commune in history and in the historical thinking of the Communist Party of Germany in the years of the Weimar Republic]. *Wissenschaftliche Zeitschrift der Karl-Marx U. Leipzig [East Germany] 1971 20(1): 69-85.* The basic idea in the historical discussion of the Paris Commune by the Communist Party of Germany was the proof that the workers of Paris had in 1871 for the first time tried to establish the dictatorship of the proletariat. The example of the Paris Commune demonstrated how the bourgeoisie allied itself with its arch-enemy in its struggle against the revolutionary proletariat. The historical analysis of the Communist Party of Germany was reached by using the comparative historical method which made it possible to establish continuity from the revolution of 1848-49 and the Paris Commune to the October revolution. Based on published documents and second-ary literature; 80 notes.   R. Wagnleitner

816. Hess, Ulrich. ZUM GESCHICHTSBILD DER SOZIALISTISCHEN DEUTSCHEN LITERATUR IN DEN JAHREN VON 1929 BIS 1932 [Views of history in German socialist literature, 1929-32]. *Jahrbuch für Geschichte [East Germany] 1977 16: 211-251.* The period 1929-32 was an important one for German socialist literature, partly as a result of the Communist Party's decision at its Essen Congress (1927) in favor of an ideological offensive and the subsequent founding of the League of Proletarian-Revolutionary Writers in 1928.

Many Communist writers at this time concentrated on antiwar themes, in compliance with the resolutions of the 6th Congress of the Third International. They expressed fear of new imperialist wars and of an attack on the USSR. Other themes were the betrayal of the working class by the Social Democrats and Independent Social Democrats and labor and political struggles of the 1920's. The rise of Nazism was not even mentioned. 147 notes. J. C. Billigmeier

817. Heyden, Günter. VOR DEM 60. JAHRESTAG DES GROSSEN OK-TOBER [Before the 60th anniversary of the great October]. *Beiträge zur Geschichte der Arbeiterbewegung [East Germany] 1976 18(6): 963-973.* Analyzes the impact of the October Revolution and the building of the Soviet Union on the development of the German Communist Party since 1917. Based on printed documents and secondary literature; 21 notes. R. Wagnleitner

818. Hortzschansky, Günter and Wimmer, Walter. EINE PARTEI DER ARBEITER FÜR DIE ARBEITER [A party of workers for workers]. *Beiträge zur Geschichte der Arbeiterbewegung [East Germany] 1976 18(2): 275-293.* During the 1920's Ernst Thälmann was a significant fighter among the German Communists who demanded that the policy of the Communist Party be acceptable to the masses. In his speeches and articles Thälmann stressed the importance of the formation of a uniform platform for the working masses and the importance of the trade unions. Basing his decisions on the world congresses of the Communist International, Thälmann tried to establish contacts with other working-class parties. Based on documents in the archives of the Institute of Marxism-Leninism, Berlin, published documents, and secondary literature; 75 notes. R. Wagnleitner

819. Hosfeldt, Reinhardt. ERNST TEL'MAN: PROLETARSKII INTER-NATSIONALIST [Ernst Thälmann: a revolutionary internationalist]. *Voprosy Istorii KPSS [USSR] 1976 (4): 110-115.* Discusses the revolutionary activities of Ernst Thälmann (1886-1944) in Germany, 1925-35, in connection with the 90th anniversary of his birth.

820. Jahnke, Karl Heinz. ERNST THÄLMANNS BEZIEHUNGEN ZUR ARBEITERJUGEND UND ZUR ARBEITERJUGENDBEWEGUNG [Ernst Thälmann's relationship to working youth and to the working youth movement]. *Beiträge zur Geschichte der Arbeiterbewegung [East Germany] 1976 18(2): 320-332.* Analyzes Ernst Thälmann's works on the position of the German Communist Party in relation to the youth of the working class, which constituted one fifth of its members, at the time Thälmann took over Party leadership in 1925, at the beginning of the world economic crisis in 1929, and shortly before the fascist takeover in autumn 1932. Based on Thälmann's works, documents in the archives of the Institute of Marxism-Leninism, Berlin, published documents, and secondary literature; 61 notes. R. Wagnleitner

821. Jahnke, Karl Heinz. MEIN STREBEN GALT DEM HÖCHSTEN DER MENSCHHEIT. CONRAD BLENKLE [My struggle was for the best of mankind: Conrad Blenkle]. *Beiträge zur Geschichte der Arbeiterbewegung [East Germany] 1973 15(1): 124-131.* At the time of the November Revolution Conrad Blenkle fought on the side of the Spartacists. In the following years he devoted himself to the organization of Communist youth and was elected chair-

man of the Youth Congress in 1924. After 1925 he belonged to the politburo of the central committee of the Communist Party of Germany and in 1928 was elected to the Reichstag. After the dissolution of parliament on 4 July 1930, Blenkle was imprisoned for publishing articles against German imperialism and preparations for war. Released at the end of 1932, Blenkle worked illegally in Germany, Belgium, France, the Netherlands, Switzerland, and Denmark. He was arrested in December 1941 and brought to Germany where he was sentenced to death in November 1942. Based on documents in the Institute for Marxism-Leninism, published documents, and secondary sources; 33 notes.

R. Wagnleitner

822.   Jahnke, Karl Heinz.   ZUM ANTEIL ERNST THÄLMANNS AN DER DURCHSETZUNG   DER   PRINZIPIEN   MARXISTISCH-LENINIS-TISCHER JUGENDPOLITIK IN DER KPD [Ernst Thälmann's part in the carrying through of the principles of a Marxist-Leninist youth policy in the German Communist Party]. *Wissenschaftliche Zeitschrift der U. Rostock. Gesellschafts- und Sprachwissenschaftliche Reihe [East Germany] 1974 23(2): 143-148.* In various articles, speeches and resolutions at Party conferences, 1925-32, Ernst Thälmann analyzes the most important tasks of Communist youth as revolutionary preorganization of the German Communist Party. Thälmann realized though, that the political activities in the youth groups had to differ from those of the adult party. Based on documents in the Institute for Marxism-Leninism, Central Party Archives, Berlin, printed documents, and secondary literature; 28 notes.   R. Wagnleitner

823.   Jendretzky, Hans.   DER RFB—ANTIMILITARISTISCHE WEHR-UND MASSENORGANISATION DER ARBEITERKLASSE   [The Red Front Fighters' League (RFB): antimilitarist defense and mass organization of the working class]. *Einheit [East Germany] 1974 29(6): 733-740.* In response to Free Corps attacks on left-wing meetings beginning in 1918, the Red Front Fighters' League was founded in July 1924 to protect Communist meetings.

824.   Jones, Arnita Ament.   PAUL LEVI AND THE COMINTERN: A POSTSCRIPT.   *Internationale Wissenschaftliche Korrespondenz zur Geschichte der Deutschen Arbeiterbewegung [West Germany] 1975 11(4): 437-451.* Following Rosa Luxemburg's critical evaluation of the Russian Revolution, Paul Levi split from the German Communists in 1921-22 by publicly criticizing the Comintern and the Bolsheviks for having become reactionary.

825.   Jongen, Jos.   TROTSKIJ EN DE SOCIALE STRUKTUUR VAN DE WEIMARREPUBLIEK   [Leon Trotsky and the social structure of the Weimer Republic]. *Kleio [Netherlands] 1977 18(5): 328-331.* Compares Trotsky's vision of Germany's social organization with the actual structure and political inclinations of German industrial workers, the lower middle class, and peasants. His vision was the product of blind faith rather than analysis. Biblio.

G. Herritt

826.   Jongh, Jos de.   HET BEGRIP "BONAPARTISME" BIJ TROTSKIJ [Leon Trotsky's concept of Bonapartism]. *Kleio [Netherlands] 1977 18(5): 331-334.* Discusses Trotsky's constantly changing concept of Bonapartism. He borrowed the concept from Karl Marx but distorted it in applying it to the German

chancellors Heinrich Brüning, Franz von Papen, and Kurt von Schleicher and to a German political situation which differed from his theoretical models. Biblio.

G. Herritt

827. Juhl, Carsten. RÅDSKOMMUNISMEN: EN PRAESENTATION OG PROBLEMATISERING [Workers' council communism: a presentation and discussion of problems]. *Meddelelser om Forskning i Arbejderbevaegelsens Hist. [Denmark] 1978 (11): 4-21.* Examines the workers' council movement among the revolutionary left in Germany, 1919-21, and its German and Dutch theoreticians, who opposed both Social Democrats and Leninist Communists.

828. Karl, Heinz. LUPTA PARTIDULUI COMUNIST DIN GERMANIA PENTRU REALIZAREA UNITĂȚII DE ACȚIUNE A CLASEI MUN-CITOARE (1918-1945) [The struggle of the German Communist Party to realize unity of action of the working class, 1918-45]. *Anale de Istorie [Rumania] 1973 19(6): 115-124.* Describes the long and futile efforts of the German Communist Party, from its founding in 1918, to establish unity of action with the Social Democratic Party, centered on the Communists' attempts to defeat reformism, a policy of collaboration with the bourgeois parties. By 1920 the left wing of the centrist Independent Social Democrats had united with the Communists (KPD) and in an open letter of 1921 the KPD began to urge a political goal of the united front. This campaign intensified as the rise of fascist strength with its anti-Communist theme made life difficult for leftists by the late 1920's, while the Social Democrats of the right joined in the rhetoric against Bolshevism, and supported only bourgeois-style social reform. Under Ernst Thälmann and later Wilhelm Pieck, the KPD at its 1935 Brussels Conference and at Bern in 1939 continued to strive for a union of all democratic forces against the Hitler regime. Only with the overthrow of fascism in 1945, however, could the united front be created. Secondary sources; 4 notes.

G. J. Bobango

829. Kikukawa, Kiyomi. VAIMARU KYOWAKOKU SHOKI RODOSHA SEIFU UNDO NO ICHI KOSATSU [The workers' government movement in the early Weimar period]. *Rekishi Hyōron [Japan] 1975 (300): 231-251.* Locates the German workers' government movement in the early 1920's as the first instance of the united front and the theory of a shift to socialism through a transitional united front government. Discusses the significance of several tactics of the united front, beginning with the crushing of the Kapp putsch, 1920. Describes the formation of the workers' government movement via the industrial democracy movement represented by the Revolutionary Council Movement and the Control Committee Movement. Traces the formation of the theory of a united front of workers, farmers, and the middle class to the epochal KPD Central Committee meeting of August 1923, the beginning of the antifascist movement, and its frustration at the fifth conference of the Comintern in June 1924. This movement could have been a new line in the shift to socialism, an alternative to the simple opposition of bourgeois democracy and proletarian dictatorship, in a highly developed capitalist country during the period of relative stability after World War I. 108 notes.

I. Matsui

830. Kinner, Klaus. AUFKLÄRUNG UND KLASSIK IM GESCHICHTS-DENKEN DER DEUTSCHEN KOMMUNISTEN IN DEN JAHREN DER WEIMARER REPUBLIK [Enlightenment and classicism in the historical

thought of the German Communists in the years of the Weimar Republic]. *Jahrbuch für Geschichte [East Germany] 1979 19: 367-390.* Emphasizes the importance of the Enlightenment and classical era in German philosophy, literature, and music for the development of Marxism in Germany. Communist writers, especially Franz Mehring, during the Weimar Republic pointed out the close connections between German classical culture and the French Revolution. Articles in the Communist newspapers and journals, like the *Rote Fahne,* claimed that the Marxist German workers' movement in the 20th century was the true inheritor of the progressive tendencies of German classicism. Based on articles in *Rote Fahne* and the published writings of Franz Mahring; 64 notes.

J. B. Street

831. Kinner, Klaus. DIE ENTSTEHUNG DER KPD IM HISTORISCHEN SELBSTVERSTÄNDNIS DER DEUTSCHEN KOMMUNISTEN IN DER ZEIT DER WEIMARER REPUBLIK   [The historic self-comprehension of the genesis of the German Communist Party during the Weimar Republic]. *Zeitschrift für Geschichtswissenschaft [East Germany] 1978 26(11): 972-982.* Leninism and the evolution of the Bolshevik Party serve as a model for the analysis of the history of the German Communist Party (KPD). The best examples for the application of Leninist principles can be found in the lectures *(Rededispositionen)* held in honor of the 10th anniversary of the KPD. With other sources, they provide a useful insight into the historic self-comprehension of the development of the German Communist movement.

S. Boehnke

832. Kinner, Klaus. DIE KPD UND REVOLUTIONÄREN TRADITIONEN DER DEUTSCHEN SOZIALDEMOKRATIE (1918-1933)   [The German Communist Party and the revolutionary traditions of German social democracy, 1918-33]. *Jahrbuch für Gesch. [East Germany] 1981 22: 309-349.* Examines the development of the revolutionary tradition within the German Communist Party during the period between the two world wars, as expressed by some of the leading Party members and theorists. The evaluation of the Erfurt program was an important issue in the interpretation of the socialist ideas and the impact of the October Revolution. Further adaptation of Lenin's theories gave new dimensions to the values of the communists. Based on writings by Marx, Engels, and other socialist and communist leaders and theorists.

T. Parker

833. Kinner, Klaus. DIE LEHREN DER DEUTSCHEN FRÜHBÜRGER-LICHEN REVOLUTION IN DER IDEOLOGISCHEN ARBEIT DER KPD (1925 BIS 1929)   [The lessons of the early German bourgeois revolution applied to the ideological activity of the Communist Party of Germany, 1925-29]. *Beiträge zur Geschichte der Arbeiterbewegung [East Germany] 1975 17(5): 873-885.* Extends the research of R. Hub which covered only the year 1925 in his 1968 article in this journal. From the earliest German revolutions the Communist Party of Germany learned the need for organization. The Party had Friedrich Engels's *German Peasants' War* and subsequent writings on this revolution and on the Protestant Reformation to guide their ideology in republican Germany. The lessons of these two 16th-century events were key points in Communist historiography during the late 1920's. Secondary sources; 53 notes.

G. H. Libbey

834. Kinner, Klaus. ZUR HERAUSBILDUNG UND ROLLE DES MARXISTISCH-LENINISTISCHEN GESCHICHTSBILDES IN DER KPD IM PROZESS DER SCHÖPFERISCHEN ANEIGNUNG DES LENINISMUS 1918 BIS 1923 [The elaboration and role of the Marxist-Leninist conception of history in the KPD during the process of the creative adaption of Leninism, 1918-23]. *Jahrbuch für Geschichte [East Germany] 1973 9: 217-280.* During the first years of the Weimar Republic, the Communist Party of Germany was able to elaborate and make more sophisticated its Marxist philosophy of history, guided in this by the great example and by the writings and thoughts of V. I. Lenin, leader of the October Revolution in Russia. Inspired by Lenin, German Marxists like Clara Zetkin were able to adapt Leninism to German conditions in a creative manner. She, and others like her, recognized the necessity of explaining the Marxist-Leninist conception of history to the workers themselves, as well as acquainting them with science and art. 177 notes.

J. C. Billigmeier

835. Klomovskij, D. S. DER KAMPF DER KPD GEGEN DIE AGGRESSIONSBESTREBUNGEN DES DEUTSCHEN IMPERIALISMUS IN DER PERIODE VON LOCARNO BIS ZUM MACHTANTRITT DES HITLERFASCHISMUS [The struggle of the German Communist Party (KPD) against the efforts of aggression by German imperialism between the Locarno treaty and the accession to power of Hitler fascism]. *Wissenschaftliche Zeitschrift der Friedrich-Schiller-U. Jena. Gesellschafts- und Sprachwissenschaftliche Reihe [East Germany] 1974 23(6): 853-864.* From the outset German Communists opposed the Locarno Treaty of 1925 because it strengthened German aggressive tendencies against Poland and began a new phase of the militarization of Germany until 1933. Based on printed documents and secondary literature; 70 notes.

R. Wagnleitner

836. Köpstein, Horst. ÜBER DIE BEZIEHUNGEN ZWISCHEN DER REVOLUTIONÄREN DEUTSCHEN UND TSCHECHOSLOWAKISCHEN ARBEITERBEWEGUNG IN DEN ZWANZIGER UND DREISSIGER JAHREN [On the relations between the revolutionary German and Czechoslovakian working class movements during the 1920's-30's]. *Beiträge zur Geschichte der Arbeiterbewegung [East Germany] 1973 15(3): 472-484.* After 1919 the Left in Bohemia tried to establish close contacts with the German Communists; by 1920 Czechoslovakian workers fought side by side with their German comrades in the Ruhr area. During the 1920's the German and Czechoslovakian communist parties organized demonstrations of solidarity. The two parties cooperated increasingly in the face of growing fascism. The Czechoslovakian Communists responded to the victory of fascism in Germany by applying the policy of the antifascist and anti-imperialist people's front, a policy which developed into the National Front. Based on documents in the Archiv Ústavu Marxismu-Leninismu, Prague, printed documents, and secondary sources; 52 notes.

R. Wagnleitner

837. Kopychev, N. I. BOR'BA NEMETSKIKH TRUDIASHCHIKHSIA V GODY VEIMARSKOI RESPUBLIKI ZA SOLIDARNOST' I DRUZHBU S SSSR [The German workers' struggle for solidarity and friendship with the USSR in the period of the Weimar Republic]. *Voprosy Istorii [USSR] 1974 (3): 68-84.* Traces the rise and development of the German workers' international

contacts and solidarity with the Soviet state in the period of the Weimar Republic. Highlights the role of the Communist Party of Germany in rallying the masses of the German working class for the struggle against the Weimar Republic's participation in the joint anti-Soviet actions of the imperialist powers, for normalizing relations, and for promoting cooperation between Germany and the Soviet Union. Examines both the mass manifestations of solidarity with the USSR and the efforts of the German Communist Party to make use of the Reichstag, the press, and other legal means for strengthening German-Soviet relations.   J

838.   Kresse, Helmut.   DER SOWJETISCHE FILM IN DER IDEOLOGISC-HEN ARBEIT DER KPD WÄHREND DER WEIMARER REPUBLIK [The Soviet film in the ideological work of the Communist Party of Germany during the Weimar Republic]. *Beiträge zur Geschichte der Arbeiterbewegung [East Germany] 1977 19(6): 1028-1036.* Describes the use of Soviet proletarian films as a medium of propaganda in Germany from 1922 to 1933. The Communist Party of Germany and the Workers' International Relief used about 120 Soviet films. The films contributed to the inculcation of class consciousness and proletarian internationalism among German workers. Analyzes the contents and impact of three exemplary films: *The Mother, The Old and the New,* and *The Man Who Lost His Memory.* Based on contemporary newspapers and journals and secondary works; 39 notes.   J. B. Street

839.   Krusch, Hans-Joachim.   ZUM ZUSAMMENWIRKEN VON KI UND DEUTSCHER SEKTION IN DER FRAGE DER ARBEITER-UND-BAU-ERN-REGIERUNG IM JAHRE 1923   [The cooperation of the Communist International and the German section in the question of a workers' and a peasants' government in 1923]. *Beiträge zur Geschichte der Arbeiterbewegung [East Germany] 1973 15(5): 757-773.* After the Comintern plenum in June 1923 the Communist Party of Germany increased its efforts to establish an alliance between workers and peasants in Germany. Although the Communists, with the help of the Comintern, had made progress in the development of a new alliance policy, they could not succeed in establishing a uniform platform. The failure to establish active unity between workers and peasants was the result of the opposition of the right Social Democrats whose counterrevolutionary policies enabled the German imperialist system to survive the revolutionary postwar crisis. Based on documents in the Institute for Marxism-Leninism, published documents, and secondary sources; 53 notes.   R. Wagnleitner

840.   Laschitza, Annelies.   "EINE NEUE, BESSERE WELT NIMMT IHREN ANFANG"   ["A new, better world is beginning"]. *Einheit [East Germany] 1977 32(3): 325-333.* To the German left-wing socialists Karl Liebknecht, Rosa Luxemburg, Franz Mehring, Clara Zetkin, Wilhelm Pieck, and Julian Marchlewski, the importance of the Russian Revolution was its role in strengthening the concept of the dictatorship of the proletariat and the struggle against imperialism in Germany.

841.   Leidigkeit, Karl-Heinz.   ZU GRUNDFRAGEN DES PARLAMEN-TARISCHEN KAMPFES DER KPD IN DER ZEIT DER WEIMARER REPUBLIK   [Basic questions of the parliamentary struggle of the German Communist Party in the period of the Weimar Republic]. *Wissenschaftliche Zeitschrift der Martin-Luther-Universität Halle-Wittenberg. Gesellschafts- und*

Sprachwissenschaftliche Reihe [East Germany] 1978 27(1): 21-29. The objectives of the German Communist Party (KPD) in the parliament of the Weimar Republic can be grouped into three phases: the struggle for the social rights of the working population and for the establishment of normal relations with the new Soviet state, 1919-23; the fight against imperialism and for a peaceful foreign policy, 1924-29; and the struggle against fascism and chauvinism. Based on printed documents and secondary literature; 17 notes.   R. Wagnleitner

842. Liening, Rudi. JAHRESTAGE DES ROTEN OKTOBER IN BERLIN [Anniversary of Red October in Berlin]. *Archivmitteilungen [East Germany] 1977 27(5): 173-176.* Charts the solidarity shown by the German working class movement with the USSR, 1917-77, with special reference to the response of the German Communist Party to the possibility of a repeated imperialist intervention in the USSR, in 1927.

843. Lindner, Heinz. ZU EINIGEN PROBLEMEN DER DEUTSCH-FRANZÖSISCHEN VERSTÄNDIGUNG NACH DEM ERSTEN WELT-KRIEG [Concerning several problems of German-French understanding after the First World War]. *R. d'Allemagne [France] 1974 6(2): 29-37.* Claims "true" German-French understanding was the achievement of Communist representatives of the workers' movement in both countries. All other attempts were capitalistic-fraudulent efforts. Based on documents and secondary sources; 9 notes.
R. K. Adams

844. Luk'ianov, K. T. and Rosenko, I. A. INTERNATSIONAL'NAIA SOLIDARNOST' TRUDIASHCHIKHSIA SSSR S RABOCHIMI GERMANII (1926-1932 GG) [International solidarity of the Soviet workers with the German workers, 1926-32]. *Vestnik Leningradskogo U.: Istoriia, Iazyk, Literatura [USSR] 1975 (2): 21-33.* After the revolution, the Soviet Union became the fatherland of the world's proletariat and supported the international revolutionary movement. The authors trace the various forms of moral, political, and material help rendered by the Soviet workers to the German workers on the eve of and during the world economic crisis. 65 notes.   G. F. Jewsbury

845. Lwunin, J. A. VERÖFFENTLICHUNGEN ERNST THÄLMANNS IN DER ZEITUNG "MOLOT" (ROSTOW AM DON) IN DEN JAHREN 1926 BIS 1928 [Publications of Ernst Thälmann in the newspaper *Molot* (Rostov), 1926-28]. *Beiträge zur Geschichte der Arbeiterbewegung [East Germany] 1976 18(2): 294-300.* Publication of three articles by Ernst Thälmann in the Russian newspaper *Molot* between 1926 and 1928. The German Communist leader stressed the importance of international cooperation among the working class and assured the Soviet Union of the solidarity of German Communists.

846. Lwunin, J. A. ZUM BRIEFWECHSEL ZWISCHEN SOWJETISCHEN UND DEUTSCHEN ARBEITERN UND ARBEITERKORRESPONDENTEN 1924-1929 [The correspondence between Soviet and German workers and worker-correspondents, 1924-29]. *Beiträge zur Geschichte der Arbeiterbewegung [East Germany] 1977 19(6): 1011-1028.* Traces the development from 1923 to 1929 of contacts between Soviet worker-correspondents and representatives of industrial collectives with German workers and worker-correspondents. The exchange of letters and articles helped to imbue the Communist Party of

Germany with Bolshevik principles, to provide the workers of both countries with accurate information on the conditions of their working-class counterparts, and to counter the propaganda lies of anti-Soviet forces. Soviet labor learned of the oppression of German workers under capitalism, and German workers learned about the revolution and building of socialist society in the USSR. Based on letters and articles from contemporary Soviet and German newspapers and journals and secondary works; 102 notes.   J. B. Street

847. Meisel, Gerhard. ZUR ENTWICKLUNG DER WISSENSCHAFTLI-CHEN AUFFASSUNG VOM SOZIALISMUS UND KOMMUNISMUS IN DER KOMMUNISTISCHEN PARTEI DEUTSCHLANDS WÄHREND DER JAHRE DER WEIMARER REPUBLIK [The development of the scientific conception of socialism and communism in the Communist Party of Germany during the years of the Weimar Republic]. *Jahrbuch für Geschichte [East Germany] 1973 9: 129-216.*

848. Meister, Rudolf. PROBLEME DER REVOLUTIONÄREN MILI-TÄRPOLITIK AUF DEM 8. PARTEITAG DER KPD IM JANUAR 1923 [Problems of revolutionary military policy at the 8th Congress of the Communist Party of Germany (KPD) in January 1923]. *Militärgeschichte [East Germany] 1982 21(2): 142-149.* Sketches the KPD's difficult problems of military policy in its struggle for mass influence at the beginning of 1923. Stresses the role of guiding resolutions for the development of militant mass struggle and for the development of a worker government at the 8th Party congress. 31 notes.
J/T (H. D. Andrews)

849. Meyer, Gertrud. DIE GRÜNDUNG UNSERER ZEITUNG "DIE SOZIALISTISCHE REPUBLIK" [The founding of our newspaper *Die sozialistische Republik*]. *Beiträge zur Geschichte der Arbeiterbewegung [East Germany] 1976 18(1): 87-91.* Personal recollections of the founding of the left-wing socialist newspaper *Die Sozialistische Republik* in December 1918 in Cologne and the first years of its publication. 4 notes.

850. Mičev, Dobrin. GEORGI DIMITROV UND DIE ENTWICKLUNG DER KOMMUNISTISCHEN PARTEI DEUTSCHLANDS (1929-1939) [Georgi Dimitrov and the development of the German Communist Party, 1929-39]. *Bulgarian Hist. Rev. [Bulgaria] 1973 1(3): 3-25.* In 1929 Dimitrov joined the leadership of the Comintern and in 1930 supported the German Communist Party (KPD) against leftist sectarians in the Comintern. Imprisoned for his alleged part in the Reichstag fire, March 1933, he was released after the Leipzig Trials. The 7th Comintern, 1934 condemned leftist sectarians, as had Dimitrov, and approved the united front policy: the KPD endorsed these measures at its 1936 Brussels conference. Dimitrov's later suggestion of a democratic republic for post-Hitler Germany was approved by the 1939 Berne Conference of the KPD. Based on Central Party Archives and secondary works; 101 notes.
A. Alcock

851. Milz, Erna. DIE ROTE HILFE—SOLIDARITÄTSORGANISATION DER INTERNATIONALEN ARBEITERKLASSE [Red Aid—solidarity organization of the international working class]. *Beiträge zur Geschichte der Arbeiterbewegung [East Germany] 1977 19(3): 453-467.* Introduces and reprints

excerpts from three memoirs by Gustav Gundelach, Mentona Moser, and Rolf Helm. They describe the work of the International Red Aid and Red Aid Germany in defending and supporting working-class political prisoners and their families in the 1920's and 1930's. The memoirs are from the Central Party Archive of the Institute for Marxism-Leninism, Berlin; 5 notes.

J. B. Street

852. Muchamedshanow, Mansur. AUS DER GESCHICHTE DER INTER-NATIONALEN ZUSAMMENARBEIT ZWISCHEN DER SOWJETISCHEN UND DER DEUTSCHEN JUGEND IN DEN JAHREN 1918 BIS 1923 [The history of the international cooperation of Soviet and German youth between 1918 and 1923]. *Wissenschaftliche Zeitschrift der U. Rostock. Gesellschafts- und Sprachwissenschaftliche Reihe [East Germany] 1974 23(2): 129-135.* The Russian youth organization Young Communist League (Komsomol) and the German Free Socialist Youth were both founded in 1918. In the cooperation of these youth organizations the Komsomol took the leading position, especially in the Communist Youth International. Based on documents in the Institute for Marxism-Leninism, Moscow, printed documents and secondary literature; 27 notes.

R. Wagnleitner

853. Müller, Dietmar. DIE HERAUSBILDUNG DER MARXISTISCHEN ARBEITERSCHULE 1927 BIS 1929 [The evolution of the Marxist workers' school, 1927-29]. *Beiträge zur Geschichte der Arbeiterbewegung [East Germany] 1979 21(1): 93-105.* Since its founding, the Communist Party of Germany has recognized the need to instruct people in Leninist thought and practice. After its eleventh Party Day in 1927, the Party began to set up workers' schools for this instruction. Horst Fröhlich, a Communist leader in Berlin, was the key figure in establishing these schools. The *Rote Fahne* publicized the instruction and urged workers to attend; until banned by the Nazis in 1933, the schools were major recruiting and organizing units for the Party. 59 notes.

G. H. Libbey

854. Natoli, Claudio. L'INTERNAZIONALE COMUNISTA, IL FRONTE UNICO E LA LOTTA CONTRO IL FASCISMO IN ITALIA E IN GERMANIA (1919-1923) [The Communist International, the United Front and the struggle against fascism in Italy and in Germany]. *Storia Contemporanea [Italy] 1976 7(1): 67-121, (2): 297-360.* Part I. Examines the reactions of the Comintern and the Italian Socialist and Communist Parties to the Italian capitalist and fascist counteroffensive in 1921. The Communist International took the position that there was little difference between bourgeois democracy and Fascism, a view that hampered the building of a united front against Fascism. 68 notes. Part II. The Comintern's line on Fascism in 1921-23 was fundamentally right, something that cannot be said for the political position of the Italian Socialist and Communist Parties. The same observations hold for the German situation, where the German Communist Party as part of the United Front's massive struggle against Fascism effectively resisted its development. 155 notes.

J. C. Billigmeier

855. Naumann, Horst. EIN NEUES DOKUMENT DES GRÜNDUNG-SPARTEITAGES DER KPD [A new document of the founding congress of the German Communist Party]. *Beiträge zur Geschichte der Arbeiterbewegung [East Germany] 1973 15(1): 95-100.* Publishes the demands for economic transition which could not be published in the protocol of the founding congress of the

Communist Party of Germany in 1919. The first part of the document elaborates on the role and duties of workers' councils in workshops, while the second part is devoted to the practical demands of the workers concerning working time, holidays, wages, and social security. Based on a brochure *Wege zum Sozialismus*; 19 notes.   R. Wagnleitner

856.   Naumann, Horst.   ERNST THÄLMANN UND DIE VEREINIGUNG DES LINKEN FLÜGELS DER USPD MIT DER KPD. ZUR TATIGKEIT DES VORSITZENDEN DER ORTSGRUPPE HAMBURG DER USPD 1919/20   [Ernst Thälmann and the union of the left wing of the Independent Social Democratic Party of Germany (USPD) with the Communist Party of Germany (KPD): activities of the chairman of the Hamburg local of the USPD, 1919-20]. *Zeitschrift für Geschichtswissenschaft [East Germany] 1978 26(2): 113-133.* Declaration of the republic in Germany in 1919 led to a sharp division in the socialist movement. The republic was a rejection by the majority of socialists of any radical change in government, since it assured that the capitalist bourgeoisie would rule Germany. The left wing of the Independent Social Democratic Party of Germany, led by Ernst Thälmann, joined the Communist Party of Germany in 1920, to form the United Communist Party of Germany. Thälmann, instrumental in the merger, was elected to the executive body of the new organization. 120 notes.   G. H. Libbey

857.   Norden, Albert.   EREIGNISSE UND ERLEBTES IN BEWEGTER ZEIT   [Events and experiences in a stirring time]. *Zeitschrift für Geschichtswissenschaft [East Germany] 1980 28(12): 1161-1173.* Recalls events in 1924, when Communists in Germany garnered 3.7 million votes in the election and sent 62 delegates to the Reichstag. Cites formerly secret documents which reveal a continuing chain of police spies in the Party and also throw light on the Kapp Putsch and other events in Weimar Germany. Based on personal reminiscences; 10 notes.   G. E. Pergl

858.   Oppermann, Sigrid.   DIE MARXISTISCH-LENINISTISCHE STAAT-SLEHRE IN DER PROPAGANDAARBEIT DER KPD (NOV. 1925 BIS MAI 1929)   [The Marxist-Leninist theory of the state and the propagandist activity of the Communist Party of Germany, November 1925-May 1929]. *Beiträge zur Geschichte der Arbeiterbewegung [East Germany] 1974 16(4): 565-586.* The Communist Party of Germany concentrated its propagandist activities on the education of its members in the classic statements of Marxism in 1925-29. V. I. Lenin's collected works began to appear in German translations during these years, and many of Karl Marx's writings were republished. The propaganda campaign stressed the closeness of Marxist-Leninist theory and the struggle of the German working class against imperialism. Based on contemporary Communist publications; 95 notes.   G. H. Libbey

859.   Orlova, M. I.   VOPROSY STRATEGII I TAKTIKI NA LEIPTSIG-SKOM S"EDZDE KPG (1923 G)   [Questions of strategy and tactics at the Leipzig Congress of the German Communist Party in 1923]. *Vestnik Moskovskogo U. Seriia 9: Istoriia [USSR] 1967 (6): 34-48.* Discusses the Leipzig Congress of the German Communist Party, 1923. Party leaders were slow to accept that the Franco-German conflict of 1923 could be the starting point of a new upsurge. Discusses the positions of various factions of the Party in relation to the

situation in the Ruhr. The failure of the Congress to find a decisive criterion for evaluating the situation led to mistakes in judging the approaching revolutionary crisis, and to delays in preparing for the struggle. 89 notes.   E. Dunn/S

860. Page, Stanley W. THE GEOPOLITICS OF LENINISM: REFLEC-TIONS. *Nationalities Papers 1981 9(1): 131-138.* During World War I, Lenin viewed Germany as the key to an all-European revolution. He conceived the idea of a victorious German army rebelling, becoming a people's army, and conquering Russia and Western Europe for the proletarian cause. Around this theme Lenin developed a series of new ideas, including that of socialism in one country and the dictatorship of the proletariat. The German revolution did not materialize and the Russian one emerged instead. By using the idea of self-determination, the Ukraine, Belorussia and the countries of Eastern Europe were included in the socialist sphere. The same principle is active in Latin America, the Middle East, and Central and Southeast Asia in the service of Communist expansion and world revolution. 13 notes.   J. V. Coutinho

861. Pavlov, E. A. VDOKHNOVLENNYI OKTIABREM: (K 90-LETIIU SO DNIA ROZHDENIIA MAKSA GEL'TSA) [Inspired by October: the 90th birthday of Max Holz]. *Voprosy Istorii KPSS [USSR] 1979 (10): 128-131.* Max Holz was born in 1889 to a working-class family. During World War I he came into contact with Spartacists and on his return to Germany took up political activity, headed a local council of the unemployed and organized military detachments. Even though the Social Democratic government of Saxony sought his arrest he did not receive the support of the local Communist leaders, many of who subsequently joined the right opportunist wing of the party. After the events of March 1921, he fled to Czechoslovakia and then Austria, continuing his revolutionary activities, including the bombing of courthouses. He was caught later that year and remained in prison until 1928. Secondary sources; 18 notes.

     L. Waters

862. Peterson, Larry. FROM SOCIAL DEMOCRACY TO COMMUNISM: RECENT CONTRIBUTIONS TO THE HISTORY OF THE GERMAN WORKERS' MOVEMENT 1914-1945. *Labour [Canada] 1980 5(Spr): 161-181.* Reviews recent works on the German labor movement and stresses their departure from traditional labor historiography, particularly in their use of new historical approaches and revisionist interpretations.   G. P. Cleyet

863. Pietschmann, Horst. ZUM PROZESS DER ENTWICKLUNG DER FREIEN SOZIALISTISCHEN JUGEND ZU EINEM KOMMUNISTISC-HEN JUGENDVERBAND (1918-1921) [The evolution of the Free Socialist Youth into a Communist youth organization, 1918-21]. *Beiträge zur Geschichte der Arbeiterbewegung [East Germany] 1975 17(6): 1045-1060.* The Free Socialist Youth organization was founded in October 1918 by young members of the proletariat who were both anti-imperialist and pacifist. Deeply influenced by the Spartacists in Berlin and by Karl Liebknecht, the organization was fully committed to Communist principles and goals by the end of 1919. By 1921 integration with the Communist Party of Germany was virtually complete, as shown by the change of name to Communist Youth of Germany. Based on publications of the Free Socialist Youth and the Communist Party of Germany; 56 notes.

     G. H. Libbey

864. Pikarski, Margot. UMSTELLUNG DER KPD AUF DIE ILLE-
GALITÄT (MAI 1932-SOMMER 1934) [The conversion of the German Communist Party (KPD) to illegality, May 1932-summer 1934]. *Beiträge zur
Geschichte der Arbeiterbewegung [East Germany] 1978 20(5): 719-733.* Despite
persecution and major setbacks the Party successfully organized itself on all
levels. New forms and feasible ways of leading the Party and maintaining contacts
between the various formations were tested. Conspiracy and illegal modes of
combat became integral parts of Party life. Thus the KPD was the only antifascist
party which was not reduced to a state of paralysis during the early years of the
Nazi regime. 72 notes.   S. Boehnke

865. Richter, Rolf. ZUR FÜHRUNG KULTURPOLITISCHER PRO-
ZESSE DURCH DIE PARTEI DER ARBEITERKLASSE [The operation of
cultural policy processes by the party of the working class]. *Wissenschaftliche
Zeitschrift Wilhelm-Pieck U.-Rostock. Gesellschafts- und Sprachwissenschaftliche Reihe [East Germany] 1976 25(2): 99-104.* Analyzes the writings and
activities of Alfred Kurella, an early member of the Communist Party of Germany who became particularly active in the 1920's in the Communist Youth
International and in the Friends of the Soviet Union organization. Kurella's
published work has been especially concerned with the problem of alienation and
the development of Communist cultural policy. Based on Kurella's published
work; 43 notes.   J. A. Perkins

866. Rodina, L. V. IZ ISTORII INTERNATSIONALISTSKOI DEIATEL'-
NOSTI KLARY TSETKIN [From the history of the international activity of
Clara Zetkin]. *Voprosy Istorii KPSS [USSR] 1979 (8): 112-116.* In the 1880's,
Clara Zetkin joined the Social Democratic movement in Germany and for many
years was the editor of the women's paper, *Gleichheit.* She was acquainted with
a number of Russian revolutionaries, including Lenin, and greeted the 1905
revolution enthusiastically. Later she defended Soviet power against its critics
within the German Socialist Party and continued, until her death on 20 July 1933,
to show great interest in events in the Soviet Union. Secondary sources; 48 notes.
                                                                      L. Waters

867. Rokotianski, Ia. G. V. I. LENIN I NEZAVISIMAIA SOTSIAL-
DEMOKRATICHESKAIA PARTIIA GERMANI [V. I. Lenin and an Independent Social Democratic Party of Germany]. *Novaia i Noveishaia Istoriia
[USSR] 1977 (2): 24-40.* A study of the Independent Social Democratic Party of
Germany (USPD) which existed from April 1917 to 1922. It arose from disagreements within the official German Social Democratic Party over World War I, and
united Left and Right oppositionists, such as Eduard Bernstein and the Spartacists. Lenin supported the Left within the USPD, which in the November Russian
Revolution called for a proletarian dictatorship. With the formation of the Comintern it became necessary to have a pure leftist Communist Party in Germany.
The USPD lost its mass support and collapsed. Based on archive material from
the Institute of Marxism-Leninism and published documents; 91 notes.
                                                                  D. N. Collins

868. Rössling, Udo. SYMPOSIUM ÜBER ERNST THÄLMANNS
KAMPF GEGEN DEN FASCHISMUS [Symposium on Ernst Thälmann's
struggle against fascism]. *Zeitschrift für Geschichtswissenschaft [East Germany]*

1976 24(8): 928-930. Reviews the lectures and discussions of the symposium held 6 April 1976 under the auspices of the Institut für Marxismus-Leninismus in Berlin, discussing Ernst Thälmann's (1886-1944) role in the struggle against fascism.

R. Wagnleitner

869. Schindler, Bärbel. ERNST THÄLMANN UND DER KAMPF GE-GEN DIE IMPERIALISTISCHE KRIEGSGEFAHR 1932 [Ernst Thälmann and the struggle against the danger of imperialist war in 1932]. *Zeitschrift für Geschichtswissenschaft [East Germany] 1976 24(11): 1278-1289.* Concerned with German rearmament, growing competition between capitalist countries during the Great Depression, and the threats of fascism and Japanese aggression with the resulting dangers to the USSR, Ernst Thälmann (1886-1944) warned the Communist Party of the danger of war in February 1932. He pointed to the interrelationship between the struggle against war and that against fascism. Consequently, the Party organized numerous antiwar activities and joined other groups in opposition to imperialist wars. 55 notes.

J. T. Walker

870. Shrainer, Albert. VSTRECHA S V. I. LENINYM [Meeting with V. I. Lenin]. *Novaia i Noveishaia Istoriia [USSR] 1976 (2): 90-93.* A recollection of V. I. Lenin's influence on the revolutionary movement in Germany from 1907 until 21 January 1924, when he died. The author, who was an active member of Germany's working-class movement, describes the memorable occasion when he met Lenin at the fourth Congress of the Comintern in Petrograd, 5 November-5 December 1922. 5 notes.

R. Permar

871. Sinowjew, A. P. AUS DER GESCHICHTE DER INTERNATION-ALISTISCHEN ZUSAMMENARBEIT ZWISCHEN DER REVOLU-TIONÄREN JUGEND RUSSLANDS UND DEUTSCHLANDS (1905-1923) [From the history of the internationalist cooperation between the revolutionary youth of Russia and Germany, 1905-23]. *Wissenschaftliche Zeitschrift der U. Rostock. Gesellschafts- und Sprachwissenschaftliche Reihe [East Germany] 1975 24(2): 167-174.* Karl Liebknecht, Rosa Luxemburg, Clara Zetkin, Wilhelm Pieck, Georg Schumann, Hermann Duncker, and V. I. Lenin after the Russian revolution of 1905-07 applied the experiences of the Russian socialist youth movement to the organization of German socialist youth. After the victory of the Bolsheviks in 1917 the cooperation between Russian and German revolutionary youth groups achieved a new quality, especially after the foundation of the Communist Youth International in 1919. Based on printed documents and newspapers; 38 notes.

R. Wagnleitner

872. Škrdle, Vladimír. NĚMECKÉ A ČESKOSLOVENSKÉ REVOLUČNÍ DĚLNICKÉ HNUTÍ V LETECH 1918-1921 [The German and Czechoslovak workers' movements, 1918-21]. *Slovanský Přhled [Czechoslovakia] 1979 65(5): 371-378.* The Czechoslovak proletariat rejoiced over the brief victory of the German workers in 1918. At that time only the Sparticists, left wing of the Social Democratic Party in Germany, understood that this revolution, though basically a bourgeois phenomena, was a step to the socialist revolution of the future. The right wing of the Social Democratic Party favored an evolutionary course in Germany, collaboration in the National Assembly, and dissolution of the workers' councils. The January 1919 fight and defeat of the Berlin workers, and the execution of Liebknecht and Luxemburg, leaders of the German Communist

Party, affected the Czechoslovak working class. Czechoslovak official institutions stood opposed to any support or sympathy for the Sparticists and therefore any real cooperation between the working class of Germany and Czechoslovakia did not take place until after the establishment of the Communist Party in Czechoslovakia in 1921. 47 notes.   B. Reinfeld

873. Škrdle,   Vladimír.   PODPORA   ČESKOSLOVENSKÉHO REVOLUČNÍHO DĚLNICKÉHO HNUTÍ NĚMECKÉMU PROLETARIÁTU V LETECH 1921-1923 [The support of the Czechoslovakian revolutionary workers' movement for the German proletariat, 1921-23]. *Slovanský Přehled [Czechoslovakia] 1980 66(4): 300-307.* Between 1921 and 1923 the Communist Party attempted to establish a dictatorship of the proletariat in a number of German cities. The support that the Czechoslovak revolutionary workers' movement gave the Communist struggle in Germany was primarily moral support and a sense of solidarity with an international Communist revolution. Although a number of meetings were called, following the German situation, no mass demonstrations occurred and the Czech government officially remained neutral. The failure of the Communist uprisings in Germany was due to a lack of discipline and organization. 31 notes.   B. Reinfeld

874. Sokolovskaia, L. B.   O SOLIDARNOSTI NEMETSKIKH KOMMUNISTOV S KITAISKOI REVOLIUTSIEI 1925-1927 GG. [The solidarity of German Communists with the Chinese revolution of 1925-27]. *Narody Azii i Afriki [USSR] 1976 (2): 129-135.* The solidarity movement with the Chinese revolution of 1925-27 by the Communist Party of Germany is a bright page in its international activity and active struggle against imperialism and colonialism. Among its achievements were the strengthening of ties between the Communist Party and the masses, the establishment of unity of action among anti-imperialist forces during certain moments of the movement, the establishment of ties between the Chinese revolutionary organizations and the Communist Party of Germany, and material assistance given by the Communist Party of Germany to the Chinese workers. Primary sources; 31 notes.   L. Kalinowski

875. Strobel, Georg W.   POLNISCHE KOMMUNISTISCHE VEREINE IN DEUTSCHLAND 1925-1935. GOTTHOLD RHODE ZUM 60. GEBURTSTAG GEWIDMET [Polish Communist associations in Germany, 1925-35: honoring Gotthold Rhode on his 60th birthday]. *Zeitschrift für Ostforschung [West Germany] 1977 26(3): 416-442.* Discusses Communist action in Germany and Poland in the organizational sphere among seasonal agricultural workers going from Poland to Germany. Communists hoped these migrant laborers would carry Communist ideas to Poland, where the Communist Party was prohibited. The Reichstag Communist Party led by Anton Jadasch supported these endeavors. The author depicts the development of the organizations involved and of the Berlin *Głos pracy,* the organ of the KPD's Polish-speaking section edited by Jadasch, until dissolved after 1933. Examines as well Polish officials' assessment of Communist activity among Polish seasonal workers and their attempts to oppose it in Germany. Socialist and Communist influence over the activities of Polish migrants crossed and overlapped. The author provides documentary material, in particular organizational statutes of the associations under discussion.

                                                                                        J

876. Sukhorukov, S. R.   NOVYI TRUD PO ISTORII GERMANO-SOVET-SKOI DRUZHBY   [A new work on German-Soviet friendship]. *Istoriia SSSR [USSR] 1978 (3): 202-204.* Reviews A. Anderle, G. Gorski, and G. Rozenfeldt, ed., *Deutsch-sowjetische Freundschaft. Ein historischer Abriss von 1917 bis zur Gegenwart* (Berlin, 1975). Using a wide range of Soviet and East German archives, published documents, and the press, the authors outline the growth of friendly relations between the German working class and the Soviet people since 1917. The authors correctly show that the aims of German antifascists and the Soviet people were the same especially during the creation of a new democratic and peace-loving Germany after 1945.   C. J. Read

877. Šuplak, P.   DIE REVOLUTIONÄRE GEWERKSCHAFTSOPPOSI-TION UND DER KAMPF DER ARBEITERKLASSE DEUTSCHLANDS GEGEN DEN ANGRIFF DER MONOPOLE IN DEN JAHREN 1930/1931 [The revolutionary trade union opposition and the struggle of the working class of Germany against the attack of the monopolies, 1930-31]. *Wissenschaftliche Zeitschrift der Friedrich-Schiller-U. Jena. Gesellschafts- und Sprachwissenschaftliche Reihe [East Germany] 1974 23(6): 827-840.* At the beginning of the Depression, when the German capitalists tried to blame the workers for the economic decline, the German Communists increased their influence in the trade unions. When the German Communists established independent trade unions, directed against the Social Democrats, they isolated themselves from the majority of the German workers. Based on printed documents and secondary literature; 74 notes.   R. Wagnleitner

878. Tregubow, A. W.   DIE PRESSE DER DEUTSCHEN KOMMUNIS-TEN IN SOWJETRUSSLAND (1918-1920)   [The German Communist press in the USSR, 1918-20]. *Beiträge zur Geschichte der Arbeiterbewegung [East Germany] 1976 18(1): 101-112.* The German Communist Party, founded on 24 April 1918 in Moscow, published numerous newspapers and journals in Russia to inform German prisoners of war about politics and to prepare them for a socialist revolution after their return to Germany. The newspapers and journals were also illegally exported to Germany, Austria, and Switzerland. Based on documents in the archives of the Institute for Marxism-Leninism, Moscow, published documents, and secondary literature; 73 notes.   R. Wagnleitner

879. Truchnov, G. M.   DER KAMPF DES DEUTSCHEN PROLETAR-IATS ZUR VERTEIDIGUNG SOWJETRUSSLANDS UND FÜR DIE NOR-MALISIERUNG DER SOWJETISCH-DEUTSCHEN BEZIEHUNGEN [The struggle of the German proletariat for the defense of Soviet Russia and for the normalization of Soviet-German relations]. *Wissenschaftliche Zeitschrift der Friedrich-Schiller-U. Jena. Gesellschafts- und Sprachwissenschaftliche Reihe [East Germany] 1974 23(6): 799-810.* After the intervention of anticommunist powers in the Russian Revolution the campaign of the German Communists under the slogan "Hands off Soviet Russia" began the development of a strong antifascist political movement. German Communists prevented the shipping of weapons and promoted the establishment of diplomatic and trading relations with the Soviets. Based on printed documents and secondary literature; 59 notes.   R. Wagnleitner

880. Trümpler, Eckhard. VOM BÜRGERLICHEN DEMOKRATEN ZUM MITBEGRÜNDER DER ANTIFASCHISTISCHEN VOLKSFRONT. RUDOLF BREITSCHEID [From bourgeois democrat to the cofounder of the antifascist popular front: Rudolf Breitscheid]. *Beiträge zur Geschichte der Arbeiterbewegung [East Germany] 1976 18(3): 513-521.* Rudolf Breitscheid (1874-1944) promoted a left-wing policy within the German Social Democrats after 1912, but opposed the union of the Independent Socialist Party with the Communists in 1920. Breitscheid fought from exile for the establishment of a people's front after 1933, until he was caught by the Nazis in France. He died in Buchenwald concentration camp during a US air force bomb attack. Based on published documents and secondary literature; 21 notes.   R. Wagnleitner

881. Tsapanov, V. I. VIL'GEL'M PIK O NEKOTORYKH PROBLEMAKH ISTORII NEMETSKOGO RABOCHEGO DVISHENIIA [Wilhelm Pieck on some aspects of the history of the German working class movement]. *Novaia i Noveishaia Istoriia [USSR] 1976 (2): 162-175.* Many ideas to be found in Pieck's rich legacy are a contribution to the study of the history, strategy, and tactics of the revolutionary German and international communist labor movement of his time. They retain their political significance today.   J

882. Ullrich, Horst. DIE KPD UND DAS REVOLUTIONÄRE ERBE HEGELS (1930-1931) [The Communist Party of Germany (KPD) and the revolutionary heritage of Hegel, 1930-31]. *Beiträge zur Geschichte der Arbeiterbewegung [East Germany] 1976 18(4): 691-700.* On the occasion of the 100th anniversary of Hegel's death the German Communist Party asserted Hegel's importance and showed that the neo-Hegelians had deformed the progressive traditions of Hegel. Based on printed documents, secondary literature, and newspapers; 19 notes.   R. Wagnleitner

883. Verner, Paul. WILHELM PIECK. ZUR 100. WIEDERKEHR SEINES GEBURTSTAGES [Wilhelm Pieck: on the 100th anniversary of his birth]. *Einheit [East Germany] 1976 31(1): 4-12.* Reviews Wilhelm Pieck's (1876-1960) activities in the German Social Democratic Party since 1895, as communal politician in Bremen before World War I, in the November revolution of 1918, as Communist politician in the Weimar Republic, and as one of the leading founders of the Socialist Unity Party of Germany (SED) after World War II.

884. Vosske, H. ÜBER DEN KAMPF WILHELM PIECKS GEGEN IMPERIALISTISCHE KRIEGSPOLITIK UND FÜR DIE VERTEIDIGUNG DES FRIEDENS [The struggle of Wilhelm Pieck against the imperialist war policy and for the defense of peace]. *Militärgeschichte [East Germany] 1975 14(6): 645-656.* Describes the contribution of Wilhelm Pieck to anti-imperialism and antifascism from his organization of the Social Democrats in Bremen in the 1900's, to his criticism of World War I and his prophecy of World War II; also examines his relations with Rosa Luxemburg and Karl Liebknecht.

885. Ward, James J. PIPE DREAMS OR REVOLUTIONARY POLITICS? THE GROUP OF SOCIAL REVOLUTIONARY NATIONALISTS IN THE WEIMAR REPUBLIC. *J. of Contemporary Hist. [Great Britain] 1980 15(3): 513-532.* Among the wide spectrum of creeds which flourished in Weimar Germany was National Bolshevism, "a doctrine that combined militant nationalist

rejection of the Versailles settlement with radical opposition to the capitalist social and economic order." Traceable to the Reichstag elections of 1928, the National Bolshevist Group of Social Revolutionary Nationalists (GSRN) was mainly formed of young men too young to have fought in the war but old enough to have experienced its effects. The group remained small and stayed on the edges of the major parties. Based on Nazi archival sources; 78 notes.

M. P. Trauth

886. Ward, James J. "SMASH THE FASCISTS..." GERMAN COMMUNIST EFFORTS TO COUNTER THE NAZIS, 1930-31. *Central European Hist. 1981 14(1): 30-62.* Seeks to modify the view of most western scholars regarding the Weimar Republic that the German Communists played a major role in bringing Hitler to power by consistently opposing only the Social Democrats. Many Communists, led by one of the most influential members of the party, Heinz Neumann, tried to circumvent Stalin's instructions to leave the Nazis alone by developing a policy of opposition to both the Social Democrats and the Nazis. The policy failed, Neumann was discredited, and the Communists were not effective in opposing Hitler's takeover in 1933. Based largely on documentary collections and contemporary periodicals; 115 notes. C. R. Lovin

887. Weber, Hermann. AKTIONISMUS UND KOMMUNISMUS. UNBEKANNTE BRIEFE VON MAX HOELZ [Actionism and communism: unpublished letters by Max Hoelz]. *Archiv für Sozialgeschichte [West Germany] 1975 15: 331-363.* Publishes eight letters by one of the most popular Communists and left-wing radicals during the Weimar Republic. Due to his ultra-left methods his reputation in the Communist Party is precarious. These letters written during his time in prison, 1924-25, and in 1929 provide new insights into Hoelz's life, political career and activities, contradicting statements in his own autobiographical writings. They also show problems of political prisoners. Primary and secondary works; 89 notes. H. W. Wurster

888. Weber, Hermann. EIN HISTORISCHES DOKUMENT IM POLITISCHEN ZWIELICHT: ZUM PROTOKOLL DES GRÜNDUNGSPARTEITAGS DER KPD [A historical document in political twilight: the protocol of the founding meeting of the German Communist Party]. *Geschichte in Wissenschaft und Unterricht [West Germany] 1973 24(10): 594-597.* The East German publication of the protocols of the first conference of the German Communist Party of 1918 is a plagiarism of an earlier publication of the author.

889. Weber, Hermann. LA KPD E L'OPPOSIZIONE DI SINISTRA IN UNIONE SOVIETICA [The German Communist Party and the Left Opposition in the Soviet Union]. *Ponte [Italy] 1980 36(11-12): 1258-1278.* Founded and adopted into the Comintern in 1919, the German Communist Party (KPD) was a mass party by 1920 and the largest outside the USSR, but financially dependent on the Soviet Party, which it took for its model. As the Comintern reflected Stalin's struggles with Right and Left opposition, the KPD started bolshevization in 1924, including attacks on the German Left opposition, which led to loss of influence in the Weimar Republic, 1924-25, and eventually (1927) to splintering, with elimination of the Trotskyites and full Stalinization by means that included ideological terror.

890.   Weber, Stefan.   ZUR HERAUSBILDUNG DES MARXISTISCH-LENINISTISCHEN ZENTRALKOMITEES DER KPD UNTER ERNST THÄLMANNS FÜHRUNG   [The formation of the Marxist-Leninist Central Committee of the Communist Party of Germany under the leadership of Ernst Thälmann]. *Beiträge zur Geschichte der Arbeiterbewegung [East Germany] 1975 17(4): 615-635.* The Communist Party of Germany moved toward Marxist-Leninist practice from its founding, but especially after 1923. Ernst Thälmann's assumption of Party leadership in September 1925 confirmed the trend, which followed from the views of Karl Liebknecht and Rosa Luxemburg. Thälmann's leadership marked the victory over both left and right political opportunists, and made the Party truly representative. 78 notes.   G. H. Libbey

891.   Wheeler, Robert F.   GERMAN LABOR AND THE COMINTERN: A PROBLEM OF GENERATIONS?   *J. of Social Hist. [Great Britain] 1974 7(3): 304-321.* Studies the German Independent Social Democrats (USPD) after World War I as a step toward a better understanding of the relationship between age and radicalism and the development of a general typology of labor politics. Can political differences within organized labor legitimately be related to generational differences? Concludes: "there is no simple causal explanation for the high correlation between youth/newness and radicalism within the USPD. . . . Consciousness of organized labor's traditions or lack thereof, wartime experience, unemployment, aspirations to higher office or influence and idealism were some of the varied factors that help explain the overwhelming commitment of the younger generation to political radicalism." 6 tables, 57 notes.   R. V. Ritter

892.   Wheeler, Robert F.   GERMAN WOMEN AND THE COMMUNIST INTERNATIONAL: THE CASE OF THE INDEPENDENT SOCIAL DEMOCRATS.   *Central European Hist. 1975 8(2): 113-139.* One reason that the Russian Revolution failed to become a world revolution was because it did not secure significant support from women outside Russia. The author uses the decision of the Independent Social Democrats not to accept the Twenty-one Demands required to become a member of the Comintern to illustrate that women in the party had strong opinions which were relatively different from those of their male colleagues. Based largely on published material; 96 notes.
C. R. Lovin

893.   Wheeler, Robert F.   REVOLUTIONARY SOCIALIST INTERNATIONALISM: RANK AND FILE REACTION IN THE USPD.   *Int. Rev. of Social Hist. [Netherlands] 1977 22(3): 329-349.* Discusses the supporters of the internationalist antiwar movement which eventually became the second largest political organization of the early Weimar Republic, the Independent Socialist Party (USPD). Among the rank and file Independents there was a strong sympathy for the USSR which provided much of the grass-roots support for the Third International. The USPD organizations registered some resistance to the Twenty-One Conditions of the Third International, notably among the predominantly female textile workers in the Rhineland and other older workers. The author concludes that the USPD and the Communist Party reached a peak in grass-roots involvement during 1919-20. Based on archival and published sources.
G. P. Blum

894. Wimmer, Walter. DIE PARTEI WAR IHM DAS HÖCHSTE, KOST-BARSTE: ZUM 95. GEBURTSAG ERNST THÄLMANNS [For him the Party was supreme and most precious: Ernst Thälmann's 95th birthday]. *Beiträge zur Geschichte der Arbeiterbewegung [East Germany] 1981 23(2): 172-183.* Ernst Thälmann became Communist Party chairman on 1 September 1925. It was his achievement to have converted the Party to Leninist principles so that it could fulfill its revolutionary mission. Thälmann displayed the highest regard for the task of the revolutionary vanguard in overcoming the split among the working-class parties. Based on holdings of Party archives and Party minutes; 65 notes.

A. Schuetz

895. Wimmer, Walter. UNTER THÄLMANNS FÜHRUNG AUF LENIN-SCHEM KURS [Thälmann's leadership on a Leninist course]. *Einheit [East Germany] 1974 29(2): 198-206.* From its founding at the end of 1918, the German Communist Party tried to follow the strategies of V. I. Lenin, a course that Ernst Thälmann strengthened when he became party leader in 1925.

896. Wimmer, Walter. ZU DEN AUFFASSUNGEN ERNST THÄL-MANNS ÜBER DEN SCHUTZ DER SOWJETUNION [On the conceptions of Ernst Thälmann concerning the defense of the Soviet Union]. *Militärgeschichte [East Germany] 1976 15(3): 261-273.* Briefly sketches the political career of Ernst Thälmann, leader of the German workers' movement, and then reviews his persistent efforts from 1919 to 1933 to rally the German working class to the defense of the Soviet Union against imperialist aggression. Thälmann correctly argued that the defense of the Soviet Union was the best support of the international revolutionary movement and the best hope for maintaining peace. Based on Thälmann's writings and secondary works; 3 photos, 38 notes.

J. B. Street

897. Wörfel, Erhard. DEUTSCH-SOWJETISCHE KAMPFTRADI-TIONEN IN DEN JAHREN DER REVOLUTIONÄREN NACHKRIEGSK-RISE IN THÜRINGEN IM ZEICHEN BRÜDERLICHER SOLIDARITÄT [German-Soviet traditions of struggle in the years of the revolutionary crisis after World War I in Thuringia in fraternal solidarity]. *Wissenschaftliche Zeitschrift der Friedrich-Schiller-U. Jena. Gesellschafts- und Sprachwissenschaftliche Reihe [East Germany] 1974 23(6): 785-798.* In the strikes of 1923 the Thuringian working class was supported by thousands of tons of Soviet wheat. Workers in numerous Soviet factories collected money for the German strikers. Based on documents in the Institute for Marxism-Leninism, Central Party Archives, Berlin, Bezirksmuseum Gera, printed documents, and secondary literature; 59 notes.

R. Wagnleitner

898. Wrobel, Kurt. MIT HERZ UND VERSTAND FÜR DIE AR-BEITERKLASSE. KÄTE DUNCKER [With heart and understanding for the working class: Käte Duncker]. *Beiträge zur Geschichte der Arbeiterbewegung [East Germany] 1973 15(2): 313-321.* Describes the political life of Käte Duncker (d. 1953) who from 1898 devoted herself to the education and organization of working-class women. While active in South German politics between 1906 and 1912 she advocated the revolutionary policy of the German Left. She worked in Berlin, the center of revolutionary activities after 1912. Together with Leo Jogiches she organized the work of the Spartacists. After the failure of the

November Revolution Käte Duncker again worked for the education of women and young people, first in Gotha and then in Berlin. She withdrew from politics after the Nazi takeover and emigrated to the United States in 1938, returning to the Soviet zone in Germany nine years later. Based on documents in the Institute for Marxism-Leninism, published documents, and secondary sources; 55 notes.

R. Wagnleitner

899.   Wrobel, Kurt.   ZUM KAMPF WILHELM PIECKS GEGEN IMPERI-ALISTISCHEN TERROR UND FASCHISMUS 1929-1932   [On the struggle of Wilhelm Pieck against imperialist terror and fascism, 1929-32]. *Zeitschrift für Geschichtswissenschaft [East Germany] 1975 23(12): 1424-1437.* Presents and elucidates three documents pertaining to Wilhelm Pieck's (1875-1960) defense of workers' rights against imperialism, fascism, and war. The first document is his testimony before the unofficial committee which investigated the clash between workers and police in Berlin during May 1929. The second and third present his analysis of the increasing fascist threat; his warnings helped mobilize the masses against the Nazi party. 32 notes, appendixes.   J. T. Walker

900.   Yoshimura, Tadao.   DOITSU KYŌSANTŌ NO SEIRITSU NI KAN-SURU ICHIKŌSATSU (1918-1920)   [The origins of the German Communist Party, 1918-20]. *Shigaku Zasshi [Japan] 1972 81(8): 61-82.*

901.   Żuraw, Józef.   DIALEKTYKA WOJNY I POKOJU W MYŚLI FILOZOFICZNEJ RÓŻY LUKSEMBURG   [The dialectic of war and peace in the philosophical thought of Rosa Luxemburg]. *Kultura i Społeczeństwo [Poland] 1980 24(3-4): 77-92.* Rosa Luxemburg's struggle against militarism, which she perceived as a bourgeois phenomenon of the capitalist system, took up a large portion of her political career. She saw the task of educating the masses and nations to respect peace as one of the most pressing needs. She was convinced that militarism could be foiled only by training the masses in the philosophies of Marx and Lenin and lasting peace achieved only by the dictatorship of the proletariat and the crushing of capitalism. Based on the works and correspondence of Rosa Luxemburg and secondary sources; 47 notes.   D. S. Lloyd

8

THE ROAD TO NAZI HEGEMONY

902. Asher, Harvey. NON-PSYCHOANALYTIC APPROACHES TO NA-
TIONAL SOCIALISM. *Psychohistory Rev. 1979 7(3): 13-21.* Reviews scholarship on the origins of Nazism in Germany. It is impossible to prove that most
Germans supported Nazism because of shared psychological pathology and common authoritarian upbringing. Explanations of Nazism based on national character and those based on the Freudian notion of collective nationality are both
reductionist. Learning theory and its concept of modeling is a more acceptable
explanation, and cognitive dissonance theory and theories of group dynamics
offer logical correctives to such nebulous psychoanalytic concepts as multiple
trauma and collective neurosis. Psychoanalytic epistemology looks first to the
individual, then to the external environment and must therefore deduce mental
processes and motivation, ignoring the impact of external events.

J. M. Herrick

903. Auerbach, Hellmuth. HITLERS POLITISCHE LEHRJAHRE UND
DIE MÜNCHENER GESELLSCHAFT 1919-1923. VERSUCH EINER BI-
LANZ ANHAND DER NEUEREN FORSCHUNG [Hitler's political ap-
prenticeship and Munich society, 1919-23: a tentative assessment on the basis of
recent research]. *Vierteljahrshefte für Zeitgeschichte [West Germany] 1977 25(1):
1-45.* An analysis of the evolution of Adolf Hitler's political goals and self-
conception as a political leader in the milieu of Bavarian folkish-nationalist
politics, 1919-23. It is now clear that in this period Hitler had as yet no far-
reaching political concepts or ambitions of his own, but fed on nationalist rhetoric
around him. Until the abortive coup of November 1923, he viewed himself
exclusively as an agitator and pathbreaker for a future national leader, presum-
ably General Erich Ludendorff (1865-1937). Secondary sources; 197 notes.

D. Prowe

904. Barkai, Avraham. WIRTSCHAFTLICHE GRUNDANSCHAUUN-
GEN UND ZIELE DER N.S.D.A.P. (EIN UNVERÖFFENTLICHTES
DOKUMENT AUS DEM JAHRE 1931) [The basic economic concepts and
goals of the Nazi Party: an unpublished document from the year 1931]. *Jahrbuch
des Inst. für Deutsche Geschichte [Israel] 1978 7: 355-385.* The author discovered
an unpublished 1931 typescript in 1974 at the American Document Center in
Berlin which is printed in full here. Partially reconstructs the factors causing the
limited circulation of the *Basic Economic Conceptions and Goals of the Nazi
Party.* The document was never published or even alluded to, which in part

reflects Nazi care for the interests of the great industrialists. But the whole Nazi economic system was already developing in 1931. 46 notes.   M. Faissler

905.   Bauer, Yehuda.   GENOCIDE: WAS IT THE NAZIS' ORIGINAL PLAN?   *Ann. of the Am. Acad. of Pol. and Social Sci. 1980 (450): 35-45.* Examination of developments that led to the Final Solution raises serious questions whether the Nazis did indeed plan the mass execution even before the 1930's. Nowhere is there any pronouncement of this before 1939. The plan the Nazis did have was to evict all Jews from Germany. Although several hundred thousand did leave, those left behind as well as the millions conquered provided a dilemma. Hitler wanted them out. No one wanted them. The Schacht-Rublee negotiations and the Nisko/Madagascar plans, efforts to clear Europe of Jews, had failed dismally before 1939. The last alternative was the Final Solution, which took form in 1941 with the adoption of the Einsatzgruppen and the Wannsee plan.
J/S

906.   Bessel, Richard and Jamin, Mathilde.   NAZIS, WORKERS AND THE USES OF QUANTITATIVE EVIDENCE.   *Social Hist. [Great Britain] 1979 4(1): 111-116.* A critique of Conan J. Fischer's quantitative analysis of the social origins of the SA membership, 1929-34, in Peter D. Stachura, ed., *The Shaping of the Nazi State* (London: Croom Helm, 1978). Fischer asserts that the SA was largely working class and helped Nazism to penetrate the working class in Germany. Fischer's samples are neither homogeneous nor statistically significant; some large cities are overrepresented; changing the nature of the storm troopers after the Nazis' rise to power is ignored; and by ignoring the social and political context of his data Fischer makes serious mistakes.   Table, 16 notes.
D. J. Nicholls

907.   Boehnert, Gunnar C.   AN ANALYSIS OF THE AGE AND EDUCATION OF THE SS FÜHRERKORPS, 1925-1939.   *Hist. Social Res. [West Germany] 1979 (12): 4-17.* Personnel files of SS (Schutzstaffel) officers show that after the Nazis gained power in Germany men from the higher social classes joined the officer corps.

908.   Bookbinder, Paul.   ITALIAN FASCISM, CARL SCHMITT AND THE DESTRUCTION OF PARLIAMENTARY DEMOCRACY IN GERMANY. *Italian Q. 1981 22(84): 85-90.* Discusses German interest in Italian political affairs, specifically the growth of Nazism in Germany during the 1920's modeled after the Fascist movement in Italy, and focuses on the work of lawyer, historian, political scientist, legal theorist, and political propagandist Carl Schmitt, who played a key role in reorienting the judiciary to function under totalitarian rule in Germany.

909.   Brown, Courtney.   THE NAZI VOTE: A NATIONAL ECOLOGICAL STUDY.   *Am. Pol. Sci. Rev. 1982 76(2): 285-302.* Two models of voting are often used to explain the Nazi vote in the Weimar Republic. The first model states that the Nazis' electoral successes resulted from Protestant petit bourgeois and peasant support for fascism. The second model argues that the Nazis gained the bulk of their support from newly mobilized voters. Previous analyses of these models are plagued with serious problems due to their limited database. This study reassesses these models with the use of complete data for all of Germany

and concludes that much of the previous work examining the Nazi vote wrongly identifies the Protestant petite bourgeoisie as the major contributor to the Nazi vote. The Nazis received important levels of support from Protestant peasants, new voters, and Catholic petite bourgeoisie. J

910. Bytwerk, Randall L. RHETORICAL ASPECTS OF THE NAZI MEETING: 1926-1933. *Q. J. of Speech 1975 61(3): 307-318.* The spectacular aspects of Nazi Party meetings, with music, banners and political speeches, were part of Nazi mass propaganda, 1926-33.

911. Cox, Vic. HITLER'S MUNICH. *Mankind 1975 5(6): 18-22, 66-68, (7): 36-39, 54-55.* Part I. 1913-1921. Post-World War I Munich provided fertile ground for the anti-Semitic political appeals of the war veteran Adolf Hitler. Joining the German Workers' Party of Anton Drexler, Hitler had within two years taken it over and merged the organization with another to form the National Socialist German Workers' Party. He thus established the basis of a mass political party of 2,500 members, set up one man rule, and created a political army that became a power to be reckoned with in Bavarian politics by 1921. Part II. The Putsch. By 1921 Adolf Hitler had gained control of the National Socialist German Workers' Party and in 1923 staged his unsuccessful beer-hall putsch in Munich, backed by the dissatisfied middle class. N. Lederer/S

912. De Felice, Renzo and Ledeen, Michael. FASCISM AND THE ITALIAN MALAISE. *Society 1976 13(3): 53-59.* Compares Fascism in Italy in the 1920's-40's to neofascism in the 1970's and to Nazism in Germany in the 1920's-40's.

913. DeWitt, Thomas E. J. THE NAZIFICATION OF WELFARE: ORGANIZATION AND POLICY, 1930-39. *Societas 1977 7(4): 303-327.* Although the Nazis had no coherent philosophy of public welfare, they did make some attempts to deal with the problems of poverty, their emphasis being on the need to make the community strong by helping its sick or impoverished members. Even so, they confined their efforts primarily to helping the temporarily disadvantaged members of the master race. Based on documents in several archives in Germany and the United States and printed primary and secondary sources; 87 notes. J. D. Hunley

914. Douglas, Donald M. THE PARENT CELL: SOME COMPUTER NOTES ON THE COMPOSITION OF THE FIRST NAZI PARTY GROUP IN MUNICH, 1919-21. *Central European Hist. 1977 10(1): 55-72.* Analyzes the only complete roster of the early Nazi Party—the Munich group from December 1919 to July 1921. The comprehensive analysis reveals that the 2,486 men and 340 women included on the roll were almost all middle class, relatively young, and politically homeless. The computerization of this list makes further analysis possible. 25 notes. C. R. Lovin

915. Faris, Ellsworth. TAKEOFF POINT FOR THE NATIONAL SOCIALIST PARTY: THE LANDTAG ELECTION IN BADEN, 1929. *Central European Hist. 1975 8(2): 140-171.* Invalidates the traditional explanation that economic depression and/or new voter participation were responsible for the rise of Nazism as a significant political force in Baden in 1929. The increase can largely be attributed to hard work at the grass roots in convincing people in the

rural, Protestant areas of Baden that Nazism was the best choice. Based on published archival sources; 79 notes.   C. R. Lovin

916. Farquharson, John. THE NSDAP IN HANOVER AND LOWER SAXONY 1921-26. *J. of Contemporary Hist. [Great Britain] 1973 8(4): 103-120.* Adolf Hitler exercised only loose control over the national socialist movement in North Germany during its formative years. This lack of control led to attempts by the northern branches to introduce a more radical program than Hitler wished. However, these branches did lay essential groundwork which contributed to the later political victory of Nazism. Based on surviving documents of the early Nazi Party branches in Hanover and Lower Saxony and secondary sources; 64 notes.   B. A. Block

917. Fiedor, Karol. THE ATTITUDE OF GERMAN RIGHT-WING ORGANIZATIONS TO POLAND IN THE YEARS 1918-1933. *Polish Western Affairs [Poland] 1973 14(2): 247-269.* Following defeat of the German army on foreign soil in World War I, right-wing organizations, appealing to the nationalism and patriotism of the Germans, began a campaign of anti-Polish propaganda which permeated nearly every institution within German society, 1918-33.

918. Fröhlich, Elke and Broszat, Martin. POLITISCHE UND SOZIALE MACHT AUF DEM LANDE. DIE DURCHSETZUNG DER NSDAP IM KREIS MEMMINGEN [Political and social power in the countryside: Nazi penetration in the district of Memmingen]. *Vierteljahrshefte für Zeitgeschichte [West Germany] 1977 25(4): 546-572.* A case study of Nazi political penetration on the village level based on statistical records of 55 rural communities in the Swabian district of Memmingen in rural Bavaria. The Nazis found it difficult to penetrate the traditional positions of authority, especially in the Catholic peasant areas, because the party was regarded as "proletarian" and socialist. Based on state archives at Neuburg and Munich, printed documents, and secondary sources; 63 notes.   D. Prowe

919. Gellately, Robert. GERMAN SHOPKEEPERS AND THE RISE OF NATIONAL SOCIALISM. *Wiener Lib. Bull. [Great Britain] 1975 28(35-36): 31-40.* Examines the support of the lower middle classes for Nazism, with reference to German storekeepers.

920. Gintsberg, L. I. GERMANSKII FASHIZM I MONOPOLII POSLE MIUNKHENSKOGO PUTCHA (1924-1929GG.) [German fascism and monopolies after the Munich putsch, 1924-29]. *Novaia i Noveishaia Istoriia [USSR] 1977 (3): 119-140.* The social roots of fascism lie in monopoly capitalism, as shown by the German experience in the 1920's. The author examines the links between the Nazi Party and big business and demonstrates how paramilitary units were established, often under the guise of sporting clubs, but in reality controlled by *Gauleiters.* These units and the whole Nazi Party were permeated with criminal types. The author outlines their attempts to gain a secure social base, and shows how the socialist tag was a front. Even the party's promise to expropriate large landholdings was only enacted when the owners were Jews. The eventual utilization of democratic processes did not change the party's basic features. The world economic crisis of 1929 laid a fruitful ground for Nazism to prosper. Based on published German documents and secondary sources; 123 notes.   D. N. Collins

921. Glees, Anthony. ALBERT C. GRZESINSKI AND THE POLITICS OF PRUSSIA, 1926-1930. *English Hist. Rev. [Great Britain] 1974 89(353): 814-834.* Examines the career of Albert C. Grzesinski as Prussian Minister of Interior, 1926-30, to demonstrate that the Social Democratic Party (SPD) was not responsible for failing to stop the rise of Hitler and other antirepublican organizations. Denies that the SPD was not energetic enough in pursuit of the enemies of the Weimar Republic, and defends the use of authoritarian methods by Grzesinski to build a pro-republic civil service. In addition to reconstituting the civil service, Grzesinski dissolved paramilitary extremist organizations of both the right and left and battled with courts and the Reich president to keep the ban on groups that used terror, violence, and intimidation to prevent others from freely exercising their democratic rights. Based mainly on published works and unpublished papers in the *Nachlasz Grzesinski,* Amsterdam; 128 notes.
R. J. Gromen

922. Goldstein, Jeffrey A. ON RACISM AND ANTI-SEMITISM IN OC-CULTISM AND NAZISM. *Yad Vashem Studies on the European Jewish Catastrophe and Resistance [Israel] 1979 13: 53-72.* Examines certain esoteric doctrines that contributed to the Nazi ideology evolving in Germany in the 1920's and 1930's. The Theosophist and Ariosophist movements, which had strong undercurrents of racism and anti-Semitism in their world views, attracted future Nazi Party members, such as Alfred Rosenberg. Especially congenial to the prejudices of these German chauvinists was the theory of Aryan racial superiority, which had long been preached in certain occult circles. In Munich the militant and clandestine activities of the Thule Society, founded by the occultist Rudolph von Sebottendorf attracted the fanatical nationalists beginning to congregate around Adolf Hitler. 59 notes.
B. Reiner

923. Gossweiler, Kurt. JUNKERTUM UND FASCHISMUS [Junkers and fascism]. *Wissenschaftliche Zeitschrift der Humboldt-U. zu Berlin. Gesellschafts- und Sprachwissenschaftliche Reihe [East Germany] 1973 22(1-2): 19-26.* Because of their strong economic and political position the East German Junkers were able to avoid structural agricultural reforms both in the Weimar Republic and during the National Socialist period. Based on documents in the Deutsches Zentralarchiv Potsdam, printed documents and secondary literature; 43 notes, annex.
R. Wagnleitner

924. Gossweiler, Kurt. ÜBER URSPRÜNGE UND SPIELARTEN DES FASCHISMUS [The origin and style of fascism]. *Jahrbuch für Geschichte der Sozialistischen Länder Europas [East Germany] 1980 24(1): 7-36.* Monopoly capitalism provided the seedbed for fascism for the period before World War I. Fascism emerged from the wartime crisis of capitalism. The failure of capitalism in Germany and its weakness in southeastern Europe paved the way for the diffusion of the Italian-born movement. Neofascism looms as a present threat. 68 notes.
D. R. Stevenson

925. Hartmann, Peter Claus. DER HITLERPUTSCH (1923) IM URTEIL DER FRANZÖZISCHEN GESANDSCHAFTS- UND BOTSCHAFTS-BERICHTE [The Hitler putsch of 1923 in reports of the French legation and embassy]. *Francia [France] 1977 5: 453-472.* French diplomats predicted the Beer-hall putsch. When it occurred, French reports from Berlin viewed the whole

story as a discharge of an old standing conflict between two large rightist groups in Bavaria, the monarchists and the militarist movement led by Erich Ludendorff and Adolf Hitler. Primary sources; 91 notes.   G. E. Pergl

926. Hennig, Eike. REGIONALE UNTERSCHIEDE BEI DER EN-STEHUNG DES DEUTSCHEN FASCHISMUS: EIN PLÄDOYER FÜR MIKROANALYTISCHE STUDIEN ZUR ERFORSCHUNG DER NSDAP (NATIONALSOZIALISTISCHE DEUTSCHE ARBEITER PARTEI) [Regional differences and the origin of German fascism: a model for a microanalytical study of the NSDAP]. *Politische Vierteljahresschrift [West Germany] 1980 21(2): 152-173.* Examines the origins of the German National Socialist Workers' Party (NSDAP) and the factors affecting its growth and development, particularly at the regional level, and reception by various sectors of the population, grouped according to profession, trade, age, and sex. Considers socioeconomic conditions in Germany for their effect on the formation of the NSDAP, and in uniting otherwise incompatible elements of society. Political activism, a climate of violence, world economic depression, and the weakness of the Weimar government also played a part. Contrary to a common view, the NSDAP is seen as appealing to both rural and urban populations. The propaganda was provincial but not geographically localized. 2 tables, 36 notes, biblio.   S. Bonnycastle

927. Hofman, J. and Stam, A. DE LEVENSLOOP VAN RUDOLPH HESS [The career of Rudolph Hess]. *Spiegel Historiael [Netherlands] 1977 12(3): 150-157.* Rudolph Hess (b. 1894) abandoned his business education to study history, economics, and geopolitics in 1920. He joined an anti-Marxist Freikorps and regarded the Germans as a sick people that a coming dictator would cure. Adolf Hitler soon enlisted him, and he became a prominent Nazi leader. Hess went to prison with Hitler, where he served as secretary during the writing of *Mein Kampf.* Hess's greatest influence was in the development of the Hitler personality cult. After 1939, he lost his former status as Hitler's sole confidant and began displaying neurotic tendencies. His political career ended in May 1941, when he made his secret flight to Scotland and authorities in Germany declared him mentally disturbed. He remained under psychiatric care in England until he was brought before the International Military Tribunal at Nuremburg in 1945. He was sentenced to life imprisonment. 10 illus.   J. E. Snellen

928. Horn, Daniel. THE NATIONAL SOCIALIST SCHÜLERBUND AND THE HITLER YOUTH, 1929-1933. *Central European Hist. 1978 11(4): 355-375.* The *Hitler Jugend* (HJ) has been thought of as unique in Nazism because of its working-class membership, equalitarianism, and revolutionary doctrines. Although it was true that as many as half the members of the original HJ were from the working class, by 1933 the HJ had basically been taken over by the more respectable and middle class Nationalsozialistischer Schülerbund (NSS). The takeover occurred in 1932 after Dr. Adrian Theodor von Renteln, who had become the first national leader of the NSS in 1929, became leader of HJ as well. He replaced most of the HJ leaders with NSS leaders and prepared the way for the merger of the two in April 1933. Based primarily on unpublished sources; 75 notes.   C. R. Lovin

929. Hovdkinn, Øystein. GOEBBELS, HITLER OG DET NASJONAL-SOSIALISTISKE VENSTRE [Goebbels, Hitler, and the National Socialist Left]. *Hist. Tidsskrift [Norway] 1976 55(3): 288-316.* The radical wing of the Nazi Party has been identified in Gregor Strasser's labor group, but not in other elements, one of which was represented by Joseph Goebbels. He believed the 20th century to be the age of the worker and thought the bourgeoisie would disappear even while he wished cooperation between them and workers. Goebbels appealed to the workers against capitalism which he defined as antinational in interest, like Communism. He opposed the Social Democrats because of their supposed treason in World War I and their revolution in 1918 which turned Germany over to capitalism and the Jews. Workers should have rights of ownership and economic participation that would solve social problems—a true national socialism. Goebbels contradicted Hitler in foreign policy (a Russian rather than an English alliance), on racist ideas, and in his anti-Communism. In 1926, Goebbels changed his opinions after meeting with Hitler. Although still opposed in theory, he supported Hitler as a person and leader. German summary.   R. E. Lindgren

930. Janner, William, Jr. NATIONAL SOCIALISTS AND SOCIAL MOBILITY. *J. of Social Hist. 1976 9(3): 339-368.* Proposes upward social mobility as incentive to support Nazism, especially among those with limited prospects under the pre-Nazi educational system with its emphasis on classical and legal studies. The author offers data on the backgrounds of middle level Nazi appointees to party, local, and national positions to show that their age, class and educational status differed from those of Weimar and Bonn era appointees. This is important now that older views of the Nazis as 1) tools of big business, 2) anti-socialists, 3) totalitarians, and 4) antimodernists are being challenged. Struggles within the party over the degree to which educational requirements for educational and civil service positions would stay loosened, or be further loosened, increased over the years. Several kinds of schools were developed to offer more widespread entry for loyal Nazis on the basis of their zeal and personal drive. All this was in keeping with a long tradition of leveling efforts in European societies.   M. Hough

931. Kater, Michael E. DER NS-STUDENTENBUND VON 1926 BIS 1928: RANDGRUPPE ZWISCHEN HITLER UND STRASSER [The National Socialist Student League, 1926-28: marginal group between Hitler and Strasser]. *Vierteljahrshefte für Zeitgeschichte [West Germany] 1974 22(2): 148-190.* Analyzes the early Nazi student organization from its lower class, anti-bourgeois origins under the leadership of Wilhelm Tempel, in close association with the Strasser Nazi left wing, to its takeover by an anti-Tempel coalition including Goebbels, Rosenberg, and Baldur von Schirach. During this time Adolf Hitler's position evolved from one of awkward avoidance to one of charismatic leadership, divide and rule, and support for the stronger pro-bourgeois group. Based on NSDSTB and other Nazi archives, contemporary Nazi press, memoirs, and secondary sources; 300 notes.   D. Prowe

932. Kater, Michael H. BÜRGERLICHE JUGENDBEWEGUNG UND HITLERJUGEND IN DEUTSCHLAND VON 1926 BIS 1939 [The middle-class youth movement and Hitler Youth in Germany, 1926-39]. *Archiv für Sozialgeschichte [West Germany] 1977 17: 127-174.* Compares middle-class youth movements and the Hitler Youth, which had the same authoritarian struc-

ture and similar ideas, though the youth movements, unlike the Hitler Youth, were elitist. The 1929 slump sent many young people to the Hitler Youth. Many youth movements were abolished in June 1933, or subsequently brought into line. Though some resisted, they were predominantly pro-Nazi, as their leaders jumped on the bandwagon. The Hitler Youth never reached more than two-thirds of German youth, though membership was compulsory after 1939. Based on the Federal Archive Koblenz, state archives in Munich, Bremen, Wolfenbüttel, Hannover, and Oldenburg, contemporary journals, and secondary works; table, 312 notes.   H. W. Wurster

933.   Kater, Michael H.   ZUM GEGENSEITIGEN VERHÄLTNIS VON SA UND SS IN DER SOZIALGESCHICHTE DES NATIONALSOZIALISMUS VON 1925 BIS 1939   [The relationship between the SA and SS in the social history of National Socialism, 1925-39]. *Vierteljahrschrift für Sozial- und Wirschaftsgeschichte [West Germany] 1975 62(3): 339-379.* An examination of the social pluralism and hierarchy within the Nazi state and their roots in pre-1933 social and power structures through a case analysis of the social origins and development of the SA (*Sturmabteilung*) and SS (*Schutzstaffel*). Initially identical in social composition and linked organizationally, the SS and SA moved apart through the SS's growing elite-consciousness and special political role. These factors led to a gradual modification of its social composition, reinforcing in turn its special role and prestige. While both organizations remained mainly lower middle class in composition, the SS boasted a far greater percentage of professionals, students, and aristocrats than either the SA or the general population and consequently increasingly reflected traditional upper middle-class values. The SA remained an organization of economically and socially unstable men which never recovered from the humiliation of the Röhm Purge (30 June 1934). Based on party and police statistics and documents in the major Bavaria, Hesse, and Baden archives and secondary works; 173 notes.   D. Prowe

934.   Keyserlingk, Robert H.   HITLER AND GERMAN NATIONALISM BEFORE 1933.   *Can. Rev. of Studies in Nationalism [Canada] 1978 5(1): 24-44.* Adolf Hitler was not simply an advocate of a more extreme version of traditional German nationalism and militarism with an anti-Semitic tinge added. He exploited German nationalism to seize and maintain power, but his vision was not limited by the bounds of Greater Germany. He was a Europe-wide, even a worldwide racial imperialist, who hoped to build a Europe, and if possible a world, dominated by an Aryan elite. All Jews and other "inferior" races would be eliminated from this world—Hitler envisaged the Final Solution from the beginning. He was in his way as much a world revolutionary as were Marx or Trotsky. Like them, he hated the liberal, bourgeois, democratic state and worked for its replacement by violent means. 81 notes.   J. C. Billigmeier

935.   Kleine, Georg H.   ADELSGENOSSENSCHAFT UND NATIONAL-SOZIALISMUS   [Association of Aristocrats and National Socialism]. *Vierteljahrshefte für Zeitgeschichte [West Germany] 1978 26(1): 100-143.* An analysis of the relationship of a significant part of the German nobility organized in the Deutsche Adelsgenossenschaft (DAG) [Association of German Aristocrats] to the Nazi movement and state. Originally composed mainly of impoverished, unpropertied aristocrats, the DAG was naturally attracted to *völkisch* ideas of a national elite and grew increasingly antirepublican in the Weimar years. After

1933 it joined the Nazi cause and attempted to create a racially pure German aristocracy in order to claim a leadership role in the new state. Based on records of the Bavarian and Saxon sections of DAG, the Deutsche Adelsarchiv, (Marburg), personal papers, DAG publications, memoirs, and secondary sources; 2 tables, 149 notes.

D. Prowe

936. Kohler, Eric D. THE RISE OF THE NAZIS. Parker, Harold T., ed. *Problems in European History,* (Durham, N.C.: Moore Publ., 1979): 251-266. Reviews the explanations offered by various writers for the rapid rise of the Nazi Party, 1924-33. These include cultural explanations emphasizing the legacy of Martin Luther, the German Romantics, or the antimodernist movement of the late 19th century, or pointing out the appeal of the fusion of nationalism and socialism, or of Nazi anti-Semitism. Contextual explanations emphasize the general revolt against a smug though discredited liberalism, the role of World War I veterans, the shock of the war and its economic aftermath, and the strong appeal of Nazism to the young. Political explanations point to foreign persecution of the Weimar Republic, to Communist activity, or to the shortcomings of the Weimar constitution. A final category of explanations emphasizes intrigue by big business, or the inept and counterproductive maneuvers of General Kurt von Schleicher. Ref.

L. W. Van Wyk

937. Koonz, Claudia. NAZI WOMEN BEFORE 1933: REBELS AGAINST EMANCIPATION. *Social Sci. Q. 1976 56(4): 553-563.* Nazi women before 1933 preferred traditional sex roles. The author seeks to identify the sources of the anti-feminist orientation.

J/S

938. Koshar, Rudy. TWO "NAZISMS": THE SOCIAL CONTEXT OF NAZI MOBILIZATION IN MARBURG AND TÜBINGEN. *Social Hist. [Great Britain] 1982 7(1): 27-42.* The German university towns of Marburg and Tübingen were structurally similar communities, but the rise of Nazism was more violent, swift, and complete in Marburg. In neither town was there a collapse or fragmentation of middle-class public life: the middle classes organized their hegemony outside the party-political sphere. But politics in Marburg had long been more violent than in Tübingen, and class conflict between students and workers intensified between 1918 and 1933. Similarly, middle-class political parties were more fragmented, and the mayor and police force protected the forces of the Right who subsequently supported Nazism. The more controlled situation in Tübingen also favored Nazism in the long run, but created a calmer context for its rise. Based on documents in the Hesse and Württemberg State Archives and printed sources; 60 notes.

D. J. Nicholls

939. Lane, Barbara Miller. NAZI IDEOLOGY: SOME UNFINISHED BUSINESS. *Central European Hist. 1974 7(1): 3-30.* Because of the influence of some of the earliest writers on Nazism who contended that Hitler was interested in power rather than programs, little of the ideology developed among Nazis before 1933 has been analyzed. The author examines the writings of early Nazi ideologists, including Dietrich Eckart, Gottfried Feder, Alfred Rosenberg, Gregor and Otto Strasser, and Richard Walther Darré. The Twenty-five Points, the agricultural program of 1930, and the full-employment program of 1932 are also considered. Includes bibliographic footnotes. Based primarily on published works of the individuals involved and official published party sources; 98 notes.

C. R. Lovin

940. Liebersohn, Harry. THE FASCIST IMAGINATION. *Radical Hist. Rev. 1979 (20): 53-58.* Review essay of Klaus Theweleit's *Maennerphantasien* (Frankfurt: Roter Stern, 1978) examines the fascist theory of sexuality, feminine roles, and the ideology of the family and marriage, espoused by members of Germany's Freikorps, 1918-45. One of 13 articles in this issue on sexuality in history.

941. Mazur, Zbigniew. KSZTAŁTOWANIE SIE KONCEPCJI PAKTU CZTERECH W LATACH 1931-1932 [The Four Power Pact: how the original concept was formed, 1931-32]. *Przegląd Zachodni [Poland] 1973 29(4): 201-229.* Germany was the first country to develop the concept of the Four Power Pact as early as 1931-32, before Benito Mussolini's proclamation of the idea made it widely known.

942. Mergner, Gottfried. LA MOBILISATION NATIONAL-SOCIALISTE PARMI LES ETUDIANTS ALLEMANDS [Nazi mobilization among German students]. *Mouvement Social [France] 1982 (120): 107-121.* The participation of German students in the counterrevolution during the years 1919-23 alongside of the *Freikorps* prefigured their later insertion in the Nazi student movement. The respect for authority and the values they experienced in the student corporations led them eventually to favor a fusion with the National Socialist German Students' League (NSDStB). Shows the evolution of this process through a case study of two corporations, Uttenruthia and Bubenruthia in the first "brown" university, Erlangen.   J/S

943. Michaelis, Meir. I RAPPORTI TRA FASCISMO E NAZISMO PRIMA DELL'AVVENTO DI HITLER AL POTERE (1922-1933) PARTE PRIMA: 1922-1928 [Relations between Fascism and Nazism before Hitler's rise to power, 1922-33: Part one; 1922-28]. *R. Storica Italiana [Italy] 1973 85(3): 554-600.* Presents new documents from Italy, Germany, and Great Britain as they relate to Nazi-Fascist relations in the period 1922-28. Considers 1) the personal relations between Mussolini and Hitler; 2) the affinity of one variety of totalitarianism for another; and 3) the secret contacts and collaboration between Nazism and Fascism over the Alto Adige (South Tyrol) question. Based on Italian, German, English, and Israeli archives and secondary sources; 208 notes. Article to be continued.   C. Bates

944. Müller, Ralf. DER REICHSLANDBUND ZWISCHEN DNVP UND NSDAP [The Imperial Land League between the German National People's Party and National Socialists]. *Wissenschaftliche Zeitschrift der U. Rostock. Gesellschafts- und Sprachwissenschaftliche Reihe [East Germany] 1974 23(9): 563-570.* Until 1928 the Imperial Land League tried to realize its aim of strengthening the position of rich landowners and peasants by cooperation with the German National People's Party (DNVP). In the Depression which caused a strong right-wing tendency in agricultural circles, the ties with the DNVP were loosened, and cooperation with Nazism strengthened the Nazis' position in rural areas. Based on secondary sources; 108 notes.   R. Wagnleitner

945. Neville, Joseph B., Jr. ERNST REVENTLOW AND THE WEIMAR REPUBLIC: A VOELKISCH RADICAL CONFRONTS GERMANY'S SOCIAL QUESTION. *Societas 1977 7(3): 229-251.* Initially a liberal, Ernst Re-

ventlow began in 1905-08 a transition through unorthodox conservatism to *völkisch* radicalism. Strongly anti-Semitic, he became determinedly anticapitalist as well, emphasizing the need to heal the social wounds capitalism inflicted. Although he opposed the *Führer* principles, these views led him to embrace the Nazi party. Based on papers in the NSDAP Hauptarchiv and printed primary and secondary sources; 93 notes.   J. D. Hunley

946. Noakes, Jeremy. NAZI VOTERS. *Hist. Today [Great Britain] 30(Aug): 44-48.* Analyzes the elections of 1928 and 1932 and concludes that it was spirit, paramilitarism, and the charisma of Hitler which attracted Nazi voters.

947. Palumbo, Michael. GOERING'S ITALIAN EXILE, 1924-25. *J. of Modern Hist. 1978 50(1): ii-iii.* The newly discovered correspondence between Hermann Goering and Negrelli helps fill the gap in the history of the relationship between the Nazi and Fascist movements during the 1920's. It also gives some new information on the Nazi movement after the setback suffered by the Nazis in Munich and suggests that Adolf Hitler was politically more active in Landsberg prison than previously believed, especially in efforts to establish ties with Fascist Italy. Abstract only.

948. Petzold, Joachim. CLASS UND HITLER: ÜBER DIE FÖRDERUNG DER FRÜHEN NAZIBEWEGUNG DURCH DEN ALLDEUTSCHEN VERBAND UND DESSEN EINFLUSS AUF DIE NAZISTISCHE IDEOLO-GIE [Class and Hitler: the advancement of the early Nazi movement through the Pan-German League and its influence on Nazi ideology]. *Jahrbuch für Geschichte [East Germany] 1980 21: 247-288.* Examines different aspects of the relationship between Adolf Hitler and Heinrich Class, president of the Pan-German League, 1918-33. In spite of ideological differences between the two, there were mutual hopes of furthering their own causes. Traces policy continuity from the Pan-German League to Nazism. Based on material in the Central State Archives, Potsdam; appendix.   T. Parker

949. Petzold, Joachim. DIE OBJEKTIVE FUNKTION DES FASCHIS-MUS IM SUBJEKTIVEM SELBSTVERSTÄNDNIS DER FASCHISTEN [The objective function of fascism in the subjective awareness of fascists]. *Zeitschrift für Geschichtswissenschaft [East Germany] 1980 28(4): 357-372.* Questions whether the fascists realized at the beginning of their rise to power in Germany that they were simply tools of monopoly capitalism and large landowners. Even the old guard with the longest record of membership in the National Socialist Party believed their own propaganda and were ignorant of the real goals of Nazism because their leaders cleverly camouflaged their close cooperation with the ruling upper middle classes, industrialists, bankers, and the military. 50 notes.
                                                          G. E. Pergl

950. Petzold, Joachim. ERNST JÜNGERS BEITRAG ZUR FASCHIS-TISCHEN KRIEGSPSYCHOLOGIE [Ernst Jünger's contribution to the fascist psychology of war]. *Militärgeschichte [East Germany] 1977 16(6): 707-715.* Jünger, a German officer in World War I, was the first to define the political-moral factor in war in a fascist way: he regarded life as expendable in pursuit of a political idea. His thought was influenced by Nietzsche. With war preparations

under way, 1924-29, Jünger became committed to German victory; by 1932 he was writing war propaganda and in 1934 urged German youth to join Hitler. His theories helped inspire the creation of the SS. 41 notes.   A. Alcock

951. Petzold, Joachim.   ZUR FUNKTION DES NATIONALISMUS [The function of nationalism]. *Zeitschrift für Geschichtswissenschaft [East Germany] 1973 21(11): 1285-1300.* Arthur Moeller van der Bruck's *Das dritte Reich* (Berlin 1923), a right-wing attack on the Treaty of Versailles, democracy, liberalism, and communism was one of the most influential ideological forerunners of German Nazism. He believed that nationalism had been used to manipulate the Germans to oppose progress. Based on Moeller's works and secondary literature; 46 notes.   R. Wagnleitner

952. Roeske, Ulrich.   ZUM VERHÄLTNIS ZWISCHEN DNVP UND NSDAP   [The relation between German National People's Party and the National Socialists]. *Wissenschaftliche Zeitschrift der Humboldt-U. zu Berlin. Gesellschafts- und Sprachwissenschaftliche Reihe [East Germany] 1973 22(1-2): 27-38.* Although the German National People's Party (DNVP) had lost its position as a mass party to the National Socialists by 1930, its leaders still hoped to retain the leading role in the opposition, only to be removed from power immediately after the Nazis took over in 1933. Based on documents in the Deutsches Zentralarchiv Potsdam, published documents and secondary literature; 45 notes.   R. Wagnleitner

953. Roth, Hermann.   DIE NATIONALSOZIALISTISCHE BETRIEBS-ZELLORGANISATION (NSBO) VON DER GRÜNDUNG BIS ZUR RÖHM-AFFÄRE (1928 BIS 1934)   [The National Socialist Shop Cell Organization (NSBO) from its founding to the Röhm affair, 1928-34]. *Jahrbuch für Wirtschaftsgeschichte [East Germany] 1978 (1): 49-66.* An anticapitalist wing within the Nazi Party was especially strong in Nazi shop cells and within the SA. After Adolf Hitler came to power the NSBO and SA agitated for a second revolution of a vaguely socialist nature. The Nazi leadership finally crushed the socialist wing of the party in the summer of 1934 in the Röhm purge. The NSBO ceased to be an independent organization. Based on published documentary collections, various business archives, and secondary works; 107 notes.
          J. B. Street

954. Roveri, Alessandro.   LA LEGGENDA STRASSER E L'AVVENTO DI HITLER AL CANCELLIERATO   [The Strasser legend and the accession of Hitler to the chancellorship]. *Studi Storici [Italy] 1980 21(3): 641-646.* Studies the activity and behavior of Gregor Strasser from 1926 until his murder by the Nazis 30 June 1934. At one time an influential Nazi member, Strasser fell out of favor after his break with Adolf Hitler in 1932. 6 notes.   E. E. Ryan

955. Saage, Richard.   ANTISOZIALISMUS, MITTELSTAND UND NSDAP IN DER WEIMARER REPUBLIK   [Antisocialism, the middle classes and the National Socialist Party in the Weimar Republic]. *Internationale Wissenschaftliche Korrespondenz zur Geschichte der Deutschen Arbeiterbewegung [West Germany] 1975 11(2): 146-177.* The German National Socialists recruited membership from those declassed by World War I with militarist, antidemocratic, and nationalist ideologies, and from petite bourgeoisie and farmers pauperized in the depression.

956. Saito, Takashi. INTERPRETATIONS OF FASCISM IN THE INTER-WAR PERIOD. *Shakai-Keizai-Shigaku [Japan] 1976 41(6): 6-17.* Of the various interpretations of fascism and its related phenomena, the Marxist proved the most comprehensive and realistic, showing it as a mere tool of declining capitalism under the guise of a revolutionary mass movement and at the same time making clear its international nature. But the subsequent Nazi seizure of power in Germany demonstrated the weakness of the Marxist interpretation. Marxists, since the latter half of the 1920's, have ignored mass psychological factors in the fascist movement. Today's task is to integrate various theories of fascism. In an attempt to pursue such integration the most important tasks are to revise Dimitrov's definition of fascism by analyzing capitalism in the fascist states of Germany, Italy, and Japan; to complement preceding theories with the socioeconomic analyses of contemporary social and behavioral scientists; and to propose a new definition of fascism that takes into account the total process of its origin, maturation, and collapse.   J/S

957. Schlicker, Wolfgang. DIE "DEUTSCHE AKADEMIE" [The German Academy]. *Jahrbuch für Volkskunde und Kulturgeschichte [East Germany] 1977 20: 43-66.* In May 1925 the *Akademie zur wissenschaftlichen Erforschung und Pflege des Deutschtums* (Deutsche Akademie) was founded in Munich with the aim of activating an aggressive nationalist and anticommunist cultural policy in Germany and abroad. Its board of directors and members combined scientists, artists, and right-wing politicians and industrialists. After 1933 the *Deutsche Akademie* was integrated into the cultural politics of the National Socialists. Based on documents in the Zentrales Staatsarchiv Potsdam and secondary literature; 90 notes.   R. Wagnleitner

958. Shiba, Kensuke. VAIMARU-MAKKI NO KOKUBŌGUN TO NA-CHISU [The Reichswehr and the Nazis in the late Weimar period]. *Rekishigaku Kenkyū [Japan] 1980 (482): 14-29.* Discusses the antagonistic and conflicting relationship between the Reichswehr (the national defense forces) and the Nazis, during the years since Hitler prohibited the battalions from participation in the border guard in December 1928 until Hitler and Defense Minister Werner von Blomberg reached a compromise to put the military training of youth under the authority of the battalions in December 1933. Thus, it is demonstrated that the German rearmament was conducted through the division of roles between the military and the party. Based on materials in the Bundesarchiv-Militär-Archiv Freiburg and other primary sources; 118 notes.   Y. Imura

959. Smelser, Ronald M. HITLER AND THE DNSAP: BETWEEN DEMOCRACY AND GLEICHSCHALTUNG. *Bohemia. Jahrbuch des Collegium Carolinum [West Germany] 1979 20: 137-155.* When the first Nazi groupings coalesced around Adolf Hitler in Munich during 1919-21, the German National Socialist Workers' Party (DNSAP) in Czechoslovakia, which dated back to 1903, considered itself an ally and mentor of the new Bavarian Nazi Party (NSDAP). By 1923, Hitler dominated the Munich movement, and the German Nazis with their dictatorial mystique overtook their Austrian and Bohemian counterparts in both numbers and importance. After his unsuccessful beer hall *putsch,* Hitler owed an unacknowledged debt to the DNSAP leaders. They taught him the parliamentary party politics which they had mastered in Czechoslovakia, and which Hitler was to find useful in Weimar Germany. Based on

German and Czechoslovak archival materials and published sources; 70 notes.
R. E. Weltsch

960.   Stachura, Peter D.   DER KRITISCHE WENDEPUNKT? DIE NSDAP
UND DIE REICHSTAGSWAHLEN VOM 20. MAI 1928   [The critical turning point? The Nazi Party and the Reichstag elections of 20 May 1928]. *Vierteljahrshefte für Zeitgeschichte [West Germany] 1978 26(1): 66-99.* The Nazi
Party's abandonment of socialism and turn to the right took place in the period
immediately after the elections of May 1928. The Nazis' most determined attempts to attract industrial workers preceded the elections, occurring between
1925 and 1928, when leftist Gregor Strasser was top party propagandist. The
party's disastrous showing in the election apparently persuaded Hitler to impose
a rightist-völkisch orientation on the party beginning with a strategy planning
session in Munich, August-September 1928. Based on Bundesarchiv (Koblenz)
records, press reports, memoirs, and secondary works; 4 tables, 156 notes.
D. Prowe

961.   Stachura, Peter D.   THE HITLER YOUTH IN CRISIS: THE CASE OF
REICHFÜHRER KURT GRUBER, OCTOBER 1931.   *European Studies
Rev. [Great Britain] 1976 6(3): 331-356.* On 29 October 1931 Adolf Hitler
announced the resignation of Kurt Gruber, who had led the Hitler Youth since
its foundation in July 1926. Although it went almost unnoted at the time, his
departure was of considerable political significance for the development of the
National Socialist Movement. The development of the Hitler youth movement
and Gruber's career before 1931 and his eventual dismissal, illustrate the ways
in which Hitler purged the National Socialists of all those leftist and social
revolutionaries who might have challenged his policy of appealing to the middle-
class and peasant vote. 127 notes.   H. Woolf

962.   Stachura, Peter D.   THE IDEOLOGY OF THE HITLER YOUTH IN
THE KAMPFZEIT.   *J. of Contemporary Hist. [Great Britain] 1973 8(3): 155-
167.* The Nazi Hitler-Jugend (HJ) developed a social-revolutionary political
ethos in 1926-33 which was nationalistic but which distinguished it from all other
National Socialist groups. The preponderance of working class youth in the HJ
gave its ideology a proletarian character. The HJ formulated policies of social,
economic, and industrial reform, some of which were carried out under Nazi rule.
Primary and secondary sources; 18 notes.   B. A. Block

963.   Stachura, Peter D.   THE POLITICAL STRATEGY OF THE NAZI
PARTY, 1919-1933.   *German Studies Rev. 1980 3(2): 261-288.* The Nazi Party
went through five distinct phases in its drive for power: 1) 1919-21, when the
party competed with a number of radical middle class groups in Bavaria; 2) from
1921 to the *putsch* of 1923, when Hitler emerged as the leader and the party was
organized more efficiently; 3) 1923-28, when Hitler decided to seek power
through constitutional means after the failure of the *putsch*; 4) 1928-32, the turn
to the right after the failure of the urban strategy in the 1928 elections; and
5) Hitler's turn to big business in 1932.   104 notes.   J. T. Walker

964.   Stachura, Peter D.   WHO WERE THE NAZIS? A SOCIO-POLITICAL
ANALYSIS OF THE NATIONAL SOCIALIST *MACHTÜBERNAHME.*
European Studies Rev. [Great Britain] 1981 11(3): 293-324. A review of scholarly

research presents a fairly accurate picture of the social composition of those who voted for National Socialism in Germany in 1933. The lower middle class constituted 75% of the party's vote. The remaining 25% was equally divided between the upper middle class and the proletariat. Religion, age, and sex are important factors in understanding the Nazi electorate. Voters were predominately Protestant and young. The female vote increased after 1930 and equaled the male vote by 1933. Nazism's drive to power was fueled by the response of the Protestant lower middle class to liberalism and modernism. Based on a paper presented to the Institut für Sozial-und Wirtschaftsgeschichte of the University of Heidelberg in Bad Homburg, October 1979; secondary sources; 117 notes.

H. M. Narducci, Jr.

965. Steger, Bernd. DER HITLERPROZESS UND BAYERNS VER-HÄLTNIS ZUM REICH 1923/24 [The Hitler trial and Bavaria's relations with the German republic, 1923-24]. *Vierteljahrshefte für Zeitgeschichte [West Germany] 1977 25(4): 441-446.* The trial following Adolf Hitler's abortive Beer Hall Putsch, November 1923-April 1924, revealed the weakness of the post-World War I republic and the antidemocratic commitment of the Bavarian administration and judiciary. In the hope of avoiding conflicts, the weakened Berlin government surrendered the case to the Bavarian people's court which, sympathetic to Hitler's goals if not methods, all but exonerated the putschists at the behest of key rightist government leaders. Based on West German Federal, Foreign Office, Bavarian, and Württemberg State, and Institute for Contemporary History (Munich) archives, printed documents, and secondary works; 73 notes.

D. Prowe

966. Stoakes, Geoffrey. 'MORE UNFINISHED BUSINESS?' SOME COMMENTS ON THE EVOLUTION OF THE NAZI FOREIGN POLICY PROGRAMME, 1919-24. *European Studies Rev. [Great Britain] 1978 8(4): 425-442.* Recent assessment of Nazi foreign policy ideas in the 1920's has been dominated by the figure of Adolf Hitler. Hitler's ideas must be placed in perspective by comparing them with the views of other Nazi writers. This article examines the questions of a German alliance with Russia and the Nazi Party's acceptance of geopolitical ideas. The writings of party philosopher Alfred Rosenberg (1893-1946) refute the recent suggestion of uncertainty in Nazi policy toward Russia. The possibility of an alliance with nationalist forces in Russia did not mitigate German territorial demands on Russia or the party's anti-Bolshevik orientation. Nor did Rosenberg use the term Lebensraum before 1926. German territorial ambition in the early 1920's owed more to Pan-German theory than to notions of geopolitics. Primary sources; 66 notes.

J. L. White

967. Stokes, Lawrence D. THE SOCIAL COMPOSITION OF THE NAZI PARTY IN EUTIN, 1925-32. *Int. Rev. of Social Hist. [Netherlands] 1978 23(1): 1-32.* Examines the social composition of a local unit of the Nazi Party in Eutin, Holstein, between 1925 and 1933. A Nazi stronghold, Eutin had a predominantly middle-class party membership, but with a very notable proletarian contingent. Entrepreneurs made up a substantial minority of party members. Handicraftsmen were numerous but contributed in a limited way to the leadership of the local unit, which was concentrated in the hands of traditional elites. The average age of the Eutin Nazis was 34.8 years. Based on the US National Archives German sources; 5 tables.

G. P. Blum

968.   Tracey, Donald R.   THE DEVELOPMENT OF THE NATIONAL SO-
CIALIST PARTY IN THURINGIA, 1924-30.   *Central European Hist. 1975
8(1): 23-50.* Presents the development of the Nazi party in Thuringia as a model
for understanding its development in Germany as a whole. The party strife, the
early, amateurish Nazi efforts, the coalition with *völkisch* elements, and the
maturing, parliamentary phase are all described in detail. The first coalition
government which included Nazis was in Thuringia. Based largely on unpublished German sources; 140 notes.   C. R. Lovin

969.   Trumpp, Thomas.   ZUR FINANZIERUNG DER NSDAP DURCH
DIE DEUTSCHE GROSSINDUSTRIE. VERSUCH EINER BILANZ
[The financing of the Nazi Party (NSDAP) by German heavy industry: attempt
at a balanced account]. *Geschichte in Wissenschaft und Unterricht [West Ger-
many] 1981 32(4): 223-241.* Summarizes the evidence on the role of German
heavy industry in financing the Nazi Party, especially in the period 1930-33, and
reviews the controversy between historians Henry Ashby Turner, Jr. and Dirk
Stegmann over this issue. This analysis concludes that it is impossible to determine the exact amount of financial support the Nazis received. Evidence indicates
most support from this group went to other nationalist parties, such as Alfred
Hugenberg's German National People's Party (DNVP). Though German heavy
industry does bear significant responsibility for the destruction of the first German republic, its financial support was probably not as decisive for Hitler's
success as the popular electoral support from middle levels of German society in
the depression of the 1930's. From a lecture at the West German Bundesarchiv,
23 October 1980. Based on primary sources; 58 notes.   L. D. Wilcox

970.   Turner, Henry Ashby, Jr.   GROSSUNTERNEHMERTUM UND NA-
TIONALSOZIALISMUS 1930-1933: KRITISCHES UND ERGÄNZENDES
ZU ZWEI NEUEN FORSCHUNGSBEITRÄGEN   [Big business and National
Socialism 1930-33: criticism and expansion of two new research contributions].
Hist. Zeitschrift [West Germany] 1975 221(1): 18-68. Two new articles are
reviving West German discussion of the relationship between big business leaders
and Nazism's rise to power. They are Axel Kuhn's "Die Unterredung zwischen
Hitler und Papen im Hause des Barons von Schröder" (*Geschichte in Wissenschaft und Unterricht* 1973 24: 709-722) and Dirk Stegmann's "Zum Verhältnis
von Grossindustrie und Nationalsozialismus 1930-1933" (*Archiv für Sozialgeschichte* 1973 13: 399-482). Kuhn's thesis that industrialists arranged a meeting
on 5 January 1933 between Adolf Hitler and Franz von Papen ignores other
factors in Hitler's decision-making at this time. Stegmann's thesis is an inadequate
variation of the "agent-theory" which portrays Hitler as an instrument of capitalists. 76 notes.   G. H. Davis

971.   Tyrell, Albrecht.   FÜHRERGEDANKE UND GAULEITERWECH-
SEL: DIE TEILUNG DES GAUES RHEINLAND DER NSDAP 1931
[The leadership idea and change of gauleiter: the division of the Nazi Rhineland
Gaue in 1931]. *Vierteljahrshefte für Zeitgeschichte [West Germany] 1975 23(4):
341-374* Nazism's leadership idea and principle guaranteed the gauleiter absolute
authority, but he earned his place through competition. The first change of office
was the succession of Heinz Haake by Robert Ley in the south Rhineland in 1925.
Ley appointed Gustav Simon to the Trier-Birkenfeld office in 1928. Simon inde-
pendently founded a newspaper and put himself forward as leader of a new area,

Koblenz-Trier. This ambition angered Ley, but in 1931 Gregor Strasser, the Reich administration leader, reconciled them by giving Ley the division of the Rhineland and Simon the Koblenz-Trier office. Based on documents in the Berlin Document Centre (BDC-OPG and PK), Federal Archives of Koblenz (BAK), and secondary works; 154 notes. A. Alcock

972. Tyrell, Albrecht. FÜHRERGEDANKE UND GAULEITERWECH-SEL. DIE TEILUNG DES GAUES RHEINLAND DER NSDAP 1931 [The Führer-idea and change of Gauleiter: the division of the Nazi Rhineland district in 1931]. *Rheinische Vierteljahrsblätter [West Germany] 1975 39(1-4): 237-271*. In summer 1931 the Nazi Party district (Gau) of the Rhineland, formerly headed by Robert Ley, was split up for organizational reasons. Josef Grohé became Gauleiter of Köln-Aachen and Gustav Simon Gauleiter of Koblenz-Trier. Based on documents in the Bundesarchiv Koblenz, printed documents and secondary literature; 154 notes. R. Wagnleitner

973. Volkmann, Hans-Erich. DAS AUSSENWIRTSCHAFTLICHE PRO-GRAMM DER NSDAP 1930-1933 [The external trade program of the NSDAP, 1930-33]. *Archiv für Sozialgeschichte [West Germany] 1977 17: 251-274*. Analyzes the Nazis' external trade policy, its place in contemporary economic and political thought, and its role in gaining the support of industrialists. Before 1930 Hitler did not believe in the necessity of an economic program. That Germany could not produce all of its necessities implied the need to extend German economic territory. Its means were to be economic, diplomatic, and eventually military. Its objectives lay mainly in South and East Europe, but extended to the whole continent and colonies. Though industry already supported the Nazis, some of its leaders were critical of this program. Based on the Federal Archive Koblenz, contemporary journals, and secondary works; 145 notes. H. W. Wurster

974. Wakefield, Kimball R. STRENGTH AND WEAKNESS: THE GER-MAN GENERALS, 1918-33. *Military Rev. 1974 54(11): 32-40*. Adolf Hitler used the German General Staff as unwitting tools in obtaining the chancellorship. Flaws within the staff led to its own destruction.

975. Walker, Lawrence. THE NAZI "YOUTH COHORT": THE MISSING VARIABLE. *Psychohistory Rev. 1980 9(1): 71-73*. Assesses Peter Loewenberg's psychohistorical analysis of the Nazi youth cohort. To the extent that Loewenberg's youth cohort thesis is dependent on demography and voting behavior, religious affiliation appears to be a stronger prediction of Nazi affiliation than Loewenberg realized. Youth cohort Catholics seem to have been consistent supporters of the Center from 1928 to 1932. The youth cohort thesis may be an incorrect explanation of group behavior toward Nazism. Secondary sources; 6 notes. J. M. Herrick

976. Wernette, Dee Richard. QUANTITATIVE METHODS IN STUDY-ING POLITICAL MOBILIZATION IN LATE WEIMAR GERMANY. *Hist. Methods Newsletter 1977 10(3): 97-101*. Reviews previous studies on the rise of Nazism, stressing the need for empirically testable data. Rejects the fallacy of transferring the characteristics of social aggregates to the characteristics of individuals. Control of the local means of political mobilization includes analyz-

ing the role of newspapers in explaining Adolf Hitler's rise to power. 15 notes.
D. K. Pickens

977. Wilcox, Larry D. HITLER DISCIPLINES HIS PRESS: "THE STRONGEST SURVIVE." *Gazette [Netherlands] 1973 19(1): 38-45.* Though Adolf Hitler in the 1920's maintained that competition between newspapers in Germany improved them, he favored news sources sanctioned by the Nazi Party and virtually forbade competition with them.

978. Winkler, Heinrich August. GERMAN SOCIETY, HITLER AND THE ILLUSION OF RESTORATION 1930-33. *J. of Contemporary Hist. [Great Britain] 1976 11(4): 1-16.* Two groups which remained largely immune to Nazi propaganda before 1933 were the Catholics and the Social Democratic workers. The majority of the National Socialist electorate came from the Protestant middle classes, especially the white collar workers, although the Nazis had to explain to them initially that the "Socialist" in the NSDAP did not mean abolition of private property. Big entrepreneurs also remained skeptical at first of the political aims of the Nazis. It was the *Reichslandbund,* representing the interests of indebted East Elbian landowners, which more directly and successfully influenced Adolf Hitler's coming to power on 30 January 1933. Small businessmen and some Protestant peasants were won over by the Fighting League against Department Stores and Consumer Cooperatives and the promise of the obliteration of class struggle, parliamentary government, and political pluralism. It was not anti-Semitism which made Nazism a mass movement in Germany. It was the hope of an authoritarian system of order. Primary and secondary sources; 19 notes.
M. P. Trauth

979. Zender, Matthias. VOLKSBRAUCH UND POLITIK. LICHTERUM-ZÜGE UND JAHRESFEUER VON 1900-1934 MIT 10 KARTEN [People's customs and politics: Light processions and year-fires, 1900-34. With ten maps]. *Rheinische Vierteljahrsblätter [West Germany] 1974 38(1-4): 355-385.* Analyzes the political exploitation of social customs in the Rhineland by German right-wing parties between 1900 and 1934.
R. Wagnleitner

9

THE END OF THE REPUBLIC

980. Abraham, David. CONFLICTS WITHIN GERMAN INDUSTRY AND THE COLLAPSE OF THE WEIMAR REPUBLIC. *Past & Present [Great Britain] 1980 (88): 88-128.* Discusses the role of German industry, 1880-1930, in the collapse of the Weimar Republic and the rise of the Nazis. Struggles within industry arose because different branches of industry supported coalitions with either organized labor or the rural sector. There were also differences over whether to incorporate, mould, or repress the attitudes and energies of the subordinate classes, and in ideology, economics, and politics industry was divided into liberal and national camps. Based on chapter 3 of the author's *Collapse of the Weimar Republic: Political Economy and Political Crisis,* (Princeton, 1980); 6 tables, 108 notes.   J. Powell

981. Bessel, Richard. THE POTEMPA MURDER. *Central European Hist. 1977 10(3): 241-254.* Describes in detail the murder by SA troops of Konrad Pietrzuch in the Silesian village of Potempa in August 1932. This was one murder among many elevated to national interest because it was a test of new antiterrorist legislation and because Hitler publicly supported the murderers. Based on Polish archival material; 44 notes.   C. R. Lovin

982. Blaich, Fritz. WIRTSCHAFTLICHER PARTIKULARISMUS DEUTSCHER LÄNDER WÄHREND DER WELTWIRTSCHAFTSKRISE 1932: DAS BEISPIEL DER AUTO-UNION AG [Economic particularism of German states during the world economic crisis of 1932: the example of Auto Union A.G.]. *Vierteljahrshefte für Zeitgeschichte [West Germany] 1976 24(4): 406-414.* Although the index sale price of automobiles during 1925-32 fell from 100 to 53.8, the Saxon government in 1932 invested six million Reichmarks in Auto Union. The finance minister, Dr. Hedrich, defended this on grounds of high unemployment in Saxony. Reinhold Maier, the Württemberg economics minister, argued that such protectionism would damage the Daimler Benz factory in Württemberg. Before Maier could take reprisals, the Nazis had gained control of Württemberg. Based on material in the State Archives in Dresden (series Saxony), and secondary works; 36 notes.   A. Alcock

983. Braatz, Werner. FRANZ VON PAPEN UND DIE FRAGE DER REICHSREFORM [Franz von Papen and the question of reform of the state]. *Politische Vierteljahresschrift [West Germany] 1975 16(3): 319-340.* Although there were good reasons in the summer and fall of 1932 for implementing constitutional and administrative reforms in Germany, Papen's attempts to increase the

autonomy of the states contributed to the weakening of state institutions. After the 1932 coup in Prussia the state leaders realized that the government saw its salvation in extreme authoritarianism. Their refusal to accept a united instead of a federal state, and their unwillingness to compromise when reform was carried out, led to insoluble difficulties. Based on archives, newspapers, and secondary works; 50 notes.   A. Alcock

984. Breitman, Richard. ON GERMAN SOCIAL DEMOCRACY AND GENERAL SCHLEICHER 1932-33. *Central European Hist. 1976 9(4): 352-378.* Discusses the tactics of the Social Democratic Party (SPD) and the labor unions regarding general Kurt von Schleicher's efforts to form a stable government in 1932-33. The SPD lacked a sense of urgency about the Nazi threat but would have probably been unable to stop Hitler's takeover legitimately since "Hitler obtained power only by way of the smoke-filled rooms to which the Social Democrats lacked entry." Based on archival sources; 93 notes.   C. R. Lovin

985. Carroll, D. F. THE ROLE OF KURT VON SCHLEICHER IN THE FALL OF THE WEIMER REPUBLIC. *Int. Rev. of Hist. and Pol. Sci. [India] 1972 9(4): 35-60.* The role of Kurt von Schleicher in the pre-Nazi period is ambiguous at best. For most of his years connected with the Hindenburg government, Schleicher operated behind the scenes and manipulated his chosen officeholders to carry out his plans. His maneuvers led to political instability which benefited the Nazis. Unable to achieve popular support in a direct cabinet office, Schleicher's government fell and Hitler became chancellor. Secondary sources; 144 notes.   E. McCarthy

986. Collotti, Enzo. LA FINE DELLA REPUBBLICA DI WEIMAR NELLE MEMORIE DI BRÜNING [The end of the Weimar Republic in Brüning's memoirs]. *Movimento di Liberazione in Italia [Italy] 1971 23(105): 79-95.* Heinrich Brüning (1885-1970), a man of learning and integrity, was Germany's last respectable chancellor before Hitler. Unable and disinclined to save a moribund democracy, he ruled by emergency decrees to cope with an unprecedented economic and political crisis. The verdict on Brüning's statesmanship has been generally unfavorable. His long-awaited *Memoiren 1918-1934* (Stuttgart: Deutsche Verlags-Anstalt, 1970) appeared shortly after his death. They were disappointing, and what little new is offered in the large volume may strengthen the position of his critics and detractors.   H. W. L. Freudenthal

987. Erdmann, Karl Dietrich. VOM SCHEITERN EINER DEMOKRATIE: FORSCHUNGSPROBLEME ZUM UNTERGANG DER WEIMARER REPUBLIK [The shattering of a democracy: problems of research on the decline of the Weimar Republic]. *Geschichte in Wissenschaft und Unterricht [West Germany] 1981 32(2): 65-78.* Summarizes a colloquium among 12 leading German historians on the problem of the failure of the Weimar Republic. Discusses the impact of the Versailles Treaty, the lack of social consensus, the economic catastrophes of 1923 and the early 1930's, the misuse of presidential powers under Article 48 of the Weimar constitution, and the political mentality of the republican parties, especially the Social Democrats. The complete papers of the colloquium have been published as Karl Dietrich Erdmann and Hagen Schulze, ed., *Weimar: Selbstpreisgage einer Demokratie: Eine Bilanz Heute— Kölner Kolloquium der Fritz Thyssen Stiftung Juni 1979* (1980). Based on a lecture delivered in Munich in May 1980.   L. D. Wilcox

988. Evans, Ellen L. and Baylen, Joseph O. HISTORY AS PROPAGANDA: THE GERMAN FOREIGN OFFICE AND THE "ENLIGHTENMENT" OF AMERICAN HISTORIANS ON THE WAR GUILT QUESTION, 1930-1933. *Can. J. of Hist. 1975 10(2): 185-208.* Examines the campaign of the *Kriegsschuldreferat,* a subdivision of the German Foreign Office, to assist American revisionists and the work of Alfred von Wegerer, editor of the office's journal, in publicizing the works of the American revisionist historians prior to Hitler's assumption of power.

989. Fejes, Judit. A MAGYAR-NÉMET POLITIKAI ÉS GAZDASÁGI KAPCSOLATOK KÉRDÉSÉHEZ AZ 1920-AS—1930-AS ÉVEK FORDULÓJÁN [Remarks on Hungarian-German economic and political relations in the late 1920's and 1930's]. *Történelmi Szemle [Hungary] 1976 19(3): 361-384.* Elaborates on the revisionist foreign policies of the Hungarian prime minister, István Bethlen, and of the German chancellor, Heinrich Brüning, whose policy is compared with Gustav Stresemann's. Explains the national interests of each country, which led to their closer political and economic relations, especially in the form of a Hungarian-German commercial treaty. Analyzes Bethlen's 1930 talks in Berlin, which were a decisive step toward concluding the commercial treaty. Based on German archival material. J/S

990. François-Poncet, A. AMINTIRILE UNUI AMBASADOR LA BERLIN [Memoirs of an ambassador to Berlin]. *Magazin Istoric [Rumania] 1975 9(12): 44-48, 1976 10(2): 56-60, 10(3): 46-51.* Part I: PAPEN-"OMUL DE ÎNCREDERE" AL LUI HINDENBURG [Hindenburg's reliable man]. Reproduces and translates into Rumanian, extracts from the diaries of a French ambassador to Berlin, which describe political developments in 1932, especially Paul von Hindenburg's choice of Franz von Papen as Chancellor and the general elections. Part II: MOARTEA LUI HINDENBURG [The death of Hindenburg]. Reproduces sections of the diaries which consider the immediate consequences of Hindenburg's death in 1934. Part III: SCHIMBAREA GĂRZII [The changing of the guard]. Reproduces those sections of the diaries which describe events leading to and the purge of German army officers in 1938, and discusses the political implications.

991. Garvy, George. KEYNES AND THE ECONOMIC ACTIVISTS OF PRE-HITLER GERMANY. *J. of Pol. Econ. 1975 83(2): 391-405.* To curb economic depression, German economists between 1931 and 1932 prescribed counter-cyclical monetary and fiscal policies later advocated by John Maynard Keynes. S

992. Gates, Robert A. GERMAN SOCIALISM AND THE CRISIS OF 1929-33. *Central European Hist. 1974 7(4): 332-359.* Examines the failure of the German Socialist Party to develop or support imaginative antidepression measures in the 1929-33 period. Their support of Heinrich Brüning's policy of deflation when it was 'financially unnecessary' and 'politically suicidal' left the field open for the Nazis. Based on archival and secondary sources; 75 notes.
C. R. Lovin

993.   Gotschlich, Helga.   REICHSBANNER SCHWARZ-ROT-GOLD UND ANTIFASCHISTISCHER WIDERSTAND (1930-1933)   [Reichsbanner Schwarz-Rot-Gold and antifascist resistance, 1930-33]. *Militärgeschichte [East Germany] 1980 19(5): 534-546.* The leaders of the Reichsbanner, reacting to the growth of the National Socialist party and the disappointment of their own membership, determined in September 1930 to strengthen the organization and mount an antifascist campaign in support of the republic. Nevertheless, their refusal to ally with the Communist Party in a common front and their support for Hindenburg in 1932 demonstrated they were deluded in thinking that German democracy could be saved in that way. Central State Archives, Potsdam; Central Party Archives, Berlin; 7 photos, 49 notes.   H. D. Andrews

994.   Graml, Hermann.   PRÄSIDIALSYSTEM UND AUSSENPOLITIK [Presidential system and foreign policy]. *Vierteljahrshefte für Zeitgeschichte [West Germany] 1973 21(2): 134-145.* Heinrich Brüning's foreign policy formed an essential part of his great effort of restoration and constituted the renunciation of Stresemann's principle of international integration. He accepted the economic crisis and utilized it in support of his policy on reparations and rearmament. The insolvency of the government was to serve as a weapon against its liabilities. Brüning's aim was to recover Germany's full freedom of action in international politics. In this respect he contributed to the progress of fascism at home and paved the way for Nazi foreign policy. Based on the Brüning memoirs and secondary works; 26 notes.   U. Wengenroth

995.   Haertel, Volker.   HITLER CONTRA HINDENBURG: ANALYSE EINES POLITISCHEN PLAKATS   [Hitler against Hindenburg: analysis of a political poster]. *Geschichte in Wissenschaft und Unterricht [West Germany] 1975 26(12): 733-743.* Analyzes a political poster and recommends its use in interdisciplinary teaching. An examination of the graphic and rhetorical methods, structure, and contents reveals the techniques of political propaganda through this medium. The poster pictures the state of Weimar: Hindenburg's supporters have already abandoned democratic values and argue against them. Primary sources and secondary works; 35 notes.   H. W. Wurster

996.   Hayes, Peter.   A QUESTION MARK WITH EPAULETTES? KURT VON SCHLEICHER AND WEIMAR POLITICS.   *J. of Modern Hist. 1980 52(1): 35-65.* Research sources on General Kurt von Schleicher are slim; he kept few records himself and those that did exist were destroyed by the Nazis or an Allied air raid on the military archives at Potsdam. Schleicher was not erratic or opportunistic but acted consistently to serve broader and more complex goals than those of the German army. But his moves alternately to contain the Nazis or kill them with kindness failed, and his political methods and maneuvering contributed to his destruction. Schleicher's pragmatism and the fact that he was accountable as chancellor to no one but President Paul von Hindenburg caused misgivings, and by 1933 he had numerous political enemies. "Kurt von Schleicher personified the schizophrenia of Weimar's political and social Establishment." 107 notes.   S

997.   Hehn, Paul N.   THE COLLAPSE OF THE WEIMAR REPUBLIC AND THE NATIONALIST SOCIALIST REVOLUTION, 1932-33, THE VIEW FROM WARSAW AND MOSCOW.   *Polish Rev. 1980 25(3-4): 28-48.*

German foreign policy underwent a diplomatic revolution in 1932 with the establishment of a cabinet under Franz von Papen (1879-1969), who was influenced by a German army fearful of a Polish invasion. Germany at this time also sought a rapprochement with France, and for a short time abandoned its eastern orientation, marking the end of the period dominated by German-Soviet friendship. As tensions with Germany mounted Poland, fearing it would be replaced by Russia as France's main ally in the East, was forced to consider its bad relations with the USSR. The latter also moved to improve relations with Poland and France. The Polish-Soviet Nonagression Pact (April 1932) was taken seriously by neither party. Josef Pilsudski continued to look upon Russia as the major enemy, and the Soviets regarded the rise of Nazism as a greater danger than did the Poles. Based on Polish, French, Soviet, and British diplomatic documents; 76 notes. W. F. Young

998. Hess, Jürgen C. GAB ES EINE ALTERNATIVE? ZUM SCHEITERN DES LINKSLIBERALISMUS IN DER WEIMARER REPUBLIK [Was there an alternative? On the destruction of left-liberalism in the Weimar Republic]. *Hist. Zeitschrift [West Germany] 1976 223(3): 638-654.* A historiographical discussion of the crisis of left-wing liberalism in the late Weimar period. Reflects on the view of about 30 books, mostly German, published during the 1960's and 1970's and relates them to the author's own research. Special emphasis is placed on Lothar Aretin's "German Liberalism and the Founding of the Weimar Republic: A Missed Opportunity?" in A. J. Nicholls and Erich Matthias, ed., *German Democracy and the Triumph of Hitler* (London, 1971). The author denies that the liberal newspapers caused the fall of liberalism. 35 notes. G. H. Davis

999. Ijūin, Ritsu. BRÜNING NAIKAKU NO SEIRITSU NI TSUITE [The formation of the Brüning cabinet]. *Rekishigaku Kenkyū [Japan] 1974 (412): 1-23.* Reorders disputed points in the formation of Heinrich Brüing's cabinet in the spring of 1930 using new historical materials. Treats four main issues: 1) the failure of the Grand Coalition cabinet of Hermann Müller caused by the essential opposition of interests between the capitalist classes and the working classes in the question of unemployment insurance; 2) the collapse of the Müller Cabinet by maneuvering of the military authorities—propulsion toward the shift to the presidential cabinet of Brüning; 3) the Brüning cabinet's financial policy; and 4) the parliamentary countermeasures for adoption of financial bills and the destruction of parliamentary democracy by the cabinet. Through analyses of the above themes, the author approaches the question of whether there were any possibility of defending democracy in Germany by mid-1930. Primary sources; 169 notes. S. Itō

1000. Jaitner, Klaus. DEUTSCHLAND, BRÜNING UND DIE FORMULIERUNG DER BRITISCHEN AUSSENPOLITIK MAI 1930 BIS JUNI 1932 [Germany, Brüning, and the formulation of British foreign policy, May 1930 to June 1932]. *Vierteljahrshefte für Zeitgeschichte [West Germany] 1980 28(4): 440-486.* Initially impressed with Chancellor Heinrich Brüning's (1930-32) leadership and competence in economic affairs, the British government was increasingly annoyed by the aggressive German pursuit of an Austro-German customs union and Brüning's unwillingness to compromise on disarmament and end of reparations. While British banking and industry circles supported Brüning's call for an immediate end of reparations, the Foreign Office worked toward a political-economic solution with significant German political concessions in exchange for ending reparations. Based on Foreign Office, Cabinet, and Prime Ministerial records of the Public Record Office; 192 notes.   D. Prowe

1001. Jones, Larry Eugene. BETWEEN THE FRONTS: THE GERMAN NATIONAL UNION OF COMMERCIAL EMPLOYEES FROM 1928 TO 1933. *J. of Modern Hist. 1976 48(3): 462-482.* Analyzes the relationship between the German National Union of Commercial Employees and smaller bourgeois parties, 1928-33, as a case study in the breakdown of functional relations between economic interests and political parties which accompanied the paralysis of Germany's parliamentary institutions.

1002. Jones, Larry Eugene. SAMMLUNG ODER ZERSPLITTERUNG? DIE BESTREBUNGEN ZUR BILDUNG EINER NEUEN MITTELPARTEI IN DER ENDPHASE DER WEIMARER REPUBLIK 1930-1933 [Concentration or disintegration? The efforts to create a new party of the center in the closing years of the Weimar Republic, 1930-33]. *Vierteljahrshefte für Zeitgeschichte [West Germany] 1977 25(3): 265-304.* In reaction to the growing disintegration of the German political center after 1930, successive and increasingly numerous and determined attempts were made to integrate the middle-class political parties of Germany and create a unified liberal-democratic party. In spite of a significant potential for integration, the dream of a single party of the center was never realized largely because of practical disagreements over the policies of the Brüning Government, the jealousies of established party leaders, the German People's Party's turn to the right after Stresemann's death, and most importantly because of the fundamentally antiparliamentary attitude of the industrial leadership. Based on archival documents, memoirs, and secondary sources; 183 notes.
D. Prowe

1003. Juhász, Gyula. AZ 1929-1933-AS GAZDASÁGI VÁLSÁG HATÁSA A NEMZETKÖZI VISZONYOKRA [The influence of the 1929-33 Depression on international relations]. *Magyar Tudományos Akad. Filozófiai és Történettudományok Osztályának Közleményei [Hungary] 1980 29(1-2): 35-40.* The most obvious political result of the Depression particularly in central and southeastern Europe was the rise of dictatorial, militaristic governments, culminating in the Nazi takeover in Germany. During the Depression years Great Britain and France expended most of their energies in maintaining their empires, and the United States adopted an isolationist stance in order to cope with its internal problems. Study of the short period from the Depression to World War II makes clear that war was inevitable.   A. M. Pogany

1004. Köhler, Henning. SOZIALPOLITIK VON BRÜNING BIS SCHLEICHER [Social policy from Brüning to Schleicher]. *Vierteljahrshefte für Zeitgeschichte [West Germany] 1973 21(2): 146-150.* The Brüning administration neither expected an early end to permanent unemployment nor believed that a future economic upswing would bring about the reabsorption of all the jobless in industry. The creation of subsistence farms for the jobless was viewed as an alternative. Hans Luther, president of the Reichsbank, developed a scheme of a moneyless economy for these settlements. Concurrently the voluntary labor service was established to gather up the jobless youth and to serve as a weapon in the struggle against radicalism. 10 notes.   U. Wengenroth

1005. Koszyk, Kurt. PAUL REUSCH UND DIE "MÜNCHNER NEUES-TEN NACHRICHTEN." ZUM PROBLEM INDUSTRIE UND PRESSE IN DER ENDPHASE DER WEIMARER REPUBLIK [Paul Reusch and the *Münchner Neuesten Nachrichten* (MNN). On the problem of industry and the press in the last years of the Weimar Republic]. *Vierteljahrshefte für Zeitgeschichte [West Germany] 1972 20(1): 75-103.* The conservative German industrialist, Paul Reusch (1868-1956), was one of a number of leaders of German industry who attempted to gain influence over newspapers in the Weimar era. Reusch, a member of the administrative committee of a firm (Knorr & Hirth GmbH) controlling various papers, tried to mould the editorial policy of the *Münchner Neuesten Nachrichten* in the years 1931-32 to conform with his political views, which at that time favored an understanding with Hitler. The editors of *MNN* were able to reject Reusch's interference. Twelve documents, Reusch's correspondence on this issue with editors and people close to Hitler, are reproduced. Based on documents in the archive of Reusch's metal works in Oberhausen, and on newspapers and secondary works; 84 notes.

J. B. Street

1006. Kuhn, Axel. DIE UNTERREDUNG ZWISCHEN HITLER UND PAPEN IM HAUSE DES BARONS VON SCHRÖDER [The conference between Hitler and Papen in the house of Baron von Schröder]. *Geschichte in Wissenschaft und Unterricht [West Germany] 1973 24(12): 709-722.* The comparison of the reports by Franz von Papen and by Baron Kurt von Schröder on the discussion between Papen and Adolf Hitler on 4 January 1933 shows that both sources differ from each other, providing a good introduction into the necessity of critical analysis of historical sources.

1007. Kulbakin, V. D. IZBIRATEL'NYE KAMPANII 1932 G. V GERMANII [The 1932 election campaigns in Germany]. *Voprosy Istorii [USSR] 1973 (6): 70-80.* Examines the 1932 reelection of the president of the Weimar Republic and the Prussian Landtag elections which are important links preceding the establishment of Germany's fascist dictatorship. Criticizes works by West German historians which present authentic historical facts in a distorted light and deliberately misrepresent the position and role of diverse social classes and groups in the period of the preparation and carrying out of the 1932 election campaigns. Steeped in their anti-Communist prejudices and adhering to the spurious "lesser evil" conception, the Social Democratic Party leaders rejected the proposal for united action advanced repeatedly by the German Communist Party, thereby enabling Hindenburg to gain the upper hand in the presidential elections and facilitating the Nazi victory in the elections to the Prussian Landtag. The experience of the 1932 elections in Germany underscores the importance of rallying all the democratic forces of society for the struggle against reaction. J

1008. Kul'bakin, V. D. PEREVOROT 1932 G. V PRUSSII I EGO OSVESH-CHENIE V ISTORICHESKOI LITERATURE FRG [The 1932 coup in Prussia and its treatment in historical literature in West Germany]. *Novaia i Noveishaia Istoriia [USSR] 1974 (4): 196-203.* Considers several works which have examined the coup d'etat of 20 July 1932 led by Franz von Papen, which removed the socialist premier of Prussia from power. Reactionary forces working to destroy the Weimar Republic engineered the coup. Although right-wing leaders of the Social Democratic Party (SPD) did not see the danger to German social democracy, the Communists saw the coup as a precursor to fascist dictatorship. The author considers the works of several historians, including E. Matthias, V. Abendrot, F. Friedenburg, K. D. Bracher, and A. Schwarz. Based on the works of the authors mentioned, articles in *Neues Deutschland,* and works by O. Braun and Fr. Stampfer; 47 notes.   A. J. Evans/S

1009. Martiny, Martin.   DIE ENTSTEHUNG UND POLITISCHE BEDEU-
TUNG DER "NEUEN BLÄTTER FÜR DEN SOZIALISMUS" UND IHRES
FREUNDESKREISES   [The origins and political importance of the *Neue Blätter für den Sozialismus* and its circle of supporters]. *Vierteljahrshefte für Zeitgeschichte [West Germany] 1977 25(3): 373-419.* The *Neue Blätter für den
Sozialismus,* a highly successful independent socialist journal of the last years of
the Weimar Republic (1929-33), brought together religious and philosophical
socialists, Youth Movement socialists (the Hofgeismar Circle), educational reformers, restless Social Democrats and unionists, and such notables as theologian
Paul Tillich and economist Eduard Heimann. Key documents relating to the
founding and development of the journal and the contributors' proposals for a
renewal of the Social Democratic Party are reprinted here. Based on contemporary publications, SPD archives, papers of editor August Rathmann, and secondary sources; 160 notes.   D. Prowe

1010. Miyazaki, Yoshio.   NACHISU SHIHAIKA NO KENPŌ JYŌKYŌ
[The Constitution and Nazism]. *Shakai Kagaku Kenkyū [Japan] 1979 31(3):
86-126.* Examines Nazi alteration of the Weimar Constitution through the Enabling Act of 1933 which granted full constitutional power to Hitler's dictatorship. Considers the vulnerability of the Weimar Constitution and the resultant
destruction of the judicial process.   105 notes.   Y. Aoki

1011. Molt, Harro.   HEGEMONIALBESTREBUNGEN DER DEUTSC-
HEN AUSSENPOLITIK IN DEN LETZTEN JAHREN DER WEIMARER
REPUBLIC: GUSTAV STOLPERS "DIENSTAG-KREIS"   [Aspirations toward a German foreign policy of hegemony in the last years of the Weimar
Republic: Gustav Stolper's "Tuesday Circle"]. *Jahrbuch des Inst. für Deutsche
Geschichte [Israel] 1976 5: 419-448.* Gustav Stolper, a Galician Jew who grew
up in Austria, moved to Weimar Germany where he exerted extraordinary political influence. In the editorial room of his *Deutsche Volkwirt* he presided over
the Tuesday Circle (Dienstag Kreis) to which came publishers, Reichstag members, high officials of the foreign office, and others influential in German foreign
policy. The *Deutsche Volkwirt* was said to be the best informed paper in Germany and its influence was enormous. The author discusses at some length such
interests of Stolper and his friends as the Mitteleuropa idea, the tariff union with
Austria, and steps toward the revision of the Versailles Treaty. 84 notes.
                                                                          M. Faissler

1012. Mommsen, Hans.   BETRACHTUNGEN ZU DEN MEMOIREN
HEINRICH BRÜNINGS   [Observations on the memoirs of Heinrich Brüning].
*Jahrbuch für die Geschichte Mittel- und Ostdeutschlands [West Germany] 1973
22: 270-280.* Although the contents of Brüning's memoirs published in 1970 will
necessitate little revision of the historiography of Weimar Germany, they do
present an unexpectedly frank exposition of the chancellor's combination of
tactical flexibility with unswerving adherence to his objectives. His objectives,

unrealized, were centralist, monarchical, and antidemocratic. His tactics contributed greatly to the weakening of the Weimar political system, and thereby helped to pave the way for the Nazi dictatorship. 20 notes.   J. A. Perkins

1013. Mommsen, Hans. DIE STELLUNG DER BEAMTENSCHAFT IN REICH, LÄNDERN UND GEMEINDEN IN DER ÄRA BRÜNING [The position of the civil service in the government, the provinces, and the municipalities during the Brüning era]. *Vierteljahrshefte für Zeitgeschichte [West Germany] 1973 21(2): 151-165.* Heinrich Brüning, influenced by the primacy of the reparations problem, decreed the cut in the civil servants' salaries to prove the insolvency of the Reich. Concurrently he brought about a financial crisis in regional government. In curtailing their subsidies he tried to push through centralization. The civil servants, victims in both cases, now felt abandoned by the state in spite of their traditional loyalty and turned increasingly to more radical alternatives. Consequently, even the slim chance of an authoritarian stabilization of the republic was forfeited. Based on documents in the Federal German Archives, and secondary works; 65 notes.   U. Wengenroth

1014. Mommsen, Hans. SOZIALISMUS UND NATIONALSOZIALISMUS: ANMERKUNGEN ZU EINER VERFEHLTEN DEBATTE [Socialism and National Socialism: observations on a misguided debate]. *Geschichtsdidaktik [West Germany] 1980 5(1): 1-7.* Examines the degree to which the Nazi movement expressed or promoted traditional German socialist principles.

1015. Morsey, Rudolf. BRÜNING UND BAYERN [Brüning and Bavaria]. *Archivalische Zeitschrift [West Germany] 1976 72: 199-208.* As German chancellor (1930-32) Heinrich Brüning (1885-1970) criticized Bavaria for its insufficient support for the German state. In Brüning's opinion the Bavarian government did not show enough understanding for the financial and economic problems of the central government in Berlin.

1016. Németh, István. AZ 1932-ES POROSZORSZÁGI ALLAMCSÍNY [The 1932 coup d'etat in Prussia]. *Párttörténeti Közlemények [Hungary] 1981 27(1): 148-182.* Between 1920 and 1932 Prussian politics were dominated by the Social Democrats led by Otto Braun. In 1932 the German National Socialist Workers' Party (NSDAP) captured 162 seats out of 423. Otto Braun's cabinet resigned and the new provincial legislation elected a Nazi president. Franz von Papen engineered a coup on July 20, declared a state of emergency, and handed all power over Prussia to General Karl von Rundstedt. Secondary sources; 95 notes.   P. I. Hidas

1017. Neveux, Jean B. LA JEUNESSE ET DES LUTTES POLITIQUES DANS "DER HITLERJUNGE QUEX" DE K. A. SCHENZINGER [Youth and political struggles in *Der Hitlerjunge Quex,* by K. A. Schenzinger]. *Rev. d'Allemagne [France] 1976 8(3): 431-448.* Describes the important but little recognized children's story, *Der Hitlerjunge Quex,* by K. A. Schenzinger, published in 1932, which perhaps unintentionally shows the psychological and political situation in Germany through the behavior of a young boy trying to decide between joining the Communist youth organization or joining the *Hitlerjugend.*

1018.   Newman, M. D.   BRITAIN AND THE GERMAN-AUSTRIAN CUSTOMS UNION PROPOSAL OF 1931. *European Studies Rev. [Great Britain] 1976 6(4): 449-472.* In March 1931 the German and Austrian governments announced their intention of establishing a customs union. British reaction was confused and ambiguous. Throws light on general British and Central European foreign policy during this period. Based on British Foreign Office reports; 60 notes.   S. P. Carr

1019.   Orde, Anne.   THE ORIGINS OF THE GERMAN-AUSTRIAN CUSTOMS UNION AFFAIR OF 1931. *Central European Hist. 1980 13(1): 36-59.* An updating of the customs union affair based on new evidence. Material in the Austrian archives hitherto not widely used allows different interpretations about the development and the announcement of the customs union. Specifically the recorded conversations of Austrian Foreign Affairs Minister Johann Schober and German Foreign Minister Julius Curtius in early March 1931 were used in this article. Although interpretations about specific portions of the events have been changed, the general consensus remains that the proposal would still have failed. Based on archival material; 76 notes.   C. R. Lovin

1020.   Petzina, Dietmar.   ELEMENTE DER WIRTSCHAFTSPOLITIK IN DER SPÄTPHASE DER WEIMARER REPUBLIK   [Elements of economic policy during the final stages of the Weimar Republic]. *Vierteljahrshefte für Zeitgeschichte [West Germany] 1973 21(2): 127-133.* Regards the pursuance of liberal economic objectives by means of a bureaucratic interventionist approach as the major inconsistency of Weimar economic policy. The fundamentals of crisis management were still determined by prewar experience. As a balanced budget remained also a crucial task with respect to foreign policy, subsidies had to be restricted. The ability to bypass parliament enabled the Brüning government to provide financial support for industry and agriculture at the expense of public welfare expenditures. 2 notes.   U. Wengenroth

1021.   Poulain, Marc.   DEUTSCHLANDS DRANG NACH SÜDOSTEN CONTRA MUSSOLINIS HINTERLANDPOLITIK   [Germany's pressure in the Southeast against Mussolini's hinterland policy]. *Donauraum [Austria] 1977 22(3): 129-153.* After the 1931 failure of the Austro-German customs union project, Germany penetrated Southeastern Europe through trade. France and Great Britain did not compete with Germany in this area, and only Italy began to counteract the German offensive because German economic policy endangered Italian interests in the Adriatic. Based on documents in the Bundesarchiv Koblenz, printed documents, and secondary literature; 18 notes.   R. Wagnleitner

1022.   Riesenberger, Dieter.   AUSSENPOLITIK UND AUSSENHANDELSPOLITIK DES NATIONALSOZIALISMUS 1933-1939 ALS DIDAKTISCHES PROBLEM   [Nazi foreign policy and international trade policy, 1933-39, as a teaching problem]. Meyers, Peter and Riesenberger, Dieter, ed. *Der Nationalsozialismus in der historisch-politischen Bildung* (Göttingen: Vandenhoeck & Ruprecht, 1979): 185-214. Examines trade and foreign policies in Germany at the end of the Weimar Republic, noting restrictions placed on Germany by the Treaty of Versailles, and continuation and expansion of trade policies under the Nazis.

1023. Ruge, Wolfgang. KRANKTE UND STARB DIE WEIMARER REPUBLIK AM ERBE DER MILITÄRISCHEN NIEDERLAGE VON 1918? [Did the Weimar Republic sicken and die because of the military defeat of 1918?]. *R. d'Allemagne [France] 1974 6(2): 38-46.* Suggests it was not military defeat but the class character of the Weimar Republic which allowed its enemies to hold positions of leadership and thus make military defeat a mortal sin for the republic. R. K. Adams

1024. Salewski, Michael. ZUR DEUTSCHEN SICHERHEITSPOLITIK IN DER SPÄTZEIT DER WEIMARER REPUBLIK [German security policy in the late Weimar Republic]. *Vierteljahrshefte für Zeitgeschichte [West Germany] 1974 22(2): 121-147.* Chancellor Heinrich Brüning's (1885-1970) security policy, officially promoting general disarmament and equality for Germany, was in reality a powerful instrument for an aggressive revision of the Versailles Treaty in the East, distinguished from Hitler's foreign policy only in its style and sense of proportion, not in principal direction. Its source was 19th-century great power thinking and its goal not a new European detente, but Germany's return to great power status. Based on documents in the political archive of the Bonn Foreign Office, West German Federal Archives (Military), Brüning's memoirs, and secondary sources; 72 notes. D. Prowe

1025. Schmidt, Manfred. DIE HALTUNG DER ADGB-FÜHRUNG ZUR FASCHISTISCHER BEWEGUNG 1932-1933 [The attitude of the German General Trade Union Federation (ADGB) toward Nazism 1932-33]. *Beiträge zur Geschichte der Arbeiterbewegung [East Germany] 1979 21 (4): 583-592.* Analyzes the national and international policy of the largest class organization in the Weimar Republic, the Allgemeiner Deutsche Gewerkschaftsbund, during the last months before the Nazi takeover. This strong organization could not prevent the rise of a fascist dictatorship because it was a prisoner of a social reformist ideology. The struggle against the extreme Right was carried on by a weak bourgeois system which collapsed in January 1933. Primary sources; 67 notes. G. E. Pergl

1026. Schönhoven, Klaus. ZWISCHEN ANPASSUNG UND AUSSCHALTUNG: DIE BAYERISCHE VOLKSPARTEI IN DER ENDPHASE DER WEIMARER REPUBLIK 1932/1933 [Between accommodation and exclusion: The Bavarian People's Party in the last phase of the Weimar Republic, 1932-33]. *Hist. Zeitschrift [West Germany] 1977 224(2): 340-378.* The activities of the Bavarian People's Party (BVP) between 30 May 1932 and its dissolution in July 1934 are described and analyzed. After the resignation of Heinrich Brüning the BVP at first opposed the cabinet of Franz von Papen but became more cooperative after Papen came to Munich for talks. Leading elements in the BVP were willing to cooperate with the National Socialists or any other party except the Communists to support a government of which Hindenburg approved and which held the confidence of the Reichstag. The BVP finally dissolved itself under the pressure of National Socialist terror. 123 notes. G. H. Davis

1027. Schulz, Gerhard. REPARATIONEN UND KRISENPROBLEME NACH DEM WAHLSIEG DER NSDAP 1930. BETRACHTUNGEN ZUR REGIERUNG BRÜNING [Reparations and problems of crisis after the election triumph of the Nazi Party in 1930: reflections on the Brüning government].

Vierteljahrschrift für Sozial- und Wirtschaftsgeschichte [West Germany] 1980 67(2): 200-222. Reflections on key questions raised by historians about the last years of Weimar Germany regarding reparations and foreign credit, the Hoover moratorium and bank crisis, and the historical role of National Bank President Hans Luther (1879-1962) and Chancellor Heinrich Bruning (1885-1970). The author confirms previous conclusions that government reparations and monetary policies grew increasingly contradictory, while the inflexible economic policy of Luther and Brüning drove Germany into ever deeper crisis. Based on Bundesarchiv, Zentralarchiv Potsdam, German Foreign Ministry, Gutehoffnungshütte, Bayer, Institut für Zeitgeschichte and secondary works; 54 notes.   D. Prowe

1028. Schumacher, Martin.   ZWISCHEN "EINSCHALTUNG" UND "GLEICHSCHALTUNG": ZUM UNTERGANG DER DEUTSCHEN ZEN-TRUMSPARTEI 1932-33   [Between inclusion and unification: the downfall of the German Center Party, 1932-33]. *Hist. Jahrbuch [West Germany] 1979 99: 268-303.* Describes the decline of the political influence of the German Center Party, the representative of German Catholics, in 1928 due to discord in the leadership. In 1932 the government of Chancellor Heinrich Brüning was dismissed. The coalition between the Center Party and the Social Democrats collapsed. The right wing of the party under the leadership of Franz von Papen tried to cooperate with the rising National Socialist Party with the intent to include Center Party politicians in a new government. The Nazis, however, rejected any cooperation with other parties and demanded unification of all politics under their leadership. As a result, the Center Party ceased to exist in 1933. Based on documents found in the literary bequest of former party members; 147 notes, appendix.   R. Vilums

1029. Stürmer, Michael.   DER UNVOLLENDETE PARTEIENSTAAT: ZUR VORGESCHICHTE DES PRÄSIDIALREGIMES AM ENDE DER WEIMARER REPUBLIK   [The unfinished party state: the previous history of the presidential regime at the end of the Weimar Republic]. *Vierteljahrshefte für Zeitgeschichte [West Germany] 1973 21(2): 119-126.* Illustrates that well before the presidential regimes, the settlement of the political crisis was largely sought in an authority independent of parliament. Various proposed reforms were directed toward dismantling the welfare state, restricting the power of parliament, and establishing a plebiscitary pseudomonarchy. The circumvention of parliament was always possible. The congenital defect of the Weimar Republic, the separation of effective power and political responsibility, was never overcome and paved the way for the destructive antiparliamentary policy after 1930. 28 notes.   U. Wengenroth

1030. Sundhaussen, Holm.   POLITISCHES UND WIRTSCHAFTLICHES KALKÜL IN DEN AUSEINANDERSETZUNGEN ÜBER DIE DEUTSCH-RUMÄNISCHEN PRÄFERENZVEREINBARUNG VON 1931: EIN BEI-TRAG ZUR VORGESCHICHTE DES DEUTSCHEN "INFORMAL EMPIRE" IN SÜDOSTEUROPA   [Political and economic calculations in the discussions over the German-Rumanian preferential treatment agreement of 1931: a contribution to the background history of the German "Informal Empire" in southeast Europe]. *Rev. des Études Sud-Est Européenes [Rumania] 1976 14(3): 405-424.* At the beginning of the 1930's, economic collapse faced the nations of the Danube Basin. Since Germany was their chief trade partner among developed nations, agreements such as the 1931 Rumanian-German preferential trade agreement made sense. These, however, paved the way for German economic and political hegemony in the area, and therefore were opposed by other powers, particularly France. 118 notes.   J. C. Billigmeier

1031. Vagts, Alfred. HEINRICH BRÜNING: A REVIEW AND A MEMOIR. *Pol. Sci. Q. 1972 87(1): 80-89.* Reviews the career, life, and ideals of Heinrich Brüning by way of his *Memoiren, 1918-1934* (Stuttgart; Deutsche Verlags-Anstalt, 1970). During his political career after World War I, he participated as a Catholic and a civilian militarist with "soldierly resoluteness, disinterest, and loyalty at all times and particularly as chancellor." He worked for the restoration of a pre-Weimar stage, for which he asked from the major beneficiaries not much more than modest sacrifices and a decent business ethos. He was doomed to disappointment, betrayed by those who stood to benefit most from his policies, including the Church. 13 notes.   R. V. Ritter

1032. Vetter, Klaus. BODO VON DER MARWITZ. DER BEITRAG EINES PREUSSISCHEN JUNKERS ZUR IDEOLOGISCHEN VORBEREITUNG DES FASCHISMUS AUF DEM LANDE [Bodo von der Marwitz: the contribution of a Prussian junker to the ideological preparation of rural areas for fascism]. *Zeitschrift für Geschichtswissenschaft [East Germany] 1975 23(5): 552-568.* Bodo von der Marwitz (1893-?) was an average East Elbian Junker, who helped lay the ideological foundation for Nazism by opposing the Weimar Republic from its inception. Marwitz assisted the Nazis by promoting anticommunism, racism, and demagoguery, though he did not accept all the tenets of National Socialism. Based on documents from the archives on the Marwitz estate at Friedersdorf, now in the State Archives in Potsdam; 35 notes.
J. T. Walker

1033. Wengst, Udo. SCHLANGE-SCHÖNINGEN, OSTSIEDLUNG UND DIE DEMISSION DER REGIERUNG BRÜNING [Schlange-Schöningen, settlement in the East, and the end of the Brüning government]. *Geschichte in Wissenschaft und Unterricht [West Germany] 1979 30(9): 538-551.* Describes part of the conflict among the Minister for Employment Adam Stegerwald, the Commissioner for the East Hans Schlange-Schöningen, and President Paul von Hindenburg about settlement in the east in the final stage of the Heinrich Brüning government. Stegerwald saw settlement as a means of creating work, whereas the commissioner regarded it as establishing eastern German agriculture on a new basis. Brüning, however, considered it of lesser importance. Despite bad luck, Schlange-Schöningen had a chance of pushing his concept through the cabinet. But Hindenburg intervened and Schlange-Schöningen offered his resignation in order to show the unity of the government on this question, because he thought that only Brüning's government could carry out his program. But Hindenburg did not react as Schlange-Schöningen expected and thus Brüning's position was weakened in the decisive talk with Hindenburg on 29 May 1932. Unpublished sources mainly from the German Federal Archive, Koblenz; 64 notes.
H. W. Wurster

1034. Wengst, Udo. UNTERNEHMERVERBÄNDE UND GEWERKSCHAFTEN IN DEUTSCHLAND IM JAHRE 1930 [Employers associations and labor unions in Germany in 1930]. *Vierteljahrshefte für Zeitgeschichte [West*

Germany] 1977 25(1): 99-119. The last promising moves toward industry-labor cooperation in Weimar Germany, June-December 1930, were not wrecked simply by the confrontation politics of Ruhr industrialists. Labor unions, frightened by growing employer power and confidence, rejected their central leadership's overtures to the employers' organizations. Yet industrialists, concerned to counteract agricultural protectionism and to stabilize the political and economic situation, seemed to favor an accommodation with labor. Based on sources in Bundesarchiv (Koblenz) and Gutehoffnungshütte Archive (Oberhausen); 69 notes.

D. Prowe

1035.   Wheeler-Bennett, John.   THE END OF THE WEIMAR REPUBLIC. *Foreign Affairs 1972 50(2): 351-371.* Reconsiders the failure of the Weimar Republic, evaluating its principal figures and events in four periods: 1) Precarious Existence, with Friedrich Ebert as leader, 1918-20; 2) Obstinate Resistance under Walther Rathenau and Hans von Seeckt, 1920-23; 3) Reconciliation, led by Gustav Stresemann, 1923-30; and 4) Fatalistic Desperation under Heinrich Brüning, 1930-33. Special attention is given to the role of Brüning. A romanticist and monarchist, he visualized a restoration of monarchy on the English model as a means of checking the Nazis and preserving constitutional monarchy in Germany. Brüning's recently published memoirs reflect not the leader of 1930-33, but rather attitudes which developed as a result of World War II and later. Primary and secondary sources; 14 notes.   T. C. Caldwell

SUBJECT INDEX

Subject Profile Index (ABC-SPIndex) carries both generic and specific index terms. Begin a search at the general term but also look under more specific or related terms.

Each string of index descriptors is intended to present a profile of a given article; however, no particular relationship between any two terms in the profile is implied. Terms within the profile are listed alphabetically after the leading term. The variety of punctuation and capitalization reflects production methods and has no intrinsic meaning; e.g., there is no difference in meaning between "History, study of" and "History (study of)."

Cities, towns, and counties are normally listed in parentheses following their respective countries; e.g., "Germany (Munich)." Terms beginning with an arabic numeral are listed after the letter Z. The chronology of the bibliographic entry follows the subject index descriptors. In the chronology, "c" stands for "century"; e.g., "19c" means "19th century."

The last number in the index string, in italics, refers to the bibliographic entry number.

A

Abetz, Heinrich Otto. Franco-German reconciliation. War crimes. 1919-58. *528*

Academic freedom. Historiography. Military history. 1779-1975. *69*

Academy of Sciences. Einstein, Albert (documents). Germany (Berlin). 1913-33. *653*

Action Committee of Revolutionary Artists. Artists. Germany (Munich). November Revolution. 1918-19. *152*

Adenauer, Konrad. Germany (Cologne). Political Theory. 1917-33. *449*

Aesthetics. Art. Dada. Germany (Berlin). Press. 1920's. *555*

—. Bauhaus. Gropius, Walter. 1919-33. *584*

Africa. Anticommunist activities. Independence movements. 1919-39. *86*

—. Colonialism (Eurafrica concept). France. International administration, unified. 1876-1954. *1*

—. Colonies. Foreign Relations. Great Britain. 1920-36. *335*

Africans. Anti-Imperialism. 1919. *230*

Agricultural Cooperatives (documents). 1918-33. *641*

Agricultural Organizations. Economic Conditions. Interest Groups. 1920's. *453*

Agricultural policy. 1924-28. *363*

—. Braun, Otto. Civil-military relations. Germany (Pomerania). Provincial Government. 1919-20. *409*

Agricultural production. Consumption. World War I. 1907-25. *10*

—. Food supply. Politics. 1914-23. *9*

Agricultural reform. Junkers. 1919-45. *923*

Agriculture. Brüning, Heinrich. Hindenburg, Paul von. Schlange-Schöningen, Hans. Settlement. Stegerwald, Adam. 1931-32. *1033*

—. Communist Party. Hoernle, Edwin. 1920's-60's. *783*

—. Economic Conditions. 1918-33. *297*

—. Economic Policy. Economic Structure. Nazism. Peasants. 1907-33. *362*

—. Historiography. 1918-33. *314*

—. Political power. Socioeconomic structure. 1907-25. *11*

—. Protectionism. 1925-39. *364*

Air Forces. Great Britain. Military Strategy. 1920-39. *457*

Albertin, Lothar. Liberalism (review article). 1918-33. *469*

All Quiet on the Western Front (film). Censorship. Germany (Berlin). 1930-31. *572*

All-German Union. Austria. Nationalism. Samassa, Paul. ca 1888-1941. *638*

Alliance policy. Comintern (3d plenum). Communist Party. Peasants. Working class. 1923. *839*

Alliances. Czechoslovakia. Foch, Ferdinand (political tour). France. Poland. Ruhr, occupation of the. 1923. *267*

Allies. Ambassadors' Conference. Diplomacy. France. Sanctions. 1923. *378*

—. Armistice. Diplomacy. Habsburg Empire. Military occupation. World War I. 1918. *142*

—. Military control policy. Rearmament. 1918-31. *379*

Ambassadors. Decisionmaking. Europe. 1922-26. *519*

Ambassadors' Conference. Allies. Diplomacy. France. Sanctions. 1923. *378*

Anarchism and Anarchists. Assassination. Rathenau, Walther. Salomon, Ernst von. 1918-33. *270*

—. Communism (left).. Working Class. 1918-23. *784*

Anglo-French Accord. 1932. *308*

Annexation. Austria. Czechoslovakia. Pan-Germanism. Parliamentarians. 1921-28. *263*

—. Austria. Pan-Germanism. 1918-33. *331*

—. Belgium (Eupen-et-Malmédy). Locarno, treaty of. Stresemann, Gustav. 1925. *223*

Anschluss. Europe, Central. Expansionism. Foreign Policy. 1918-19. *203*

Anti-Americanism. Right. 1917-33. *507*

Anticapitalism. Conservative Revolution. Mohler, Armin. Youth movements. 1920's. *334*

Anticommunist activities. Africa. Independence movements. 1919-39. *86*

Anti-Fascism. Comintern. Communist Parties. Italy. Socialist Parties. United Front. 1919-23. *854*

Anti-Fascist Movements. Anti-Imperialism. Pieck, Wilhelm. Political Leadership. 1900-60's. *884*

—. Breitscheid, Rudolf. Popular front. 1874-1944. *880*

—. Communist Party. Historiography (East German). 1919-33. 1970's. *795*

—. Communist Party. Thälmann, Ernst. United front strategy. 1929-33. *788*

Auto Union. Automobile Industry and Trade.
Depressions. Germany (Saxony, Württemberg).
Government Enterprise. Protectionism. 1932.
982
Autobiography. Diaries. Mann, Thomas. 1918-36.
610
Autobiography and Memoirs. Gundelach, Gustav.
Helm, Rolf. International Red Aid. Moser,
Mentona. 1921-40. *851*
Automobile Industry and Trade. Auto Union.
Depressions. Germany (Saxony, Württemberg).
Government Enterprise. Protectionism. 1932.
982
Automobile Industry and Trade (rationalization
plans). Consumer attitudes. 1924-29. *294*
Autonomy. Federalism. Germany (Bavaria).
1918-75. *23*
—. France. Rhineland. Ruhr crisis. Stresemann,
Gustav. 1923-24. *397*
Avant-garde (term). Expressionism. 20c. *659*

B

Badia, Gilbert. Luxemburg, Rosa (review article).
1890's-1919. *155*
—. Luxemburg, Rosa (review article). 1898-1919.
159
Balance of payments. Economic Theory. Graham,
Frank D. Ohlin, B. Reparations. 1925-29.
549
Balance of power. Europe. 1800-1945. *82*
—. Foreign Policy. Rapallo Treaty (1922).
Revisionism. USSR. 1922. *268*
—. Foreign Relations (review article). 18c-20c.
59
Balkans. Foreign Policy. *Tat* (magazine). 1918-33.
477
Ballin, Günther. Jews. Mayer, Paul "Yogi".
Nationalism. Youth Movements. 1932-34.
714
Baltic states. Germans. Haller, Johannes.
Propaganda. Russia. World War I. 1914-30.
374
Bank of England. Business. Europe, Central.
1918-24. *523*
Banks. Foreign deposits. Inflation. Reparations.
1918-23. *393*
Barclay, C. N. (personal narrative). Army Staff
College. Germany (East Prussia). Great Britain.
Travel. 1931. *278*
Barth, Karl. Ethics. Liberalism. Niebuhr,
Reinhold. 1920's-60. *735*
Barth, Karl (letters). Bultmann, Rudolf (letters).
Theology. ca 1920-40. *744*
Bauhaus. Aesthetics. Gropius, Walter. 1919-33.
584
—. Architecture. Gropius, Walter. 1919-30's.
558
Baur, Erwin. Blakeslee, Albert F. Eugenics.
1921-23. *582*
Bavarian People's Party. Politics. 1932-33. *1026*
Beer-hall putsch. Coups d'Etat. Germany (Munich).
Hitler, Adolf. Nazi Party. 1913-23. *911*
—. Diplomatic dispatches (French). Germany
(Bavaria). 1923. *925*
Behavior. Catholics. France (Alsace). Germany
(Baden). Jews. Protestants. Religion.
1871-1939. *759*
Beimler, Hans. Political activities. 1918-36. *810*
Belgium. Diplomacy. Ruhr occupation. 1920-23.
380
Belgium (Eupen-et-Malmédy). Annexation.
Locarno, treaty of. Stresemann, Gustav. 1925.
223
—. Boundaries. France. Great Britain. 1924-26.
370

Beneš, Eduard. Czechoslovakia. Economic
cooperation. Schubert, Carl von. 1928. *419*
Berlin Journal. Parliaments. Union of Poles in
Germany. 1919-33. *482*
Berlin, University of. Theater Science, Institute for.
1919-22. *617*
Bernstein, Eduard. Europe, Western. Socialism.
1850-1932. *621*
—. Political Factions. Revisionism. Social
Democratic Party. 1850-1932. *808*
Bible, Buber-Rosenzweig. Jews. Philosophy of
History. Religion, fundamentalist. Translation.
1918. *692*
Bibliographies. 1920-45. 1975-79. *36*
—. Archives. Research. 1918-78. *77*
—. Austria. Economic History. Social history.
19c-20c. *85*
—. Hilferding, Rudolf. 1899-1941. *423*
—. Historiography. 1871-1945. *114*
—. Historiography. 1918-33. 1972-77. *37*
—. Methodology. Political participation. Weber,
Max. ca 1889-1920. *573*
—. Middle Classes. Politics. 1871-1933. *68*
—. Moses, Julius (papers). Public Health (policy).
Socialism. ca 1920-42. *619*
—. Navies. Revolution. 1917-19. *793*
Biographies. Rathenau, Walther. 1900-72. *662*
Biography. Historiography. Stresemann, Gustav
(review article). 1878-1929. 1978. *338*
Bishop, office of. Evangelical Church. 16c-20c.
739
Blakeslee, Albert F. Baur, Erwin. Eugenics.
1921-23. *582*
Blau-Weiss. Youth movement. Zionism. 1907-22.
718
Blenkle, Conrad (biography). Communist Party.
1901-42. *821*
Bloch, Joseph. Europe. Socialism. *Sozialistische
Monatshefte* (periodical). World War I.
1888-1936. *17*
—. European unity. Social Democratic Party.
Sozialistische Monatshefte (periodical). Zionism.
1871-1936. *674*
—. Politics. *Sozialistischen Monatshefte*
(periodical). 1919-33. *296*
Bolsheviks. Comintern. Levi, Paul. 1921-22.
824
Bolshevism. Communist Party. Leftism. Political
Factions. Spartacism. 1918-23. *775*
Bonapartism. Trotsky, Leon. 1930-33. *826*
Bond market. Local government. Public Finance.
1925-30. *407*
Bonhoeffer, Dietrich. Nazism. 1920-45. *750*
Book Industries and Trade. Jews. Olschki family.
Rosenthal family. 1859-1976. *716*
Boundaries. Belgium (Eupen-et-Malmédy). France.
Great Britain. 1924-26. *370*
—. Czechoslovakia. Foreign Relations. Locarno
Conference. 1925. *361*
—. Diplomacy. Poland. 1919. *154*
—. Foreign Policy. Germany (Rhineland).
Millennium celebration. 1919-24. *480*
Boundaries (revision). Danish-German Border
Stream Commission. Versailles, Treaty of.
1920-22. *377*
Bracher, Karl Dietrich. Fascism. Historiography.
1920's-30's. 1960's-70's. *128*
Braun, Otto. Agricultural policy. Civil-military
relations. Germany (Pomerania). Provincial
Government. 1919-20. *409*
—. Coups d'Etat. Germany (Prussia). Nazi Party.
Papen, Franz von. Rundstedt, Karl von. Social
Democratic Party. 1932. *1016*
Braun, Otto (letters). Exiles. Politics. Wirth,
Joseph (fall of). 1920's-45. *505*
Braun, Otto (review article). Germany (Prussia).
Schulze, Hagen. 1919-32. *447*

Brecht, Alfred (memoirs). Protestantism. Urach Theological Seminary. 20c. *737*
Breitscheid, Rudolf. Anti-Fascist Movements. Popular front. 1874-1944. *880*
Brockdorff-Rantzau, Ulrich von. Diplomacy. Trade. USSR. 1922-28. *265*
—. Foreign policy. Kopp, Viktor. USSR. 1918-19. *185*
—. Historiography. ca 1900-28. *332*
Brüning, Heinrich. Agriculture. Hindenburg, Paul von. Schlange-Schöningen, Hans. Settlement. Stegerwald, Adam. 1931-32. *1033*
—. Cabinet (formation of). 1930. *999*
—. Center Party (review article). Historiography. 1928-33. 1950's-70's. *341*
—. Centralization. Civil Service. Financial crisis. 1930-32. *1013*
—. Depression. Economic Policy. Nazis. Socialist Party. 1929-33. *992*
—. Economic Policy. Foreign policy. 1930-32. *1000*
—. Economic policy. Luther, Hans. Reparations. 1930-32. *1027*
—. Foreign Policy. Presidency. 1930-32. *994*
—. Foreign policy. Versailles, Treaty of (revision). 1930-32. *1024*
—. Germany (Bavaria). Intergovernmental Relations. 1930-32. *1015*
—. Periodization of History. Political Leadership. 1918-33. *1035*
Brüning, Heinrich (dismissal). Hindenburg, Paul von. Lobbying. Neudeck estate, gift of. 1927-34. *533*
Brüning, Heinrich (memoirs). 1918-1934. *1031*
—. 1918-34. *986*
—. Government. 1918-34. *413*
—. Political system. ca 1924-32. *1012*
Buber, Martin. Jews. 1913-57. *683*
—. Jews. Youth Movements. 1914-38. *719*
—. Judaism. Theology. Translating and Interpreting. 1906-62. *697*
—. Landauer, Gustav. Youth Movements. 1920's. *612*
Bulgaria. Austria. Disarmament. Hungary. World Disarmament Conference. 1932-33. *525*
—. Dimitrov, Georgi. Labor unions. Social Democrats. World War I. ca 1890-1919. *211*
Bultmann, Rudolf (letters). Barth, Karl (letters). Theology. ca 1920-40. *744*
Bureaucracies. Class consciousness. Consumption. Labor, white-collar. Middle classes. 1920's. *566*
Bureaucracy. Political leadership. Public Finance. 1918-24. *539*
Business. Bank of England. Europe, Central. 1918-24. *523*
—. Economic policy. Emergency Union of German Science. Haber, Fritz. Science. 1920-33. *636*
—. Economic Policy. Government regulation. Rathenau, Walther. 1907-22. *448*
—. Economic Regulations. Germany, West. Government. Social Policy. 1918-77. *33*
—. Foreign policy. Houghton, Alanson B. Reconstruction. USA. 1920's. *316*
—. France. Great Britain. Leadership. Recruitment. USA. 1760-1970. *74*
—. Subsidies. 1925-32. *295*
Business cycle. Capital imports. 1920's. *342*
Business History. Foreign policy. Government. Krupp, Gustav. Stresemann, Gustav. 1925. *478*
—. Historiography. 1918-74. *70*
Business leaders. Historiography. Hitler, Adolf. Nazism. Papen, Franz von. 1933. *970*
Businessman, small. Middle Classes (Mittelstand). Nazism. Social protectionism. 1848-1945. *134*

C

Cabinet discussions. Locarno, treaty of. Stresemann, Gustav. 1925. *324*
Cabinet (formation of). Brüning, Heinrich. 1930. *999*
Cabinet (minutes). Documents (review article). 1919-33. *458*
Cabinet of Dr. Caligari (film). Expressionism. Films. 1910-20. *560*
Calwer, Richard. Europe. Imperialism. Quessel, Ludwig. Socialism. *Sozialistische Monatshefte* (journal). 1905-18. *180*
Camparter, Eduard. Anti-Semitism. 1860-1945. *755*
Canada. Europe. Industrial unionism. Labor Unions and Organizations. Syndicalism. USA. 1900-25. *103*
Capital imports. Business cycle. 1920's. *342*
Capitalism. Economic Theory. Luxemburg, Rosa. 1870-1919. *146*
—. Fascism, interpretations of. Historiography. 1920's-30's. *956*
—. Nazism (review article). 1920's-30's. 1976-77. *101*
—. November Revolution. Working Class. 1918-19. *187*
Capitalism, managerial. Rathenau, Walther. Socialism. 1880-1922. *656*
Capitalism, Monopoly. Europe, Eastern. Fascism. Italy. 1900-80. *924*
—. Nazi Party. Social Conditions. 1924-29. *920*
Cartoons. Versailles, Treaty of. 1917-30's. *565*
Cartoons and Caricatures. Art and Society. Grosz, George. Socialism. 1917-32. *596*
Cartoons and Caricatures (political). Art. Expressionism. Graphics. Kollwitz, Käthe. Kubin, Alfred. Weber, Paul. 1920-70. *614*
Catholic Church. Center Party. Educational policy. Social Democratic Party. 1918-33. *752*
—. Germany (southern, western). Separatism. 1918-23. *736*
—. Nazi Party. Political Attitudes. 1930-33. *732*
Catholicism. Socialist movement. 1918-33. *749*
—. World War I. 1914-20's. *741*
Catholics. Behavior. France (Alsace). Germany (Baden). Jews. Protestants. Religion. 1871-1939. *759*
—. Schmitt, Carl. Theology, political. 1920's. *757*
Causality. Culture. Forman, Paul. Physics. Quantum mechanics. 1918-27. *588*
Censorship. *All Quiet on the Western Front* (film). Germany (Berlin). 1930-31. *572*
—. Authors. Kläber, Kurt (*Barrikaden an der Ruhr*). Political Protest. 1925. *607*
—. Communist Party. Films. Social Democratic Party. 1920-33. *660*
—. Competition. Hitler, Adolf. Newspapers. 1920's. *977*
Center Party. Catholic Church. Educational policy. Social Democratic Party. 1918-33. *752*
—. Nazism. Political strategy. 1928-33. *1028*
Center Party (review article). Brüning, Heinrich. Historiography. 1928-33. 1950's-70's. *341*
Central Association of German Industrialists (CDI). Hugenberg, Alfred. Industrial associations. League of Industrialists (BdI). Politics. Stresemann, Gustav. 1876-1918. *113*
Central Committee for the Promotion of Popular and Youth Games. Gymnastics. Jahn, Friedrich Ludwig. Youth Movements. 1892-1921. *633*
Centralization. Brüning, Heinrich. Civil Service. Financial crisis. 1930-32. *1013*
—. Liebknecht, Karl. Police. ca 1891-1919. *193*

Confiscation. Property, enemy. Versailles, Treaty of. World War I. 1914-23. *222*
Conflict of interest theory. Italy. Politics. 1919-31. *349*
Conservatism. 1918-19. *251*
—. Engineers. Modernism. Technocracy. 1920-35. *631*
—. Farmers' Union. Labor Unions and Organizations. Peasants (councils). 1918. *213*
—. Fascism. Political Theory. 19c-20c. *359*
—. Historiography. Nazism. 1920's-30's. 1950-82. *446*
—. Hitler, Adolf. Jung, Edgar Julius. Nazism. 1920's-30's. *475*
—. Hoetzsch, Otto (memorandum). 1900-18. *255*
—. Industry. *Münchner Neuesten Nachrichten* (newspaper). Newspapers. Reusch, Paul. 1930-33. *1005*
—. Paramilitary Organizations. Peasants. Political organizations. 1918-22. *356*
—. Political role. Wartburg Foundation. 1922-30. *663*
Conservative Party. Political Change. 1918. *244*
Conservative Revolution. Anticapitalism. Mohler, Armin. Youth movements. 1920's. *334*
Conservatives. Class, Heinrich. Nazism. Youth Movements. 1920's-33. *476*
Constitution. Enabling Act. Judicial process. 1930-39. *1010*
Constitution, Weimar. 1918-33. *143*
—. Legislation. Schools. 1918-19. *635*
Constitutions. Jews. Preuss, Hugo. 1919-25. *686*
—. Kelsen, Hans. Political Theory. Schmitt, Carl. 1931. *473*
Consulate. Germany (Hamburg). November Revolution. USSR. Workers' councils. 1918-19. *253*
Consumer attitudes. Automobile Industry and Trade (rationalization plans). 1924-29. *294*
Consumption. Agricultural production. World War I. 1907-25. *10*
—. Bureaucracies. Class consciousness. Labor, white-collar. Middle classes. 1920's. *566*
Coudenhove-Kalergi, Richard. Attitudes. Europe. Pan-European Union. Political Integration. 1924-32. *417*
—. Europe. Foreign Relations. Pan-European Union. 1924-29. *416*
Coups d'Etat. Beer-hall putsch. Germany (Munich). Hitler, Adolf. Nazi Party. 1913-23. *911*
—. Braun, Otto. Germany (Prussia). Nazi Party. Papen, Franz von. Rundstedt, Karl von. Social Democratic Party. 1932. *1016*
—. Germany (Prussia). Historiography (West German). Papen, Franz von. 1932. *1008*
—. Hindenburg, Paul von. Kapp, Wolfgang. Ludendorff, Erich. Seeckt, Hans von. 1918-23. *202*
Courts. Jews. 1919-33. *707*
Courts, jury. Reform. 1918-73. *72*
Craig, Gordon A. Historiography (review article). Sheehan, James J. Stern, Fritz. Wehler, Hans-Ulrich. 1800-1945. *83*
Cultural criticism. Curtius, Ernst Robert. Intellectuals (definition of). Lepsius, Rainer. ca 1920-56. *561*
Cultural development. Working class. 1918-33. *643*
Cultural History (review article). Germany, West. 1858-1980. *65*
Cultural policy. Communist Party. Kurella, Alfred. 1920's. *865*
—. German Academy. Germany (Munich). 1925-45. *957*

Culture. Causality. Forman, Paul. Physics. Quantum mechanics. 1918-27. *588*
—. Jews. 1920's-30's. *684*
—. Politics. Society. 1920's. *622*
—. Sports. ca 1880's-1930's. *657*
Curtius, Ernst Robert. Cultural criticism. Intellectuals (definition of). Lepsius, Rainer. ca 1920-56. *561*
Customs union. Austria. 1931. *1019*
—. Austria. Foreign policy. Great Britain. 1931. *1018*
Czechoslovakia. Alliances. Foch, Ferdinand (political tour). France. Poland. Ruhr, occupation of the. 1923. *267*
—. Annexation. Austria. Pan-Germanism. Parliamentarians. 1921-28. *263*
—. Beneš, Eduard. Economic cooperation. Schubert, Carl von. 1928. *419*
—. Boundaries. Foreign Relations. Locarno Conference. 1925. *361*
—. Communist Parties. 1919-40. *836*
—. Communist Parties and Movements. Rebellions. 1921-23. *873*
—. German National Socialist Workers' Party. Hitler, Adolf. 1919-23. *959*
—. Germans, Sudeten. Nationalism. World War I. 1918. *156*
—. Germany (Bavaria). Local Government. Sudeten Germans. 1918. *158*
—. Imperialism. 1918-33. *360*
—. Imperialism. Propaganda. 1918-19. *182*
—. Kreibich, Karel. Self-determination. Sudeten Germans. Unification. 1918-19. *51*
—. Political cooperation. Revolutionary Movements. 1918-21. *872*

D

Dada. Aesthetics. Art. Germany (Berlin). Press. 1920's. *555*
Daily life. Women. 1890-1980. *112*
Dairy cattle. *Committee zur Hilfeleistung der Notleidenden in Deutschland und Österreich.* Economic Aid. USA. 1921. *629*
Danish-German Border Stream Commission. Boundaries (revision). Versailles, Treaty of. 1920-22. *377*
Danube Basin. Europe. Hungary. Trade. 1918-28. *486*
—. Germans. Minorities. 1918-30's. *524*
Danzig (Free City 1919-39). Ethnic Groups. Jews. Refugees. Sagalovich, Jaakov Meir. 1923-33. *725*
—. Foreign Relations. France. Great Britain. 1918-39. *310*
—. Foreign Relations. League of Nations. 1919-26. *224*
Dawes Plan. Economic reconstruction. Foreign Investments. USA. 1919-29. *392*
—. Reparations. 1923-24. *460*
Debts, revaluation of. Legislation. 1922-25. *514*
Decisionmaking. Ambassadors. Europe. 1922-26. *519*
—. Historiography. Military. Political leadership. War policy. 1914-45. *58*
Defense policy. Communist Party. Social Democratic Party. 1920's. *796*
Demobilization. Koeth, Joseph. Revolution. 1918-19. *258*
Democracy. Döblin, Alfred. 1919-20's. *444*
—. Fascism. Italy. Nazism. Schmitt, Carl. 1910-20's. *908*
—. Germany (Prussia). Kapp Putsch. Social Democrats. 1920. *468*
—. Germany, West. 1918-33. 1945-53. *87*
Democratic Party. Political Factions. 1918-33. *682*

Economic Integration. Europe. Stresemann, Gustav. 1925-27. *358*
—. France. Paris Peace Conference. Reparations. Revisionism. 1919-24. *260*
—. Habsburg Empire (successor states). 1919-38. *510*
Economic mobilization. Interest groups. World War I. 1914-16. *177*
Economic planning. Moellendorf, Wichard von. 1918-19. *279*
Economic Policy. 1930-32. *1020*
—. Agriculture. Economic Structure. Nazism. Peasants. 1907-33. *362*
—. Brüning, Heinrich. Depression. Nazis. Socialist Party. 1929-33. *992*
—. Brüning, Heinrich. Foreign policy. 1930-32. *1000*
—. Bruning, Heinrich. Luther, Hans. Reparations. 1930-32. *1027*
—. Business. Emergency Union of German Science. Haber, Fritz. Science. 1920-33. *636*
—. Business. Government regulation. Rathenau, Walther. 1907-22. *448*
—. Europe, Southeastern. Italy. 1930's. *1021*
—. Industrial concentration. 1871-1945. *104*
—. Nazi Party. 1929-40. *904*
Economic Policy (review article). Depression. 1918-33. *396*
—. Diplomacy. Europe. 1914-39. *302*
Economic power. Inflation. Monetary policy. 1918-24. *418*
Economic reconstruction. Dawes Plan. Foreign Investments. USA. 1919-29. *392*
Economic Regulations. Business. Germany, West. Government. Social Policy. 1918-77. *33*
Economic relations. Foreign Policy. Hungary. Revisionism. 1920's-30. *989*
—. France. Ruhr, occupation of the. 1918-27. *517*
Economic stabilization. Gessler, Otto (memorandum). Martial law. Politics and the Military. 1923-24. *330*
Economic Structure. Agriculture. Economic Policy. Nazism. Peasants. 1907-33. *362*
—. Economic Growth. Germany (Southwest). 1918-45. *410*
Economic system. Germany (Württemberg). Zetkin, Clara (speech). 1919. *163*
Economic Theory. Balance of payments. Graham, Frank D. Ohlin, B. Reparations. 1925-29. *549*
—. Capitalism. Luxemburg, Rosa. 1870-1919. *146*
—. Hilferding, Rudolf. Marxism. Political Theory. 1902-41. *368*
—. Keynes, John Maynard. Rathenau, Walther. 1800's-1922. *348*
—. Korsch, Karl. Social Theory. Workers' councils. 1920's. *495*
Economic Theory (underdevelopment). Luxemburg, Rosa *(Accumulation of Capital)*. 1912-18. *165*
Economists. Keynes, John Maynard. Monetary and fiscal policies, counter-cyclical. 1931-32. *991*
Education *See also* Colleges and Universities, Elementary Education, Religious Education, Scholars, Schools, Secondary Education, Teachers, and Textbooks.
—. Germany, West. Military officers. Social Classes. 1900-79. *6*
—. Nazism. Social mobility. 1930-40. *930*
—. Poland (Warmia). Polish People's Council (School Commission). 1919-20. *563*
Education, Experimental Methods. Geheeb, Paul. Germany (Oberhambach). Odenwald School. 1910-34. *604*

Education (review article). Fishman, Sterling. Reform. Steinberg, Michael S. 1890-1935. *590*
—. Nazism. Science. Youth. 1918-45. *598*
Educational policy. Catholic Church. Center Party. Social Democratic Party. 1918-33. *752*
Educational Reform. Elementary education. Jews. Religion. 1890-1928. *576*
Educational Reform *(Mittlere Reife)*. Authoritarianism. 1928-31. *603*
Educational theories. 1870-1974. *591*
Educational theory. Locke, John. Research. 17c-19c. 1860-1970. *62*
Eight-hour day. Industrial Relations. 1922-24. *346*
Einstein, Albert. ca 1900-55. *688*
—. Anti-Semitism. Europe. Scientists. War. Zionism. 1879-1955. *580*
Einstein, Albert (documents). Academy of Sciences. Germany (Berlin). 1913-33. *653*
Election, landtag. Germany (Baden). Nazism. 1925-30. *915*
Elections. Ebert, Friedrich (death). Jews. Press. 1925. *722*
—. Nazi Party. Socialism, abandonment of. Strasser, Gregor. 1925-30. *960*
—. Nazism. Voting and Voting Behavior. 1928-32. *946*
—. Political Campaigns. Social Democratic Party. 1932. *1007*
—. Politics. Quantitative Methods. Women. Working Class. 1924-25. *472*
Electoral system. Germany, West. 1919-70's. *456*
Electrical industry. Industrial development. Jews. Rathenau, Emil. Rathenau, Walther. 19c-1922. *721*
Electricity. Germany (Saxony). Government Enterprise. 1916-36. *462*
Elementary education. Educational Reform. Jews. Religion. 1890-1928. *576*
Elites. Middle Classes. 1919-32. *546*
Emergency Union of German Science. Business. Economic policy. Haber, Fritz. Science. 1920-33. *636*
Emigration. Historians. Jews. Levison, Wilhelm. 1876-1947. *720*
Emperor Wilhelm Society for the Advancement of Science. Chemical industry. Farben, I. G. Scientific research. 1918-1933. *627*
Empire, idea of. History teaching. 1918-33. *554*
Employers' associations. France. Industrial Relations. Labor movement. Labor Unions and Organizations. 1914-78. *126*
—. Labor unions. 1930. *1034*
Enabling Act. Constitution. Judicial process. 1930-39. *1010*
Engineers. Conservatism. Modernism. Technocracy. 1920-35. *631*
—. Ideology. Middle classes. Nazism. 1918-33. *488*
Enlightenment. Classicism. Communists. Mehring, Franz. Philosophy of History. 1918-33. *830*
Equality. National unity. 1848-1973. *19*
Erlangen, University of. Nazism. Student corporations. 1919-33. *942*
Esperanto movement. Working Class. 1917-33. *772*
Essen Program. Political Parties. Stegerwald, Adam. 1919-33. *399*
Ethics. Barth, Karl. Liberalism. Niebuhr, Reinhold. 1920's-60. *735*
Ethnic Groups. Danzig (Free City 1919-39). Jews. Refugees. Sagalovich, Jaakov Meir. 1923-33. *725*
Ethnic minorities. Europe, Eastern. Nationalism. St. Germain Treaty. Trianon Treaty. World War I. 1919. *220*

H

M

N

S

—. Europe, Central. Historiography. Military. Revolution. Spartacists. 1917-19. *231*

Socialization (review article). Dissertations. Revolution. 1918-22. *184*

Society. Culture. Politics. 1920's. *622*

Socioeconomic change. Middle Classes. Political attitudes. 1918-25. *394*

Socioeconomic structure. Agriculture. Political power. 1907-25. *11*

Sociology. Jews. Kreutzberger, Max. 1932-79. *696*

—. Weber, Max. 1910's-30's. *668*

—. Weber, Max. 1920-33. *639*

—. Weber, Max (research goals). 1893-1922. *618*

Soldiers' Councils. Germany (Württemberg). 1918-19. *200*

—. Germany (Württemberg). November Revolution. 1918-19. *233*

Solf, Wilhelm. Foreign Relations (restoration). Japan. Knorr, Captain von. Public opinion. 1919-22. *300*

Sorbs. Nationalities. 1919-32. *405*

Sozialistische Monatshefte (journal). Calwer, Richard. Europe. Imperialism. Quessel, Ludwig. Socialism. 1905-18. *180*

Sozialistische Monatshefte (periodical). Bloch, Joseph. Europe. Socialism. World War I. 1888-1936. *17*

—. Bloch, Joseph. European unity. Social Democratic Party. Zionism. 1871-1936. *674*

Sozialistische Republik (newspaper). Germany (Cologne). Meyer, Gertrud (memoirs). Socialism. 1918-21. *849*

Sozialistischen Monatshefte (periodical). Bloch, Joseph. Politics. 1919-33. *296*

Spartacism. Bolshevism. Communist Party. Leftism. Political Factions. 1918-23. *775*

Spartacists. Communist Party. Middle Classes. 1918-20's. *181*

—. Duncker, Käte (biography). Jogiches, Leo. Politics. Women, working-class. 1898-1953. *898*

—. Europe, Central. Historiography. Military. Revolution. Socialists. 1917-19. *231*

Spengler, Oswald (*Decline of the West; review essay*). World and Universal History (theory). ca 850 BC-1970. *577*

Sports. Culture. ca 1880's-1930's. *657*

—. Jews. 1933-39. *702*

SS *(Schutzstaffel)*. SA *(Sturmabteilung)*. · Social origins. 1925-39. *933*

—. Social classes. 1920's-45. *907*

Stahlhelm. Germany (Magdeburg). Militarism. 1918-24. *293*

State, theory of the. Communist Party. Propaganda campaign. 1925-29. *858*

Steel industry. France. Mayrisch, Émile. 1919-29. *284*

Stegerwald, Adam. Agriculture. Brüning, Heinrich. Hindenburg, Paul von. Schlange-Schöningen, Hans. Settlement. 1931-32. *1033*

—. Essen Program. Political Parties. 1919-33. *399*

Stegmann, Dirk. Finance. Historiography. Industry, heavy. Nazi Party. Turner, Henry Ashby. 1929-33. *969*

Steinberg, Michael S. Education (review article). Fishman, Sterling. Reform. 1890-1935. *590*

Stern, Fritz. Craig, Gordon A. Historiography (review article). Sheehan, James J. Wehler, Hans-Ulrich. 1800-1945. *83*

Stinnes-Legien Agreement. Industrial Relations (documents). World War I. 1918. *176*

Stolper, Gustav. *Deutsche Volkwirt* (newspaper). Foreign policy. Tuesday Circle. 1914-33. *1011*

Storekeepers. Middle Classes. Nazism. 1920-39. *919*

Strasser, Gregor. Elections. Nazi Party. Socialism, abandonment of. 1925-30. *960*

—. Germany (Rhineland). Haake, Heinz. Ley, Robert. Nazism. Political Leadership (gauleiter). Simon, Gustav. 1925-31. *971*

—. Hitler, Adolf. National Socialist Student League. Tempel, Wilhelm. 1926-28. *931*

—. Hitler, Adolf. Nazism. 1926-34. *954*

Streicher, Julius. Anti-Semitism. Germany (Nuremberg). Newspapers. *Stürmer* (newspaper). 1923-33. *675*

Stresemann, Gustav. Annexation. Belgium (Eupen-et-Malmédy). Locarno, treaty of. 1925. *223*

—. Autonomy. France. Rhineland. Ruhr crisis. 1923-24. *397*

—. Business History. Foreign policy. Government. Krupp, Gustav. 1925. *478*

—. Cabinet discussions. Locarno, treaty of. 1925. *324*

—. Central Association of German Industrialists (CDI). Hugenberg, Alfred. Industrial associations. League of Industrialists (BdI). Politics. 1876-1918. *113*

—. Colonization. Great Britain. Locarno, treaty of. 1925. *317*

—. Diplomacy. Historiography. 1925-29. *337*

—. Economic Integration. Europe. 1925-27. *358*

—. Europe. Iron Cartel. 1923-29. *479*

—. European security. Foreign policy. Versailles, Treaty of (revision). 1925-32. *492*

—. Foreign policy 1918-29. *502*

—. Foreign policy. France. 1924-29. *283*

—. Foreign Policy. Lithuania. 1923-29. *511*

—. Foreign Policy (review article). Maxelon, Michael-Olaf. Walsdorff, Martin. Weidenfeld, Werner. 1923-29. *369*

—. League of Nations. Nationalities policy. 1926-29. *353*

—. Political Leadership. 1920's. *340*

—. Public Opinion. 1878-1929. *530*

Stresemann, Gustav (review article). Biography. Historiography. 1878-1929. 1978. *338*

—. France. Maxelon, M. O. 1914-29. *285*

Strike movement. Germany (Berlin). Merker, Paul (recollections). Restaurant workers. 1920-21. *442*

Strikebreaking. *Technische Nothilfe*. 1919-45. *406*

Strikes. Economic Aid. Germany (Thuringia). USSR. 1923. *897*

—. Germany (Berlin). Left. Russia. World War I. 1918. *147*

—. Germany (Brunswick). Labor movement. Socialism. 1914-18. *153*

—. Germany, West (Ruhr). Great Britain. Labor Unions and Organizations. 1918-29. *347*

—. Great Britain. Labor Unions and Organizations. 1918-21. *252*

Strikes and Lockouts. Arbitration, industrial. Germany (Ruhr). Mining industry. 1924. *289*

Student corporations. Erlangen, University of. Nazism. 1919-33. *942*

Students. Free Corps (Marburger Studentencorps). Germany (Thuringia). Kapp Putsch. Mechterstädt, massacre at. 1919-20. *531*

—. Labor, manual. *Werkstudenten*. 1918-34. *600*

AUTHOR INDEX